21st International Conference Mobile Learning (ML 2025) and 10th Educational Technologies (ICEduTech 2025)

Madeira Island, Portugal
1-3 March 2025

Editors:

Inmaculada A. Sánchez
Piet Kommers
Tomayess Issa
Pedro Isaías
Luís Rodrigues

ISBN: 979-8-3313-1621-1

Printed from e-media with permission by:

Curran Associates, Inc.
57 Morehouse Lane
Red Hook, NY 12571

Some format issues inherent in the e-media version may also appear in this print version.

International Association for Development of the Information Society (IADIS)
Rua Sao Sebastiao Da Pedreira
No. 100, 30, 1050-209
Lisbon, Portugal

Phone: 351 21 3151373
Fax: 351 21 3151244

secretariat@iadis.org

Additional copies of this publication are available from:

Curran Associates, Inc.
57 Morehouse Lane
Red Hook, NY 12571 USA
Phone: 845-758-0400
Fax: 845-758-2633
Email: curran@proceedings.com
Web: www.proceedings.com

INTERNATIONAL CONFERENCES PROCEEDINGS

2025

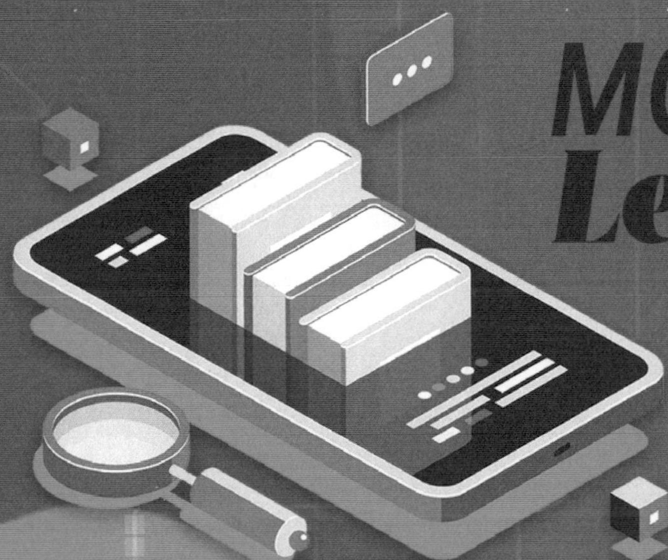

MOBILE Learning

1 - 3 March
Madeira Island,
PORTUGAL

Educational Technologies

Edited by

Inmaculada Arnedillo Sánchez
Piet Kommers
Tomayess Issa
Pedro Isaías

INTERNATIONAL CONFERENCES
ON
MOBILE LEARNING 2025
AND
EDUCATIONAL TECHNOLOGIES 2025

PROCEEDINGS OF THE INTERNATIONAL CONFERENCES

on

MOBILE LEARNING 2025

AND

EDUCATIONAL TECHNOLOGIES 2025

1- 3 MARCH, 2025

MADEIRA ISLAND, PORTUGAL

Organised by

iadis

international association for development of the information society

As a member of Crossref (a non-profit membership organization for scholarly publishing working with the purpose to make content easy to find, link, cite and assess) each published paper in this book of proceedings will be allocated a DOI (Digital Object Identifier) number for its fast and easy citation and indexation.

Edited by Inmaculada Arnedillo Sánchez, Piet Kommers, Tomayess Issa and Pedro Isaías

Associate Editor: Luís Rodrigues

TABLE OF CONTENTS

Educational Technologies

SHORT PAPERS

Mobile Learning

Educational Technologies

FOREWORD

These proceedings contain the papers and posters of 21th International Conference on Mobile Learning (ML 2025) and 10th International Conference on Educational Technologies 2025 (ICEduTech 2025), organised by the International Association for Development of the Information Society in Madeira Island, during 1-3 March 2025.

The Mobile Learning 2025 Conference seeks to provide a forum for the presentation and discussion of mobile learning research which illustrate developments in the field. In particular, but not exclusively, we aim to explore the theme of mobile learning under the following topics:

- Learning analytics and mobile learning
- Cloud computing and mobile learning
- Pedagogical approaches, models and theories for mLearning
- mLearning in and across formal and informal settings
- Strategies and challenges for integrating mLearning in broader educational scenarios
- User Studies in mLearning
- Learner mobility and transitions afforded by mlearning
- Socio-cultural context and implications of mLearning
- Mobile social media and user generated content
- Enabling mLearning technologies, applications and uses
- Evaluation and assessment of mLearning
- Research methods, ethics and implementation of mLearning
- Innovative mLearning approaches
- Tools, technologies and platforms for mLearning
- mlearning: where to next and how?

The International Conference on Educational Technologies 2025 (ICEduTech 2025) is the scientific conference addressing the real topics as seen by teachers, students, parents and school leaders. Scientists, professionals and institutional leaders are invited to be informed by experts, sharpen the understanding what education needs and how to achieve it.

Topics for this conference were:

- **Education in Context:** Education in the Network Society, Educational Games, Social Media in Education, Home Schooling, Students' Rights, Parents' Rights, Teachers' Rights, Student-Safe Searching, School Violence, Education and Tolerance for Peace and Education in Developing Countries.
- **Education as Professional Field:** Teacher Education, Teachers' Professional Development, Teachers' Workload, Teacher Support for Grading, Time Tabling, Grading, Learning Tools, and Online Learning Software, Teachers' learning in Communities of Practice, Web-based Communities for Teacher Support, Teachers' Career Planning, Legal and Financial Issues, Conflict Resolution and Mediation, Governance and Servant Leadership and Educational Policies.

- **Curricular Evolution:** Problem-based Learning, Critical Thinking Skills, Creativity Skills, Learning Citizenship, Global Education, Media Literacy / Pedagogy, Multicultural Education and Alternative Assessment Methods.
- **Learner Orientation:** Student-Oriented Learning, Peer- and Collaborative Learning, Learning Strategies: Learn how to Learn, Motivating Students, Recognizing Students' Learning Styles and Special Education.
- **Integrating Educational Technologies:** Social Media and Social Networking, The Semantic Web 3.0, Podcasting for Broadcasting Video Lectures, Podcasting feedback to students, Wiki and blogs in Higher Education, Mobile, Virtual and Vicarious Learning and Simulations and Modeling.
- **International Higher Education:** Marketing Higher Education as a Business Case, Pitfalls and Solutions in Joint and Double Degree Programs, Enculturation and International Teacher Accreditation, Web-based, Mobile, Virtual Presence and Social Media to Overcome Student Mobility, Blended Learning and Student Assessment at a Distance, Student Mobility and Distance Education, New-Emerging Standards and Benchmarks for Higher Education, Education, Research, Exchange an Capacity Building, 21st Century Academic and Industrial Brain Exchange, Academic Salaries, Faculty Contracts, Residence Permits and Legal Issues, International Student Exchange Funding Programs: Erasmus Mundus, the U.S. Council on International Educational Student Exchange, and the Euro-American "Atlantis" program, Networks for International Higher Education in the Pacific, Australia, Europe, Asian and European countries and Higher Education, Cultural Diversity, Tolerance and Political Conflict.

These events received 131 submissions from more than 23 countries. Each submission has been anonymously reviewed by an average of 4 independent reviewers, to ensure the final high standard of the accepted submissions. Out of the papers submitted, 24 received blind referee ratings that signified acceptability for publication as full papers (acceptance rate of 18%), while some other papers were published under the following categories: short and poster. The best papers will be selected for publishing as extended versions in the IADIS Journal on Computer Science and Information Systems (ISSN: 1646-3692) and also in the IADIS International Journal on WWW/Internet (ISSN: 1645-7641).

In addition to the papers' presentations, the conferences also feature one keynote presentation. We wish to thank Professor Mike Sharples, Emeritus Professor of Educational Technology, Institute of Educational Technology, The Open University, United Kingdom for accepting our invitation as keynote speaker. Furthermore, it is included a Talk by Christian Rudloff, Anna Kapsalis, Christiane Gesierich, Alexandra Efstathiades and José Miguel Rodrigues de Sousa and a Tutorial entitled "AI-Generated Rubrics: Enhancing Assessment in Higher Education" by Anne Jantos, Dresden University of Technology, Germany.

As we all know, a conference requires the effort of many individuals. We would like to thank all members of the Program Committee for their hard work in reviewing and selecting the papers that appear in this book. We would also like to thank all the authors who have submitted their papers to this conference. We wish to thank all members of our organizing committee.

Last but not least, we hope that everybody enjoyed the presentations, and we invite all participants for next year's editions of the International Conferences on Mobile Learning and Educational Technologies.

Inmaculada Arnedillo Sánchez, Trinity College Dublin, Ireland
ML 2025 Program Chair

Piet Kommers, UNESCO Professor of Educational Technology, The Netherlands
ICEduTech 2025 Conference Chair

Tomayess Issa, Curtin University, Perth, Australia
ICEduTech 2025 Program Co-Chair

Pedro Isaías, Universidade Aberta (Portuguese Open University), Portugal
ML 2025 Conference Chair and ICEduTech 2025 Program Co-Chair

March 2025

PROGRAM COMMITTEE

MOBILE LEARNING

PROGRAM CHAIR

Inmaculada Arnedillo Sánchez, Trinity College Dublin, Ireland

CONFERENCE CHAIR

Pedro Isaías, Universidade Aberta (Portuguese Open University), Portugal

COMMITTEE MEMBERS

Abdullah Al-zaghameem, Tafila Technical University, Jordan
Abeer Salim Jamil, Al-Mansour University College, Iraq
Adamantios Koumpis, University Hospital Cologne, Germany
Ademiotan Laleye, Adekunle Ajasin University, Akungba-akoko, Nigeria
Agostino Marengo, University of Foggia, Italy
Aiman Ayyal Awwad, Faculty of Information and Communications Technology, Jordan
Alessandro Pagano, University of Bari, Italy
Angelos Michalas, University of Western Macedonia, Greece
Antoanela Naaji, Vasile Goldis Western University, Romania
Antonella Carbonaro, Universiy of Bologna, Italy
Aslı Gonenç, Istanbul University, Turkey
Bertil P. Marques, ISEP/IPP, Portugal
Boriss Misnevs, Transport and Telecommunication Institute, Latvia
Celine Llewellyn-Jones, London Metropolitan University and University of East London, United Kingdom
Charalampos Karagiannidis, University of Thessaly, Greece
Chiu-Kuo Liang, Chunghua University, Taiwan
Christos Bouras, University of Patras, Greece
Claudia Steinberger, University of Klagenfurt, Austria
Daniyar Sapargaliyev, University of Nottingham, United Kingdom
Diana Bratić, Faculty of Graphic Arts, University of Zagreb, Croatia
Elliot Soloway, University of Michigan, USA
Emad Bataineh, Zayed University, United Arab Emirates
Emet Gurel, Ege University, Turkey
Euripides Loukis, University of the Aegean, Greece
Fadi Abuamara, Shenandoah University, United States
Fahriye Altinay, Near East University, Cyprus
Farshad Badie, Aalborg University, Denmark
Gabor Kiss, J. Selye University, Slovakia
Gazi Zahirul Islam, Southeast University, Bangladesh
George Magoulas, Birbeck College, United Kingdom
Gülcan Erçetin, Bogaziçi University, Turkey
Gwo-Jen Hwang, National Taichung University of Education, Taiwan

EDUCATIONAL TECHNOLOGIES

CONFERENCE CHAIR

Piet Kommers, UNESCO Professor of Educational Technology, The Netherlands

CONFERENCE PROGRAM CO-CHAIRS

Tomayess Issa, Curtin University, Perth, Australia
Pedro Isaías Universidade Aberta (Portuguese Open University), Portugal

COMMITTEE MEMBERS

Aderbal Correa, Maneschy Correa & Associates, United States
Adrian Bruch, SAE Creative Institute, Australia
Alba Torrego, Complutense University of Madrid, Spain
Alexander Vaninsky, City University of New York/Hostos Community Colle, USA
Ana María de Las Heras Cuenca, Universidad Complutense de Madrid, Spain
Annette Deschner, Pädagogische Hochschule Karlsruhe, Germany
Augustin Prodan, Iuliu Hatieganu University, Romania
Beatrice Pudelko, Téluq-université du Québec, Canada
Boris Vazquez-Calvo, University of Málaga, Spain
Christa Tigerstedt, Arcada, Finland
Christos Troussas, University of West Attica, Greece
Dale Kirby, Memorial University of Newfoundland, Canada
Dessislava Vassileva, Sofia University St. Kliment Ohridski, Bulgaria
Elena Bañares, Maravillas School of Madrid, Spain
Eugenia Smyrnova-Trybulska, University of Silesia in Katowice, Poland
Evdokia Karava, National and Kapodistrian University of Athens, Greece
Farshad Badie, Aalborg University, Denmark
Gabriela Grosseck, West University of Timisoara, Romania
Gabriela Prelipcean, University, Romania
Gayle Calverley, Independent, United Kingdom
Gemma Tur Ferrer, Universitat de Les Illes Balears, Spain
Giovanni Fulantelli, National Research Council of Italy - ITD, Italy
Iuliana Zsoldos-Marchis, Babes Bolyai University, Romania
James Uhomoibhi, Ulster University, United Kingdom
Janerik Lundquist, Linkoping University, Sweden
Jerzy Moscinski, Silesian University of Technology, Poland
Jiao Jianli, South China Normal University, China
José Hernández Ortega, Complutense University of Madrid, Spain
Kuki Singh, Edith Cowan University – Perth, Australia
Kyparisia Papanikolaou, School of Pedagogical and Technological Education, Greece
Laura Marinas, Bucharest Academy of Economic Studies, Romania
Lavinia Suteu (Haiduc), Babes Bolyai University, Romania
Liudmila Shafirova, Aveiro University, Portugal
Malinka Ivanova, Technical University of Sofia, Bulgaria
Manoj Kumar Saxena, Central University of Himachal Pradesh, India
Manuel Ramiro Munoz, Pontificia Universidad Javeriana, Colombia

KEYNOTE LECTURE

SOCIAL LEARNING WITH GENERATIVE AI

Professor Mike Sharples,
Emeritus Professor of Educational Technology, Institute of Educational Technology, The Open University, United Kingdom

Abstract

In 2005, Josie Taylor, Giasemi Vavoula and I developed and published a Theory of Learning for the Mobile Age. The essence of that theory is that we need to re-conceive learning for an era of networked mobility, where people are continually connected with and through personal and embedded technologies. Twenty years later, we again need to re-think learning, for a world infused by AI. In my presentation I shall discuss the emergence of "social generative AI" – AI systems that interact with humans and with other AI tools in complex social networks. Social AI will have profound implications for education. Young people will have lifelong AI companions, mentors and tutors. They will command AI agents to solve problems and represent them in conversations and on social media. Social AI will break down language barriers and connect people across cultures. Companies will compete with traditional education in providing online classes, tutorials and group seminars facilitated by AI. Social AI may also erode trust in information and create networks of interacting machines beyond human control. I will propose we should explore education for an AI-infused world that is not only effective but also empowers human teachers and extends human care and empathy.

TALK

STEP FORWARD WITH FOOTT PRINTTS: YOUR COMPANION IN TEACHER TRAINING

Christian Rudloff[1], Anna Kapsalis[2], Christiane Gesierich[1], Alexandra Efstathiades[1] and José Miguel Rodrigues de Sousa[3]
[1]PH Wien, Austria
[2]Bezirksregierung Arnsberg, Germany
[3]DTIM, Portugal

Abstract

FOOTT PRINTTS, standing for 'Focus on Teacher Training - Practical Guidelines for In-Service Teacher Trainers', is an EU-funded Erasmus+ cooperation partnership with seven countries focussing on teacher training across Europe. The Arnsberg District Government brings together teacher training institutions and organisations to establish a holistic quality approach to national and international continuous professional development (CPD). With global issues like teacher shortages and teacher dropouts, the importance of in-service teacher training has become increasingly prominent.

We focus on in-service teacher trainers and the organisational structure of teacher training to combine research-based results and practical needs in CPD. Our goal is to ensure international understanding and agreement on quality standards for teacher CPD. This includes the identification of proven methods and structures, the development of a comprehensive and easily accessible guidance framework concentrating on practical implementation, and the exchange of successful strategies.

Therefore, we consider the following key milestones:

1. **Theory and Literature Review**: Establishment of hypotheses and indicators for quantitative analysis.
2. **Sequential Mixed Methods Data Collection**: Quantitative and qualitative data collection in all participating countries.
3. **Framework**: Development of a guidance framework for teacher trainers based on the research.
4. **Practical Guidelines**: Interactive, adaptable, and ready-to-use input within the framework modules for teacher training.
5. **Peer Learning and Networking**: **Conferences** and other events to peer review, disseminate, and further develop the tool to ensure sustainability.

This process ensures applicability in diverse contexts across participating countries. We are also supported by pan-European education associations and the European Commission in order to create an interactive platform that not only offers support to teacher trainers, but also provides guidance on how to improve the quality of teacher training. With the initiation of a network for teacher trainers, we also promote peer-to-peer learning and therefore support the development of key competences for teacher trainers across Europe.

Keywords: Teacher Education, Professional Development, Quality of Teaching

TUTORIAL

AI-GENERATED RUBRICS: ENHANCING ASSESSMENT IN HIGHER EDUCATION

Anne Jantos
Dresden University of Technology, Dresden, Germany

Abstract

A **rubric matrix** is a structured framework that defines performance criteria for assessments, providing clear expectations for learners and evaluators. It facilitates **transparent grading, meaningful feedback, and consistency** in evaluation processes. In digital and mobile learning environments, rubrics play a crucial role in enabling **scalable, autonomous, transparent and interactive assessment methods**, including **self-assessment, peer feedback, and instructor-led evaluation**. This interactive 90-minute tutorial introduces educators to rubric matrices and the transformative potential large language models (LLMs).

The rise of mobile learning has amplified the need for adaptive and scalable assessment solutions. With students engaging in learning across multiple platforms and contexts, traditional assessment methods often fail to provide timely and personalized feedback since this flexibility also presents challenges. Without direct interaction with educators or peers, learners may struggle to reflect and self-regulate their progress without prompt feedback. Mobile learning encourages multimodal assignments such as videos, podcasts, blog posts, short films, presentations, discussions, essays, reflection texts, and even social media posts. However, grading these diverse formats consistently is a challenge for educators.

By leveraging AI-generated rubrics, educators can easily create clear, structured, and adaptable evaluation criteria for a wide range of learning activities. Instead of generic grading, rubric-guided feedback supports reflection, self-improvement, and deeper engagement with learning materials. GenAI tools like ChatGPT and Claude can generate customized rubrics based on educator-defined quality criteria, ensuring that assignments – regardless of format – are evaluated fairly and systematically.

This tutorial is particularly relevant at M-Learn, as mobile learning environments demand flexible, technology-enhanced solutions that can support self-regulated learning, peer interaction, and structured feedback. This session will provide hands-on experience in using GenAI to design assessment frameworks suited for mobile education. This tutorial is designed for educators, instructional designers, and EdTech professionals who are exploring AI-supported teaching and assessment for mobile and digital learning.

Table 1. Example of an AI-generated Rubric Matrix for a Blog Post

Criteria	Excellent	Good	Needs Improvement	Poor
Content & Relevance	The blog post presents a deep, original, and well-supported discussion of the topic.	The blog post is relevant and informative but could be more precise or expanded in some areas.	The blog post touches on the topic but lacks depth or clarity. Some parts are off-topic or weakly supported.	The blog post is largely off-topic, lacks coherence, or fails to present a strong argument.
Structure & Clarity	The post has a clear and logical structure. Ideas flow smoothly, and arguments are well-developed.	The structure is mostly logical, but some sections could be better organized or transitions improved.	The post lacks clear organization, making it difficult to follow. Arguments are inconsistent or incomplete.	The structure is unclear or missing, making the content hard to understand.
Writing Style & Language	The writing is engaging, well-suited to the audience, and easy to read. Vocabulary is rich and precise, with minimal grammar or spelling errors.	The writing is clear and appropriate but could be more fluent. Some minor grammar or spelling mistakes.	The writing is sometimes unclear, repetitive, or contains several grammatical errors that impact readability.	The writing is confusing, with frequent errors that make comprehension difficult.
Use of Media & Formatting	The blog post effectively incorporates media to enhance understanding. Formatting is professional and visually appealing.	Media is present and relevant but could be better integrated or formatted.	Limited or poorly integrated media. Formatting inconsistencies make reading difficult.	No media is included, or the formatting is inconsistent and unprofessional.
Reflection & Critical Thinking	The post demonstrates reflection, original insights, and a critical perspective on the topic. Arguments are well-reasoned and supported.	The post includes some reflective elements but lacks depth or stronger justification in arguments.	Reflection is superficial, with weak or unsupported arguments. Little critical analysis is present.	The post lacks reflection or critical engagement, and arguments are unclear or missing.

Full Papers

TOOLS, METHODOLOGIES AND BEST PRACTICES FOR M-LEARNING COURSES TO SUPPORT TOURISM MANAGERS IN DESIGNING AND MANAGING TOURISM PROJECTS

Anícia Rebelo Trindade[1,3], Ana Amélia Carvalho[1,2] and Célio Gonçalo Marques[3]
[1]*Universidade de Coimbra, LabTe, Coimbra, Portugal*
[2]*CEIS20, Coimbra, Portugal*
[3]*Instituto Politécnico de Tomar, Centro de Tecnologia, Restauro e Valorização das Artes, Portugal*

ABSTRACT

There is a notable gap in mobile learning courses designed to guide tourism managers in adopting digital innovation and sustainable practices. This research proposes a mobile learning course informed by recent studies on the topic, addressing the characteristics and needs of seven tourism institutions in the Abrantes Municipality region of Portugal. The research question examines the most suitable methodology for designing a course that equips tourism managers with the skills to design and manage sustainable tourism projects. Additionally, it explores the themes and activities essential for achieving this goal. The study provides valuable insights into the key subjects that should be incorporated into a mobile learning program, enabling tourism managers to apply digital innovation and sustainability in their projects. Considering their limited availability to attend onsite or traditional eLearning courses, this research offers a practical solution and meaningful contribution to the field. To achieve these objectives, a qualitative and descriptive approach was employed, including a systematic literature review and two online surveys. These methods helped identify the specific learning needs related to digital innovation and sustainable tourism projects. This study advances the understanding of mobile learning courses within the tourism sector.

KEYWORDS

Mobile Learning, Tourism Managers, Sustainable Tourism, Digital Innovation, Project Design

1. INTRODUCTION

Digital innovation and sustainability are increasingly emphasized in today's tourism landscape (Varju et al., 2014; Quinta-Nova & Ferreira, 2022; Rezvani et al., 2022). Tourism managers face growing pressure to design and manage projects that incorporate these elements to meet the expectations of stakeholders and communities (Farinha et al., 2019; Trindade et al., 2024; UNWTO, 2005). However, significant gaps remain in understanding how to effectively integrate digital innovation and sustainable practices into their businesses. This is particularly crucial given the diverse nature of the tourism industry, where digital tools can transform operations, enhance stakeholder engagement, and optimize resource consumption (Trindade et al., 2024). Our research questions aim to investigate:

1. which themes and activities should be incorporated into a mobile learning (m-learning) course to assist tourism managers in designing and managing sustainable tourism projects?
2. which tools, methodologies, and best practices should be considered to achieve this goal?

The purpose of our study is to: i) identify and evaluate m-learning tools, methodologies, and best practices for effectively training tourism managers in digital innovation and sustainable practices for designing and managing tourism projects; ii) compile best practices from high-impact studies that showcase the successful implementation of m-learning courses, with a focus on enhancing long-term sustainability and digital innovation practices among tourism managers; iii) propose an m-learning matrix to assist tourism managers in designing and managing sustainable tourism projects through digital innovation; and iv) uncover existing gaps in this field. To achieve these objectives, our research employs a systematic literature review spanning two decades (2003–2024), using the PRISMA protocol (Preferred Reporting Items for Systematic Reviews and

Meta-Analysis). PRISMA is a set of guidelines designed to help researchers report systematic reviews and meta-analyses clearly and transparently, aiming to enhance the quality and consistency of the review (Banomyong et al., 2019; Boell & Cecez-Kecmanovic, 2015; Dwan et al., 2013; Jiravichai & Banomyong, 2022). Additionally, data were collected through two online surveys conducted with seven tourism institutions in the Abrantes Municipality region of Portugal.

This research advances understanding of how m-learning can be integrated into the tourism sector to encourage tourism managers to adopt digital innovation and sustainable practices in the digital era, while promoting awareness of sustainable development goals (SDG). It offers a model for a m-learning course that serves as a blueprint for unlocking the tourism sector's potential by fostering digital innovation and sustainable practices. Besides this introduction, the paper presents the theoretical framework underpinning the research, details the methodology, and discusses the results achieved. It also examines the implications of these findings and provides recommendations for future research.

2. LITERATURE REVIEW AND HYPOTHESES/ASSUMPTIONS

The literature reveals that archaeological tourism holds particular significance, offering valuable insights into centuries of human history and cultural heritage (Trindade et al., 2022; Trindade et al., 2024; UNWTO, 2005). On the other hand, the advent of digital innovation and information systems underscores the need to explore how these technological advancements can be effectively integrated into the design and management of archaeological tourism projects (Gössling, 2021; Marian & Jacob, 2022; Vaz et al., 2012; Vaz, 2016; Trindade et al., 2022; Trindade et al., 2024). In light of this, we present: (i) the body of knowledge supporting the analysis and research of tools, methodologies, and best practices for developing mobile learning (m-learning) courses in the tourism sector; (ii) the hypotheses and assumptions that delineate the research's motivation; and (iii) the contributions and implications for this field, examining its past, present, and future while clarifying the literature's directions.

2.1 Advancing Sustainable Tourism and Digital Innovation: A Comprehensive Approach

Some scholars refer to the concept of sustainable tourism as having emerged in the 1970s in response to growing dissatisfaction with government and industry practices in the tourism sector, focusing on the need to balance economic development with environmental and social well-being (Farinha et al., 2019; Varju et al., 2014; Trindade et al., 2024). Initially, this definition was primarily viewed as an environmental concern, emphasizing conservation and responsible tourism practices. Indeed, the World Tourism Organization (UNWTO, 2005) provides a foundational definition that primarily highlights the preservation of local cultures, heritage, and ecosystems. Nevertheless, sustainable tourism has since evolved into a multidimensional concept that encompasses political, economic, social, technological, legal, and environmental dimensions (Trindade et al., 2024). These dimensions aim not only to minimize the negative impacts of tourism operations but also to maximize the positive contributions of these various dimensions to tourism sustainability (Trindade et al., 2024). On the other hand, emerging technologies such as augmented reality (AR), artificial intelligence (AI), and advanced data analytics promise even more immersive, personalized, and sustainable experiences (Gössling, 2021). Practically, AR offers augmented experiences by combining digital and physical elements, while AI contributes to i) personalized visitor experiences and optimized resource management; ii) catering to visitor preferences in a responsible manner, promoting ethical tourism behavior. Additionally, data analytics can drive sustainable practices by reducing environmental impact, preserving heritage sites, bolstering social benefits for local communities, and facilitating real-time monitoring of visitor behavior (Gössling, 2021). Considering this approach to sustainable tourism and digital innovation, it is important to identify which mobile learning methodologies can effectively train tourism managers to acquire the necessary skills for designing and managing sustainable tourism projects while leveraging these technological advancements. Indeed, in low-density population areas such as Abrantes, Portugal, where the need for balanced development is crucial, sustainable tourism takes on added significance in addressing multiple dimensions of concern. This leads to the following hypothesis: **H1**: The integration of sustainable tourism and digital innovation themes into a mobile learning course for tourism managers will contribute to achieving long-term sustainability in their respective regions (UNWTO, 2005; Trindade et al., 2024).

2.2 Mobile Learning Tools, Methodologies and Best Practices to Train Tourism Managers

Before addressing the existing mobile learning methodologies and best practices for training tourism managers, it is essential to first understand the skill set required by these professionals to design and manage sustainable and digitally innovative projects. Based on these competencies, a mobile learning curriculum can be proposed to achieve this goal (Trindade, Carvalho & Marques, 2024).

2.2.1 Skills Required by Tourism Managers

In the past, tourism management primarily revolved around traditional business and hospitality skills. The emphasis was on maximizing profits and enhancing customer satisfaction, with limited regard for sustainability or digital innovation. Sustainable tourism was not a prevalent concept, and digital competence played a minimal role in managerial skill sets (Darcy et al., 2010). This historical approach had social and economic implications, including potential negative impacts on local communities and the environment (Strzelecka et al., 2017).

The evolution of skills required by tourism managers, as well as their current demands, has significantly shifted over time, reshaping the industry's landscape. According to Trindade et al. (2024), there are currently seven essential skills that tourism managers must possess to effectively design and manage sustainable tourism projects: digital competence, sustainability knowledge, community engagement, information systems usage, business intelligence (BI), communication competence, and systems thinking (see Trindade et al., 2024, for a description of each mentioned skill).

Looking to the future and considering this set of skills proposed by Trindade et al. (2024), tourism managers will need to be increasingly innovative, particularly in a post-pandemic environment. They will play a pivotal role in managing and mitigating the impacts of climate change on tourism destinations, thereby shaping new tourism demands.

Considering the above, this leads to the following hypothesis: **H2**: A mobile learning course for tourism managers should address competencies such as digital competence, sustainability knowledge, community engagement, information systems usage, business intelligence (BI), communication competence, and systems thinking.

2.2.2 M-Learning Tools, Best Practices and Methodologies for Tourism Sector

Despite the growth of m-learning in tourism, applied methodologies often draw from broader educational or corporate training models rather than tourism-specific studies (Ahmad et al., 2020; Arrasyid et al., 2020; Trindade et al., 2024). A literature review covering studies from 2003 to 2024 revealed multiple approaches associated with innovative m-learning tools, methodologies, and best practices. Despite presenting various tools and methodologies, the literature lacks a detailed focus on contributions specific to the tourism sector, particularly in critical areas such as digital innovation and sustainability.

Designing an effective m-learning course for tourism managers on digital innovation and sustainable practices requires a comprehensive evaluation of tools and methodologies that support this goal. Such an evaluation is essential for crafting a course that effectively engages tourism managers, who often lack the time to participate in onsite or traditional eLearning courses. In this context, m-learning has emerged as a transformative approach, providing tourism professionals with the flexibility and accessibility needed for continuous learning. The widespread availability of smartphones and Wi-Fi makes m-learning a feasible and scalable solution, particularly suited to the tourism sector (Arrasyid et al., 2020).

According to various scholars (Arrasyid et al., 2020; Cheng & Shao, 2022; Huang & Chiu, 2015; Lee et al., 2020; Li et al., 2024; Moya & Camacho, 2021; Zhu & Huang, 2023), the tools, methodologies, and practices selected for an m-learning course significantly impact its effectiveness.

In terms of tools supporting m-learning courses, podcasts, Global Positioning System (GPS), and the integration of real-world contexts with learning systems and mobile applications can provide personalized support for learners, especially tourism managers. These tools enable managers to observe and experience real-world situations, thereby enhancing their personal knowledge construction (Ahmad et al., 2020; Arrasyid et al., 2020; Huang & Chiu, 2015). For instance, some scholars have developed mobile applications that encourage learners to interact with immersive environments (Arrasyid et al., 2020; Tan & Law, 2015). One example is the VirTEd mobile learning application for tourism education in Indonesia, developed and evaluated by Arrasyid et al. (2020). Their study highlighted the usability and effectiveness of interactive tools, such as 360-degree videos, which significantly enhance user engagement and promote effective learning in tourism education. Another valuable tool is cloud computing. According to Ahmad et al. (2020), integrating cloud-based platforms facilitates regular content updates and resource scalability. However, this requires tourism organizations to prioritize and allocate resources for digital infrastructure. Artificial Intelligence (AI) can also significantly enhance m-learning for tourism managers by personalizing content to their specific needs, skills, and goals (Gössling, 2021). AI enables real-time feedback and adaptive learning experiences, making training more efficient and impactful. AI-powered simulations allow managers to explore different tourism scenarios and understand the implications of their decisions in a risk-free environment (McGrath et al., 2020).

Regarding m-learning methodologies, Huang and Chiu (2015) identified that the context-aware mobile learning (CAML) methodology, based on meaningful learning theory, holds tremendous potential across various learning scenarios. According to Huang and Chiu, CAML comprises the following elements: (1) spontaneous learning, (2) learning mobility, (3) situated instructional activity, (4) context awareness, (5) personalized learning, (6) self-regulated learning, (7) collaborative learning (Huang et al., 2010), (8) learning community, (9) virtual interaction, and (10) physical interaction. These elements are particularly relevant given the seven competencies identified by Trindade et al. (2024) and address tourism managers' limited time for onsite or traditional eLearning courses. Another innovative methodology is the Open-set Learning Context Recognition Model (OLCRM). According to Li et al. (2024), this model uses smartphone sensor data to determine learning contexts in real time, enabling personalized and contextually appropriate content delivery. This approach benefits tourism professionals by distinguishing between known and unknown learning contexts. Based on a Dual Discriminator Generative Adversarial Network (DDGAN), OLCRM creates high-quality simulated examples, helping learners improve context recognition accuracy. This is particularly valuable for tourism managers, as it provides insights to enhance project management and understanding in tourism. Although not an m-learning methodology per se, the Unified Theory of Acceptance and Use of Technology (UTAUT) helps evaluate user acceptance and adoption factors in organizational contexts of specific technologies (Zhu & Huang, 2023). UTAUT provides valuable insights into critical adoption factors—such as performance expectancy, ease of use, and technological readiness—relevant for the success of an m-learning course aimed at tourism management training. This model is also useful for predicting user engagement and satisfaction (Zhu & Huang, 2023). For instance, m-learning adoption is often influenced by learners' technical skills and readiness to engage in different environments, which is applicable to tourism contexts (Lee et al., 2020; Moya & Camacho, 2021). A study in Bangladesh, for example, found that self-efficacy and innovativeness significantly impact students' acceptance of m-learning in tourism education (Fatima et al., 2019). This finding underscores the need to integrate content that is both personally and technologically relevant to learners. It is also essential to develop applications accessible to tourism managers with varying levels of digital proficiency. Information quality, system quality, and service quality should be carefully balanced using a combination of tools and methodologies to make necessary context-specific adjustments (Fatima et al., 2016; Lee et al., 2020). Despite the advantages of diverse tools and methodologies, in developing regions—such as the Abrantes region in Portugal—connectivity limitations often hinder m-learning adoption. In such cases, partnerships between tourism organizations, government agencies, and technology providers could play a crucial role in making m-learning more accessible to target audiences.

Based on the points described above, the following hypothesis is proposed: **H3:** Effective m-learning courses for tourism managers should integrate diverse tools, methodologies, and practices tailored to the competencies required in their roles.

3. METODOLOGY

3.1 Data Selection and Analysis

The choice of Abrantes Municipality for the development of this study can be explained by several compelling factors. First and foremost, Abrantes Municipality is renowned for its wealth of archaeological remains and ancient artifacts spanning a wide range of historical periods, from the Neolithic era, as evidenced by settled communities and transformations in the territory, to the Modern Age (Trindade et al., 2022). Furthermore,

Abrantes Municipality's archaeological sites and historical artifacts have the potential to attract tourists interested in history and culture (Trindade et al., 2022). This aligns with the research focus on effectively integrating these heritage sites into sustainable tourism projects, as emphasized by Quinta-Nova and Ferreira (2022), Rezvani et al. (2022), and Varju et al. (2014). Such integration can stimulate economic growth, job creation, and socio-economic development in the region.

The tourism management institutions selected for this study underwent a selection process that started with 152 tourism institutions encompassing a diverse range of tourism businesses, such as hospitality, restaurants, event venues, and sports companies. Only private tourism business institutions were selected, reducing the sample size to 123 institutions. Then, only those tourism institutions with at least an institutional email and a website were included in the final sample of thirteen tourism institutions, with only seven institutions responding to each survey. The implementation of both surveys considered for the writing of this article is well documented in our previous study (Trindade et al., 2024). These surveys were revisited to reflect on tools, methodologies, and best practices for m-learning courses. The aim is to assist tourism managers in designing and managing tourism projects aligned with digital innovation and sustainable practices. These surveys used Cronbach's alpha to determine their accuracy and measure their intended constructs, internal consistency, and reliability as psychometric instruments (Trindade et al., 2024). The first survey focuses on personal and professional characterization, detailing the personal and professional characteristics of tourism managers, as well as the characterization of the tourism institution employing the tourism manager (Trindade et al., 2024). The second survey evaluates the views of tourism managers on sustainability, innovation, and digital competence, examining their attitudes regarding sustainability in project design and management, along with their familiarity with innovation and digital competence. It also evaluates the competencies of tourism managers (Trindade et al., 2024).

As stated earlier, the research employs a qualitative and descriptive approach, also based on a systematic literature review covering two decades (2003–2024), using the PRISMA protocol (Preferred Reporting Items for Systematic Review and Meta-Analysis). This protocol is characterized as a set of guidelines designed to help researchers report systematic reviews and meta-analyses in a clear and transparent manner, aiming to enhance the quality and consistency of the review conducted (Boell & Cecez-Kecmanovic, 2015; Jiravichai & Banomyong, 2022).

4. RESULTS AND DISCUSSION

4.1 Literature Review and Surveys Results

The literature review conducted highlights several tools, methodologies, and best practices that could be integrated into the design of an m-learning course, emphasizing their roles in enhancing the effectiveness of such a course (Table 1, Table 2, and Table 3). These tools, methodologies, and best practices can be used to develop the competencies identified in our previous study (Trindade et al., 2024). The results of both online surveys are well documented in our previous study (Trindade et al., 2024). They show that some tourism managers have significant gaps in key competencies, highlighting an opportunity for strategic interventions. One such intervention is the design of m-learning courses that focus on tools, methodologies, and best practices to enhance the capacity of tourism managers to lead sustainable and innovative projects. These m-learning courses should emphasize a deeper understanding of their role in fostering resilience, promoting constructive and proactive behaviors, and addressing the seven competencies proposed in the aforementioned study (Trindade et al., 2024).

Table 1. M-learning tools to develop tourism managers competencies

Category	Description	Supporting Authors	Related Competencies
M-learning tools			
Podcast	Utilization of audio content to provide flexible and on-the-go learning experiences.	Arrasyid et al., 2020	Communication Competence
Global Positioning System (GPS)	Enhances contextual learning by linking learning content to specific locations, making real-world application easier for tourism managers.	Ahmad et al., 2020; Arrasyid et al., 2020	Information Systems (IS)
Cloud Computing	Allows for scalable access to learning resources and materials without hardware limitations.	Huang & Chiu, 2015	Digital Competence
Real-World Context Integration	Combines actual scenarios with digital learning, allowing learners to interact with immersive, situational contexts.	Arrasyid et al., 2020; Tan & Law, 2015	Systems Thinking; Community Engagement
Mobile Applications & Technology	Enables personalized learning experiences, where tourism managers can engage with interactive and customized learning modules.	Ahmad et al., 2020; Arrasyid et al., 2020; Huang & Chiu, 2015	Digital Competence; Business Intelligence (BI)

Source: The authors

Table 2. M-learning methodologies to develop tourism managers competencies

Category	Description	Supporting Authors	Related Competencies
M-learning methodologies			
Context-Aware Mobile Learning (CAML)	Based on meaningful learning theory and comprises the following elements: (1) spontaneous learning, (2) learning mobility, (3) situated instructional activity, (4) context awareness, (5) personalized learning, (6) self-regulated learning, (7) collaborative learning (Huang et al., 2010), (8) learning community, (9) virtual interaction, and (10) physical interaction.	Huang & Chiu, 2015.	Digital Competence; Systems Thinking
Open-Set Learning Context Recognition Model (OLCRM)	Uses smartphone sensors to recognize learning contexts in real-time for personalized content delivery.	Li et al., 2024	Business Intelligence (BI); Information Systems (IS)
Unified Theory of Acceptance and Use of Technology (UTAUT)	Evaluates technology adoption factors like ease of use and performance expectations.	Zhu & Huang, 2023	Communication Competence; Digital Competence

Source: The authors

Table 3. M-learning best practices to develop tourism managers competencies

Category	Description	Supporting Authors	Related Competencies
M-learning best practices			
Interactive and Immersive Tools	Use of 360-degree videos and other immersive tools to increase engagement and promote experiential learning.	Arrasyid et al., 2020	Digital Competence; Community Engagement
Context-Specific Adjustments	Tailoring learning applications to the digital proficiency levels of tourism managers to ensure accessibility and relevance.	Fatima et al., 2019	Digital Competence; Communication Competence
Collaboration with Local Partners	Form partnerships with tourism organizations, government agencies, and technology providers to ensure m-learning accessibility.	Fatima et al., 2019	Community Engagement; Sustainability Knowledge
Emphasis on Digital Readiness	Considering digital readiness and self-efficacy in adoption strategies to enhance m-learning acceptance among tourism professionals.	Moya & Camacho, 2021	Digital Competence; Communication Competence

Source: The authors

5. CONCLUSION

Derived context-aware learning models, such as those explored by Huang and Chiu (2015), use an open-set learning approach to recognize varied environmental contexts. This allows m-learning courses to adapt dynamically to the diverse tourism sector. By integrating a variety of methodologies and tools into the design of an m-learning course, tourism education can deliver personalized, context-sensitive content that enhances its relevance and impact. In conclusion, while mobile learning methodologies for tourism are heavily drawn from general e-learning and corporate training models, specific adaptations, such as the incorporation of context-aware technologies and a focus on user readiness, are essential. Integrating sustainable practices, interactive tools, and user-centered design ensures that m-learning can meet the unique demands of the tourism sector, promoting learning experiences that are both flexible and impactful (Fatima et al., 2019).

While mobile learning offers multiple benefits, its implementation in the tourism sector is not without challenges. One significant hurdle is ensuring content relevance and context adaptation, as tourism professionals operate in diverse environments where pre-set learning contexts may not be applicable. The Open Learning Context Recognition Model (OLCRM) by Li et al. (2024) addresses the challenge of recognizing unfamiliar learning contexts. However, such advanced technology may require substantial investment and integration efforts, potentially creating barriers for smaller tourism operators.

While this research offers valuable insights into identifying the appropriate tools, methodologies, and best practices to help tourism managers acquire necessary skills, it has certain limitations and presents opportunities for further study. A key limitation is the small sample size of tourism institutions, which not fully represent tourism managers in the Abrantes Municipality region, being that further research to validate the findings is required. To gain a more comprehensive understanding of the actual impact of each tool, methodology, and best practice, it is essential to create a specific m-learning program tailored to each competency that tourism managers need to acquire. Furthermore, it is crucial to analyse how each approach, as highlighted in the literature, meets its intended objectives. This broader scope could offer a more accurate perspective on the most suitable tools, methodologies, and best practices for designing an effective m-learning course.

ACKNOWLEDGMENTS

Work funded by national funds through the Portuguese National Funding Agency for Science, Research and Technology (FCT).

REFERENCES

Ahmad, N. et al, (2020). Developing a cloud-based mobile learning adoption model to promote sustainable education. *Sustainability*, Vol. 12, No. 3126, pp.1-18. https://doi.org/10.3390/su12083126

Arrasyid, R. et al, (2020). Design, development, and evaluation of a mobile learning application for tourism education. *Journal of Engineering Science and Technology*, Vol. 15, No. 6, pp.3859-3875.

Banomyong, et al., (2019). A systematic review of humanitarian operations, humanitarian logistics and humanitarian supply chain performance literature 2005 to 2016. *Annals of Operations Research*, Vol. 283, pp.71–86. https://doi.org/10.1007/s10479-017-2549-5

Boell, S. K., & Cecez-Kecmanovic, D., (2015). On being 'systematic' in literature reviews in IS. *Journal of Information Technology*, Vol. 30, No.2, pp.161–173. https://doi.org/10.1057/jit.2014.26

Cheng, G. & Shao, Y., (2022). Influencing factors of accounting practitioners' acceptance of mobile learning. *International Journal of Emerging Technologies in Learning*, Vol. 17, No. 1, pp.90-101. https://doi.org/10.3991/ijet.v17i01.28465

Darcy, S., et al., (2010). Accessible tourism and sustainability: a discussion and case study. *Journal of Sustainable Tourism*, Vol. 18, No. 4, pp. 515-537. https://doi.org/10.1080/09669581003690668

Dwan, K. et al, (2013). Systematic review of the empirical evidence of study publication bias and outcome reporting bias—An updated review. *PloS One*, Vol. 8, No.7, pp.1-37. https://doi.org/10.1371/journal.pone.0066844

Fatima, J.K. et al, (2019). Mobile learning adoption for tourism education in a developing country. *Current Issues in Tourism*, Vol. 22, No. 4, pp.420-427. https://doi.org/10.1080/13683500.2018.1434135

Farinha, F., et al, (2019). Selection Process of Sustainable Indicators for the Algarve Region—OBSERVE Project. *Sustainability*, Vol. 11, N. º 2, pp. 2-24. https://doi.org/10.3390/su11020444

Gössling, S., (2021). Technology, ICT and tourism: from big data to the big picture. *Journal of Sustainable Tourism*, Vol. 29, No. 5, pp.849-858. https://doi.org/10.1080/09669582.2020.1865387

Huang, Y.-M. & Chiu, P.-S., (2015). The effectiveness of a meaningful learning-based evaluation model for context-aware mobile learning. *British Journal of Educational Technology*, Vol. 46, No. 2, pp.437-447. https://doi.org/10.1111/bjet.12147

Jiravichai, A., & Banomyong, R., (2022). A Proposed Methodology for Literature Review on Operational Risk Management in Banks. *Risks*, Vol. 10 No. 5, 108, pp. 2-18. https://doi.org/10.3390/risks10050108

Lee, E.Y. & Jeon, Y.J.J., (2020). The difference of user satisfaction and net benefit of a mobile learning management system according to self-directed learning: An investigation of cyber university students in hospitality. *Sustainability*, Vol. 12, No. 2672, pp.1-13. https://doi.org/10.3390/su12072672

Li, J., et al, (2024). Open-set learning context recognizing in mobile learning: Problem and methodology. *ICT Express*, 10, pp.909-915. https://doi.org/10.1016/j.icte.2024.04.006

McGrath, G. M., et al., (2020). Teaching sustainability in tourism education: A teaching simulation. *Journal of Sustainable Tourism*, pp. 1–18. https://doi.org/10.1080/09669582.2020.1791892

Marian, CV. & Iacob, M. (2022). The ArchTerr Project—A GIS-Based Integrated System for Cultural and Archaeological Heritage Protection (Pilot Phase Tested in Romania). *Applied Sciences-Basel*, Vol. 12 No. 16, pp.1-24. https://doi.org/10.3390/app12168123

Moya, S. & Camacho, M., (2021). Identifying the key success factors for the adoption of mobile learning. *Education and Information Technologies*, Vol. 26, pp.3917-3945. https://doi.org/10.1007/s10639-021-10447

Quinta-Nova, L., & Ferreira, D., (2022). Analysis of the suitability for ecotourism in Beira Baixa region using a spatial decision support system based on a geographical information system. *Regional Science Policy & Practice*, pp.1–21. https://doi.org/10.1111/rsp3.12583

Rezvani, et al., (2022). A risk-based decision-making approach for identifying natural-based tourism potential areas. *Journal of Outdoor Recreation and Tourism-Research Planning and Management*, Vol. 37, No. 100485, pp.2-13. https://doi.org/10.1016/j.jort.2021.100485

Strzelecka, M., et al., (2017). Using PP GIS interviews to understand residents' perspective of European ecological network Natura 2000. *Tourism Geographies*, Vol. *19*, No. 5, pp.848-877. https://tinyurl.com/3483mh59

UNWTO, (2005). *Making Tourism More Sustainable: A Guide for Policy Makers. Madrid: World Tourism Organization*. https://doi.org/10.18111/9789284408214

Varju, et al., (2014). Geographic Information Systems in the Service of Alternative Tourism - Methods with Landscape Evaluation and Target Group Preference Weighting. *International Journal of Tourism Research*, Vol. 16, No. 5, 496-512. https://doi.org/10.1002/jtr.1943

Vaz, E. (2016). The future of landscapes and habitats: The regional science contribution to the understanding of geographical space. *Habitat International*, 51, 70-78. https://doi.org/10.1016/j.habitatint.2015.10.004

Vaz, ED., et al. (2012). Urban heritage endangerment at the interface of future cities and past heritage: A spatial vulnerability assessment. *Habitat International*, Vol. 36, No. 2, pp.287-294. https://doi.org/10.1016/j.habitatint.2011.10.007

Tan, E. & Law, R., (2016). mLearning as a softer visitor management approach for sustainable tourism. *Journal of Sustainable Tourism*, Vol. 24, No. 1, pp.132-152. https://doi.org/10.1080/09669582.2015.1049610

Trindade, A. R., Carvalho, A. A. A., & Marques, C. G. (2022). Proposal of a Methodological Approach for Digital Innovation in Sustainable Tourism Project Design and Management. *Proceedings of 22ª Conferência da Associação Portuguesa de Sistemas de Informação* (CAPSI 2022), Ilha de Santiago, pp. 282-294. http://dx.doi.org/10.18803/capsi.v22.282-294

Trindade, A.R. et al, (2024). Competencies to digital innovation and the design of sustainable tourism projects: Challenges and risks for tourism sustainability. In Seabra, C. & Korstanje, M. (eds.) *A Research Agenda for Tourism and Risk*. Edward Elgar Publishing (forthcoming).

Vidal García, M. et al, (2019). Determinants of the acceptance of mobile learning as an element of human capital training in organisations. *Technological Forecasting & Social Change*, Vol. 149, No. 119783, pp.1-16. https://doi.org/10.1016/j.techfore.2019.119783

Zhu, Z. & Huang, W., (2023). A meta-analysis of mobile learning adoption using extended UTAUT. *Information Development,* pp.1-17. https://doi.org/10.1177/02666669231176428

ROADBLOCKS AND OPPORTUNITIES FOR CHINESE TOWNSHIP TEACHERS USING MOBILE LEARNING FOR BALANCES AND HIGH-QUALITY EDUCATIONAL DEVELOPMENT

Yuxia Tan, Jiachao Wei and Mengqi Su
School of Educational Sciences, Nanning Normal University, Guangxi, China

ABSTRACT

As a relatively new and independent learning method that replaced traditional classroom instruction, mobile learning has now steadily evolved into a cutting-edge, future learning mode. It is crucial to use mobile learning to support China's compulsory education system's balanced development to maintain a high standard of education. There is still a gap between the requirements and standards of the balanced development of compulsory education in China, which cannot meet the needs of the entire process of education fairness and the overall improvement of education quality. This is especially true of China's township primary and secondary schools, especially in remote areas, where there is a lack of educational facilities, inadequate capital investment, and other objective factors. This means that to support teachers' professional development and the balanced advancement of mandatory education, township primary and secondary school teachers must improve their knowledge of and proficiency with mobile learning, optimize the learning model, increase the availability of learning resources, and fortify their training.

KEYWORDS

Mobile Learning, High Quality Balance, Township Primary and Secondary Schools

1. INTRODUCTION

"We should promote education equity, accelerate the balanced development of compulsory education and urban-rural integration, and optimize the allocation of regional education resources," the Chinese Education Department's 2023 report said. Based on the fundamental balance of compulsory education, the balanced development of compulsory education aims to further seek the fairness of the entire educational process and the general enhancement of the quality of education (Feng, 2013). Examining the evolution and restructuring of mandatory education in China, the following phases can be summed up: China's compulsory education has achieved significant progress in popularization between 1986 and 2006 thanks to policy orientations that prioritize popularization and quality enhancement. The fundamentally balanced growth of mandatory education will be supported between 2006 and 2022 under the direction of fair quality policy. China's 2895 counties will have met the requirements for fundamental balanced development by the end of 2021. Following 2022, China will embark on a new phase of policy orientation centered around high-quality balance to develop education to a higher level based on basic balance. However, as science and technology advance, mobile learning—a new approach to learning that is becoming more and more popular in the digital age—becomes more and more significant. Mobile learning can offer us a fresh perspective on the current disparity between the balanced growth of compulsory education and the expansion of primary and secondary education in towns and villages.

To put it briefly, township teachers should use mobile learning to their advantage to advance. The two main components of education are teachers and pupils. Teachers can only educate pupils more effectively and take on the duty of producing socialist builders and successors for the nation when they are at the forefront of education.

2. LITERATURE REVIEW

2.1 Studies on The Connection Between Mobile Learning Technologies and High-Quality Equilibria

To support the balanced growth of compulsory education, Chinese scholars Liu, Y.Q. (2014) and Lu, F.K. (2018) proposed mobile learning technology. First and foremost, mobile learning technology may enhance the classroom teaching environment and encourage the sharing of excellent educational content. The second goal is to support the balanced development of mandatory education, which includes implementing in-class and school communication, using information technology for teaching, and so on. The final goal is to support gender equality in the educational process and close the achievement gap, particularly in developing nations like India.

2.2 Studies on The Enhancement of Teachers' Professional Growth Using Mobile Learning

Respectively, Chinese scholars Cao, Y.H. (2017) and Yang, Q.G. (2021) suggested using mobile learning in the sphere of education. The first is to support teachers' professional development and transform the traditional classroom setting through mobile learning; the second is to offer contemporary distance learning to give teachers the chance to further their education and professional growth; and lastly, it assists teachers in shifting from being traditional preachers to facilitators, mentors, and supporters of learning to better prepare them for the teaching profession.

3. RESEARCH DESIGN

3.1 Theoretical Foundation

This paper selects the Unified Theory of Acceptance and Use of Technology (UTAUT). The Unified Theory of Acceptance and Use of Technology (UTAUT), as presented in Figure 1, was developed in 2003 by American scholars Venkatesh et al. based on the integration of multiple technology acceptance models, which included the four aspects of performance expectations, effort expectations, social impact, and convenience conditions (Pan & He, 2024). The acceptance of different educational technologies by instructors and students, including mobile learning aids, educational software, and online learning platforms, can be examined using the UTAUT paradigm. By conducting research and analysis, we can identify the variables that influence how instructors and students utilize these tools, and we can then implement the necessary changes to encourage the use of technology in the classroom and raise educational standards and productivity (Liu, Li, & Wang, 2020).

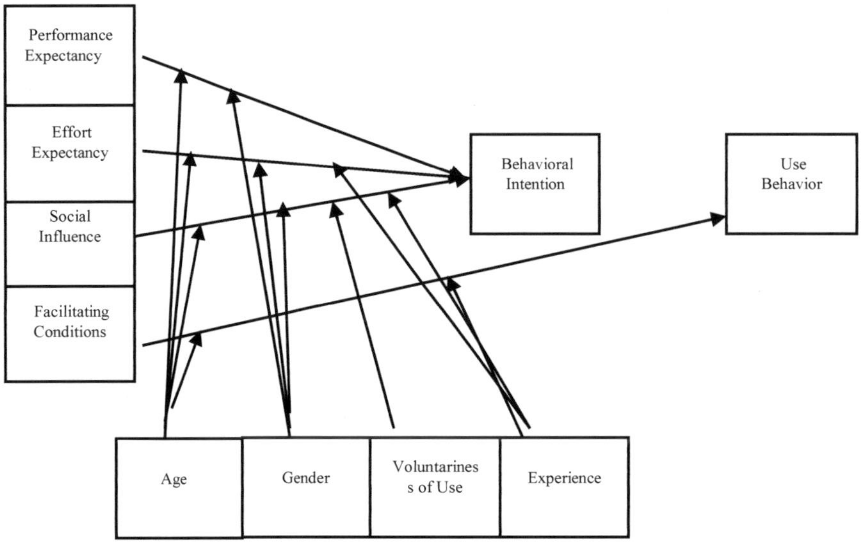

Figure 1. UTAUT model

3.2 Research Hypothesis

The integrated information technology acceptance model (UTAUT), put forth by Venkatesh et al., is the theoretical framework that this study attempts to use to investigate and study the current state of mobile learning for primary and secondary school teachers in China's villages and towns, as well as the relationship between mobile learning and the balanced development of compulsory education. The research hypothesis is that there is a positive correlation between mobile learning and the balanced development of compulsory education in China's villages and towns. This conclusion is based on the reading and analysis of pertinent literature and data.

3.3 Research Objects and Research Tools

In Southwest China, primary and secondary school teachers in villages and cities are the study subjects. 782 of the 820 questionnaires that were distributed were found. 760 valid questionnaires—an effective recovery rate of 95.37%—were obtained after invalid questionnaires were eliminated. Teachers of primary and high schools in townships made up the respondents.

4. RESEARCH RESULTS

4.1 Raise the Bar for Primary and Secondary School Instructors in Township Schools

To begin with, the majority of educators concur that mobile learning technologies can enhance the caliber of instruction and learning. To increase students' learning outcomes, mobile learning technology can be used to enhance instructional materials, vary instructional approaches, and offer flexible teaching strategies. Second, most educators are aware of how mobile learning technologies can boost students' motivation and excitement for studying. The features of mobile learning—interactivity, engagement, and personalization—have the power to grab students' interest and pique their passion for learning. Lastly, educators feel that mobile learning technology can overcome geographic barriers to provide high-quality education to towns and villages and close the achievement gap between urban and rural education, all while supporting the balanced quality of required education. Teachers' performance expectations have been continuously raised as a result of their growing knowledge of and experience with mobile learning. As Figure 2 illustrates, teachers have gradually come to see the potential of mobile learning in enhancing instruction, stimulating students' interests, and advancing the caliber and balance of compulsory education.

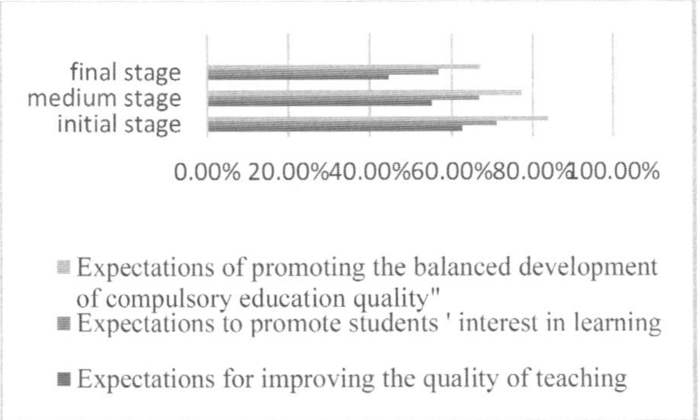

Figure 2. Performance expectancy of teachers

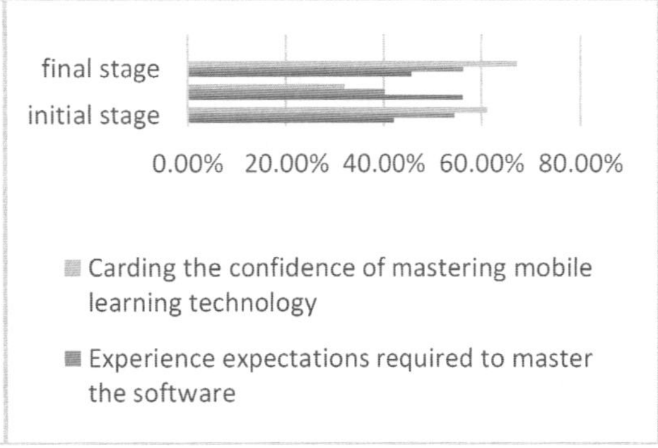

Figure 3. Effort expectancy of teachers

4.2 Lower the Effort Requirements for Instructors in Township Primary and Secondary Schools

Particularly young educators who are more open to new technology, some teachers think using mobile learning tools is quite simple. It takes more time and effort to learn new mobile learning tools, though, and some senior teachers find it challenging. Though the degree of confidence varies depending on individual technical level and experience, teachers are generally confident in their ability to master mobile learning technology and use it in teaching. Teachers' expectations of work have increasingly improved along with their expertise in mobile learning technologies as a result of more training and hands-on experience. They believe that learning the technology is more confident and that it is simpler to get started. In addition, they believe that less time and effort are needed, as Figure 3 illustrates.

4.3 Amplify the Social Influence of Elementary and High School Teachers in Townships

First of all, teachers are more likely to be influenced and attempt to use mobile learning tools if their colleagues use them frequently and do well with them. This demonstrates that, in addition to the importance of peer example and communication in fostering mobile learning, school administrators' attitudes also have a significant influence on teachers' adoption of mobile learning. Teachers will participate more fully in mobile learning when leaders support and encourage them to do so. Lastly, instructors' approval of mobile learning is also influenced to some extent by public opinion and educational trends. With the increasing use of contemporary information technology in the classroom, educators are gradually coming to understand the value of mobile learning. As time goes on, educators' favorable attitudes and behaviors about mobile learning are increasingly influenced by leaders and colleagues; this has led to a progressive growth in social impact, as Figure 4 illustrates.

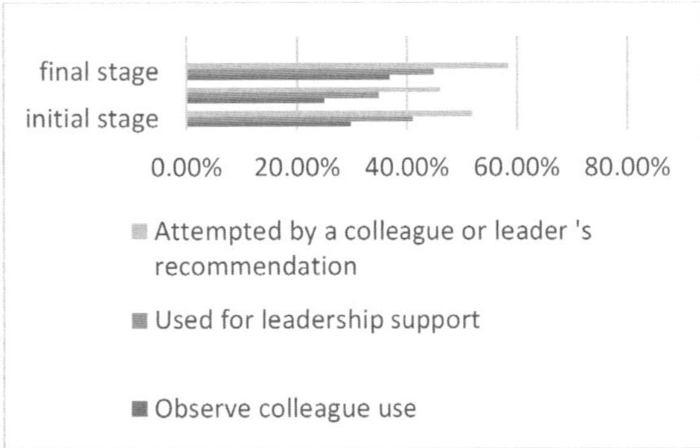

Figure 4. Social influence of teachers

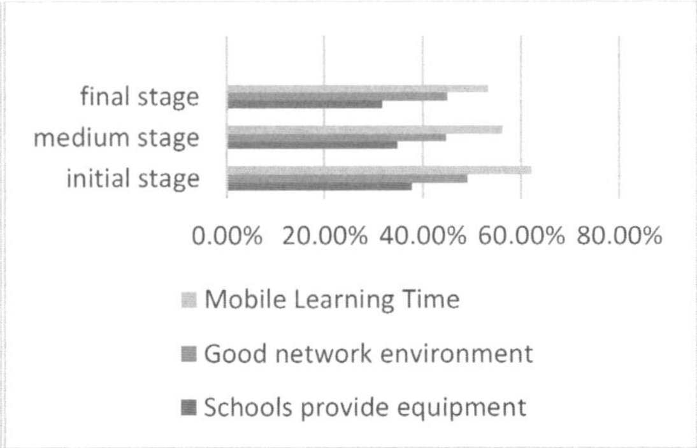

Figure 5. Facilitating conditions of teachers

4.4 Better Accommodations for Elementary and Secondary School Teachers in Townships Should Be Provided

First and foremost, reliable tools and networks are essential for instructors to employ mobile learning technologies. Still, there are certain issues with several local schools in this area. Second, training and support resources are essential for teachers to understand mobile learning technology. Objective issues like aging equipment and unstable networks impair teachers' user experience. While some schools have offered instructors pertinent training, there is still room for improvement in terms of both content and delivery techniques to better serve teachers' needs. Finally, time management is a critical consideration for educators. Some teachers are overburdened with tasks, leaving them with little time to experiment with and implement mobile learning. It is essential to give teachers more time for learning and to organize the curriculum reasonably. As demonstrated in Figure 5, the school has progressively prioritized and enhanced the infrastructure that supports mobile learning, given instructors more tools, and enhanced the network environment while logically allocating tasks to them and giving them more time for mobile learning.

In conclusion, it is evident from the examination of the questionnaire survey results that primary and secondary school teachers in townships have a basic awareness of the role that mobile learning plays in the development of high-quality and well-rounded compulsory education, but there are still certain issues and difficulties with its actual implementation. We will further encourage the use of mobile learning technology and support the balanced growth of compulsory education by raising instructors' performance demands, lowering effort expectations, boosting social effects, and improving convenience circumstances.

5. SUGGESTIONS

5.1 Precision Targeting Performance

Economic progress, advanced network technologies, and smartphone ubiquity in rural areas facilitate mobile learning. Users can independently select advanced mobile devices and access the internet anytime, anywhere. Engaging in learning through feedback and coaching is pivotal for improving educational outcomes and advancing education. Rural educators must understand active learning to excel in modern teaching. They should adopt teaching strategies suited to real-world contexts and leverage mobile learning's practicality, feasibility, and flexibility to enhance their teaching standards and social competitiveness. Additionally, they should deepen their understanding of mobile learning to effectively use it for independent study (Chen, 2017).

5.2 Stimulate Endogenous Motivation

Mobile devices have revolutionized education through mobile learning, enabling ubiquitous access to educational content. This approach encompasses various styles, firstly, autonomous learning--individuals select and schedule their learning based on personal interests and needs. Secondly, socially interactive learning--platforms enable communication and collaboration, fostering a community-like environment for learning. Thirdly, personalized learning--utilizing big data, platforms offer tailored content aligned with users' objectives and preferences. Finally, gamified learning--educational content is integrated into games, enhancing engagement through competition and rewards. These modalities underscore the versatility of mobile learning in accommodating diverse learning preferences and enhancing educational engagement.

5.3 Expand Multi-Radiation

Mobile learning technology has transformed education by enhancing access to a broad spectrum of educational materials, transcending geographical limitations and enabling global educational resource sharing. It personalizes learning by allowing users to select content based on individual interests and needs.

Furthermore, this technology has refined teaching practices. Educators can assign tasks, interact with students, and manage courses via mobile devices, leveraging real-time student progress data to adjust instructional strategies. Mobile learning has also facilitated innovative pedagogies such as blended learning and the flipped classroom, where students conduct independent study outside of class and engage in interactive activities within the classroom, thereby boosting student participation and instructional effectiveness.

5.4 Make Good Use of Convenient Conditions

Learning is now more than just listening in class and reading books—mobile learning has revolutionized traditional education. Users can make use of fragmented time to learn in parks, subways, and buses by utilizing mobile learning technology. Learning may be made more engaging and vivid with the use of mobile learning applications, which typically include engaging features like social learning, online testing, learning games, and other features. Furthermore, mobile learning facilitates both independent and group learning. To enhance the learning process, users can interact and collaborate with classmates, teachers, or other learners, as well as learn at their own pace.

6. CONCLUSION

Due to the small sample size, this study may not accurately reflect the circumstances facing primary and secondary school teachers in towns and villages as a whole. In the future, there will be opportunities to increase the survey's sample size, enhance its representativeness and accuracy, and track and evaluate teachers' mobile learning habits over an extended time. This will create a more robust scientific foundation for supporting primary and secondary school teachers' mobile learning in urban and rural areas, as well as the balanced and high-quality development of compulsory education.

To put it briefly, the features of mobile learning—namely, its great flexibility, robust engagement, and personalization—offer a more practical and effective method of instruction. Users are free to select the mobile learning mode that best suits their requirements and tastes. Primary and secondary school teachers in townships, particularly those who work in remote areas, can enhance their professional development by utilizing mobile learning technologies to raise the standard of teacher education. This will not only help to reduce regional disparities but also advance the balanced growth of mandatory education.

ACKNOWLEDGMENT

This article is a phased result of the key project of Guangxi Undergraduate Education Reform Project in 2024: Construction and Practice of "Three Learning" and "Four Party" Collaborative Practice Teaching System for Normal Majors under the Background of Professional Certification(2024JGB266).

REFERENCES

Cao, Y. H., &Yang, Q. G. (2017). Mobile Learning for Education Quality and Education Equality: Some New Trends of the Overseas Study and Practice. *International and Comparative Education, 39(03)*,60-66+88. DOI:10.20013 / j. cnki. ice. 2017.03.008

Chen, Z. C. (2017). Innovation of mobile learning model for adult education in underdeveloped rural areas. *China Adult Education, (07),*157-160

Feng, J. J. (2013). Theoretical Study on High—quality Balanced Development of Compulsory Education. *Global Education, 42(1)*,84-94+61.

Lu, F. K., Hao, Z. Y., & Zhang, H. J. (2018). Research on the effective ways of information technology to promote the balanced development of schools in the region. *Compilation of scientific research results of the 13th Five-Year Plan, Vol.4*, 73-77.

Liu, J. D., Li, Q. X., & Wang, J. (2020). Research on the influencing factors of online office APP users ' behavior based on UTAUT mode. *Information Science, 38(09)*,49-55+68.

Liu, Y. Q. (2014). Research on the Impact of Information Technology on the Balanced Development of Compulsory Education in Area of China. *China Education Technology, (04)*,43-47.

Pan, Y., & He, W. (2024). Research on the influencing factors of promoting flipped classroom teaching based on the integrated UTAUT model and learning engagement theory. *Sci Rep* 14, 15201. https://doi.org/10.1038/s41598-024-66214-7

Yang, Q. G., &Xu, T. T. (2021). Mobile Learning Promotes Teacher Professional Development: Change, Challenge and Response. *Journal of Capital Normal University (Social Sciences Edition)*, *(03)*,171-180.

COMPARISON OF STUDENT ATTENDANCE RATES AND ANALYSIS OF THEIR IMPACTS ON STUDENTS' ACADEMIC PERFORMANCE: BLENDED LECTURES (ONLINE PLUS OFFLINE) VS PURELY OFFLINE LECTURES

Victor K. Y. Chan[1] and Hio Man Lei[2]
Macao Polytechnic University
[1]Faculty of Business, Macao Polytechnic University, Rua de Luís Gonzaga Gomes, Macao, China
[2]Centre for Gaming and Tourism Studies, Macao Polytechnic University, Avenida Padre Tomás Pereira, Taipa, Macao, China

ABSTRACT

This paper empirically compares, for the same series of courses, the student attendance rates in blended lectures (i.e., comprising on-and-off online and offline lectures) and those in purely offline lectures and analyzes the impact of such student attendance rates on students' academic performance and such impact's moderation by the blended versus purely offline paradigms. Two samples respectively of blended lecture attendance rates together with academic performance from the academic year 2022/2023 ($n = 78$) and purely offline lecture attendance rates together with academic performance from 2023/2024 ($n = 83$) were collected from students at the authors' university in Chinese-culture-oriented Macao, both samples covering the same series of four senior undergraduate courses in disciplines ranging from software engineering to management. Students' academic performance in a course was appraised by their final examination scores or their coursework scores, depending on whether the course concerned included any final examination. It was found with statistical significance that the mean overall attendance rate (covering both online and offline lectures) in the blended lectures was higher than that in the purely offline lectures ($p < 0.05$), the mean attendance rates in both the online and offline lectures out of the blended lectures were respectively higher than those in the comparable lectures out of the purely offline lectures ($p < 0.01$ and $p < 0.05$ respectively), a high overall attendance rate for a student was associated with his/her good academic performance ($p < 0.01$), and this association was stronger in the case of purely offline lectures than blended lectures ($p < 0.05$), at least among students in Chinese-culture-oriented Macao. These findings offer guidance to universities, educators and students on the benefits of blended lectures.

KEYWORDS

Online Attendance Rates, Offline Attendance Rates, University Courses, In-dependent Samples *t*-test, Regression, Moderator

1. INTRODUCTION

Alongside the emergence of online lectures or classes (of course, inclusive of and dominated by mobile lectures or classes in recent years), researchers in the education discipline have been investigating the pedagogical efficacy of online lectures (probably, with respect to that of traditional, offline lectures) and the relationship between online lecture (probably, versus traditional, offline lecture) attendance and academic performance (Michinov et al, 2011; Galyon et al, 2016; Kauffman et al, 2018; Nieuwoudt 2020; Diab-Bahman, 2022; Chan, 2023). Some others pinpointed the advantages and disadvantages of online lectures vis-à-vis offline ones. In particular, advantages were typified by convenience (Chan, 2023; Jensen, 2011; Almahasees, 2021), more engagement in quantitative analysis (Chan, 2023; Dumford and Miller, 2018), flexible learning environment (Nieuwoudt, 2020; Chan, 2023; Almahasees, 2021; Bdair, 2021), academic achievement (Chan, 2023; Bdair, 2021), student-centered learning (Chan, 2023; Bdair, 2021), self-learning, and low costs (Chan, 2023; Almahasees, 2021). Disadvantages include difficulty in maintaining attention in the less structured environment of online lectures in comparison with offline counterparts (Chan, 2023; Jensen, 2011), demotivation of students in terms of their learning effort (Chan, 2023; Jensen, 2011; Almahasees, 2021), less engagement in collaborative learning, student-faculty interactions and discussions with diverse others (Chan, 2023; Dumford and Miller, 2018), less exposure to effective teaching practices (Chan, 2023; Dumford and Miller, 2018), lower quality of interactions between students and between students and faculty (Chan, 2023; Almahasees, 2021; Dumford and Miller, 2018; Bdair, 2021), inadequacy of behavioral control, online lecture training, Internet connectivity, and platform standardization (Chan, 2023; Bdair, 2021), academic integrity compromise (Chan, 2023; Bdair, 2021), learning environment trading off engagement, teamwork and social interaction and overloading students with assignments (Chan, 2023; Bdair, 2021), family burden in respect of the demand for computers and Internet access (Chan, 2023; Bdair, 2021), technical and Internet issues, data privacy, and security (Chan, 2023; Almahasees, 2021). Contingent upon the contexts, these researches, inter alia, rendered conflicting findings, for example, some upholding the online paradigm being superior to the offline counterpart whilst some favoring the contrary.

In the face of the COVID pandemic spanning the years from 2020 to 2023, universities virtually globally, reluctantly or not, were expediently compelled to the recourse of online lecturing, almost regardless of the courses' natures. Even "more" unprecedented was that some of the courses' lectures were delivered partially online and partially offline, for example, when the governments' lockdown policies were tightened and relaxed over the courses' semesters or terms as the pandemic developed. Such a situation of chance set the stage for collection of empirical data on student attendance in blended (i.e., on-and-off online and offline) lectures for various courses, which could otherwise be also impossible without the pandemic. In fact, Chan (2023) compared students' online lecture attendance rates with their offline lecture attendance rates for courses delivered via such blended lecturing and found the former's mean exceeding the latter's. However, even more intriguing context emerged toward the end of the pandemic when all expediencies tapered off and most lectures, if not all, reverted to the purely offline (i.e., totally in-person) paradigm. This endowed researchers with a once-several-decades occasion to collect empirical data on student attendance in purely offline lectures for a series of courses one semester or one year after analogous data had been collected for the blended lectures of the same series of courses. Thereby, contrast and comparison of students' attendance were enabled between the blended lecture paradigm and the purely offline lecture paradigm for the same series of courses, the two paradigms' practice being merely one semester (or term) or one year apart and thus any exogenous variables possibly impinging on attendance rates (other than the variable about blended lectures versus purely offline lectures) presumably remaining rather constant over such a short period of time. Jumping at this transitional opportunity, this article aims to fulfill the following objectives:

1. To compare students' overall attendance rates between the blended and purely offline lecture paradigms.
2. To compare students' attendance rates in the online lectures of the blended lecture semester with those in comparable lectures (i.e., lectures delivering the same instructional content of the same courses as the online lectures of the blended lecture semester) of the purely offline semester, i.e., to compare the online-attendance-corresponding rates between the blended and purely offline semester.
3. To compare students' attendance rates in the offline lectures of the blended lecture semester with those in comparable lectures (i.e., lectures delivering the same instructional content of the same courses as the offline lectures of the blended lecture semester) of the purely offline semester, i.e. to compare the offline-attendance-corresponding rates between the blended and purely offline semester.
4. To uncover how the overall attendance rate of a student in a course impacted his/her academic performance in the course and how the course comprising blended lectures versus purely offline lectures moderated such impact.

In particular, this study focused on a series of software engineering and management courses administered to students of predominantly Chinese culture at the authors' university. Though generalizability to students of other cultures and elsewhere might be subject to extension of the research to universities worldwide, this study did exemplify an investigation into a niche area in the broader domain of student attendance in online versus offline lectures and students' ensuing academic performance.

2. THE PRESENT STUDY

2.1 Materials

For the study, two empirical data samples were collected in two respective stages from the Faculty of Business at the authors' university in the city of Macao[1] (Special Administrative Region), China, the two stages being in the first semester of the academic years 2022/2023 and 2023/2024 respectively. These two semesters' lecturing lasted from 19 August 2022 to 24 November 2022 and 24 August 2023 to 29 November 2023. Each of these two samples from each of these two semesters was composed of the four undergraduate courses, specifically, one entitled "System Analysis and Design," one entitled "E-commerce Project Management," and two entitled "Operations Management." The contents, structures, and assessments of these courses were in essence, if not absolutely, identical across the two semesters so that the two data samples were comparable, independent samples. Table 1 delineates some characterizing features of these four courses.

Table 1. Characterizing features of the four courses in the present study

Course title	Language of instruction	Regular weekly lecture frequency	Program specialization, year of undergraduate study	Number of students in the semesters of 2022/2023, 2023/2024
System Analysis and Design	English	Two 1.5-hour lectures	E-commerce, 3	20, 21
E-commerce Project Management	English	Two 1.5-hour lectures	E-commerce, 3	20, 21
Operations Management	English	Two 1.5-hour lectures	Management, 3	19, 20
Operations Management	Chinese/ English (bilingual)	Two 1.5-hour lectures	Management, 3	19, 21

By design, all these courses were originally to deliver purely offline lectures in physical lecture rooms or computer laboratories. Nevertheless, amid the COVID-19 pandemic since early 2020, Macao was particularly plagued by a bout in mid-June 2022. As a precaution in the aftermath during the first semester of academic year 2022/2023, the authors' university imposed the expedient policy of online lectures in place of the otherwise offline counterparts. As such, approximately a quarter of all the lectures for these four courses in that semester of 2022/23 were conducted online, the rest adhering to the offline paradigm as usual. Hence, it was by chance that these courses in that semester of 2022/23 were partly online and partly offline, i.e., adopting a blended lecture paradigm. By the first semester of 2023/2024, the same four courses were offered again while most, if not all, pandemic expedients were lifted such that all the lectures of the four courses reverted to their purely offline lecture paradigm as originally designed. Therefore, over these two academic years, there so happened to be a very rare opportunity for the authors to collect data to contrast and compare the student attendance rates for these four courses between the scenario of expediently enforced blended lectures (i.e., on-and-off online and offline lectures) and that of back-to-normal, purely offline lectures.

At the authors' public university, it was a "statutory" requirement that attendance be taken by the professor-in-charge for each student in each lecture. Such attendance was recorded university-wide on an Internet/Intranet-based, specialized attendance system, from the attendance data for this study were collected. The online lectures were in the form of Zoom (Zoom, 2024) sessions with the professor-in-charge being the host and students being invited to the Zoom sessions over the Internet by means of an "Assignment" on the university's Canvas learning management system (Instruture, 2024). This way of inviting students to attend online lectures on Zoom had been practiced occasionally for around two years since the pandemic for quite some other courses prior to the above four courses, so all students were supposed to be so well versed in the platform that no operational impediment could likely preclude them from attending the online lectures for the four courses of this study. Locally in Macao, ownership of and access to such information and communications technology (ICT) as notebook/laptop computers, desktop computers, mobile phones and Internet connectivity

[1] "Macao" is sometimes also known as "Macau."

were commonplace (Xie et al., 2020) and so was those of and to Zoom sessions. In view of students' mastery of online courses' operation and the handiness of ICT equipment for that purpose, there was no environmental, operational, or resource-related limitation on students' voluntary choice to be present at any online lectures. In other words, the attendance records collected were truthful about the students' behaviors and decisions as opposed to such extraneous factors as operational hurdles, ICT equipment handiness, etc.

As for attendance taking, owing to its "statutory" nature, the procedure was carried out rigorously and formally during each lecture. For online lectures on Zoom, the professor-in-charge read out the name of each student for the student to report presence by voice before marking the student as present on the specialized attendance system, which stored such attendance records immediately on the university's server(s), the technological data integrity being safeguarded by a series of security measures inherent in the system. In case of suspected impersonation, the professor could choose to match the student's live appearance on Zoom against his/her official picture on the attendance system. Even if no camera was on the student's side, the professor could still question the student for identification purposes. For offline lectures, the professor read out the name of each student for the student to report presence either by voice or show of his/her hand before marking him/her as present on the attendance system and could simply tally the student's physical outlook with his/her official picture on the system to deter students from impersonation. Hence, the credibility of the attendance records for this study was beyond reasonable doubt.

It turned out that the sizes of the blended lecture sample from 2022/2023 and the purely offline lecture sample from 2023/24 were respectively 78 and 83.

2.2 Methods

For the student attendance in 2022/23 when there were blended (i.e., on-and-off online and offline lectures), an online-attendance-corresponding rate (r_n), an offline-attendance-corresponding rate (r_f) and an overall attendance rate (r_a) were calculated for each student in each course as in Table 2:

Table 2. The online-attendance-corresponding rate (r_n), the offline-attendance-corresponding rate (r_f) and the overall attendance rate (r_a) defined for 2022/2023

Rate	Definition
r_n	$\frac{\text{Total number of online lectures attended by the student in the course}}{\text{Total number of online lectures in the course}}$
r_f	$=\frac{\text{Total number of offline lectures attended by the student in the course}}{\text{Total number of offline lectures in the course}}$
r_a	$\frac{\text{Total number of (online and offline) lectures attended by the student in the course}}{\text{Total number of (online and offline) lectures in the course}}$

For the student attendance in 2023/24 when there were purely offline lectures, the online-attendance-corresponding rate (r_n), the offline-attendance-corresponding rate (r_f) for each student in each course were redefined by reference to the comparable online and offline lectures in 2022/23 in Table 3 whereas the definition of the overall attendance rate (r_a) was unchanged:

Table 3. The online-attendance-corresponding rate (r_n) and the offline-attendance-corresponding rate (r_f) redefined for 2023/24

Rate	Definition
r_n	$\frac{\text{Total number of lectures in 2023/2024 that were comparable to the online lectures in 2022/2023 by instructional content and were attended by the student in the course}}{\text{Total number of lectures in 2023/2024 that were comparable to the online lectures in 2022/2023 by instructional content}}$
r_f	$\frac{\text{Total number of lectures in 2023/2024 that were comparable to the offline lectures in 2022/2023 by instructional content and were attended by the student in the course}}{\text{Total number of lectures in 2023/2024 that were comparable to the offline lectures in 2022/2023 by instructional content}}$

To determine whether the overall attendance rate r_a in 2022/2023 (with blended lectures) differed from that in 2023/2024 (with purely offline lectures), an independent samples t-test was conducted. The test results would reveal whether the population mean r_a in the population of students in the four courses in 2022/2023 (with blended lectures) differed from that in 2023/2024 (with purely offline lectures) with statistical significance. Collaterally, the sample mean r_a for the students in the four courses in 2022/2023 (with blended lectures), that in 2023/2024 (with purely offline lectures) and the difference between them with its 95% confidence interval (CI) were derived.

To ascertain whether each of the online-attendance-corresponding rate r_n and offline-attendance-corresponding rate r_f in 2022/2023 (with blended lectures) correspondingly differed from each of those in 2023/2024 (with purely offline lectures), an independent samples t-test was applied to each of r_n and r_f between the two academic years. The test results would reveal whether the population mean r_n and r_f in the population of students in the four courses in 2022/2023 (with blended lectures) correspondingly differed from each of those in 2023/2024 (with purely offline lectures) with statistical significance. Collaterally, the sample mean r_n and the sample mean r_f for the students in the four courses in 2022/2023 (with blended lectures), those in 2023/2024 (with purely offline lectures) and the difference of each of them between the two academic years with its 95% confidence interval (CI) were derived.

To compare the overall attendance rate r_a for a student in a course as a predictor of his/her academic performance in the course in 2022/2023 (comprising blended lectures) with that in 2023/2024 (comprising purely offline lectures), regression as presented by the following equation was carried out:

$$p = \beta_0 + \beta_a r_a + \beta_{ay} r_a y + \epsilon \quad (1)$$

where p = the academic performance in the case, i.e., the final examination score or the overall coursework score, as applicable, of the student in the course;

$y = \begin{cases} 0 \text{ if the case was in 2022/2023 (with blended lectures)} \\ 1 \text{ if the case was in 2023/2024 (with purely offline lectures)} \end{cases}$

ϵ = the error term in the case; and

β_0, β_a and β_{ay} were the constant regression coefficients to estimate.

In other words, y is a moderator or moderating variable moderating the impact of r_a on p. Please note that in a very rigorous and formal sense, variables p, r_a, y, and ϵ in equation (1) should be subscripted by, for example, i, which indicates each case i in the two data samples as pooled. For the sake of simplicity, this subscript is omitted and understood.

The coefficient of determination (R^2) was calculated in order to estimate the proportion of the variation of p being explained the variations of r_a and $r_a y$. The higher R^2, the better r_a and $r_a y$ predicted p. The goodness-of-fit F-statistic to test the null hypothesis H_0: $\beta_a = \beta_a y = 0$ was also calculated so as to affirm whether either r_a or $r_a y$ or both predicted p with statistical significance. The t-statistics to test the individual null hypotheses H_0: $\beta_a = 0$ and H_0: $\beta_a y = 0$ were also computed so as to affirm whether r_a and $r_a y$ individually predicted p with statistical significance. In particular, the latter of these two t-statistics was to verify whether and probably also in what way y was a moderator moderating the impact of r_a on p with statistical significance.

3. RESULTS

Table 4 enumerates the sample mean overall attendance rate r_a (covering both online and/or offline lectures) for the students in the four courses in 2022/2023 (with blended lectures), that in 2023/2024 (with purely offline lectures), the difference between them with its 95% confidence interval (CI) and the t-statistic of the t-test to test such a difference with its p-values (two-tailed) and degrees of freedom.

Table 4. The sample mean overall attendance rate r_a in 2022/2023, that in 2023/2024, the difference between them with its 95% confidence interval (CI) and the corresponding t-test results

Sample mean r_a in		Difference / [95% CI]	t (p-value) / degrees of freedom
2022/2023	2023/2024		
.8147	.7578	.05688 / [.01074, .10301]	2.436 (.016*) / 148.491

* $p < 0.05$

The population mean overall attendance rate r_a for the students in the four courses in 2022/2023 (with blended lectures) is higher than that in 2023/2024 (with purely offline lectures) at the 5% significance level.

Table 5 lists the sample mean online-attendance-corresponding rate r_n and the sample mean offline-attendance-corresponding rate r_f for the students in the four courses in 2022/2023 (with blended lectures), those in 2023/2024 (with purely offline lectures), the difference of each of them between the two academic years with their 95% confidence intervals (CIs) and the t-statistics of the t-tests to test such differences with their p-values (two-tailed) and degrees of freedom.

Table 5. The sample mean online-attendance-corresponding rate r_n and the sample mean offline-attendance-corresponding rate r_f for the students in the four courses in 2022/2023 (with blended lectures), those in 2023/2024 (with purely offline lectures) and the difference of each of them between the two academic years with their 95% confidence intervals (CIs) and the corresponding t-test results

r_n or r_f	Sample mean r_n or r_f in		Difference / [95% CI]	t (p-value) / degrees of freedom
	2022/2023	2023/2024		
r_n	.9188	.8153	.10354 / [.02940, .17768]	2.758 (.006**) / 158.239
r_f	.7920	.7371	.05493 / [.00196, .10790]	2.049 (.042*) / 150.947

* $p < 0.05$
** $p < 0.01$

The population mean online-attendance-corresponding rate r_n and the population mean offline-attendance-corresponding rate r_f for the students in the four courses in 2022/2023 (with blended lectures) are higher than those in 2023/2024 (with purely offline lectures) at the 1% and 5% significance levels respectively.

For the regression corresponding to equation (1), Table 6 depicts the estimates of β_0, β_a and β_{ay}, their 95% confidence intervals (CIs), their two-tailed t-statistics (alongside their p-values and degrees of freedom), R^2 and the F-statistic (alongside its p-value and degrees of freedom).

Table 6. Estimates of β_0, β_a, β_{ay}, their 95% confidence intervals (CIs), their t-statistics, the R^2 and the F-statistic for the regression of equation (1).

		t (p-value), degrees of freedom
β_0 / [95% CI]	34.211 / [15.716, 52.705]	3.654 (.000**), 158
β_a / [95% CI]	56.190 / [33.852, 78.528]	4.970 (.000**), 158
β_{ay} / [95% CI]	8.551 / [.680, 16.422]	2.146 (.033*), 158
R^2	0.154	
F (p-value), df	13.959 (0.000**), (2, 153)	

* $p < 0.05$
** $p < 0.01$

In view of R^2 being equal to 0.154, the variations of r_a and r_{ay} explain 15.4% of the variation of p. The F-statistic is statistically significant ($p < 0.01$), so the overall attendance rate r_a for a student in a course together with the product between his/her overall attendance rate r_a and the course being in 2023/2024 (with purely offline lectures) predicted his/her academic performance in the course with statistical significance. Also, both the t-statistics for β_a ($p < 0.01$) and β_{ay} ($p < 0.05$) are statistically significant after controlling for each other. Therefore, in a sense, not only did the overall attendance rate r_a for a student in a course predict his/her academic performance in the course but also such prediction was moderated by the course being in 2023/2024 (with purely offline lectures). Also, the CIs for both β_a and β_{ay} are positive and do not span the zero point, so it is confirmed with statistical significance that a high overall attendance rate r_a for a student in a course tended to boost his/her academic performance in the course and that the course being in 2023/2024 (with purely offline lectures) strengthened the boost as manifested by substituting the values of β_a and β_{ay} into (1),

$p = 34.211 + 56.190r_a + \epsilon$ if in 2022/2023 (with blended lectures), i.e., $y = 0$ and

$p = 34.211 + 56.190r_a + 8.551r_a + \epsilon$ or $p = 34.211 + 64.741r_a + \epsilon$

if in 2023/2024 (with purely offline lectures), i.e., $y = 1$

4. CONCLUSION AND DISCUSSION

Against the backdrop of Macao's students with Chinese culture and in senior undergraduate courses in diverse disciplines, it transpired that their mean overall attendance rate (covering both online and/or offline lectures) in blended lectures was higher than that in the purely offline lectures. Subject to further research's verification, such findings may be explicable in terms of the online lectures' advantage of convenience (Chan, 2023; Jensen, 2011; Almahasees, 2021), which facilitates students' attendance and thus motivates their higher attendance rates in the online lectures out of the blended lectures vis-à-vis purely offline lectures.

Moreover, again for Macao's students with Chinese culture, this study revealed that the mean attendance rates in both the online and offline lectures out of the blended lectures were respectively higher than those in the comparable lectures out of the purely offline lectures where lectures were defined as "comparable" if they delivered the same instructional content of the same course. In other words, not only does the blended lecture paradigm render higher attendance rates in its online lectures than the purely offline paradigm in its comparable offline lectures but also the former even gives rise to higher attendance rates in its offline lecture than the latter in its comparable offline lectures.

In additional, again for Macao's students with Chinese culture, it was ascertained that a high overall attendance rate for a student in a course was associated with his/her good academic performance in the course, and this association was stronger in the case of purely offline lectures than blended lectures. This association between the overall attendance rate and the academic performance is conceivable in view of Nieuwoudt (2020) and various education theories, for instance, the agency theory (Westerman *et al.*, 2011). As for the enhancing effect of purely offline lectures on the association, it may be conjectured subject to further analysis that with the advantages of convenience (Chan, 2023; Jensen, 2011; Almahasees, 2021) and low costs (Chan, 2023; Almahasees, 2021), online lecture attendance (even as a component of blended lecture attendance) necessitates far less student commitment when compared with purely offline lecture attendance. Even a student with high online lecture attendance in a course should not necessarily be equated with his/her devotion to the course or concomitantly any high likelihood of his/her good academic performance in the course. In contrast, purely offline lecture attendance demands way more student commitment and thus more student devotion to the course, thereby escalating the odds of good academic performance substantially.

This study is not without its critics. First, the portfolio of course disciplines, though already omnibus, could still be broader. Second, the statistical results could have been more discerning if the number of students in the study was increased. Third, part of this study drew on the student attendance rates in the academic year 2022/23 (with blended lectures) and those in the academic year 2023/2024 (with purely offline lectures) to compare blended lecture attendance rates with purely offline lecture attendance rates. This is premised on the assumption that all exogenous variables possibly impinging on attendance rates (other than the variable about blended lectures versus purely offline lectures) remained fairly constant over the brief year in between. This may be true of most exogenous variables in the relatively stable educational context. However, 2022/2023 was pandemic-stricken whereas 2023/24 was "back to normal." Students' time management across the two academic years might differ substantively in that they might have almost no option whatsoever other than their courses in spending their time in 2022/23 whilst, for example, the revived extra-curricular activities in 2023/2024 might divert a considerable proportion of their time from their courses. Therefore, any variable(s) about students' time management probably being exceptions to the constant exogenous variable assumption may not be totally ruled out.

Having said this, this study affirms that the blended lecture paradigm is superior to the purely offline paradigm when it comes to student attendance rates and thus their academic performance. These findings offer guidance to universities, educators, and students on the benefits of blended lectures.

REFERENCES

Almahasees, Z., (2021). Faculty's and Students' Perceptions of Online Learning during COVID-19. *In Frontiers in Education,* Vol. 6, No. May, pp. 1–10. Available at: https://doi.org/10.3389/feduc.2021.638470

Bdair, I. A., (2021). Nursing Students' and Faculty Members' Perspectives about Online Learning during COVID-19 Pandemic: A Qualitative Study. *In Teaching and Learning in Nursing*, Vol. 16, No. 3, pp. 220–226. Available at: https://doi.org/10.1016/j.teln.2021.02.008

Chan, V. K. Y., (2023). Online vs Offline Attendance Rates: Are They Correlated and How Do They Compare? *Proceedings of International Conference on e-Learning and Digital Learning 2023 (ELDL 2023)*. Porto, Portugal, pp. 125–130.

Diab-Bahman, R. et al, (2022). The Effect of Attendance on Student Performance: Implications of Using Virtual Learning on Overall Performance. *In Journal of Applied Research in Higher Education*, Vol. 14, No. 3, pp. 1175–1192. Available at: https://doi.org/10.1108/JARHE-04-2021-0135

Dumford, A. D. and Miller, A. L., (2018). Online Learning in Higher Education: Exploring Advantages and Disadvantages for Engagement. *In Journal of Computing in Higher Education*, Vol. 30, No. 3, pp. 452–465. Available at: https://doi.org/10.1007/s12528-018-9179-z

Galyon, C. E. et al, (2016). Comparison of Group Cohesion, Class Participation, and Exam Performance in Live and Online Classes. *In Social Psychology of Education*, Vol. 19, No. 1, pp. 61–76. Available at: https://doi.org/10.1007/s11218-015-9321-y

Instruture, (2024). Amplifying Awesomeness: You. To the Power of the Canvas Learning Management Platform. Available at https://www.instructure.com/en-au/canvas, last accessed 2024/08/31.

Jensen, S. A., (2011). In-Class versus Online Video Lectures: Similar Learning Outcomes, but a Preference for In-Class. *Teaching of Psychology*, Vol. 38, No. 4, pp. 298–302. Available at: https://doi.org/10.1177/0098628311421336

Kauffman, C. A. et al, (2018). Relationship between Classroom Attendance and Examination Performance in a Second-Year Medical Pathophysiology Class. *In Advances in Physiology Education*, Vol. 42, No. 4, pp. 593–598. Available at: https://doi.org/10.1152/advan.00123.2018

Michinov, N. et al, (2011). Procrastination, Participation, and Performance in Online Learning Environments. *In Computers and Education*, Vol. 56, No. 1, pp. 243–252. Available at: https://doi.org/10.1016/j.compedu.2010.07.025

Nieuwoudt, J. E., (2020). Investigating Synchronous and Asynchronous Class Attendance as Predictors of Academic Success in Online Education. *In Australasian Journal of Educational Technology*, Vol. 36, No. 3, pp. 15–25. Available at: https://doi.org/10.14742/AJET.5137

Westerman, J.W. et al., (2011). The Relationship Between Undergraduate Attendance and Performance Revisited: Alignment of Student and Instructor Goals. *In Decision Sciences Journal of Innovative Education*, Vol. 9, No. 1, pp. 49–67. Available at: https://doi.org/10.1111/j.1540-4609.2010.00294.x.

Xie, Y. J. et al., (2020). Relationships between the Usage of Televisions, Computers, and Mobile Phones and the Quality of Sleep in a Chinese Population: Community-based Cross-Sectional Study. *In Journal of Medical Internet Research*, Vol. 22, No.7. Available at: https://doi.org/10.2196/18095.

Zoom, (2024). Zoom Workplace: Zoom Online Video Conferencing Homepage. Available at https://explore.zoom.us/en/lp/video-conferencing/?creative=649288063628&keyword=web%20conference%20plat-forms&matchtype=e&network=s&device=c&zcid=6095&utm_id=19735288070_649288063628&gclid=Cj0KCQjwn9CgBhDjARIsAD15h0B9FdK_h6JAkHpGIK60d6ylhxW1MraG0S380gFnavqaAEo, last accessed 2024/08/31.

A STRATEGIC STUDY OF LABOUR EDUCATION PRACTICES IN PRIMARY AND SECONDARY SCHOOLS IN URBAN GUANGXI (CHINA) BASED ON MOBILE LEARNING

Yue Zhao[1], Jiachao Wei[1] and Shujian Wei[2]
[1]*School of Education Science, Nanning Normal University, Nanning, Guangxi, China*
[2]*Menggong Central Primary School in Qintang District, Guigang, China*

ABSTRACT

In the new era of rapid development of globalised economy, mobile learning has become an important influence on labour education. In this study, labour education courses in primary schools in Guangxi towns in China were selected as research objects, and EXCEL tables were used to explore the relationship between labour education practices in primary and secondary schools in Guangxi towns (China) in the context of mobile learning. The study concludes that labour education practices in primary and secondary schools in Guangxi towns (China)appear to have shallow labour concepts, lack of initiative and learning-use disconnection among Chinese adolescents' labour education. Therefore, the three dimensions of enhancing adolescents' perception of labour and cultivating students' labour spirit; multiple incentives to enhance motivation; bridging the gap and building a curriculum system Which are presented as their suggestions.

KEYWORDS

Mobile Learning, Labour Education, Curriculum, Students

1. INTRODUCTION

Nowadays, m-learning is a kind of supplement to solidified learning in traditional teaching mode, providing convenience for students to acquire knowledge in today's fast-developing era. On March 20, 2020, the Central Committee of the Communist Party of China (CPC) and the State Council issued the Opinions on Comprehensively Strengthening the Labour Education in Universities, Schools and Primary Schools in the New Era, which emphasizes that labour education is an important content of the socialist education system with Chinese characteristics, and that it is necessary to include labour education in the cultivation of talents. The whole process of labour education should be integrated into the cultivation of talents. Therefore, the combination of mobile teaching and labour education is crucial. Based on this, the author analyzes the current situation of labour education practice in Guangxi towns (China), finds out the value embodiment and specific problems in the implementation of labour education in the context of m-learning, and then explores the practical path of labour education in primary schools.

2. LITERATURE REVIEW

In this study, taking 30th September 2024 as the time point, on the journal search of China Knowledge Network (CNKI: www.cnki.net), firstly inputting the keyword: m-learning, 14,260 academic journals are displayed online, among which 14,260 are from the Chinese Social Sciences Citation Index with those originating from the selection of the Peking University Library. There are 993 articles from core journals. Secondly, inputting the keyword: labour education, China Knowledge Online shows 30895 academic journals, of which 2478 are from the core journals of Chinese Social Sciences Citation Indexi. Entering the keyword: primary schools in Guangxi towns again, 6 academic journals are displayed, including 0 core journal papers from Chinese Social Sciences Citation Indexi and Peking University Library. Finally, the keyword: strategy research on labour education practice in primary schools in Guangxi towns (China) based on mobile learning showed 0 academic journals. This study combed through the above papers and concluded that the research on mobile learning mainly focuses on the following parts.

2.1 Research on the Value

Scholars have concentrated on the positive impact of mobile learning on subject education in primary and secondary schools, but little has been done to address the study of labour education time in primary schools. For mobile learning, many scholars have given their own insights, such as the American scholar Harris (2001) (USA), who believes that the two-way combination of mobile learning network technology and online learning allows people to carry out learning anytime and anywhere. Chinese scholars Liu Chunyan, Zhu Shuting, and Li Meishu (2024) (China) believe that m-learning can replace face-to-face learning, replacing the physical classroom experience by learning from a remote location or a mobile device at a different time. It can also complement face-to-face learning through the use of mobile devices to deliver content in a classroom lecture setting, and in the use of mobile devices to operate student project collaborations. The combination of m-learning and labour education is thus an important and crucial part of exploring new teaching models and advancing the digitalisation of education. The aim of this study is to combine the two and propose new thinking about their development.

2.2 Research on the Challenges

Scholars have focused on the negative impacts of mobile learning on the process of labour education practice in primary schools today. For example, Chinese scholars Tang Su'e and Wu Yanjiao (2024) (China) point out that the use of mobile learning tools in labour education has led to an imbalance in the value of the goal due to the overloading of educational technology, a loss of the main body of labour triggered by the reliance on educational intelligence, a loss of labour emotions due to the deconstruction of education into the virtual world, and a loss of order in the process of education due to the overstepping of the logic of capital, which are the four losses of education. The problem of 'four losses'. Chinese scholars Liu Yongmei (2024) (China) pointed out that in the context of mobile learning, the environment, means and evaluation overly lead to the dilution of the concept of student labour, the degradation of the body and brain and the decline in the quality of teaching and other issues. Primary school labour education in the specific implementation process, due to the alienation of teachers' labour concepts and students' labour concepts fade, in the process of implementation of the form and superficiality, the evaluation system appears to be monotonous, fixed, thus leading to primary school students' labour education in the context of m-learning laxity, perfunctory.

2.3 Research on the Implementation Path

Scholars have focused on the study of the realization path of mobile learning on the practice of labour education in primary schools in urban Guangxi, and three theoretical levels have emerged. First, at the macro level, the government should promote labour education in depth and ensure the establishment of the labour system. China has proposed in 2024 to cultivate new quality productivity. Therefore, the top-level design should be implemented to ensure that a scientific and perfect labour education guarantee system is put in place. Secondly, at the meso-level, Chinese scholars Chen Siyin, Qi Mingming and Peng Yanying (2024) (China) pointed out that schools should become the main venue for the dissemination of labour education, and teachers should change their teaching concepts, make full use of teaching resources, and set up the awareness of the combination of labour education and mobile learning in the new era. Thirdly, micro level: Student groups should take the initiative, improve their sense of social responsibility, and continue to accumulate labour knowledge and skills in order to adapt to future social needs.

At present, the academic research on labour education mainly focuses on three aspects, one is to combine labour education with education of other disciplines. Secondly, labour education is regarded as an independent discipline. Thirdly, labour education can be integrated with advanced fields, such as the development path of labour education in the era of artificial intelligence, or labour education can be combined with the National Education Conference for theoretical and practical exploration. In view of these, this paper will explore students' attitudes towards labour education in the context of m-learning, the implementation of labour education in the m-learning client learning and progress, explore its problems and give suggestions.

3. RESEARCH DESIGN

3.1 Theoretical Foundations

In 2004, Siemens (Canada) proposed the Connectionist Learning Theory. This theory is used to explain how human beings learn in complex networked environments, so it is also known as the learning theory of the digital age. The theory argues that in the era of rapid knowledge change and the rapid development of networks, complexity theory, self-organisation theory, chaos theory and network theory are the basic theories, and argues that learning is based on the relationship between people, networks, and digital products. Siemens (2004) (Canada) pointed out that connectionist learning theory is suitable to be applied to complex learning and learning in the midst of change. Thus, connectivism presents a completely different perspective from traditional behaviourism, cognitivism and constructivist cognitivism.

3.2 Research Hypothesis

Based on the literature review and the analysis of the problem, this study attempts to use Siemens' connectivism theory as the theoretical framework, conduct a survey study through the prepared questionnaire to explore the current situation of labour education in Chinese towns and cities (Guangxi), the impact of m-learning on the development of labour education in primary and secondary schools in Chinese towns and cities (Guangxi), and put forward the research hypotheses: m-learning has a positive correlation with the practice of labour education in primary and secondary schools in Guangxi towns and cities (China) relationship.

4. RESEARCH OBJECTS AND RESEARCH TOOLS

4.1 Research Sample

The object of this study covers primary and secondary school students in the townships of Guangxi Province, China. Nearly 30,000 questionnaires were distributed to primary and secondary school students in Guangxi Province, and relevant analyses and surveys were conducted based on the questionnaires. Until 25 September 2024, 31,592 questionnaires were distributed to students and 31,592 questionnaires were recovered. Therefore, the following table can be derived:

Table 1. Statistics on students' labour education in the context of mobile learning (%)

	Most agreeable	**More agreeable**	**agreeable**	**Less agreeabl e**	**Disagreeable**
I think students should be taught about labour	85.6	12.8	1	0.4	0.2
Students can use mobile devices for learning labour education	78.9	16.8	2.9	0.8	0.6
	4 times in a month	**3 times in a month**	**Twice in a month**	**Once in a month**	**Never**
Frequency of using mobile devices to learn about labour education	16.2	30.4	36.8	12.9	3.7
	Above 10 minutes	6-9minutes	1-5minutes	Below 1 minute	Never
Total time spent on labour education per use of mobile devices	3.2	45.6	41.8	5.3	4.1
	More difficult	**Difficult**	**Normal**	**Easy**	**Eaiser**
Ease of performing labour practices after learning on mobile devices	27.9	24.9	38.9	7.2	1.1
	Always maintain	Usually maintain	Often maintain	Seldom maintain	Never
Frequency of labour practices following learning on mobile devices	1.7	15.3	20.9	30.1	32

	Teacher requirements	Life requirements	Parental requirements	Hobby	None of the above.
Use of mobile devices for learning about labour education content topic selection	70.2	13.8	3.2	1.5	11.3

4.2 Research Instrument

The research tools for this study were self-administered questionnaire and EXCEL version.

The self-administered questionnaire is based on the theory of connectivism, and mainly includes three dimensions to explore: the background information part, the attitude of labour education, and the development of labour education in the context of mobile learning. For example, the student questionnaire mainly covers the students' education level; the students' recognition of labour education; the status of using mobile devices to learn labour education; and the results and continuity of the subsequent development of labour education.

5. RESEARCH RESULTS AND ANALYSIS

Using EXCEL software, this study firstly analysed the current situation of labour education practice in urban primary and secondary schools in Guangxi (China), and secondly attempted to explore the correlation relationship between m-learning and labour education practice in urban primary and secondary schools in Guangxi (China).

Firstly, based on the background survey of primary and secondary school students in urban Guangxi, it was concluded that the number of primary school students was 18,713, accounting for 59.2%; the number of junior high school students was 8,630, accounting for 27.3%; and the number of senior high school students was 4,249, accounting for 13.5%. There were 16,329 male students, accounting for 51.7 per cent, and 15,263 female students, accounting for 48.3 per cent. The survey shows that, although the degree of students' recognition of labour education is high, in reality, the enthusiasm for labour practice is not high, even the continuity of labour practice is greatly reduced, so that correct labour values have not yet been formed.

6. DISCUSSION OF THE FINDINGS

In summary, the research hypotheses were verified, and (Chinese) m-learning showed a positive correlation with the practice of labour education in urban primary and secondary schools in Guangxi. There are three aspects:

6.1 Shallow Labour Concepts

According to the results of the survey, students believe that they should carry out labour education flying shovel agree with and relatively agree with the proportion of 85.6% and 12.8%, which shows that the concept of labour of adolescents in the context of mobile learning is shallow. The reason is that in today's world, the international situation is changing rapidly, the economy and science and technology are developing at a fast pace, and the connotation of youth for labour and the way to carry it out is also changing. As a result, we cannot evaluate the concept of labour and labour awareness from the traditional point of view, but rather we need to pay more attention to the idea of youth on labour education.

6.2 Lack of Motivation

In this study, a questionnaire was asked about 'students' choice of topics for labour education on mobile devices'. The results showed that 70.2% of students chose the topics of labour education according to the requirements of teachers, 13.8% according to the needs of students' lives, 3.2% according to the requirements of parents, only 1.5% chose the topics they were interested in, and 11.5% chose the topics of labour education randomly and without any purpose at all. In view of this, the setting of labour courses, the assignment of labour tasks and the evaluation of labour in the mobile learning terminal are mostly controlled by teachers. This leads to a passive state of acceptance and a lack of opportunities for students to independently explore the meaning and value of labour.

6.3 Disconnection Between Learning and Use

The phenomenon of 'disconnection between learning and use' occurs after labour education is carried out on mobile devices. The study shows that only 1.7% of the students have always maintained the labour practice after learning on mobile devices, 15.3% have always maintained it, 20.9% have always maintained it, 30.1% have occasionally maintained it, and 32% have never maintained the labour practice. After students have conducted labour education on mobile clients, they put their knowledge and skills on the back burner once they are removed from the real-life labour environment.

7. STRATEGIC RECOMMENDATIONS

Mobile learning, as an indispensable support and means to achieve education modernization, which expands the connotation of labour education, extends the space of labour education, enriches the content of labour education, and at the same time brings brand new challenges. Based on the above analysis, the author will put forward suggestions:

7.1 Enhancement of Knowledge and Spirit Building

In the context of mobile learning, students can easily use mobile learning devices to actively search for labour knowledge and then practice to form a correct view of labour. Therefore, this study proposes the following points:

Firstly, the status of the subject should be clarified. Therefore, educators should actively guide students to experience the fun and sense of achievement of labour in the process of practice. In turn, students are guided to reflect on specific labour practices, about the relationship between personal cognition and technology application, the relationship between personal behaviour and intelligent technology in mobile learning, and the shortcomings and progress of individuals in labour practices. So that teachers should cultivate students' creativity. Secondly, injecting the spirit of labour model into students' personal shaping. In the context of mobile learning, teachers can adopt rich means to help students know the model workers, understand the model workers, and learn from the model workers. For example, teachers can use AI intelligent method to let model workers communicate with students in dialogue, use animation, short videos, including AR technology to let students personally experience the hardship of the model worker's working process.

7.2 Multiple Incentives to Enhance Motivation

In the context of mobile learning, the labour skills of mobile learning are different from the presentation of classroom labour knowledge and skills, and have the characteristics of labour such as diversity, progression and innovation.

Collaborative parenting between home, school and society is essential to increase the frequency of labour education. Firstly, at the school education level, the labour curriculum should be incorporated into the regular teaching system, and diversified practical labour activities should be carried out during regular weekly class hours, such as school clean-up days, handicrafts classes, and planting and breeding experiences. Secondly, in terms of family education, parents should change their mindset, abandon excessive pampering, and assign appropriate amounts of household chores to their children, such as washing dishes, sweeping the floor, etc., as well as giving correct guidance and encouragement. Finally, the social level can organize youth labour public welfare activities, such as community volunteer services, environmental protection actions, etc.

7.3 Bridging the Gap and Building a System

At present, there is a gap between learning and use in the field of labour education, which has two meanings. On the one hand, labour knowledge and skills are detached from labour practice. On the other hand, the continuity of labour practice is not strong, so that it is difficult to be sustained. Based on this, the author puts forward the following suggestions:

Make the curriculum better. Based on the background of mobile learning, teachers can make use of mobile learning resources, and make use of network resources and social resources to integrate labour time projects into the labour education curriculum. Teachers' labour education curriculum reduces the content of specific labour courses and introduces project-based integrated labour content into the task assignment. For example, the teacher set the theme like using agricultural planting knowledge, planting their favorite crops based on which students in the mobile device terminal or choose crops or choose flowers and fruits and vegetables, from the planting space to planting varieties, from turning the soil, sowing, fertilising to harvesting every step of the bucket of theoretical knowledge is closely integrated. So that students can have more planting experience.

8. CONCLUSION

With the background of the mobile learning era and the theoretical basis of connectivism, this paper argues that mobile learning is positively related to labour education. However, the shortcoming of this paper is that questionnaire survey was conducted on students only, which is a single target. In the future, teachers and parents can be taken as the target of the survey, which will help to make a clearer investigation on the implementation of labour education and the actual expectation of parents in primary and secondary schools in Guangxi (China).

ACKNOWLEDGMENT

The author is grateful to the 2022 (China) Guangxi Education Science Planning Research Base "Research on the implementation strategy of labour education curriculum in Guangxi urban primary schools under the background of 'Double Reduction'" (2022JD19).

REFERENCES

Chen, S.Y., Qi, M. M.* & Peng,Y. L. (2024). Exploration of labour education reform in colleges and universities led by artificial intelligence. *Journal of Guangdong Light Industry Vocational and Technical College,* 23(4), 46-49.

Harris, G. (2001). 50th Statistical Report on the Development Status of China's Internet. CHINA INTERNET NETWORK INFORMATION CENTER. http://www.cnnic.net.cn/NMedi-aFile/2022/0926/MAIN1664183425619U2MS433V3V.pdf

Liu, C. Y., Zhu, S. T. & Li, M. S. (2024). Research on the application of mobile learning in education industry. *Science and Technology Wind Theory Research,* 37(26), 145-147.

Liu, Y. M. (2024). The difficulties and breakthroughs of artificial intelligence-enabled labour education. *Teaching and Management,* 41(33), 35-39.

Siemens, G. (2005). Connectivism: A learning theory for the digital age. *International Journal of Instructional Technology and Distance Learning,* 2(1), 3-10.

Tang, S. E., & Wu, J. Y. (2024). Artificial Intelligence Embedded in Labour Education:Value, Risk and Relief. *Research on Electrochemical Education,* 45(9), 76-78.

DEVELOPMENT OF PRE-SCHOOL CHILDREN'S MATHEMATICAL AND GEOMETRIC IMAGINATION THROUGH DIGITAL TECHNOLOGIES

Kristýna Kiliánová, Petra Kočková and Kateřina Kostolányová
University of Ostrava, Faculty of Education, Department of Information and Communication Technologies
Frani Sramka 3, 709 00 Ostrava, Czech Republic

ABSTRACT

The article's primary focus is on the utilization of digital technologies in the context of preschool education, with a particular emphasis on their contribution to the nurturing of mathematical and geometric imagination. The article discusses the importance of pre-mathematics education in the context of children's cognitive development and presents the characteristics of children's thinking in preschool as described by developmental psychology theory. Furthermore, the article presents concrete tools, such as interactive applications, robotic toys and multimedia games, which have been demonstrated to enhance spatial orientation, logical reasoning and creativity. Additionally, the importance of a balanced approach that integrates traditional manipulative activities with digital technologies is emphasized. Finally, the article identifies the challenges associated with the implementation of these tools and the necessity for collaboration between educators and parents. The objective is to facilitate the meaningful use of technology that contributes to the harmonious development of children in a digital environment.

KEYWORDS

Mathematical Imagination, Geometric Imagination, Digital Technology, Kindergarten, Digital Literacy

1. INTRODUCTION

Digital technologies are now integral to modern education, playing a key role in developing 21st-century skills. As Mercader & Sallán (2017) and Pinto & Leite (2020) note, integrating these technologies is a priority across all education levels, from primary to higher education. This shift is not merely about upgrading technical equipment but responding to evolving societal and labor market demands for digital literacy. While basic tools like visual presentations and video platforms are widely used, the adoption of more advanced tools—such as social networks, interactive software, and robotics—is approached with greater caution (Mercader & Sallán, 2017).

Educational institutions must not only modernize infrastructure but also actively foster digital literacy, as children today are socialized in a technology-driven world. Research highlights the importance of early digital literacy development, as young children use technology for both entertainment and learning (Pöntinen & Räty-Záborszky, 2020). Factors such as age, social environment, and access to technology influence digital literacy levels (Styenhantseva, 2022). Consequently, educators must strategically integrate digital tools to enhance the learning process (Pöntinen & Räty-Záborszky, 2020). In the Czech Republic, research underscores the need for a comprehensive approach to digital literacy education that includes curricular, procedural, and organizational elements (Rambousek et al., 2015). This is particularly relevant in preschool education, where early experiences with technology shape children's problem-solving skills and approach to learning.

Digital tools effectively support cognitive and spatial development in early education. Interactive games and activities have been shown to enhance pre-math skills, geometric imagination, and logical reasoning (Havlaskova et al., 2020; Pereira, 2017; Nikulin, 2019). Robotic tools like Bee-Bot introduce fundamental algorithmic principles while fostering logical thinking and digital literacy (Havlaskova et al., 2020). Additionally, digital games encourage cooperative learning and improve cognitive abilities through Feuerstein's mediation criteria (Pereira, 2017). To advance digital literacy among educators and students, a structured approach is needed, including the development and assessment of digital learning materials

(Hostovecký & Zat'kova, 2011). This article explores the potential of digital technologies in fostering mathematical and geometric imagination in preschool children, offering theoretical insights, practical applications, and recommendations for educators and parents on meaningful technology integration.

2. THE USE OF DIGITAL TECHNOLOGIES IN EARLY CHILDHOOD EDUCATION

The integration of modern didactic technology, including digital tools, is becoming increasingly prevalent in preschool education. Interactive whiteboards, data projectors, robotic toys, and building blocks provide new opportunities for learning and skill development. However, concerns persist regarding the necessity and potential risks of digital technologies in early education. Despite these reservations, digital tools are deeply embedded in daily life, and many children already have access to tablets and smartphones at home. Early childhood education presents an opportunity to utilize this access meaningfully, fostering digital literacy from an early age.

When used appropriately, digital technologies can be both beneficial and motivating. Gjelaj et al. (2020) highlight their potential to enhance engagement, cognitive development, and creativity, while multimedia games offer interactive learning experiences with immediate feedback (Krezhevskikh & Mikhailova, 2019). Additionally, digital tools can be tailored to individual needs, promoting inclusivity in education. However, concerns remain about excessive screen time, which has been linked to reduced physical activity, poor sleep, and overstimulation (Straker et al., 2018; Holloway et al., 2015). Discrepancies also exist between educators, who often favor traditional activities, and parents, who report high levels of children's technology use at home (Gjelaj et al., 2020). Research suggests that the focus should be on the quality of content rather than the duration of screen exposure (Holloway et al., 2015).

Balancing digital tools with traditional activities is essential. Digital drawing apps can enhance fine motor skills, while interactive tasks support logical thinking, spatial awareness, and pre-mathematical abilities, crucial for school readiness (Familyarskaya, 2021). Digital tools also provide immediate feedback and interactive experiences that traditional methods may lack. For example, the Explain Everything app allows children to manipulate shapes dynamically, which is not possible with physical materials. Collaboration between educators and parents is key to maximizing benefits while minimizing risks, ensuring the appropriate use of technology in early education (Straker et al., 2018; Gjelaj et al., 2020). When effectively integrated, digital tools can complement traditional teaching methods, making learning more engaging and fostering cognitive and social development.

3. MATHEMATICAL AND GEOMETRIC IMAGINATION

Mathematical and geometric imagination play a crucial role in developing logical thinking, problem-solving skills, and understanding abstract concepts. Mathematical imagination involves working intuitively with abstract relationships, while geometric imagination focuses on recognizing and manipulating geometric objects. According to Nikulin (2019), geometric imagination bridges abstract concepts and their physical representations, enabling mental image generation and modification. Jirotková (2012) highlights the role of "spatial intelligence," which includes shape recognition, understanding transformations in position or size, and the ability to manipulate mental images. These skills are essential not only for understanding geometry but also for practical applications.

Young children process information differently from older students and adults. As Piaget (1964) explains, preschoolers are in the preoperational stage, where concrete and situation-based reasoning dominates. Generalization and classification are still developing, with children beginning to compare and evaluate objects based on prior experiences (Kaslová, 2010). Pre-mathematics education emphasizes play as a natural learning tool, helping children develop foundational skills such as sorting, recognizing similarities, and interacting with geometric objects. Digital technologies enhance this process by integrating engaging activities with effective learning. Interactive apps, such as Explain Everything, Canva, and Google's Jamboard, allow children to engage with geometric objects and develop spatial imagination (Krezhevskikh & Mikhailova, 2019). Similarly, applications like GeoBoard, Tangram for Kids, and GeoGebra improve children's ability to visualize relationships between geometric parts and the whole.

Robotic toys like Bee-Bot support spatial and algorithmic thinking by teaching children to plan movement trajectories and understand basic geometric concepts, such as direction and distance (Havlaskova et al., 2020). Interactive whiteboards and robotic building blocks further bridge abstract geometry and real-world objects, fostering analytical and intuitive thinking (Kmetova, 2020). Spatial orientation, a foundation of geometric thinking, develops through interactive games linking visual, motor, and verbal experiences. McCollum (2022) asserts that visual-motor experiences enrich mental imagery, enhancing intuitive understanding. Multimedia games involving geometric transformations (e.g., rotation, resizing) improve children's grasp of geometric operations. Additionally, integrating digital tools with physical models, such as 3D printing, facilitates the transition from two-dimensional representations to three-dimensional objects.

Developing mathematical and geometric imagination in preschool is vital for future success in mathematics and geometry. Digital tools provide engaging, hands-on learning experiences, but their use should be balanced with traditional activities like clay modeling, drawing, and hands-on construction. Fuchs et al. (2015) emphasize that working with physical materials fosters cognitive development and creativity. By combining digital and traditional methods, educators can create a comprehensive learning environment that nurtures both abstract reasoning and hands-on exploration.

4. ACTIVITIES DEVELOPING MATHEMATICAL AND GEOMETRIC IMAGINATION

The development of mathematical imagination in preschool children relies on cognitive abilities that support mathematical thinking and creativity (Diachenko, 2011). Mathematical concepts are essential for broadening a child's worldview and preparing them for school (Mamjonova Khushroy Shavkatovna et al., 2020), much like geometric imagination. Jirotková (2012) defines geometric imagination as the ability to recognize geometric figures and their attributes, conceptualize their interrelationships, recall their various forms, and visualize them based on descriptions, even when material models are unavailable.

Geometry occupies a distinctive position within the mathematical domain, as it is founded upon a distinct set of abilities that fall outside the purview of mathematical-logical intelligence. These abilities collectively constitute spatial intelligence, which can be further delineated as follows:

a) the ability to recognize the same shape,
b) the ability to identify similarities between disparate forms,
c) the capacity to discern alterations in the position or dimensions of a spatial object, and
d) the capacity to create and manipulate mental images,
e) the ability to represent two-dimensional spatial information in a visual format (drawings, plans, sketches, etc.),
f) the ability to express three-dimensional spatial information (building blocks, models, gestures, etc.).

The development of these abilities is reflected in the typology of activities used to create activities that support mathematical and geometric imagination. The typology of activities includes activities focused on comparing, matching, sorting, classifying, perceiving space, quantity and number series.

Kaslová (2010) defines comparison as a cognitive process in which a child perceives or recalls two distinct objects. Initially, comparisons involve tangible three-dimensional objects, such as people, animals, and everyday items, which can be touched. Later, children compare two-dimensional representations like pictures, shadows, and photos, followed by sounds, movements, and meanings. Through comparison, children develop an understanding of relationships such as size, length, height, and volume. Matching, another key cognitive process, involves forming ordered tuples (pairs, triples) from a set of objects based on predefined criteria. This is commonly practiced in kindergarten, where children pair homogeneous items (e.g., child-child, sock-sock) or non-homogeneous ones (e.g., theater seat-ticket, picture-word) (Kaslová, 2010).

Sorting is another essential activity, leading to the categorization of objects into distinct groups based on relationships within a set (Kaslová, 2010). Children sort objects by criteria such as colour, type, size, and shape, often using familiar items like food, clothing, and animals. Sorting also helps with recognizing geometric shapes, starting with basic forms like squares and circles and progressing to rectangles and triangles. Similarly, spatial perception activities help children understand directional concepts (e.g., up, down, behind) through exploration of their surroundings, nature walks, and block-building exercises. Additionally, quantity-based activities support early mathematical understanding through comparisons (e.g., "Which glass has more water?") and numerical concepts, helping children grasp terms like "a lot," "a few," and "too much." Lišková (2018) emphasizes that preschoolers learn numerical sequences verbally, often reinforced through rhymes and chants, ensuring that numbers are linked to meaningful real-world applications.

To reinforce these concepts, we utilized the Explain Everything app to create interactive tasks that develop mathematical and geometric understanding. Its compatibility with both PCs and iPads makes it accessible and engaging for young learners, supporting real-time collaboration, annotation, and multimedia integration. The app functions as an interactive whiteboard and a tool for instructional videos, though alternatives like Canva and Jamboard offer similar features. The choice ultimately depends on the teacher's and students' preferences and educational goals.

5. INTRODUCTION OF SPECIFIC ACTIVITIES

As a preliminary exercise designed to facilitate the advancement of mathematical and geometric concepts, we selected the Sorting by Color activity. The objective of this exercise is to arrange the images into the grey box, matching them to the corresponding colors. Through this activity, children will revisit the fundamental colors, and, due to the interactive nature of all the activities, their fine motor skills will also be enhanced.

Figure 1. Color and shape sorting activity (Kočková, 2019)

Another activity that engages children in sorting is the one connected with the recognition of shapes. The objective of this activity is to guide the children in the process of categorizing the objects (pictures) into the groups that correspond to their intrinsic characteristics. This activity allows children to practice recognizing geometric shapes.

From the category of activities focused on matching, we chose the activity on pair matching. This activity is one of the most basic and easiest activities to develop pre-math ideas. It is suitable even for the youngest children, so almost every preschooler should be able to do it. The aim of the activity is to create a pair with the same animals. The child's cognitive skills are developed at the same time.

Figure 2. Matching or pairing activity (Kiliánová, 2019)

The subsequent activity entails numerical operations. The objective is to select the corresponding number on the right-hand side, based on the number indicated in the image on the left. In this activity, the children are required to enumerate the animals depicted in the image and identify the corresponding number on the number line. This activity is designed to facilitate the recognition of numbers and to enhance counting abilities.

Figure 3. Number line activity (Kočková, 2019)

The following activity is exclusively dedicated to the instruction of geometric shapes. The objective of this activity is to facilitate the recognition of geometric shapes by associating them with objects that are familiar to the children from their immediate surroundings.

Figure 4. Learning geometric shapes (Kočková, 2019)

Once the child can recognize and name the basic geometric shapes, the following activity is offered for work. Preschool children love to put together different objects from building blocks, so it is no wonder that they enjoy this type of activity. Their task in this case is to build an animal from geometric shapes such as circles, triangles, rectangles, etc., while repeating their names.

Figure 5. Composing animals from geometric shapes (Kiliánová, 2019)

6. THE RESULTS OF THE OBSERVATIONS

The activities were tested in practice in three kindergartens in the Czech Republic with a total of 45 childrens aged 4 to 6 years. The observations conducted during the implementation of the proposed digital activities in preschool education yielded several key findings. The children demonstrated active engagement with the interactive tasks proposed in the Explain Everything app, particularly in activities that combined visual stimuli with manual manipulation of digital objects.

The activities utilizing the Explain Everything app enabled children to interact with geometric shapes, thereby facilitating a more profound comprehension of the relationships between the constituent parts and the whole. To illustrate, children assembled patterns comprising discrete shapes (e.g., triangles, squares) or rotated objects to generate a particular configuration. These activities facilitated the development of visualization skills and spatial perception. The completion of interactive tasks aimed at sorting objects according to shape, color or size proved instrumental in the development of classification skills and logical thinking. The children were able to rapidly discern the rules of classification and apply them to novel tasks, thereby demonstrating the acquisition of fundamental generalization skills. In tasks that required children to construct their own patterns or create scenes, they demonstrated a capacity for creative problem-solving. The tasks set provided motivation for the children to devise their own methods for completing the tasks and to utilize the tools available in the app. In pairs, children shared their ideas and discussed potential solutions to the tasks. This collaboration not only promoted social interaction but also facilitated a deeper comprehension of the concepts through peer learning.

The results demonstrate that more than 80 % of the children were able to complete the interactive tasks in the Explain Everything independently after their third attempt, indicating a high level of children's adaptability to the digital geometric imagination in preschool children. App is an efficacious instrument for fostering mathematical and geometric imagination in preschool children. Due to the interactive character of the activities and the capacity to manipulate digital objects, it assists children in developing essential competencies such as visualization, classification and creative problem-solving. These findings substantiate the assertion that digital tools, when judiciously integrated, can facilitate learning in a playful manner and enhance children's engagement in the learning process.

7. CONCLUSION

Integrating digital technologies into preschool curricula equips children with essential skills for the digital age. Research shows that interactive applications, robotic toys, and multimedia games enhance mathematical imagination, logical thinking, and digital literacy while fostering creativity and curiosity.

However, a balanced approach is crucial, combining digital tools with hands-on activities like construction blocks and natural materials to support motor and cognitive development. A thoughtful blend of both methods ensures comprehensive growth.

Future research should explore digital technology's impact on cognitive and social skills and optimize collaboration between educators and parents. A responsible approach will maximize technology's benefits for early childhood development.

REFERENCES

Diachenko, O. M., (2011). On major development in preschoolers' imagination. *International Journal of Early Years Education.* No. 19, pp. 19-25.

Familyarskaya, L., (2021). Integration of Digital Technologies in the Educational Environment of Preschool Education Institutions. *Open Educational E-Environment of Modern University.*

Fuchs, E., Lišková, H. & Zelendová, E., (2015). *Rozvoj předmatematických představ dětí předškolního věku. Předškolní vzdělávání očima praxe.* 1. Vyd. Praha: Jednota českých matematiků a fyziků.

Gjelaj, M., Buza, K. A., Shatri, K. & Zabeli, N., (2020). Digital Technologies in Early Childhood: Attitudes and Practices of Parents and Teachers in Kosovo. *International Journal of Instruction.*

Havlaskova, T., Homanova, Z. & Kostolanyova, K., (2020). Activities for developing digital literacy.

Holloway, D., Green, L. & Stevenson, K., (2015). Digitods: Toddlers, Touch Screens and Australian Family Life. *M/C Journal,* 18.

Hosťovecký, M. & Zaťková, T. Š., (2011). Supporting the development of digital competences of pupils and teachers. *2011 9th International Conference on Emerging eLearning Technologies and Applications (ICETA)*, pp. 75-78.

Kaslová, M., (2019). Cesty ke zkvalitňování výuky geometrie.

Kaslová, M., (2010). *Předmatematické činnosti v předškolním vzdělávání*. Praha: Portál.

Kiliánová, K., (2019). *Podpora rozvíjení geometrické představivosti v předškolním vzdělávání.* Bakalářská práce (Bc.). Ostrava: Ostravská univerzita, Pedagogická fakulta.

Kočková, P., (2019). *Podpora rozvíjení matematických představ u dětí předškolního věku pomocí ICT.* Bakalářská práce (Bc.). Ostrava: Ostravská univerzita, Pedagogická fakulta.

Kmetová, M., (2020). Intuition, Imagination and Visual Evidence in Geometry.

Krezhevskikh, O. V. & Mikhailova, A. I., (2019). Digital technologies in preschool education: on the way to democratization. *Pedagogical Education in Russia.*

Lišková, H., (2018). *Rozvíjíme předmatematické myšlení dětí.* Praha: Raabe.

McCollum, G., (2022). Sensorimotor Underprintings of Mathematical Imagination: Qualitative Analysis. *Frontiers in Psychology*, 12.

Mercader, C. & Sallán, J. G., (2017). Cómo utiliza el profesorado Universitario las technologías digitales en sus aulas.

Nikulin, D., (2019). *Imagination and Mathematics Neoplatonism in Late Antiquity.*

Pereira, A. B., (2017). Uso de jogos digitais no desenvolvimento de competências curriculares da matemática.

Piaget, J., (1964). Cognitive Development in Children: Development and Learning. *Journal of Research in Science Teaching*, 2, pp. 176-186.

Pinto, M. & Leite, C., (2020). Digital technologies in support of students learning in Higher Education: literature review. *Digital Education Review.*

Pöntinen, S. & Räty-Záborszky, S., (2020). Pedagogical aspects to support students' evolving digital competence at school', *European Early Childhood Education Research Journal*. 28, pp. 182-196.

Rambousek, V., Figulík, V. & Stípek, J., (2015). Selected outcomes of research of digital competency development on elementary schools.

Shavkatovna, M. K., Muhiddinovna, M. S. & Ahunovna, A. G., (2020). Reflections on the formation of mathematical imagination in preparing children for school.

Straker, L. M., Zabatiero, J., Danby, S., Thorpe, K. J. & Edwards, S., (2018). Conflicting Guidelines on Young Children's Screen Time and Use of Digital Technology Create Policy and Practice Dilemmas'. *The Journal of Pediatrics.* 202, pp. 300-303.

Styenhantseva, V. V., (2022). Formation of information and digital competence of primary school pupils in the context of their cyber socialization. *Bulletin of Alfred Nobel University Series "Pedagogy and Psychology".*

THE CURRENT STATE OF TECHNOLOGY USE IN LOWER SECONDARY SCHOOLS AS BASIS FOR HYBRID LEARNING

Magdalena Zavodna, Tatiana Havlaskova, Tomas Javorcik and Kateřina Kostolányová
University of Ostrava, Czechia

ABSTRACT

The use of modern technology in education brings new possibilities for teaching and learning. Among the most dynamically developing technologies in education are mobile technologies that allow students to access information anytime and anywhere. Combined with a hybrid learning approach, where traditional classroom presence is blended with online learning, the door is opening to more interactive and personalized learning. This research focused on the current state of technology use in lower secondary schools in the Czech Republic. The aim was to find out what technologies teachers use in their teaching, for what purpose and how often. The intention was also to find out whether mobile classrooms are used in schools and whether students have the opportunity to use their own mobile devices in lessons. The research was carried out through a questionnaire survey among lower secondary school teachers in the Czech Republic. The results of the survey showed that the use of technology in teaching is at a very good level and most teachers allow their students to use their own mobile devices at least occasionally in lessons. In the case of hybrid teaching, teachers and pupils can thus use their experience and, in a similar way as in face-to-face teaching, integrate these technologies into their teaching. Thanks to mobile apps based on augmented or virtual reality, the online part of learning can be improved.

KEYWORDS

Technology, Mobile Devices, BYOD, Lower Secondary Schools, Czech Republic, Teachers

1. INTRODUCTION

Mobile technologies such as smartphones and tablets support information sharing and collaboration between students and teachers (Abazova et al., 2024). On the other hand, the hybrid model of learning allows for effective use of both physical presence in the classroom and digital tools that can enhance the learning experience (Gamage et al., 2022; Bickle et al., 2019). This combination represents an innovative way to adapt the educational process to the needs of today's generation of learners, who have digital technologies as an integral part of their lives. The use of technology in education is changing as dynamically as the development of the technologies and applications themselves. As a basis for further research, it was therefore necessary to conduct a survey of the current state of technology use in lower secondary schools.

1.1 Technology in Learning

Technology has become a key factor influencing contemporary education. Since the introduction of computers into school classrooms in the late 20th century, digital technologies and applications have evolved and now offer not only access to information but also innovative forms of learning. From the original computer classrooms that contained only desktop computers, there is now a shift to so-called mobile classrooms that can include laptops or tablets as well as other portable digital devices. There is also a developing trend where students can use their own mobile devices in the classroom, the so-called BYOD model (Shafik, 2024; Slepankova & Kotyrba, 2024). Thus, today's educators and students have a wide range of digital tools at their disposal, from conventional learning apps and web-based platforms to virtual or augmented reality, which is growing in popularity (Koumpouros, 2024).

Augmented reality is particularly applicable in technical or medical fields where it allows to bring into the digital environment real objects that the student has to learn to work with, such as different machines and structures of the human body (Taher, 2024). This allows, for example, in a virtual or even real environment, using a device such as a mobile phone or a tablet, one can get more information about a particular object and try to operate it without having to be physically present in classroom or having the student actually manipulate it (Di Fuccio et al., 2024).

Nowadays, almost anything can be done on mobile devices and the development of educational applications is still moving forward. The trend of m-learning is still growing, mainly due to its positive impact on learners' learning outcomes. M-learning allows continuous access to educational content from anywhere, and also allows learners to progress at their own pace and adapt to their own needs (Abazova et al., 2024). Mobility has become an indispensable part of the daily lives of billions of people. Thus, as the number of mobile phone users increases, so does the number of people who have embraced m-learning. It is the freedom and convenience of learning on the go that is why its popularity continues to grow (Jay, 2023).

However, not every pupil or student has a mobile device. Another problem can be the internet connection that is required for most mobile apps. Not every school has a Wi-Fi connection. In addition, some lower secondary schools are not allowed to use their own mobile devices in class, or the school does not own any mobile devices for students to use. Therefore, we set out in our research to find out how lower secondary schools are currently equipped with digital technology, internet connectivity and whether they allow their students to use their own mobile devices.

1.2 Forms of Teaching

Four main forms of teaching are used in contemporary education. These are face-to-face, online, blended and hybrid learning. Each of these forms has its own specificities that determine how the learning process takes place, what technologies can be used and how they can be used in teaching.

Face-to-face teaching has been a traditional form of education for generations, where students and teacher are physically present in the classroom. This form allows for direct interaction and feedback between teacher and students and the opportunity to engage in a variety of hands-on activities. The main disadvantage of this form remains its time and space constraints and the need for physical aids. On the other hand, online (synchronous) learning takes place entirely in a virtual environment using various platforms such as MS Teams, Google Meet, or Zoom. This form of learning provides students with greater flexibility and allows access to learning materials from anywhere and at any time (Bickle et al., 2019). Online learning is often supported by various tools, apps, and other digital materials. Lack of face-to-face contact and poor quality or dysfunctional technology can be a problem in this form of learning.

Blended and hybrid learning can address the shortcomings of face-to-face and online learning (Gamage et al., 2022). Both of these forms combine elements of face-to-face and online learning, but each in a different way. In a blended learning environment, the two modes of learning, namely face-to-face and online, are treated as distinct entities, with no overlap between the two. In contrast, hybrid instruction combines the two parts into a single unit (Rijst et al., 2023). This means that both online and face-to-face instruction is implemented at the same time and the choice of how to participate in the lesson is delegated to the students. This model has become increasingly popular in recent years (Gamage et al., 2022).

2. METHODOLOGY

The research was conducted in the form of a questionnaire survey. The questionnaire would be created and sent electronically to randomly selected lower secondary schools in the country. The questionnaire contained a total of ten questions. Two questions were open-ended and eight questions were closed-ended. Of these, two questions were dichotomous, the others contained a wider range of responses. For only one question could respondents mark multiple answers at the same time. The research sample consisted of current lower secondary school teachers with varying lengths of teaching experience and subject area (Figure 1). In total, we obtained responses from 206 respondents. The size of the schools (by number of students) at which respondents teach also varies, see Figure 2.

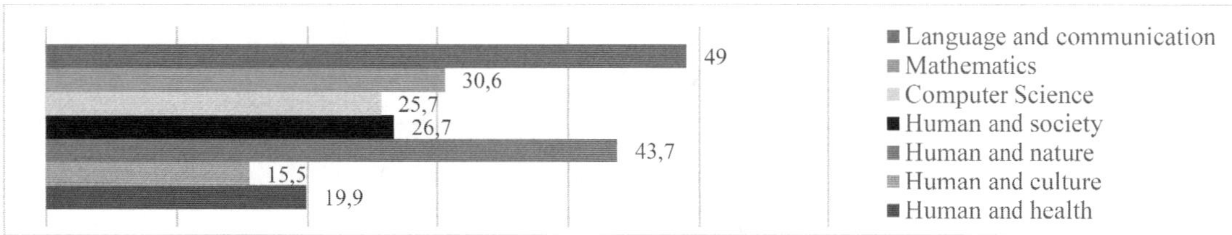

Figure 1. Composition of the research sample in terms of field of study (%)

Respondents from the fields of language (native and foreign) and science (physics, chemistry, natural history, geography) were the most represented. On the other hand, the lowest number of respondents was in the field of culture (art education, music education) and health care (physical education, health education).

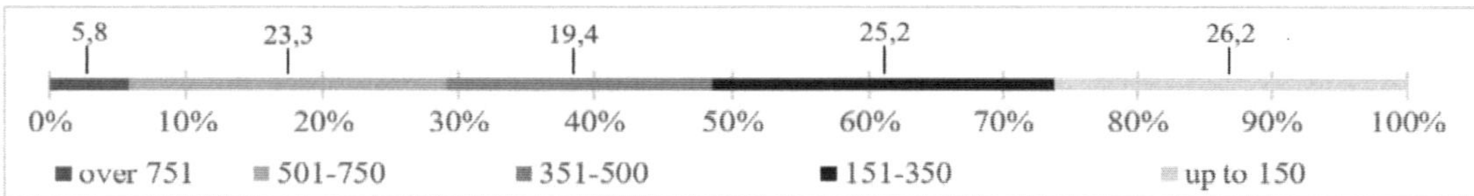

Figure 2. Composition of the research sample in terms of school size by number of students (%)

Respondents were active teachers in schools of varying sizes in terms of student numbers at the time of the research. Thus, teachers from small schools as well as medium and large schools were represented.

Our research sample was diverse both in terms of the length of teaching experience, which also influences the diversity of the age of the respondents, and in terms of their social background, as our respondents come from all areas (regions) of the Czech Republic and different lower secondary schools (state and private).

The research survey was conducted during the school year 2023/2024. PAST4 was used to analyze the data collected. The purpose of the research was to obtain current information and the use of technology in teaching as a basis for its use in hybrid teaching. Four research questions and three hypotheses were established for this research:

RQ1: Is the length of teacher experience related to the frequency of technology use in teaching?
RQ2: Is school internet connectivity related to the use of the BYOD model in teaching?
RQ3: Is the school's technology equipment related to the use of the BYOD model in teaching?
RQ4: What technologies are teachers currently using in their teaching?

H1: Teachers' length of experience has an impact on the frequency of technology use in teaching.
H2: The school's internet connectivity has an impact on the use of the BYOD model in teaching.
H3: The school's equipment has an impact on the use of the BYOD model in teaching.

3. RESULTS

The overview of the data and calculations is divided according to the research questions. All data are presented in percentages. There were cases where the respondent did not answer the question or could indicate more than one answer.

3.1 Frequency of Technology Use in Teaching

Current teachers already use technology in teaching quite frequently. 30.6% of the respondents use technology in teaching every lesson. Another 43.8% of respondents use technology several times a week and 10.8% of respondents try to use technology in teaching at least once a week. Only 9.4% of respondents use technology in teaching several times a month, 2.5% of respondents use it at least once a month and another 2.5% of respondents use it only a few times a school term. There was also one respondent who stated that they do not use technology at all in their teaching. The frequency of technology use in teaching was summarised into four categories and compared with the length of teaching experience of the teachers, see Table 1.

Table 1. Distribution of respondents by length of experience in relation to frequency of use of technology in teaching

	up to 5 years	6-10 years	11-15 years	16-20 years	21-30 years	over 31 years
very often	15 %	11,2 %	6,3 %	11,7 %	17,5 %	12,6 %
sometimes	4,4 %	2,9 %	2,9 %	1,5 %	4,4 %	3,9 %
hardly at all	0,5 %	0,5 %	0,5 %	1,9 %	1 %	0,5 %
at all	0 %	0 %	0 %	0 %	0 %	0,5 %

Based on the contingency table (Table 1), the chi-square was calculated (Table 2). The null hypothesis was accepted and the stated hypothesis H1 was therefore rejected. The results of the research showed that there is no statistically significant relationship between the length of teaching experience and the frequency of technology use in teaching. Therefore, the length of teachers' experience does not affect the frequency of technology use in teaching.

Table 2. Chi-square calculation for Table 1

Chi squared				
Rows, columns:	3, 6		Degrees freedom:	10
Chi2:		4,803	p (no assoc.):	0,90394

3.2 Using the BYOD Model in Education

The use of BYOD in lower secondary schools has become quite widespread, but in some cases it is prohibited. The most common option is only occasional use of own mobile devices, as teachers fear that students will misuse this opportunity to play games and browse social networks instead of completing assignments. On the other hand, teachers perceive the potential of the BYOD model (students are used to their devices, they know how to use them, it motivates them), and therefore they diversify the lessons with a quiz, practice in apps, quick search for short information, or on the contrary, they want to show them that they can use their mobile phone for other activities than playing games and browsing social media.

In most cases, students are only allowed to use the internet in class under the supervision of a teacher. There are very few schools that do not allow students to access the internet anymore. But there are also schools with a modern approach that allow students to access the internet at all times. It can be seen that most of these schools allow students to use their own devices in school.

Table 3. Comparison of schools' internet connectivity and BYOD usage

use of BYOD	Every student has access to the internet at all times.	Students have access to the Internet only under the supervision of a teacher.	Students at the school do not have access to the internet.
yes	12,1 %	12,1 %	1 %
no	0,5 %	23,3 %	0,5 %
sometimes	6,3 %	38,3 %	1 %
total	18,9 %	73,7 %	2,5 %

Based on the chi-square calculation to H2 (Table 4) from the contingency table (Table 3), the null hypothesis was rejected. The stated hypothesis of H2 was confirmed. The results of the research showed that there is a statistically significant relationship between schools' internet connectivity and the use of BYOD model in teaching. This implies that school's internet connectivity endowment has an effect on the use of BYOD model in teaching.

Table 4. Chi-square calculation for Table 3

Chi squared			
Rows, columns:	3, 3	Degrees freedom:	4
Chi2:	21,306	p (no assoc.):	0,0002753

As part of the calculations for H3, it was necessary to split the data into two contingency tables. The first table (Table 5) contains information on the current number of tablets in the schools studied in relation to the use of the BYOD model in teaching.

Table 5. Comparison of schools with tablets and BYOD

use of BYOD	up to 15 tablets	16 to 20 tablets	21 to 30 tablets	over 31 tablets
yes	4,4 %	8,3 %	3,9 %	6,8 %
no	6,3 %	3,4 %	5,3 %	6,8 %
sometimes	7,3 %	9,7 %	9,7 %	14,1 %

The first part of the chi-squared calculation to H3 (Table 6) led to the acceptance of the null hypothesis. The research results showed that the number of tablets available to the school does not affect the frequency of using the BYOD model in the classroom.

Table 6. Chi-square calculation for Table 5

Chi squared			
Rows, columns:	3, 4	Degrees freedom:	6
Chi2:	4,2163	p (no assoc.):	0,64743

The second contingency table to H3 shows the number of computer classrooms in relation to the use of the BYOD model in teaching.

Table 7. Comparison of the availability of computer classrooms in schools and the use of the BYOD model

use of BYOD	1 classroom	2-3 classrooms	more than 4 classrooms
yes	12,1 %	11,2 %	0 %
no	9,2 %	15 %	1 %
sometimes	18,9 %	21,8 %	2,4 %

Based on the chi-square calculation (Table 8) for the second part of H3, the null hypothesis was also accepted. Both parts of hypothesis H3 were rejected. The results of the research showed that the number of computer labs available in the school does not affect the frequency of using the BYOD model in teaching. Based on the data analysis: there is no statistically significant relationship between the technological equipment of the school and the use of the BYOD model in teaching.

Table 8. Chi-square calculation for Table 7

Chi squared			
Rows, columns:	3, 3	Degrees freedom:	4
Chi2:	2,1688	p (no assoc.):	0,70475

3.3 Type and Use of Technology in Teaching

Although desktop computers (79.1%) are still the most frequently used technology in teaching, they are far from being the only technology used by teachers. So what technologies (Figure 3) are teachers currently using in their teaching? The use of interactive whiteboards is now very common (74.3%), which may not only be used to passively convey information, but can also activate and motivate students to further their learning.

Portable devices in mobile classrooms are already very popular and frequently used, in the form of laptops or chromebooks (43.7%), tablets or iPads (61.7%), but also smartphones (45.1%). There are also teachers who use e-book readers (1.5%).

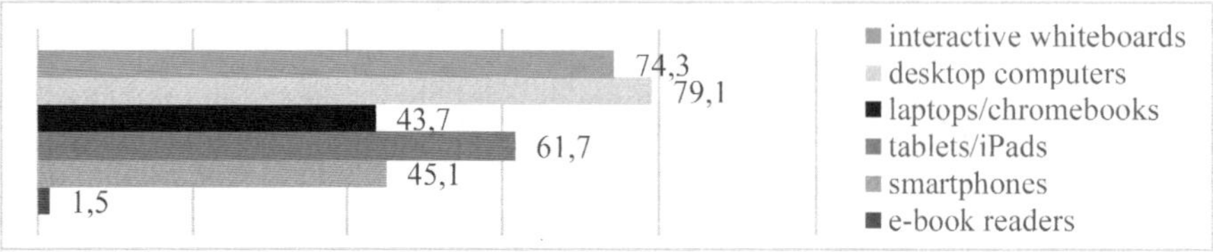

Figure 3. The most commonly used technologies in education (%)

The variety of technologies also offers a variety of possibilities for their use in education (see Figure 4). This research also identified the purposes for which teachers use technology in their teaching. The most frequent use of these technologies is for initial motivation of learners (63.6%), whether it is the creation of mind maps, an introductory quiz or a thematic video. Playful or competitive quizzes are also common (60.7%), used to review and remember the material. Technology is also used in the classroom for independent (54.4%) or group (46.6%) work by students, and in some cases technology is used for online assignments (39.8%).

A number of these activities make use of mobile technology, which allows for some flexibility and immediacy. When students are given the task of looking up specific information (51.5%), need to document an item, procedure or laboratory experiment, either as part of an individual or group assignment, or need to practice what they are learning on their own (50%) or in groups (49%) using apps, there is nothing easier and faster than using mobile technology to do so, whether it be school tablets or their own smartphones.

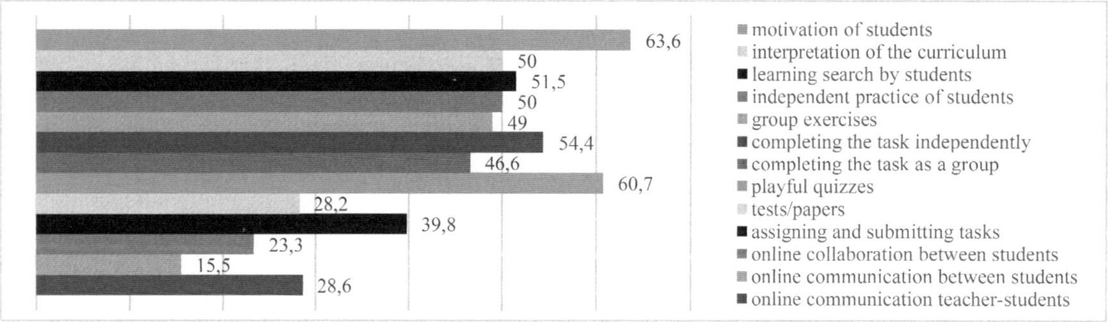

Figure 4. The purpose of using technology in teaching (%)

4. CONCLUSION

Technology is slowly becoming a common part of teaching in lower secondary schools and is widely used by teachers regardless of the length of their teaching experience and the amount of experience they have. They take advantage of the variety of technologies and applications and the possibilities they offer for a variety of activities. The use of the BYOD model is also increasing, but the use of this model is dependent on the availability of an internet connection in the school.

The finding that there is no direct relationship between equipping schools with technology and the adoption of the BYOD model offers valuable insights. It indicates that the success of technology integration depends less on the sheer availability of resources and more on how these resources are utilized. Schools with limited devices can still achieve effective integration by fostering a culture of digital literacy and encouraging creative uses of existing tools. For policymakers and educational leaders, this emphasizes the need for strategies that focus on teacher training, structured guidelines for technology use, and creating a supportive environment for experimentation with digital tools. These findings suggest that even schools with limited budgets or availability of digital devices can, if necessary, implement hybrid learning if they focus on maximising the use of existing devices and leveraging the BYOD model.

The current use of diverse technologies (e.g., interactive whiteboards, desktops, tablets, and smartphones) demonstrates teachers' willingness to experiment with their integration into the learning process and their potential use in hybrid teaching. Hybrid teaching can benefit from combining these technologies. For example, the use of tablets for hands-on augmented reality exercises, or interactive applications on smartphones that can be run by both online and face-to-face learners. It is also the use of computers for group work, where students can be divided into online and face-to-face groups, but also mixed groups, so that everyone (online and face-to-face students) can be connected to each other online.

The fact that teachers are already incorporating technology into their teaching quite frequently, regardless of their length of experience, shows that educators are open to innovation, including the possible implementation of hybrid teaching. This may be the key to the successful implementation of hybrid teaching. The frequent use of technology in teaching also suggests that teachers have already built the basic skills needed to implement hybrid teaching. Therefore, further research on hybrid teaching could explore methods that integrate technologies used in the classroom with tools appropriate for the online environment.

Teachers allow students to use their devices mostly under supervision and only for certain activities. The effectiveness of this model remains questionable. While some educators recommend and endorse this method because of its merits, others are concerned about its negative impact and prefer to use school devices equipped with security features in the classroom, either in terms of virus protection or in the form of blocking prohibited, inappropriate or disruptive sites and applications.

Mobile apps offer huge potential for use in hybrid learning. Specifically, apps based on augmented or virtual reality provide an unparalleled experience, easier and deeper understanding of the learning compared to conventional learning (Di Fuccio, 2024; Taher, 2024; Koumpouros, 2024). For example, just pointing a mobile phone at a plant and digital elements or illustrations appear on the screen to explain and present basic information about it (Koumadoraki, 2022). Many researchers have identified the biggest drawback of online learning, which is also taken up by hybrid learning itself, is precisely the unsuitability for hands-on learning (Gamage, 2022). However, due to the possibilities offered by these mobile applications, online learning can equal real-life practice and can thus be used as a substitute for hands-on activities in hybrid learning.

This research contributes significantly to the understanding of the integration of digital technologies in lower secondary education, especially in the context of the Czech Republic. A systematic analysis of the current state of technology use and availability highlights key areas that can contribute to the integration of hybrid learning. For educators, the results of the study show the importance of a balanced approach to integrating mobile technologies, such as tablets or BYOD models, into teaching. Teachers should use these technologies not only for motivational activities such as quizzes, but also to promote collaboration and independent learning. The key is to design lesson plans that effectively incorporate digital tools, while establishing clear rules so that technology serves as a facilitator, not a distraction.

Adequate provision of digital technologies in schools and their active use in face-to-face teaching is essential for the successful implementation of hybrid learning. On the basis of this research, it can be concluded that both of these conditions are currently being fulfilled, especially due to the experience of online teaching during the Covid-19 pandemic and the impact it had on the widespread use of technology in teaching. Teachers are using technology for many different purposes that could also be implemented in a possible hybrid education. However, their specific uses still offer enormous scope for research, as well as the area of hybrid learning and its potential deficiencies or limitations.

REFERENCES

Abazova, L., Gutaeva, Z., & Kochesokova, M. (2024). The effects of mobile technologies on the level of student involvement. *International Journal of Evaluation and Research in Education*, *13*(6), 4321-4329.

Bickle, M. C., Rucker, R. D., & Burnsed, K. A. (2019). Online Learning: Examination of Attributes that Promote Student Satisfaction. *Online Journal of Distance Learning Administration*, *22*(1).

Di Fuccio, R., Kic-Drgas, J., & Woźniak, J. (2024). Co-created augmented reality app and its impact on the effectiveness of learning a foreign language and on cultural knowledge. *Smart Learning Environments*, *11*(2), 1-29.

Gamage, K. A. A., Gamage, A., & Dehideniya, S. C. P. (2022). Online and Hybrid Teaching and Learning: Enhance Effective Student Engagement and Experience. *Education Sciences*, *12*(10), 651. https://doi.org/10.3390/educsci12100651

Jay, A. (c2023). *11 New Elearning Trends & Predictions for 2023*. FinancesOnline. Retrieved October 20, 2024, from https://financesonline.com/elearning-trends/

Koumadoraki, A. (c2023). *10 eLearning Trends That Will Go Big in 2023*. LearnWorlds. Retrieved October 20, 2024, from https://www.learnworlds.com/elearning-trends/

Koumpouros, Y. (2024). Revealing the true potential and prospects of augmented reality in education. *Smart Learning Environments*, *11*(2), 1-62.

Molnar, G., & Orosz, B. (2019). Visual, own device and experience-based educational methods and possibilities in VET. In *10th IEEE International Conference on Cognitive Infocommunications, CogInfoCom 2019 - Proceedings* (pp. 517-520). Institute of Electrical and Electronics Engineers. https://doi.org/10.1109/CogInfoCom47531.2019.9089915

Moya, S., & Camacho, M. (2024). Leveraging AI-powered mobile learning: A pedagogically informed framework. *Computers and Education: Artificial Intelligence*, *7*(1).

Rijst, R. van der, Guo, P., & Admiraal, W. (2023). Student engagement in hybrid approaches to teaching in higher education. *RIE-REVISTA DE INVESTIGACION EDUCATIVA*, *41*(2), 315-336. https://doi.org/10.6018/rie.562521

Shafik, W. (2024). Enhancing AI-enabled education through mobile learning and bring your own device (BYOD) integration. In *Exploring Youth Studies in the Age of AI* (pp. 140-173). IGI Global.

Slepankova, M., & Kotyrba, M. (2024). Overview of Teachers' and Students' Perceptions of the BYOD Implementation: An Outcome of a Systematic Literature Review. In *International Conference of Numerical Analysis and Applied Mathematics 2022*. American Institute of Physics. https://doi.org/10.1063/5.0210592

Taher, S. M. (2024). Application of Improved PSO in Augmented Reality for Dental Healthcare. *Journal of Advanced Research in Applied Sciences and Engineering Technology*, *50*(2), 90-102.

A STUDY ON THE INNOVATIVE PATH OF EDUCATOR SPIRIT OF CHINESE TOWNSHIP SECONDARY SCHOOL TEACHERS BASED ON MOBILE LEARNING

Jiachao Wei[1], Fuling Shi[1] and Yafang Liu[2]
[1]*School of Education Science, Nanning Normal University, Nanning, China*
[2]*Bozhou Vocational and Technical College, Bozhou, China*

ABSTRACT

With the development of the new era, mobile learning provides a new platform for teachers to promote the spirit of educator, help teachers to improve themselves and promote educational progress. In this study, teachers in township secondary schools in South China were selected as survey respondents, and SPSS 24.0 software as well as Excel tools were used to explore the relationship between mobile learning and teachers' innovative path of educator spirit. The study concludes that the integration of mobile learning content of Chinese township secondary school teachers has yet to be improved, the synergy of computation has yet to be strengthened, there are deficiencies in the systematization of access, and the coherence of communication still needs to be perfected, and so on. Therefore, it is crucial to organize the content to promote integration and efficiency, build a synergistic structure to enhance computational efficiency, plan the access path to build a knowledge network, and improve the communication link to unite the educational synergy. These initiatives are extremely crucial for rural secondary school teachers to make full use of mobile learning, cultivate educator's spirit and improve educational effectiveness.

KEYWORDS

Mobile Learning, Pedagogy, Township Secondary Schools

1. INTRODUCTION

In today's era, mobile learning, with the help of smart terminals and networks, breaks through the limitations of time and space, makes the acquisition of knowledge more convenient and efficient, and reshapes the ecology of education. The spirit of educator in the new era is rich in connotation, including the determination to love education, the perseverance to be indifferent to fame and fortune, and the courage to innovate and explore, etc. In the context of mobile learning, the spirit of educator inspires education practitioners to actively integrate the two. In terms of mLearning, the spirit of educator inspires education practitioners to actively integrate the two, open up new paths in education, and take up the mission of cultivating new generations. The rationale for the topic of m-learning and the innovative path of educator's spirit among Chinese township secondary school teachers is that m-learning is increasingly becoming an important learning mode in the new era of education, and is a powerful tool to promote educational change and development, for example, how to disseminate educator's spirit through m-learning platforms. Therefore, it is of great practical significance and theoretical value to study the innovation path of mobile learning and educator spirit of teachers in Chinese township secondary schools.

2. LITERATURE REVIEW

2.1 A Study of The Significance of M-Learning for Teacher Educators' Spirituality

Scholars have focused on the positive impact of mobile learning on the spiritual enhancement of teacher educators. Mobile learning platform is an important way to promote teacher educator spirit, for example, Chinese scholars Ye-lin, Wu and Han, Xu (2023) pointed out that mobile platform can further open up the path of teachers' growth, and promote the exchange and collision between teachers and students by building online courses and constructing an online learning platform, which is also an important path for the promotion of educator spirit. Chinese scholar Ying-xu, Gao (2024) believes that in the context of globalization and informationization, the application and innovation of teaching methods and technologies can effectively improve the quality of education and play a leading role in the spirit of teacher educators. Jian, Zhang (2024), a Chinese scholar, said that changes in human technology, such as artificial intelligence and ChatGPT, can effectively improve the choice of educators' own logical and academic abilities. The countryside is in an area of relative economic deprivation, educational resources are relatively backward, rural teachers are bound by the environment, science and technology and other factors, the road to development is difficult. When focusing on the plight of rural schools, to help the countryside to overcome the problems of teaching and learning development, and to face the dilemma of mobile learning of rural teachers, this study is committed to contributing to the development of a little bit of wisdom.

2.2 A Study on The Impact of Secondary School Teachers in Townships

Scholars have focused on the negative impact of mobile learning on teachers in economically relatively backward township areas. For example, Chinese scholar Jin-pin, Hu (2013) pointed out that township areas are relatively backward in terms of educational development due to their special geographic location, hardware conditions, and the richness. Chinese scholar Yan, Yu (2020) suggests that teachers are less capable of applying mobile terminals, know less about mobile learning, cannot use mobile learning to provide timely guidance and effective feedback to students, and are still keen on the traditional mode of teaching, so it poses a challenge to the development of teachers, and is not conducive to the promotion of the spirit of teacher educators. Chinese scholar Wei, Chang (2021) proposed that in the mobile learning mode, the identity of the teacher, resulting in a lack of self-control ability of the students, and the huge pile of resources for mobile learning, which can easily lead to the loss of student learning.

2.3 Research on The Innovative Path of Teacher Educator Spirit

Scholars have focused on the possible paths of mobile learning to enhance teacher educator spirit, first, the subject theory, Chinese scholars Qig-uang, Yang and Ting-ting, Xu (2021) pointed out that to enhance the educator spirit of teachers in township secondary schools, the focus should be on stimulating the intrinsic motivation of teachers to use mobile learning, enhancing teachers' ability to use big data for teaching and learning, and perfecting the teachers' mobile learning systematic evaluation, etc. Second, institutional theory, Chinese scholars Hong-xiu, Li and Xiao, Liu (2024) believe that in order to promote the integration of the spirit of educator into the teacher education curriculum, we should scientifically plan the teacher education curriculum under the guidance of the spirit of educator. Thirdly, methodology, Chinese scholars Chun-jiao, Jiang and Han-wen, Li(2024) suggest that China's unique educator's spirit is not only a summary of China's excellent traditional culture, but also a measure of teacher literacy in the new era, and that the dissemination of educator's spirit should be adapted to China's national conditions.

In summary, it can be seen that the path of most of the literature is based on the assumption of the function of m-learning itself. By analyzing the innovative path of mobile learning resources on the dissemination of teachers' educator's spirit, it provides new ideas and directions for the development of education in the new era. Thus highlighting the importance of this study.

3. RESEARCH DESIGN

3.1 Theoretical Foundation: Clark Quinn 4C Model

Clark Quinn first proposed the 4C model, the 4Cs are Content, Compute, Capture and Communicate. In m-learning in schooling, content refers to the learning resources used for learners in m-learning, computation refers to the data that learners get and process from m-learning, acquisition refers to the ideas that learners get from m-learning, and communication refers to the exchanges between learners, and between learners and teachers.The 4C model states that m-learning systems require certain learning content, and that the data are captured and processed through the device, the Learners and learners can exchange with each other.

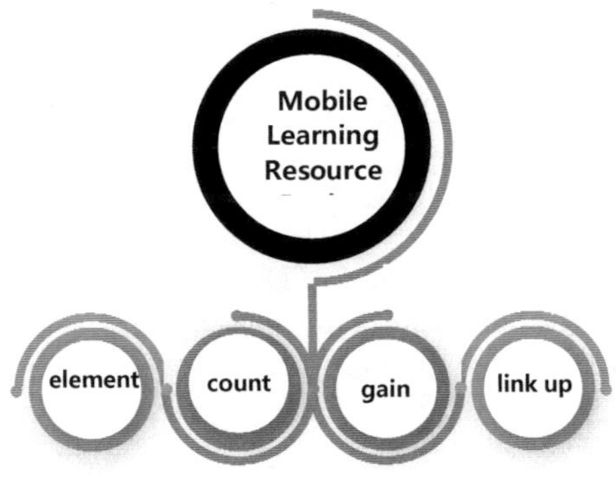

Figure 1. Clark-Quinn 4C Model

3.2 Research Hypothesis

Based on the literature review and the analysis of the problem, this study tries to use Clark Quinn's analytical model about mobile learning as the theoretical framework, conducts a survey study through the prepared questionnaire to find out the current situation of mobile learning of Chinese township secondary school teachers, the impact of mobile learning on the development of spiritual innovation path of township secondary school teacher educators, and puts forward the research hypotheses: there is a positive correlation between the development of spiritual innovation path of Chinese township secondary school teacher educators and the development of mobile learning ability are positively correlated.

3.3 Research Objects and Research Tools

3.3.1 Research Objects

The target population of this study covers the teachers of township secondary schools in South China. 630 questionnaires were distributed and 622 were recovered; excluding the invalid questionnaires, 612 valid questionnaires were obtained, with an effective recovery rate of 98.70%. The respondents were all township secondary school teachers, including 330 males and 282 females; the basic information characteristics of the teacher sample are shown in Table 1.

Table 1. Frequency analysis results

Classification	Length of teaching experience				Academic		
	1-3years	4-9years	10-15years	15+ years	Specialized and below	Bachelor's Degree	Postgraduate
Number of people	77	218	202	115	355	190	67
Ratio (%)	12.6	35.6	33.0	18.8	58.0	31.0	11.0

Classification	Qualifications Title			
	Not rated	Secondary Level 2 Teacher	Secondary Level 1 Teacher	Senior Secondary Teacher
Number of people	45	190	365	12
Ratio (%)	7.4	31.0	59.6	2.0

Classification	Level of information technology				
	Poor	Fairly Poor	Average	Fairly Good	Good
Number of people	30	69	130	263	120
Ratio (%)	4.9	11.3	21.2	43.0	19.6

3.3.2 Research Tools

The research instrument of this study is a self-administered questionnaire. The questionnaire questions were designed from sources such as China's Professional Standards for Secondary School Teachers (Trial) (2012), The questionnaire mainly consists of three parts: basic information, mobile learning, and teacher educator spirit, as shown in (Table 2). The second and third parts are based on the five-point scale of Likert, an American scholar, where each statement has "not at all consistent", "not at all consistent", and "not sure", "basically consistent", "fully consistent" composition, scoring 1-5 points in order.

Table 2. Questionnaire dimensions

Level 1 indicators	Secondary indicators
Basic Information	Gender, years of teaching experience, title, education, information technology level
element	Mobile Learning Course Resources Educational Spirituality Thematic Learning Materials Personalized Instructional Content Creation
count	Statistical analysis of mobile learning data Quantitative calculation of teaching effectiveness Calculation of resource allocation to education
gain	Access to mobile learning resources Access to Teacher Education Philosophy Cutting-edge educational knowledge acquisition
link up	Teacher-Student Mobile Learning Interaction Sharing and communication of educational experiences among teachers Home-School Mobile Communication Platform

4. FINDINGS AND ANALYSIS

Using SPSS 24.0 software as well as Excel tools, this study firstly analyzed the basic situation of m-learning among teachers in township secondary schools in China, and secondly attempted to explore the correlation level of m-learning to analyze the relationship between m-learning and teachers' educator spirit in township secondary schools.

4.1 Overall Situation of Mobile Learning Among Teachers

The overall situation of Chinese township secondary school teachers who effectively used m-learning tools in the survey was average, and the popularization of the use of m-learning tools in township areas needs to be improved. As a whole, the level of m-learning among males is slightly higher than that of females. In terms of academic qualifications, since in townships, specialties and below occupy the majority, followed by undergraduates and postgraduates. There are significant differences in m-learning among Chinese township teachers of different teaching ages. Teachers with different levels of information technology (IT) showed significant differences in m-learning.

4.2 The Relationship Between Mobile Learning Skills and Teacher-Educator Spirit

Based on Clark Quinn's theoretical analysis framework, the relationship between mobile learning and the development of teacher educator spirituality was explored in terms of each of the four aspects of mobile learning: content, computation, access, and communication.

4.2.1 Calculation of Model Validity

Pearson's correlation coefficient is applicable to the study of continuous linear data, therefore, before analyzing the correlation empirically, it is necessary to verify the scientific validity of the Pearson's correlation coefficient used in this paper. The linear correlation between the variables "mobile learning" and "teacher educator spirit" was verified by using SPSS 24.0 scatterplot.

By calculating the Cronbach's alpha reliability coefficient, the cronbach's values were all greater than 0.9. Therefore, the measures of the study variables have high internal consistency reliability.

Table 3. Reliability analysis

Variable	Number of question items	Cronbach's alpha reliability coefficient
Content	3	0.932
Calculation	3	0.913
Acquisition	3	0.916
Communication	3	0.909

Then the corresponding regression analysis proved that the KMO validity value is 0.901, which is greater than 0.8, indicating that the research data is valid; the probability significance value of Bartlett's spherical test is 0.000 (Sig), which is less than 0.01, thus it can be seen that there is a significant correlation between the variables; therefore, the data of the current study has a better validity and it is suitable to do factor analysis.

Table 4. Validity analysis

KMO	.901
Bartlett's test of sphericity	604.118
	15
	.000

4.2.2 The Content Dimensions of Mobile Learning

The study found that the degree of utilization of m-learning course resources was closely related to the level of personalized content creation. In terms of learning materials on the topic of the spirit of education, teachers who had studied such materials in depth for a certain amount of time (more than 6 hours per month) were 85% more likely to proactively reflect the spirit of education in their personalized content creation. Further analysis shows that when teachers make full use of curriculum resources and in-depth study of thematic materials at the same time, the overall quality index of their personalized teaching content creation increases by 55%, which indicates that curriculum resources provide materials and methods for creation.

4.2.3 The Computational Dimension of Mobile Learning

In terms of mLearning data analysis, teachers who conduct in-depth data analysis more than three times a week can improve students' knowledge mastery by 40% on average in the quantitative calculation of teaching effectiveness. Meanwhile, teachers with excellent results in quantitative calculation of teaching effectiveness are 45% more reasonable than other teachers in the calculation of educational resource allocation, and they are able to rationally allocate resources according to their teaching effectiveness.

4.2.4 The Relationship Between the Access Dimension

The study shows that the diversity of mLearning resource access channels is significantly correlated with the richness of cutting-edge educational knowledge acquisition methods. When teachers acquire rich resources through multiple channels, the probability of them coming into contact with different educational concepts and cutting-edge knowledge increases, so as to build up a close connection network between the level of m-learning acquisition and the spirit of teacher educators, and to enhance the level of their educational practice and spiritual realm.

4.2.5 The Relationship Between the Communicative Dimension

According to the research and analysis, in terms of teacher-student mobile learning interaction and communication, teachers who have more than 10 interactions per week are 40% more active in sharing and communicating with each other about their educational experiences. Meanwhile, teachers who frequently share their educational experiences with each other can answer parents' questions more professionally on the home-school mLearning platform, and their satisfaction with the effectiveness of communication is 35% higher than that of other teachers. This suggests that teacher-student interaction stimulates teachers' communication and enhances educational effectiveness.

5. ANALYSIS OF PROBLEMS

In summary, the research hypothesis was verified, that is, there is a positive correlation between teachers' m-learning ability and their teacher educator spirit. Meanwhile, Chinese township secondary school teachers' m-learning is deficient in four dimensions: content, computation, access and communication.

5.1 Mobile Content Integration Has to Improve

According to the results of the study, m-learning is highly positively correlated with the cultivation of teachers' educator spirit, for example, in the face of rich online course platforms, they only browse occasionally without formulating a systematic learning plan, which makes the effect of mobile learning greatly reduced. The study also shows that the situation of teachers' mobile learning is closely related to their cognitive level, and teachers with different cognitive levels show significant differences in mobile learning, and some teachers in township secondary schools have low initiative in using mobile learning devices, which can't meet the requirements of the era of informationization development.

5.2 Computing Synergy to Be Strengthened

From the results of the study, the mobile learning computing synergy of teachers in Chinese township secondary schools needs to be strengthened. This is mainly reflected in the fact that teachers are independent of each other and have less interaction during mobile learning. For example, in the statistical analysis of mobile learning data, only 18% of teachers share data resources and discuss analysis strategies with colleagues, while 82% of teachers process data on their own, which makes it difficult to achieve efficient integration and optimization of data in the quantitative calculation of teaching effectiveness and the calculation of educational resource allocation, resulting in a waste of computational resources, and computational results cannot be effectively shared and improved.

5.3 Deficiencies in The Systematic Nature of Mobile Learning Access

According to the survey data, there is a positive correlation between the school's material access on mobile learning and the educator spirit of rural secondary school teachers. Teachers in rural secondary schools are very concerned about factors such as the status of classroom networks, the performance of mobile devices, and the quality of learning resources to support their mobile learning. Due to the relative backwardness of the local economy, many advanced mobile devices have not been introduced to rural secondary schools. In the survey on mobile learning in China's township middle schools, more than 70% of the teachers gave feedback on the lack of systematic access to resources.

5.4 Communication Coherence Still Needs Improvement

In the practice of m-learning in China's township middle schools, the problem of communication consistency is more prominent. In the survey on "the main problems of communication in m-learning", it is found that as many as 85% of teachers believe that there is a lack of coherence in communication at present. for example, only 25% of teachers regularly discuss their learning experience with their students. There is also a gap in the sharing of educational experiences among teachers, which is mostly occasional, without a regular and organized communication mechanism. This lack of communication consistency hinders the full realization of the effectiveness of mLearning and the cultivation of educator spirit among teachers.

6. STRATEGIC RECOMMENDATIONS

Mobile learning is closely linked to educator spirit. Educator's spirit implies a love for education and plays a key leading role. Based on the above analysis, four dimensions are proposed to improve the mobile learning of secondary school teachers from the four dimensions of sorting out the content vein to promote integration and efficiency; building a synergistic architecture to enhance the computational effectiveness; planning the access path to build a knowledge network; and sound communication links to unite the educational synergy.

6.1 Sorting Out the Content Lineage To Promote Integration And Efficiency

In the context of mobile learning, the steps for teachers to carry out mobile learning should be clearly defined, and each link should be carefully designed from resource recommendation to learning task arrangement to assessment of teaching results to ensure that mobile learning is carried out efficiently. for example, to determine the amount of teaching tasks to be accomplished weekly through the mobile learning platform, and the stage-by-stage assessment standards. Secondly, optimize teaching resource management, classify and organize mobile learning resources and update them in a timely manner to ensure the quality and applicability of the resources. Then, new educational resources, such as the latest teaching videos and online courses, are constantly introduced to keep the learning content fresh and up-to-date, and to provide support for educational innovation in order to cultivate educator spirit.

6.2 Building a Synergistic Architecture to Enhance Computational Efficiency

In the environment of mobile learning, it is crucial to build a perfect computing synergy system. A unified computing platform should be constructed to integrate the functions of mobile learning data statistics analysis, quantitative calculation of teaching effect and calculation of educational resources allocation. Teachers can upload all kinds of teaching data to the platform, such as students' learning hours, homework completion and other data, and the platform conducts comprehensive analysis with the help of intelligent algorithms to break the data silos and make the calculation process more coordinated and orderly. Secondly, it is necessary to standardize the calculation process standards to ensure the accuracy and completeness of the data. By standardizing the process and improving the effectiveness of calculation, it provides a reliable basis for educational decision-making and highlights the practical value of educator spirit in mobile learning calculation.

6.3 Planning Access Routes and Building Knowledge Networks

Integrate excellent educational resources and produce high-quality catechism courses to provide rich learning opportunities for areas with relatively insufficient educational resources, such as township secondary schools. The quality of catechism content should be improved, the teaching ability of teachers should be strengthened, the quality of teachers should be improved, and the cultivation of educator's spirit through catechism should be promoted. Secondly, the construction of the catechism platform should be strengthened, the functions and user experience of the catechism platform should be optimized, the efficiency of resource sharing should be improved, and personalized learning recommendation functions should be set up. At the same time, the platform interactivity is strengthened to facilitate communication and discussion between students and teachers, promoting students' learning progress and educator's spirit promotion.

6.4 Improving Communication Links and Building Synergies in Education

Through the mobile learning platform to establish interactive channels, timely understand the confusion and needs of teachers in the teaching process. Continuously create a new path of educator's spirit innovation from the interactive feedback between teachers and teachers. Multiple communication channels should be established to spread and promote the educator spirit beyond time and space limitations through the online discussion forums, private messaging functions and regular video conferences of the mobile learning platform. Secondly, feedback should be handled in a timely manner to improve teachers' competence in applying the mobile learning platform and strengthen their ability to use the mobile learning platform for dissemination, so that the mobile learning platform can be used as a medium to realize dissemination efficacy and to unite educational synergy.

7. CONCLUSION

In this study, there are deficiencies in integration, synergy, systematicity and coherence in content, computing, access and communication. Based on this, it is proposed to organize the content, build a collaborative structure, plan the access path and improve the communication link. These initiatives can help rural secondary school teachers to better cultivate educator spirit and improve educational effectiveness in the mobile learning environment. The study reveals the current situation of m-learning among secondary school teachers in townships, provides a theoretical basis and practical guidance for the subsequent use of m-learning to promote the development of educator's spirit.

ACKNOWLEDGEMENT

The author thanks for the support of the 2024 Guangxi Undergraduate Education Reform Project: Under the background of professional certification, the construction and practice of the "three lessons" and "four directions" collaborative practice teaching system for normal majors (project No. 2024JGB266).

REFERENCES

Chang, W. (2021). Construction of mobile learning mode of university English based on smart phone[J]. *Journal of Shanxi University of Finance and Economics*, 43(S2):171-174.

Gao, Y. X. (2024). Research on the construction of university faculty under the guidance of educator's spirit[J]. *Public Relations World*, (19):148-150.

Hu, J. P. (2013). Research on the role of mobile learning in promoting the development of education informatization in minority areas[J]. *Teaching and Management*, (21):81-83.

Jiang, C. J. & Li., H. W. (2024). On the Historical Logic and Realization Path of China's Unique Educator's Spirit[J]. *Ideological Education*, (01):106-111.

Li, H. X. & Liu, X. (2024). Reconstruction and realization of teacher education curriculum under the leadership of educator spirit[J]. *College Education Management*, 18(02):84-92.

Rocco S. (2012). Book Review: 'The Mobile Academy' by Clark Quinn[J]. *eLearn*, 2012(1):3.

Wu, Y. L. & Xu, H. (2023). Integration of educator's spirit into teacher education in colleges and universities: logic, function and mode[J]. *Heilongjiang Higher Education Research*, 41(04):1-7.

Yang, Q. G. & Xu, T. T. (2021). Mobile Learning for Teachers' Professional Development: Practice, Challenges and Responses[J]. *Journal of Capital Normal University (Social Science Edition)*, (03):171-180.

Yu, Y. & Zhu, P. W. (2020). Research on mobile learning mode of colleges and universities based on cell phone terminals under the environment of "Internet+"[J]. *Intelligence Science*, 38(02):125-128.

Zhang, J. (2024). Paradigm change of teachers' on-site learning driven by educators' spirit: cultural empowerment and school-based practice[J]. *Journal of Huaiyin Normal University (Natural Science Edition)*, 23(03):247.

A STUDY ON THE RELATIONSHIP BETWEEN HANDHELD TECHNOLOGY AND LEARNING EFFICIENCY OF MIDDLE SCHOOL STUDENTS

Xixi Lu[1], Dongling Chen[2] and Jiachao Wei[3]
[1]Nanning Normal University, College of materials and chemistry, Major in chemistry
No. 508 Xinning Road, Wuming District, Nanning City 530100, China
[2]The College of Teacher Education, Wuzhou University
82 Fumin Third Road, Wanxiu District, Wuzhou City,543002, China
[3]School of Education Science, Nanning Normal University
No.3 Hexing Road, Qingxiu District, Nanning City 530299, China

ABSTRACT

Digital technology is becoming an important traction to lead the transformation of education, and secondary education as a cradle of scientific and technological talents, and further promote the development of digital technology. Based on a number of case studies on the application of digital technology in teaching and learning, this paper makes a data visualization analysis through SPAA, this paper probes into the realistic predicament of the application of mobile technology in middle school teaching at present: (1) the low penetration rate of digital technology in middle school classroom; (2) the significant regional difference in the application of intelligent technology in classroom; (3) the students' attention to study is distracted; PCCI model is proposed to design the implementation path.

KEYWORDS

Digital Technology, Project-Based Learning, Social Constructivist

1. INTRODUCTION

"The convergence of cloud computing, big data, the Internet of things, and artificial intelligence is driving network effects, leading to exponential change."(Yu Ying & Song Ruyue, 2024) In the past few decades, the spread of the Internet has reshaped everyday communication in a way that allows people to transcend time and space through instant messaging and social platforms, the realization of high-speed interaction of information and immediate transmission of emotion greatly expands the scope and depth of interpersonal communication, and changes the structure and operation logic of traditional social ecology.

In the field of consumption, the booming development of e-commerce platform has revolutionized the way of shopping. Online shopping has become one of the mainstream consumption patterns because of its convenience, richness and efficiency, at the same time, it also drives the rapid development of logistics and distribution and other related industries, and further affects the micro-and macro-economic patterns.

As far as education is concerned, internet penetration has given birth to the rise and prosperity of online education. Teachers can be digitized through intelligent devices, transforming interpersonal relationships into abstract relationships between objects. Algorithm through the "Digital I" data analysis, calculation, planning and impact of various digital platforms, products, teachers and students of teaching resources and learning paths, finally through the control of data to achieve the control of teaching and learning (Lu hanxue, 2024). Digital learning is becoming a mainstream way of learning is accepted by the public, and becomes an important support for citizens to realize life-long learning in modern society. This paper analyzes the influence of mobile digital technology on the learning efficiency of middle school students according to the results of many surveys, and puts forward the optimized scheme. Hope to be able to other regions will be more efficient digital technology into secondary school classroom teaching to provide reference.

2. THEORETICAL FOUNDATION

2.1 Project-Based Learning

Project-Based Learning, referred to as PBL, is an important way in many countries and regions to cultivate students' comprehensive literacy and key abilities and achieve modern teaching goals. PBL is a kind of student-centered teaching activity which is carried out according to a specific project activity and aims at improving students' literacy. It emphasizes the real situation and product orientation, which is very important and effective for the development of students' problem-solving ability (Hu Jiakang & Tian Li, 2023). This teaching activity is based on a project activity with certain practical application value and real situation, and the project has clear goals and expected results. For example, in the chemistry class of middle school, students took designing a simple battery as a project. According to the project objectives, students explored the internal working mechanism, constituent conditions, electron flow and other knowledge contents of the battery in a group, and completed the design scheme of the galvanic battery, and finally verified the rationality of the scheme through experiments. In May 2023, the Ministry of Education of the People's Republic of China issued the Opinions on Strengthening Science Education in Primary and Secondary Schools in the New Era, proposing to "explore project-based and interdisciplinary learning to enhance students' problem-solving ability" (Ministry of Education of the People's Republic of China, 2023). In the same period of 2023, the Ministry of Education issued the "Action Plan for Deepening the Reform of Basic Education curriculum Teaching", which said: "The demonstration will drive the majority of teachers to change the way of teaching and learning, respect the principal position of students, and pay attention to heuristic, interactive and inquision-based teaching."(Ministry of Education of the People's Republic of China, 2023). Both of these programs emphasize and advocate project-based teaching.

In the study of Hart Joanne Louise, project tasks are divided into disciplinary tasks (integration of knowledge content with a high degree of correlation within the discipline, such as integration of linear algebra and statistics) and narrow interdisciplinary tasks (integration of disciplines in different disciplines but belonging to a unified discipline field) according to disciplines. E.g. Integration of biology and chemistry), broad interdisciplinary tasks (integration of different disciplines and interdisciplinary fields, e.g. Integration of language and physics) (Hart Joanne Louise, 2019). This theory greatly expands the scope of project-based teaching and provides a theoretical basis for interdisciplinary teaching. Krajcik. It emphasizes project-based learning, a kind of inquisitorial teaching method that focuses on the theme tasks derived from the real world. It is a kind of inquiry teaching method in which students show the process of participating in complex and real world theme tasks and developing world products to the public, so as to acquire knowledge and improve their own skills (Krajcik, J. S., & Shin, N, 2014). Juebei Chen integrated 108 articles on PBL in the past 40 years and found that PBL is not limited to one course, and PBL is one of the main learning methods in the undergraduate or graduate courses of a higher education institution (Chen, J., Kolmos, A., & Du, X, 2020).

2.2 Social Constructivist Theory

Constructivist teaching methods have been valued as a student-centered paradigm. This approach emphasizes the active participation of learners in the learning process, with teachers acting as facilitators, sharing knowledge and authority with students (FaridiM., & IzadpanahS, 2024). Constructivism emphasizes that learning is a process of active construction by learners, rather than a process of one-way output of knowledge and information by passive educators. Piaget emphasized that the learning of knowledge is constructive, and believed that "both the occurrence without structure and the structure without occurrence are wrong" (Kang Hing-hung, 1988). From the perspective of the system, any system has its internal structure, which determines the function of the system, if there is no structure, the system cannot be stable and normal operation. From a philosophical point of view, "the occurrence of no structure" means that matter is chaotic and irregular, for example, in physics, the motion of matter is believed to follow the laws of relativity or other physical laws, and if a matter jumps outside of all laws, it is not in line with the scientific cognitive system. "The structure that does not happen" means that the structure needs a certain practical performance, emphasizing that knowledge comes from practice, and if it cannot happen in practice, it is not in line with the actual speculation rather than the theory of the law of reaction matter. On the basis of Piaget's theory, Vygotsky divided human psychological function into lower psychological function and higher psychological function. The lower psychological function represents the animal instinct, while the higher psychological function is the product of social, historical and cultural development. That is to say, higher mental functions develop in the interaction of sociocultural and historical contexts in which the individual learns. Therefore, Vygorsky emphasized that in the process of individual learning, that is, the transformation of low-level psychological functions to high-level psychological functions, the impact of social, historical and cultural situations on learners is quite important (Qian Jiayu, 2011).

Another landmark figure in the theory of cognitive development, Jerome Bruner, Bruner's discovery learning method expects students to "discover" the internal connection of changes in things through their own exploration and discovery under the guidance of scientists to find the law of matter, so as to form concepts and obtain principles. The discovery learning method mainly consists of several steps: finding problems, designing situations, carrying out exploration activities, guiding evaluation and drawing conclusions. It emphasizes that learning should be a process of students' active discovery and self-construction.

3. METHOD

3.1 Teacher: Equipment Coverage and Urban-Rural Differences

Hu Jia relies on the National Education resources public service platform and the teaching and research platform jointly launched by Jiangsu Primary and Secondary School Teaching Research Laboratory and Jiangsu Provincial Department of Education Basic Education: "One teacher, one Excellent course" and "New Teaching Space and Time". Select high school chemistry classroom teaching examples from 2018 to 2024 as research objects to carry out a survey on the coverage rate of handheld technology in high school chemistry classrooms. The equipment data of handheld technology are shown in Table 1 (Hu Jia, 2022).

Table 1. Hand held technology coverage statistics

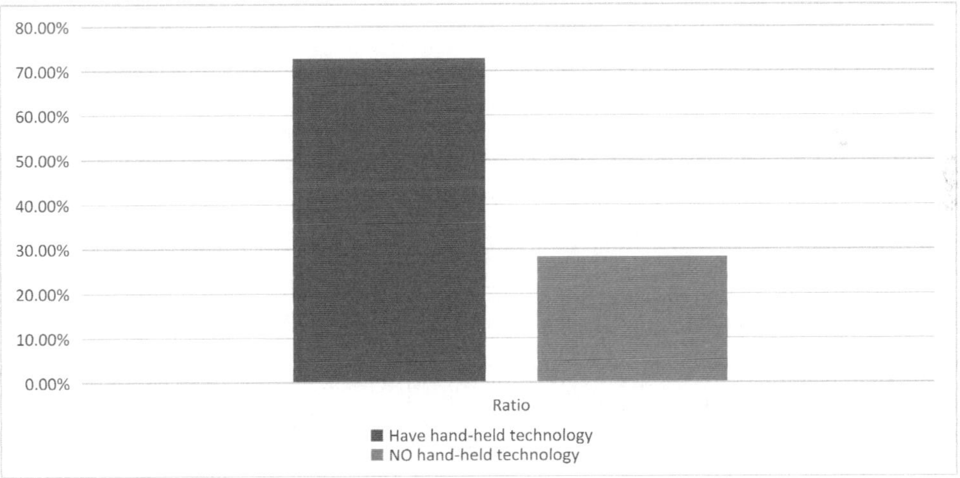

"One teacher and one Excellent Course" is China's national public service platform for education resources. The teaching resources included in the platform are excellent teaching cases at or above the ministerial level from all over the country, which is authoritative and representative. "Teaching New Time and Space" is a teaching and research platform launched by the provincial level, which has the title of "leading the innovation of teaching and research mechanism for 61 primary and secondary school teachers in the province", which is leading and innovative. Through the investigation of the teaching cases of these two teaching and research platforms, it can be found that the class cases without handheld technology support accounted for 73.33%, while the class cases equipped with handheld technology accounted for only 26.67%, indicating that there is a low utilization rate and a narrow popularization of handheld technology in the current class application.

The use of digital technology in the classroom varies from place to place. Because of the difference of hardware facilities and software resources sharing, the situation of using digital technology to assist teaching in middle school classroom is also different. Based on Liu Jihua's questionnaire survey on human-computer interaction teaching of teachers in Zhejiang province, the data of human-computer interaction teaching ability of teachers were analyzed by one-way Anova. It can be seen that the situation of man-machine cooperation teaching in rural areas is obviously different from that in urban areas, which means that there is an imbalance between the use of digital technology in rural areas and the development of cities. Especially in the implementation of teaching, urban teachers and township teachers have more obvious differences.

Table 2. Regional differences of man-machine collaborative teaching ability in schools

project	Rural school	Township school	County-level school	Municipal school	F
Man-machine cooperative teaching ability	2.6252	2.609	2.8188	3.0503	6026
Cognitive ability of man-machine collaborative teaching	2.5769	2.5208	2.7246	2.9136	3.657
Man-machine cooperative teachingdesign ability	2.5214	2.6528	2.7705	2.9792	5.301
Implementation ability of man-machine collaborative teaching	2.6897	2.6583	2.8667	3.1368	6.057
Evaluation ability of man-machine collaborative teaching	2.6538	2.5417	2.8502	3.0686	5.886

3.2 Student: The Focus of The Study Is Distracted

Imane Elimadi et al. conducted a survey to examine how engaged students are with digital learning and the significant benefits of digital learning. Participants in the survey participated in a variety of e-learning activities, such as online lectures, forums, and multimedia resources. Participants communicated with each other through online communication tools as well as with professors, using multimedia resources such as video, interactive simulations, and online forums. The results of the survey are shown in Table 3 (Elimadi Imane, Chafiq Nadia & Talbi Mohammed, 2024). It can be seen that more than half of the students think that digital learning is more interesting and convenient, and can achieve higher efficiency and more conducive to the mastery of knowledge through online application learning. Overall, online learning provides students with a better learning experience, and the digital learning environment keeps students interested and engaged in the course. In today's society, more and more institutions and schools choose to use digital technology to assist teaching, because digital technology makes curriculum content more and more personalized, a growing number of students believe that learning in a digital environment is more effective. For example, students are more likely to accept content presented in animations or audio than in a straightforward course introduction.

Table 3. How E-Learning Can Enhance Student Learning and Engagement

Items	Strongly agree %	Strongly disagree%
I found the e-learning lessons to be interesting and engaging.	77	6
The e-learning platform was simple to use.	81	4
I was able to understand the course material better thanks to the multimedia resources used in the e-learning lessons.	75	7
The e-learning lessons assisted me in remembering and applying the course material.	87	10
In the e-learning environment, I felt in command of my learning.	60	12
The e-learning platform's feedback was beneficial to my learning.	69	14
The e-learning environment seemed conducive to my learning.	78	13
I would recommend e-learning to other students as a method of instruction.	80	17

4. STRATEGY

On the one hand, digital technology has a powerful function of information dissemination and integration. As a rich carrier of learning resources, it can break the limitation of traditional learning resources in time, space and region with massive knowledge databases and diversified multimedia learning materials. On the other hand, the problem of information overload is serious, and the information in the network environment is complex and uneven in quality. When students lack the ability of effective information screening, they are easy to get lost in a large number of invalid, redundant and even wrong information. The 20th report of the Communist Party of China pointed out that in order to "promote the digitalization of education", Internet technology should not only revolutionize the way of production and life, but also update the way of education and teaching of students. Based on social constructivism and project-as-instruction theory, this study will propose meaningful integration of digital technology into middle school classrooms from three dimensions of curriculum, teaching and evaluation.

4.1 Courses Covering Digital Technologies

Since the creation of the computer, the rapid development of digital technology from the computer to the Internet to artificial intelligence has given contemporary education a new task. In order to improve students' information literacy, the following measures are put forward: (1) Add a special course to teach information technology and programming. Taking robot production as an example, students are asked to learn the working principle of robots, simple robot programming methods, and make a simple robot activity program as a test at the end of the course. Robot competition can also be held at the end of the semester to stimulate students' enthusiasm for learning information technology and improve students' digital literacy through group cooperation and healthy competition. (2) The use of digital resources as teaching content, such as pre-class preview or after-class review through the "Xuetang Online" initiated by Tsinghua University, which gathers high-quality educational resources of many colleges and universities, or the "National Smart Education Platform for primary and secondary schools" sponsored by the Ministry of Education, which covers all course content resources of primary and secondary schools, to complete the transformation of science and education, and collaboration between production and education. Promote the updating of practice teaching content and teaching model (Liu Jinku, Zhang Haoran & Huang Jie,2024).

4.2 Problem-Oriented Project-Based Teaching

The teaching should be problem-oriented, context-oriented and aimed at improving students' comprehensive moral, intellectual, physical, American and labor literacy. In today's society, many scholars have designed a variety of teaching models and methods. Big concept teaching is a teaching form advocated by the new curriculum standards. It is a teaching method centered on core concepts, emphasizing beyond specific facts and skills, focusing on deep-level concepts that can integrate subject knowledge, so as to help students establish connections between knowledge and form knowledge networks. Enable students to move more effectively in real situations. In the design of big concept teaching process, WHERETO, seven stages of concept inquiry, four stages of learning deep pit theory and four elements of teaching process are all representative models or frameworks (Liu Hui, 2020). W (goal) H (attraction and retention) E (exploration) R (reflection) E (evaluation) T (adjustment) O (organization) teaching concepts can be used to plan teachers' teaching design more systematically. This study proposes a learning cognitive model supported by digital technology based on WHERETO model——PCCI, as shown in Figure 1.

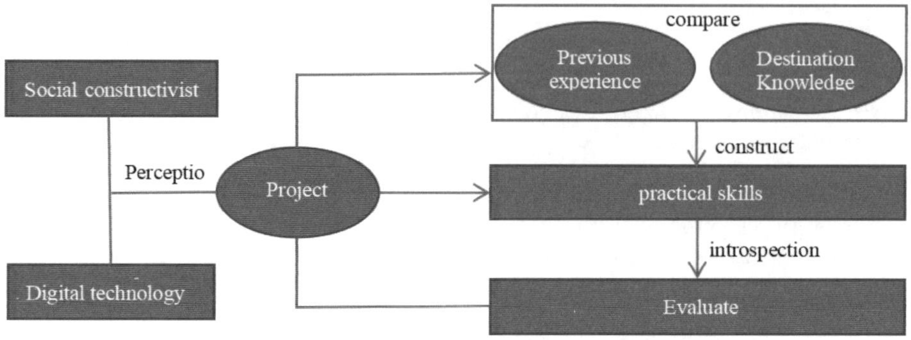

Figure 1. PCCI teaching process model

With constructivism as the theoretical basis, mobile digital technology as the means, and project-based teaching method, on the one hand, students perceive the new knowledge brought by digital devices in the learning process, compare with the existing experience in their minds, summarize the similarities and differences, and construct their own knowledge framework. On the other hand, the knowledge is transferred to practice or experiment, and the learning loop is completed through academic evaluation. This model conforms to the characteristics of openness, integration and sharing in the era of big data, which not only improves the digital literacy of teachers, but also increases the information learning ability of students, and achieves a win-win outcome of teaching and learning.

4.3 Student-Centered Academic Evaluation

Digital literacy and skills-oriented learning evaluation focuses on students' learning performance in real situations, so as to depict students' thinking process in solving problems, analyze students' comprehensive application of knowledge and skills, and realize the true mapping between students' individual literacy performance and core literacy requirements (Li Feng, Xi Shao Jian & Xiong Zhang, 2024). Compared with the results-based evaluation that pays more attention to the final grades, student-oriented academic literacy evaluation pays more attention to the progress of students themselves. It is a longitudinal, comprehensive and comprehensive academic evaluation that aims to track the learning situation of students at the current stage in real time through mobile data, classify and summarize the obstacles in the development of students at the current stage, and check the gaps at any time with the help of online tools. Improve students' knowledge ability and skill level. For example, performance tasks can be designed that have authenticity and are directed towards literacy goals (Revelle, K. Z, Wise, C. N. Duke, N. K,2020). The students' feedback on the task is evaluated in a targeted manner. According to the GRASPS task design template proposed by Wiggins team, this study designed task-based evaluation criteria for primary cell content learning, and the standard content is shown in Table 4.

According to this evaluation standard, it not only feedbacks the students' learning situation of galvanic battery subject knowledge, improves their chemical literacy, but also improves their mobile learning ability. The task-based evaluation criteria reflect the students' internalization of new knowledge, the degree of transfer, the ability of model building and other qualities in the process of completing the design of the galvanic cell model.

Table 4. Evaluation criteria for primary cell content learning

Evaluation aspect	evaluation item	score
Design scheme	1.Whether the positive and negative battery equations are correctly written in the design scheme.	15 points
	2.Whether the selection of electrode material and electrolyte conforms to the principle of galvanic cell generation.	Ten points
	3.Whether the galvanic reaction can occur.	15 points
Works	1.The galvanic cell is the pathway that can make the diode light up.	20 points
	2.The structure of galvanic cell model is safe, stable and beautiful.	20 points
demonstration	1.When explaining on stage, whether the language is clear, smooth and logical, and whether the key points and design innovations are highlighted.	Ten points
	2.Whether the content of the PPT presentation is complete, it is required to cover the complete content of the design and the characteristics of the model, and whether the layout is beautiful.	Ten points

ACKNOWLEDGEMENT

The author thanks for the support of the 2024 Guangxi Undergraduate Education Reform Project: Under the background of professional certification, the construction and practice of the "three lessons" and "four directions" collaborative practice teaching system for normal majors (project No. 2024JGB266).

REFERENCES

Chen, J. Kolmos, A. & Du, X, (2020). Forms of implementation and challenges of PBL in engineering education: a review of literature. *European Journal of Engineering Education*, *46*(1), 90–115.

Elimadi Imane, Chafiq Nadia & Talbi Mohammed, (2024). How E-Learning Can Enhance Student Learning and Engagement: Case study faculty of sciences Ben M'sick, Casablanca. (eds.)

FaridiM., & IzadpanahS. (2024). The Study of EFL Learners' Perception of Using E-learning, Self-Regulation and Constructivism in English Classrooms: Teachers, Intermediate and Advanced Learners' Attitude. *Journal of Language and Education*, *10*(2), 45-58.

Hart Joanne, (2019). Interdisciplinary project-based learning as a means of developing employability skills in undergraduate science degree programs. *Journal of Teaching and Learning for Graduate Employability,* (2),50-66.

Hu Jia, (2022). Teachers conduct research on the evaluation of chemistry classroom teaching practices based on handheld technology experiments (master's, dissertation, East China Normal University).

Hu Jiakang & Tian Li, (2023). Exploration of project-based learning in Japanese primary and secondary schools: development process, practical dilemma and experience review. *Studies in foreign education,* (08), 35-50.

Kang Hing-hung, (1988). A preliminary study of the structure of thought. *Journal of Inner Mongolia Normal University* (philosophy and social sciences edition) (04), 52-60 + 36.

Krajcik, J. S., & Shin, N, (2014). Project-Based Learning. In R. K. Sawyer (Ed.), The Cambridge Handbook of the Learning Sciences (pp. 275–297). chapter, Cambridge: Cambridge University Press.

Li Feng, Xi Shao Jian & Xiong Zhang. (2024). Digital literacy and skills-oriented information technology curriculum standards and teaching implementation. *China distance education,* (11), 52-59 + 96.

Liu Hui., (2020). The whole unit teaching structure from the perspective of"Big concept"-- also on the accomplishment-oriented classroom reform. *Education Research*, (06), 64-77.

Liu Jinku, Zhang Haoran & Huang Jie. (2024). The connotation development of practice teaching in the new era of digital empowerment. University teaching in China (06), 68-74.

Lu hanxue, (2024). The digital existence and educational existence of educational digitization transformation. *Open Education Research*, (04), 62-70.

Ministry of Education of the People's Republic of China, (2023). Opinions on strengthening science education in primary and secondary schools in the new era.

Ministry of Education of the People's Republic of China, (2023). Action Plan for deepening the teaching reform of Basic Education Curriculum [EB/OL].

Qian Jiayu, (2011). A comparison between Bruner's discovery learning and research learning -- a reflection on Bruner's discovery learning. *Foreign Primary and secondary education,* (08), 55-58.

Revelle, K. Z. Wise, C. N. Duke, N. K, et al, (2020). Realizing the Promise of Project-Based Learning [J]. *The Reading Teacher*, (6):697-710.

Yu Ying & Song Ruyue, (2024). Algorithmic thinking teaching in the Digital Age: Reverse Design Framework and action practice. *Journal of Distance Education,* (05), 86-94.

EVALUATION OF MOBILE EDUCATION APPS BY POPULAR GENERATIVE ARTIFICIAL INTELLIGENCE (GENAI) SYSTEMS: AN EXTENDED STUDY ON ITS CONSISTENCY AND THUS CONVERGENT VALIDITY

Victor K. Y. Chan
Macao Polytechnic University
Faculty of Business, Macao Polytechnic University, Rua de Luís Gonzaga Gomes, Macao, China

ABSTRACT

As an extension to a previous pilot study, this article aims to analyze the consistency between and thus the convergent validity of a few popular generative artificial intelligence (GenAI) systems in evaluating popular mobile education apps' usability, effectiveness, and efficiency. The three GenAI systems examined were Microsoft Copilot, Google PaLM, and Assistant, which were individually prompted to award rating scores to the eight major dimensions of usability, effectiveness, and efficency, namely, (1) content/course quality, (2) pedagogical design, (3) learner support, (4) technology infrastructure, (5) social interaction, (6) learner engagement, (7) instructor support, and (8) cost-effectiveness of 100 popular mobile education apps. A paired sample *t*-test was applied to the rating score difference in each of the above eight dimensions between each GenAI system pair out of the above three GenAI systems over all the 100 apps. Then, Cronbach's coefficient alpha of the rating scores was computed for each of the above eight dimensions between all the three GenAI systems across all the 100 apps. The computational results were to confirm whether the GenAI systems, with respect to each other, systematically overrated or underrated any dimension over the 100 apps and whether there were high consistency between and thus convergent validity of the three GenAI systems in evaluating each dimension across the 100 apps. Among other collateral finding, it was revealed that the consistency between and thus the convergent validity of the three GenAI systems was basically sufficiently high in evaluating all the eight dimensions across the 100 apps, with those in the dimension (8) cost-effectiveness being at least marginally high enough, and thus the three GenAI systems may be rather reliable in evaluating all the eight usability, effectiveness, and efficiency dimensions across mobile education apps.

KEYWORDS

Convergent Validity, Mobile Education Apps, Generative Artificial Intelligence (Genai), Evaluation

1. INTRODUCTION

1.1 Recent Development of Mobile Education Apps

The landscape of education has undergone a significant transformation with the advent and proliferation of mobile education apps (Camilleri and Camilleri, 2020; Fan and Wang, 2020; Chan, 2024; Akour et al, 2021). These apps have revolutionized the way students learn and teachers instruct (Zhang and Liao, 2015), offering a plethora of benefits such as personalized learning, increased accessibility, and engaging content. The rise of mobile apps in education has bridged gaps, making learning more flexible, dynamic, portable, and accessible than ever before (Adanır and Muhametjanova, 2021). With the proliferation of smartphones and tablets (Adanır and Muhametjanova, 2021), students can now access educational content anytime and anywhere (Fan and Wang, 2020), breaking down the barriers of traditional classroom settings. The integration of technologies such as augmented reality (AR) and virtual reality (VR) has further enhanced the learning experience (Al-Ansi et al, 2023), providing immersive and interactive environments that foster deeper understanding and engagement. Additionally, the use of gamification techniques has made learning more enjoyable and motivating for students (Adanır and Muhametjanova, 2021; Al-Ansi et al, 2023; Fan and Wang, 2020).

1.2 Difficulty in Evaluating Mobile Education Apps

Despite the numerous advantages, evaluating the usability, effectiveness, and efficiency of mobile education apps through traditional methods poses significant challenges. Traditional evaluation methods such as questionnaire surveys, interviews, and focus groups (Maramba et al, 2019; Chan, 2024) are often time-consuming and may not capture the full spectrum of user experiences (Chan, 2024). These methods rely heavily on self-reported data, which can be biased and may not accurately reflect the actual usability, effectiveness, efficiency of the apps. Moreover, the rapid pace of technological advancements and the diverse range of mobile educational apps available make it difficult to conduct comprehensive evaluations using manual methods. The lack of standardized evaluation tools further complicates the process, making it challenging for educators and researchers to assess the pedagogical affordances of these apps accurately.

1.3 Role of Generative Artificial Intelligence in Evaluation

Generative artificial intelligence (GenAI) offers a promising solution to the challenges associated with evaluating mobile education apps (Chan, 2024). GenAI can analyze vast amounts of data from user interactions, providing insights into the usability, effectiveness, and efficiency of such apps in real time. By leveraging machine learning algorithms but unlike typical AI technologies primarily designed for analysis and pattern recognition, GenAI can create novel outputs based on the data the GenAI systems have been trained on (Xia et al, 2024).

GenAI, and AI in general, as applied in education have already been rather thoroughly analyzed in the current literature (Chan, 2024). For instance, Gligorea et al (2023) is an overall literature review of major AI categories' application to education and learning. More specifically, Leiker et al (2023) addresses the gap concerning the impact of using GenAI to create learning videos with synthetic virtual instructors. The experiment with $n = 83$ adult learners, including those in both the experimental group (employing an AI-generated learning video with a synthetic virtual instructor) and the control group (featuring a traditionally produced instructor video), demonstrated significant improvement from pre- to post-learning ($p < .001$), with no significant differences in gains between the two groups ($p = .80$), and with no qualitative differences in the perceived learning experience. These findings suggest that AI-generated learning videos have the potential to be a viable substitute for videos produced via traditional methods in online educational settings, making high quality educational content more accessible across the globe. Ilieva et al (2023) pinpoints another application domain. The authors explore and compare the main characteristics of existing educational chatbots untilizing GenAI. They further propose a new theoretical framework for blended learning with intelligent chatbots integration enabling students to interact online and instructors to create and manage their courses using GenAI tools. The advantages of the proposed framework are as follows: (1) it provides a comprehensive understanding of the transformative potential of AI chatbots in education and facilitates their effective implementation; (2) it offers a holistic methodology to enhance the overall educational experience; and (3) it unifies the applications of intelligent chatbots in teaching-learning activities within universities. Despite all these publications, the author is not aware of any existing literature specifically evaluating mobile education apps' usability by means of generative AI robots (Chan, 2024).

1.4 The Current Study

The author had not been aware of any existing literature head-on evaluating mobile education apps' usability, effectiveness, and efficiency by GenAI systems until he himself conducted such an evaluation in a limited-scale pilot study, which consisted of only 17 mobile learning apps (or equivalently, mobile education apps) (Chan, 2024). Albeit it transpired that the findings were encouraging, fundamental theories of statistics indicated that such a small sample might not be able to render some statistical significances even if corresponding significances would have manifested themselves in a substantially larger sample (Weiss, 2016). Being an extension of the pilot study, the current study is exactly to fill this gap of too small a sample size.,. As with the pilot study, the current study is to apply multiple popular GenAI systems to the evaluation of the various usability, effectiveness, and efficiency dimensions or perspectives of a sample of popular mobile education apps on the market, drawing on global users' comments on the apps' dimensions as appear on the web. These dimensions are rigorously upheld by the literature. The ultimate objective is to determine whether the various evaluations by the systems are consistent, or in a more technical parlance, whether the convergent validity of such evaluations is high. Such consistency or convergent validity matters because it is almost logically impossible to define the superiority of any particular system's evaluation over others in view of the non-existence of any neutral "yardstick" of evaluation as the paramount reference for any system's evaluation to benchmark against. At best, to decide which evaluation to be regarded as reliable, one can measure the consistency between various evaluations. If several evaluations happen to be consistent, it will be likely, if not absolute, that all of them are reliable. This is exactly the concept of convergent validity of an operationalized instrument or scale (e.g., questionnaire questions) to measure an abstract construct (e.g., happiness) in most social or behavioral sciences. For example, logically, there is no absolute way to define what questionnaire questions are the best instrument to gauge any particular person's degree of happiness. One criterion to judge that a set of questionnaire questions are likely, if not absolutely, to be a good instrument to measure happiness is the high consistency between or the high convergent validity of the questionnaire question set and other questionnaire question sets also designed to gauge happiness. Both the pilot study and the current study seek to explore such consistency between and such convergent validity of a few popular GenAI systems in evaluating popular mobile education (or learning) apps' usability, effectiveness, and efficiency.

However, it is noteworthy that the 17 mobile learning apps in the pilot study were chiefly generic and content-neutral. In other words, the 17 mobile learning apps were primarily, if not absolutely exclusively, mobile learning platforms with their contents up to the instructors and learners to upload. The number of popular mobile learning apps of this categories were far from plenty. To extend the pilot study, the current study includes 100 mobile education apps, the majority being content-specific and aiming at educating learners on particular subject areas and/or skills. With minimal effort, this fine-tuning of the scope enables the increase from 17 popular mobile learning apps to 100 mobile education apps.

2. METHODOLOGY

2.1 Data and Materials

The present study experimented in December 2024 with six very popular GenAI systems, namely Microsoft Copilot (Cambon et al, 2023), Google PaLM (Anil, 2023), Assistant (Anonymous, 2024a; Sridharan and Sequeira, 2024), Claude-3-Haiku and 1 bot (Schmidl et al, 2024), Gemini-1.5-Pro (Anonymous, 2024b; Masalkhi et al, 2024), and GPT-3.5-Turbo (Lin et al, 2023) as candidates for the evaluation of mobile education apps' usability, effectiveness, and efficiency, the first being bundled with Microsoft Windows or the Microsoft Edge browser and the other five being accessible through the GenAI portal poe.com. Eight major dimensions to evaluate a mobile education app's usability, effectiveness, and efficiency were adopted (Albelbisi, 2020; Hew and Cheung, 2014; Khalil and Ebner, 2014; Kizilcec et al., 2013; Liyanagunawardena et al., 2013), they being (1) content/course quality, (2) pedagogical design, (3) learner support, (4) technology infrastructure, (5) social interaction, (6) learner engagement, (7) instructor support, and (8) cost-effectiveness, which were rated by each of the above systems. (1) Content/course quality measures the overall quality and relevance of the course content, including the course design, instructional strategies, and assessment methods. It is essential to ensure that the course content is up-to-date, accurate, and relevant to the learners' needs. The quality of the mobile education app's content is a critical factor that affects learners' satisfaction with the course. (2) Pedagogical design refers to the design of the courses, including the teaching methods, assessment strategies, and learning outcomes. It is essential to ensure that the courses are designed in a way that encourages active learning and promotes learner engagement. The (2) pedagogical design of a mobile education app's courses is a critical factor that affects learners' engagement and motivation. (3) Learner support includes the support provided to learners throughout the courses on the mobile education app. It is essential to ensure that learners have access to adequate support, including technical support and academic support. (3) Learner support is a critical factor that affects learners' completion rates and overall satisfaction with a mobile education app's courses. (4) Technology infrastructure measures the technological capabilities of the mobile education app, including its ability to deliver course content, interact with learners, and manage learner data as well as how user-friendly, accessible, and reliable it is. (4) Technology infrastructure may be assessed by metrics like a mobile education app's uptime, speed of content delivery, compatibility with different devices, and security measures. (5) Social interaction refers to the opportunities for learners to interact with each other and with the instructors. It is essential to ensure that learners have opportunities to collaborate, discuss, and share ideas with each other. (5) Social interaction is a critical factor that affects learners' engagement and satisfaction with a mobile education app's courses. (6) Learner engagement measures the level of interaction between learners and the course content. Engagement is a crucial factor in determining the effectiveness of a mobile education app as it affects the learning outcomes of learners. It can be appraised by such metrics as the average time spent on the course content, the number of interactions with the course materials, the number of forum posts and comments by learners, and the average completion rate of the mobile education app's courses. (7) Instructor support measures the level of support provided to learners by the instructors. (7) Instructor support is important because it fosters a sense of community and increases learner engagement. It can be gauged by metrics such as the response time to learners' queries, the quality of responses to learners' queries, the availability of instructors during course hours, and the frequency of instructor-led sessions. (8) Cost-effectiveness measures the cost of delivering the course content and the benefits derived from it. (8) Cost-effectiveness is important because it determines the viability of a mobile education app as a mode of delivering education. It can be translated into metrics, namely, the cost per learner, the return on investment of the mobile education app, the cost savings compared to traditional modes of education delivery, and the revenue generated by the mobile education app. (Chan, 2024).

The data collection commenced with the identification of 100 popular mobile education apps. This study simply referred to the website of similarweb at https://www.similarweb.com, which was a commercial website ranking the apps listed in the two major app stores, namely, Google Play Store and Apple App Store, as classified by the apps' app stores (where the apps were listed), countries (in which the apps were available from the app stores), categories (e.g., education, entertainment, etc.), and some other minor attributes. The ranking algorithms were proprietary and presumably based on online traffic, which could roughly be a proxy for each app's popularity. Whether such commercial ranking was equitable would not bear on the study's findings as the ranking was only a means to sample popular apps whereas the ranking spots were not any variable in the data analysis. This study sampled the top 50 apps in the app store of "Google Play Store," the category of "Education," the country of the "United States," and being "Top Paid" (i.e., to include the top-ranked paid apps) as well as the top 50 apps in the app store of "Apple App Store," the category of "Education," the country of the "United States," being "Top Paid," and to be installed on "iPhone" (as opposed to "iPad"). The country of the "United States" was selected as an example for the sampling process just because of its being the largest economy and thus app market globally but with no denigration of other countries or markets. These double top 50 apps turned out to include:

Star Walk 2 - Night Sky View (Android version), Toca Hair Salon 3 (Android version), Fighter Verses (Android version), SkyView® Explore the Universe (Android version), ..., SkyView® (iOS version), AnkiMobile Flashcards (iOS version), Prepware Aviation Maintenance (iOS version), Star Walk 2: Stars and Planets (iOS version), …

Then, a prompt was submitted to the above six GenAI systems individually for giving "a rating score to each of the… popular mobile education apps" "for each of the eight dimensions (1) content/course quality, (2) pedagogical design, (3) learner support, (4) technology infrastructure, (5) social interaction, (6) learner engagement, (7) instructor support, and (8) cost-effectiveness" "based on a scale of 1 to 10 (1 being the worst and 10 the best)." The prompt accentuated deriving the "scores from global users' textual comments on these eight dimensions of these apps as appear all around the web." In order words, the systems were instructed to derive their scores from global users' textual comments appearing all around the web instead of parroting any analogous scores already published somewhere on the web or elsewhere. Also, the above 100 popular mobile education apps were explicitly spelt out in the prompt. It happened that only the three GenAI systems Microsoft Copilot, Google PaLM, and Assistant replied with their rating scores in all the above eight dimensions for all the above 100 apps. The remaining three GenAI systems declined to rate either all or some of the 100 apps on the alleged grounds of, for instance, being "unable to fetch real-time data or scrape textual comments from the web," a "limited scope" of apps, "subjectivity" of ratings, "dynamic nature of apps," and the lack of "substantial research, user testing, and subject matter expertise."

It is noteworthy that all GenAI systems' outputs are as good as the data on which they were trained, and such training data were unavoidably updated up to a certain cutoff date. Any outputs are thus reflective of what the world was as of the cutoff date. By additionally submitting to the above three systems a simple prompt about their training data cutoff dates, it was discovered that PaLM and Assistant of this study were trained on data up to somewhere around April 2023 and October 2023, respectively whilst Copilot stressed that its knowledge was continuously updated, and it could always search for the most up-to-date information. In other words, the rating scores from these three systems Copilot, PaLM, and Assistant related to the 100 apps as of December 2024, April 2023, and October 2023 respectively. Equally noteworthy is that this study aimed to examine the consistency between and thus the convergent validity of GenAI systems in evaluating mobile education apps' eight dimensions, so its original objective did not encompass (and, as a matter of fact, its research resources were far insufficient to support) microscopically and technically unravelling the way these systems interpreted, comprehended, and measured each dimension of such apps. Rather, such microscopic and technical (or even algorithmic) details were treated as black boxes such that this study focused on the ultimate evaluation results in the form of rating scores as what they were and on the consistency between and thus the convergent validity of GenAI systems' rating scores awarded to each dimension of such apps irrespective of such microscopic and technical details.

2.2 Analysis

Unlike the pilot study, the current study skips the basic computation of the minimum, the maximum, the range, and the standard deviation of the rating scores accorded by any particular GenAI system in each of the above eight dimensions across all the mobile education apps and the kindred quantities.

Rather, the analysis started off with the application of a paired sample *t*-test to the rating score difference in each of the above eight dimensions between each GenAI system pair out of the above three GenAI systems over all the above 100 apps. If the *t*-test is significant and the corresponding mean difference is positive (negative), it is revealed that the first GenAI system in the pair systematically overrates (underrates) the dimension with respect to the second GenAI system.

For more statistically rigorous confirmation of the consistency between and thus the convergent validity of all the above three GenAI systems' evaluations, Cronbach's coefficient alpha (DeVellis, 2005) of the rating scores was computed for each of the above eight dimensions between all the three GenAI systems across all the 100 apps. If Cronbach's coefficient alpha is high, for instance, over 0.5 or 0.6 (Ling et al, 2021; Nunnally, 1967) for a particular dimension, it is implied that there is consistency between and thus high convergent validity of all the above three GenAI systems in rating the dimension across all the above 100 apps.

3. RESULTS

Table 1 enumerates the paired sample *t*-tests of the rating score differences in each of the above eight dimensions between each pair of GenAI systems out of the above three GenAI systems over all the above 100 mobile education apps. Vis-à-vis Assistant, Copilot tended to systematically overrate the three dimensions (3) learner support (at the 1% significance level or $p < 0.01$), (5) social interaction ($p < 0.05$), and (7) instructor support ($p < 0.01$) and systematically underrate another three dimensions (1) content/course quality ($p < 0.01$), (2) pedagogical design ($p < 0.01$), and (4) technology infrastructure ($p < 0.01$) whilst PaLM inclined to systematically overrate the four dimensions (2) pedagogical design, (3) learner support, (6) learner engagement, and (7) instructor support ($p < 0.01$ for all) and systematically underrate the two dimensions (1) content/course quality and (5) social interaction ($p < 0.01$ for all). With respect to PaLM, Copilot leaned toward systematically overrating the dimension (5) social interaction ($p < 0.01$) and systematically underrating the four dimensions (2) pedagogical design, (4) technology infrastructure, (6) learner engagement, and (7) instructor support ($p < 0.01$ for all). Otherwise, relative to each other, the three GenAI systems neither overrated nor underrated systematically any other dimensions. In this study, the 5% significance level is opted for in all hypothesis tests, so all tests with $p < 0.05$ or $p < 0.01$ are regarded as statistically significant.

Table 1. The paired sample *t*-test of the rating score differences in each of the eight dimensions between each pair of GenAI systems over all the 100 mobile education apps

Differences (sample size *n*)	Dimension	Mean difference / [95% confidence interval]	*t* (*p*-value) / degrees of freedom
	(1) Content/course quality	.007 / [-.121, .135]	.109 (.914) / 99
	(2) Pedagogical design	-1.182 / [-1.308, -1.056]	-18.626 (.000**) / 99
	(3) Learner support	.129 / [-.014,.272]	1.793 (.076) / 99
Copilot – PaLM	(4) Technology infrastructure	-.257 / [-.411, -.103]	-3.305 (.001**) / 99
(*n* = 100)	(5) Social interaction	.580 / [.408,.752]	6.700 (.000**) / 99
	(6) Learner engagement	-.442 / [-.673, -.211]	-3.803 (.000**) / 99
	(7) Instructor support	-.633 / [-.758, -.508]	-10.052 (.000**) / 99
	(8) Cost-effectiveness	-.052 / [-.170,.066]	-.873 (.385) / 99
	(1) Content/course quality	-.290 / [-.432, -.148]	-4.057 (.000**) / 99
	(2) Pedagogical design	-.730 / [-.906, -.554]	-8.240 (.000**) / 99
	(3) Learner support	1.000 / [.811, 1.189]	10.488 (.000**) / 99
Copilot – Assistant	(4) Technology infrastructure	-.230 / [-.387, -.073]	-2.913 (.004**) / 99
(*n* = 100)	(5) Social interaction	.230 / [.045,.415]	2.472 (.015*) / 99
	(6) Learner engagement	.170 / [-.043,.383]	1.583 (.117) / 99
	(7) Instructor support	2.410 / [2.274, 2.546]	35.283 (.000**) / 99
	(8) Cost-effectiveness	.110 / [-.126,.346]	.926 (.357) / 99
	(1) Content/course quality	-.297 / [-.451, -.143]	-3.838 (.000**) / 99
	(2) Pedagogical design	.452 / [.263,.641]	4.758 (.000**) / 99
	(3) Learner support	.871 / [.684, 1.058]	9.248 (.000**) / 99
PaLM – Assistant	(4) Technology infrastructure	.027 / [-.178,.232]	.262 (.794) / 99
(*n* = 100)	(5) Social interaction	-.350 / [-.533, -.167]	-3.800 (.000**) / 99
	(6) Learner engagement	.612 / [.381,.843]	5.249 (.000**) / 99
	(7) Instructor support	3.043 / [2.871, 3.215]	35.115 (.000**) / 99
	(8) Cost-effectiveness	.162 / [-.068,.392]	1.396 (.166) / 99

* $p < 0.05$; ** $p < 0.01$

Table 2 delineates Cronbach's coefficient alpha of the rating scores for each of the above eight dimensions between all the above three GenAI systems over all the 100 mobile education apps. All the eight dimensions rendered a value of Cronbach's coefficient alpha sufficiently high (Nunnally, 1967) to signify consistency between and thus high convergent validity of the three GenAI systems in evaluating all the eight dimensions. In summary, the convergent validity of the three GenAI systems was basically sufficiently high for all the eight dimensions, and that for the dimension (8) cost-effectiveness was at least marginally high enough. Therefore, the three GenAI systems may be rather reliable in evaluating all the eight usability, effectiveness, and efficiency dimensions of mobile education apps.

Table 2. Cronbach's coefficient alpha of the rating scores for each of the eight dimensions between all the three GenAI systems over all the 100 mobile education apps

Sample size *n*	(1) Content/ course quality	(2) Pedagogical design	(3) Learner support	(4) Technology infrastructure	(5) Social interaction	(6) Learner engagement	(7) Instructor support	(8) Cost-effectiveness
100	.753	.733	.671[a]	.653	.672	.749	.734	.574

4. CONCLUSION AND DISCUSSION

In contrast to the author's earlier pilot study (Chan, 2024), the current study ended up with more lucid and definite findings. Specifically, whilst there was systematic overrating or underrating of quite some dimensions by one GenAI system versus another GenAI system in the pilot study, there were not a large proportion of dimensions exhibiting such overrating or underrating to the extent of statistical significance at the 5% or even 1% significance level. On the contrary, the current study was able to "discern" such overrating or underrating not only for the majority of dimensions but also within most possible pairs of GenAI systems analyzed. More likely than not, this contrast was a statistical consequence of an appreciably larger sample in the current study than in the earlier pilot study (Weiss, 2016). The implication is that any particular GenAI system usually, if not always, overrates or underrates any dimension of mobile education apps in comparison with any other particular GenAI system. Stated differently, any pair of GenAI systems very often evaluate the same dimension of mobile education apps on rather disparate scales. For example, one GenAI system may accord a rating score of 9 to a certain high level of (1) content/course quality whereas another GenAI system may consider the same high level worth a rating score of merely 8. Please note that this discrepancy in the alignment of a dimension's levels with rating scores between any pair of GenAI systems may not necessarily prejudice the consistency between and thus the convergent validity of the GenAI system pair. For instance, suppose that whenever one GenAI system rates any particular mobile education app favorably (or unfavorably) in a certain dimension, the other GenAI system also rates as such. Even if the first GenAI system's rating score is 9 (or 2) whilst the second GenAI system's rating score is 8 (or 1), i.e., the two GenAI systems' rating scores for that dimension of that mobile education app are linearly shifted, the two GenAI systems' rating scores can still be consistent in that whenever the first GenAI system's rating score for that dimension of that mobile education app is high (or low), the second GenAI system's corresponding rating score is also high (or low) though the degrees of highness and lowness may differ between the two GenAI systems.

The current study's comparative lucidity and definiteness are also manifested in the consistency between and thus the sufficiently high convergent validity of all the three GenAI systems in evaluating all the eight dimensions of the mobile education apps whereas the pilot study only attested to similar consistency and convergent validity at a marginal level in the dimension (1) content/course quality. This contrast might also be due to the way larger sample size in the current study. After all, the promising consistency and convergent validity uncovered in this study strongly indicate the likeliness of all the three GenAI systems concerned being trustworthy in evaluating the eight dimensions of mobile education apps.

This study itself is not without its critics. First, even with some effort, only three popular GenAI systems Copilot, PaLM, and Assistant were found in this study to be "willing" to reply with rating scores in all the eight dimensions over all the 100 apps. The study's findings could have been more cogent if more out of the profuse GenAI systems in operation worldwide had participated in the study. Second, these three GenAI systems were trained on data up to some cutoff dates, so even their rating scores collected in this study were not reflective of the latest mobile education apps and their versions then but merely those as of the systems' cutoff dates. Therefore, there was room for improving the timeliness of the findings. Third, the sample in this study focused on the 100 apps most popular in the United States as ranked by similarweb and thus was not sufficiently global to enable worldwide generalization of the findings.

In view of the high convergent validity of GenAI systems ascertained in this study and other sanguine findings elsewhere, GenAI systems are believably to be an invaluable means of opinion evaluation whether in academia or industry and whether for mobile education apps or otherwise. Such evaluation is far less time-consuming, less expensive, less subjective, and broader in the coverage of diverse opinions from a large population and from more geographic locales globally than traditional evaluation methods.

REFERENCES

Adanır, G. A. and Muhametjanova, G., (2021). University Students' Acceptance of Mobile Learning: A Comparative Study in Turkey and Kyrgyzstan. *In Education and Information Technologies*, Vol. 26, No. 5, pp. 6163–6181. Available at https://doi.org/10.1007/s10639-021-10620-1

Akour, I. et al, (2021). Using Machine Learning Algorithms to Predict People's Intention to Use Mobile Learning Platforms during the COVID-19 Pandemic: Machine Learning Approach. *In JMIR Medical Education*, Vol. 7, No. 1. Available at https://mededu.jmir.org/2021/1/e24032/

Al-Ansi, A. M. et al, (2023). Analyzing Augmented Reality (AR) and Virtual Reality (VR) Recent Development in Education. *In Social Sciences and Humanities Open*, Vol. 8, No. 1.

Albelbisi, N. A., (2020). Development and Validation of the MOOC Success Scale (MOOC-SS). *In Education and Information Technologies*, Vol. 25, No. 5, pp. 4535–4555. Available at https://doi.org/10.1007/s10639-020-10186-4

Anil, R., (2023). PaLM 2 Technical Report. *In arXiv:2305.10403v3*. Accessed December 10, 2024 at https://doi.org/10.48550/arXiv.2305.10403

Anonymous, (2024a). Assistant. Accessed December 10, 2024 at https://poe.com/Assistant

Anonymous, (2024b). Gemini - chat to supercharge your ideas. Available December 10, 2024 at https://gemini.google.com/

Cambon, A. et al., (2023). Early LLM-based Tools for Enterprise Information Workers Likely Provide Meaningful Boosts to Productivity. Accessed December 10, 2024 at https://www.microsoft.com/en-us/research/uploads/prod/2023/12/AI-and-Productivity-Report-First-Edition.pdf

Camilleri, M. A. and Camilleri, A. C., (2020). The Students' Readiness to Engage with Mobile Learning Apps. *In Interactive Technology and Smart Education*, Vol. 17, No. 1, pp. 28–38. Available at https://doi.org/10.1108/ITSE-06-2019-0027

Chan, V. K. Y., (2024). The Convergent Validity of Mobile Learning Apps' Usability Evaluation by Popular Generative Artificial Intelligence (AI) Robots. *Proceedings of 20th International Conference on Mobile Learning*. Porto, Portugal, pp. 247–254.

DeVellis, R. F., (2005). Inter-rater reliability. In Kempf-Leonard, K., *Encyclopedia of Social Measurement*. Elesvier.

Fan, J. and Wang, Z., (2020). The Impact of Gamified Interaction on Mobile Learning APP Users' Learning Performance: the Moderating Effect of Users' Learning Style. *In Behaviour & Information Technology*, pp. 1–14. Available at https://www.tandfonline.com/doi/full/10.1080/0144929X.2020.1787516

Gligorea, I. et al, (2023). Adaptive Learning Using Artificial Intelligence in e-Learning: A Literature Review. *In Education Sciences*, Vol. 13, No. 12, pp. 1216. Available at https://doi.org/10.3390/educsci13121216

Hew, K. F. and Cheung, W. S., (2014). Students' and Instructors' Use of Massive Open Online Courses (MOOCs): Motivations and Challenges. *In Educational Research Review*, Vol. 12, pp. 45–58. Available at 10.1016/j.edurev.2014.05.001

Ilieva, G. et al, (2023). Effects of Generative Chatbots in Higher Education. *In Information*, Vol. 14, No. 9, pp. 492. Available at https://doi.org/10.3390/info14090492

Khalil, H. and Ebner, M., (2014). MOOCs Completion Rates and Possible Methods to Improve Retention - A Literature Review. *Proceedings of EdMedia 2014--World Conference on Educational Media and Technology*, Tampere, Finland. pp. 1305–1313.

Kizilcec, R. F. et al, (2013). Deconstructing Disengagement: Analyzing Learner Subpopulations in Massive Open Online Courses. *Proceedings of the Third ACM International Conference on Learning Analytics and Knowledge*, Leuven, Belgium pp. 170–179. Available at 10.1145/2460296.2460330

Leiker, D. et al, (2023). Generative AI for Learning: Investigating the Potential of Learning Videos with Synthetic Virtual Instructors. In Wang, N. et al (eds), Artificial Intelligence in Education: Posters and Late Breaking Results, Workshops and Tutorials, Industry and Innovation Tracks, Practitioners, Doctoral Consortium and Blue Sky. *Proceedings of 24th International Conference in Artificial Intelligence in Education, Tokyo, Japan, Communications in Computer and Information Science*, Vol 1831. Available at https://doi.org/10.1007/978-3-031-36336-8_81

Lin, J. C. et al, (2023). Comparison of GPT-3.5, GPT-4, and Human User Performance on a Practice Ophthalmology Written Examination. *In Eye*, Vol. 37, pp. 3694–3695. Available at https://doi.org/10.1038/s41433-023-02564-2

Ling, H.-C. et al, (2021). Exploring the Factors Affecting Customers' Intention to Purchase a Smart Speaker. *In Journal of Retailing and Consumer Services*, Vol. 59.

Liyanagunawardena, T. R. et al, (2013). MOOCs: A Systematic Study of the Published Literature 2008-2012. *In The International Review of Research in Open and Distributed Learning*, Vol. 14, No. 3, pp. 202–227. Available at 10.19173/irrodl.v14i3.1455

Maramba, I. et al, (2019). Methods of Usability Testing in the Development of eHealth Applications: A Scoping Review. *In International Journal of Medical Informatics*, Vol. 126, pp. 95–104. Available at https://doi.org/10.1016/j.ijmedinf.2019.03.018.

Masalkhi, M. et al, (2024). Google DeepMind's Gemini AI versus ChatGPT: A Comparative Analysis in Ophthalmology. *In Eye*, Vol. 38, pp. 1412–1417. Available at https://doi.org/10.1038/s41433-024-02958-w

Nunnally, J. C., (1967). *Psychometric Theory*. McGraw-Hill, New York, USA.

Schmidl, B. et al, (2024). Assessing the Use of the Novel Tool Claude 3 in Comparison to ChatGPT 4.0 as an Artificial Intelligence Tool in the Diagnosis and Therapy of Primary Head and Neck Cancer Cases. *In European Archives of Oto-Rhino-Laryngology*, Vol. 281, pp. 6099–6109. Available at https://doi.org/10.1007/s00405-024-08828-1

Sridharan, K. and Sequeira, R. P., (2024). Evaluation of Artificial Intelligence-Generated Drug Therapy Communication Skill Competencies in Medical Education. *In British Journal of Clinical Pharmacology*. Available at https://doi.org/10.1111/bcp.16144

Weiss, N. A., (2016). *Introductory Statistics*, 10th Edition (Global Edition). Pearson.

Xia, Q. et al, (2024). A Scoping Review on How Generative Artificial Intelligence Transforms Assessment in Higher Education. *In International Journal of Educational Technology in Higher Education*, Vol. 21, 40. Available at https://doi.org/10.1186/s41239-024-00468-z

Zhang, J. and Liao, B., (2015). Learning on the Fingertips: The Opportunities and Challenges of Educational Apps. *In Journal of Education and Practice*, Vol. 6, No. 20, pp. 62–67.

ADAPTING TO PERSONALIZED DIGITAL LEARNING ENVIRONMENT: A COMPARATIVE STUDY OF TEACHER PRACTICES BETWEEN ROMANIA AND ISRAEL

Moshe Facler and Madalina Cristea
Babes-Bolyai University
Mihail Kogalniceanu street no. 1, Cluj-Napoca, Romania

ABSTRACT

The reality of our time has accelerated with technological innovations that are very convenient and exciting, allow for high-level actions, and create better understanding at a personal level tailored to almost everyone. The education system has also experienced this in practice. In a personalized learning approach, the responsibility for implementation lies in leading the student's journey. However, the teacher has a critical role in this leadership and mentoring, alongside the student and technology as an integral part of the personal learning journey. Personalized learning was conceived more than a century ago. However, since then, the education system has operated with a One-Size-Fits-all teacher approach, treating all students in the classroom as if they were the same and uniform. This picture is changing in the digital age. This paper will present a quantitative study with school teachers in Romania and Israel regarding their knowledge and skills in the virtual environment today and their familiarity and experience with the personalized learning approach in the digital age. Education is required to lead the student into the era of tomorrow and not lag. The teacher becomes a mentor and also a self-learner, involving a lifelong learning approach, which means leading students to personalized learning according to their profile in their journey and, alongside this, endless learning of digital learning skills and existing tools and applications in favor of integrating it in the correct dose and balance to promote personalized learning for students in both countries. This comparative analysis provides essential insights into how teachers can adapt to the learning demands of the 21st century and offers practical and necessary recommendations for pre-service teacher training programs, especially in this technological period. Teachers are required to lead the challenges of tomorrow in the digital age, which is becoming personalized. The paper discussed digital means for the teacher to help and conduct the learners in the virtual learning environment. Therefore, they must master them with high skills in general and, in particular, personalized ones. The One-Size-Fits-All learning approach is moving slowly away from the education system classes in light of tomorrow's challenges and possibilities for personalized learning paths for future generations. This study examines the status of this critical learning approach for teachers in Romania and Israel.

KEYWORDS

Personalized Digital Learning (PDL), Learning Path, Comparative Study, AI

1. INTRODUCTION

Personalization, a concept gaining ground in every field, has led to the emergence of personalized learning as a significant educational revolution in the digital era. This approach, which tailors teaching processes to each student's unique needs, pace, and characteristics, is a departure from the traditional uniform One-Size-Fits-all approach. Instead, it generates a personalized learning path for each student and creates distinct learning experiences that foster engagement, motivation, and deeper understanding, making it a compelling study area. Against this opening, teachers become facilitators or mentors and play a crucial role in implementing the personalized learning approach in the education system. Their ability to combine pedagogical knowledge, understanding of the content, and the ability to use advanced technologies is a key factor in the success of this learning model. Furthermore, the differences between education systems in different countries and diverse cultural and social approaches constitute fertile ground for research that compares how teachers familiarize themselves with and implement personalized learning approaches in practice. The present article compares the familiarity, skills, approaches, and tools teachers in Romania and Israel use to implement personalized learning. The two countries, which differ in cultural, educational, and technological background, constitute an interesting basis for examining how teachers integrate into the transition to personalized learning in the digital era. The study is based on a questionnaire conducted among teachers from both countries and includes a quantitative analysis of the data collected. The findings, which highlight the challenges and opportunities in implementing personalized learning, have the potential to significantly impact the field of education by suggesting ways to improve teaching and learning processes in diverse education systems in the era of rapid digital transformation.

2. BACKGROUND

As early as the end of the 18th century, more than 250 years away from digital capabilities, Rousseau's philosophical approach to personalized learning began, emphasizing the child's experiential learning over the imposition of information (Rousseau, 1762). Rousseau proposed adapting education to the child's developmental stages, not necessarily to his age, and preventing the imposition of knowledge in a way that is not appropriate for the student. He emphasized naturalness, freedom, and autonomy in the learning process, which does not need to be uniform for everyone. Montessori further emphasized the child's freedom to explore while supporting necessary skills, including practical ones, in a laboratory environment independently under the supervision of the teacher (Montessori, 1912). The emphasis was on independent and student-centered learning, using interactive materials tailored to the child's needs. Similarly, Dewey emphasized experiential learning, a process that allows students to actively participate in the construction and discovery of knowledge (Dewey, 1916). In modern times, Bloom presented the important and critical approach of establishing a minimum level of acquired knowledge, and that the transition to the next level will be accompanied by the student's acceptance of a minimum threshold to move to it, i.e., the student's achievements are mapped into the learning path. Students progress at their own pace according to their achievements or by dividing into groups (Bloom, 1956). There is not one intelligence, but many, and therefore, learning must be planned to include diverse approaches; Gardner presented and, in fact, officially presented the concept of personalized learning in combination with different learning approaches about existing resources (Gardner, 1983). Earlier, experiments had already begun in the world of computing, also through the PLATO system, which was one of the first computing systems that tried to offer personalized learning and computerized systems have the potential to provide content adapted to the learner's pace (Bitzer, 1961). The world began to operate with computing infrastructures significantly from the beginning of the 2000s, and the UDL concept produces anchors and tools for creating learning environments adapted to each student while providing a variety of ways, through computing tools, to represent knowledge, to express understanding (CAST, 2024). In the last decade, digital platforms have come to the teacher's disposal to feed online learning materials to students in the classroom and home learning, and a concept has been established that combines holistic concepts, such as TPACK (Technology-Pedagogical Content-Knowledge), or blended learning which combines an integration approach between knowledge, the learning approach, and technology that is already available to the general public for learning in the classroom and anywhere in the online learning era. TPACK allows the establishment of a model for the integration format (which is flexible for everyone) of technology in the education system (Schmidt, 2009).

Organizational tools in the education system as a whole, such as those of technology giants and platforms such as Google Classroom or MS Teams, including in the academic community with Moodle, have become available tools in the world of education as well. In the last five years, we have witnessed a significant breakthrough in the world of AI (Artificial Intelligence) and a revolution in the world of information and network resources, data processing, and the resulting products, shaking up the world of education and academia for higher education. Yilmaz described virtual reality as creating an experiential environment in which students control the pace of learning (Yilmaz & Goktas, 2022). The AI algorithm allows, including AR, to promote the learning experience and its resources. Teachers are a central part of this process and are required to lead learning and not lag behind, despite the momentum of technology companies in every field and for the benefit of training students for future skills in front of IT companies at the level of control, skill, and knowledge within the framework of teaching training in all institutions and in practice on an ongoing basis. Advanced tools enable adaptive learning according to the student's profile, algorithms matching his achievements to the necessary adjustments, and the resources required for enrichment/supplementation. Historically, we are already in an era in which full personalization for the student is within reach, and the teacher plays a central role in the student's advancement. The teacher's training is also critical to the implementation of this learning approach in all aspects following the PL approach that will be chosen. Today, the trend is for the widespread use of AI (Artificial Intelligence) tools in implementing personalized learning paths in the digital environment. These AI tools, when fully integrated, offer several advantages. They enable more personalized learning experiences, use wearables and sensors for precise adaptation to learning, and are expected to revolutionize the world of education for the personalized learning experience that is not only specific to the field of study. Figure 1 below outlines an overview of the implementation process for creating a personalized learning path for a student. This process involves defining the student's profile, traits, hobbies, SWOT, and learning style. It also includes identifying inspirational figures, gathering resources related to the fields of study, and manually filtering and recommending materials using AI tools with a content expert. Finally, the process uses algorithmic rules to create a personalized learning path for each learner or group with similar characteristics. This process is a key part of implementing a unique learning approach in the digital era, as practiced by some teachers who responded to the questionnaire in Israel. It is about the idea that no person is average (Rose, 2013). We are deeply in the digital era, and personalization, with its emphasis on learner choice and lifelong learning, challenges educators to provide innovative, student-centric educational experiences. New technologies have great potential to support personalized learning paths (O'Donoghue, 2010). The learning path for each student is impressive ability followed by adaptive learning, such as feedback, results, and improvement. Adaptive learning theory follows a teaching approach that tailors the educational experience to the individual of each student (Contrino et al., 2024). The teacher's role changed with the combination of technology, even from the 60s in the former century, when machine learning was started between teachers and students. Most of the students preferred programmed learning, which enhanced the student interests and student pace (Watters, 2021).

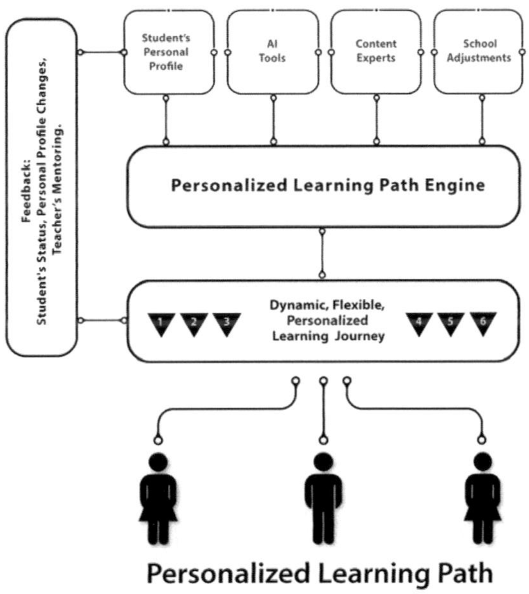

Figure 1. A schematic workflow example for a personalized digital learning path (PL system approach)

Note: AI tools help content experts find and present any resource on the learning subject for inclusion in personalized digital learning paths. These tools are adaptable to the learner's profile, embedding the appropriate resource (manually or automatically according to a pre-planned algorithm). Learner results can update the resources better to understand digital feedback and get back to the learner path.

3. PURPOSE

The study aims to explore the relationship between Romanian and Israeli teachers' familiarity with and use of the Personalized Digital Learning (PDL) approach in class using the virtual environment in the digital era.

4. RESEARCH QUESTIONS

Q1. Are there any significant differences between Romanian and Israeli teachers' perceptions on implementing the Personalized Digital Learning (PDL) approach in their practice?
Q2. What are the differences in PDL usage among Romanian and Israeli teachers according to their teaching environment?
Q3. What are the differences in PDL usage among Romanian and Israeli teachers according to their teaching level?
Q4. What are the differences between Romanian and Israeli teachers' PDL usage according to their academic background?

5. RESEARCH HYPOTHESIS

H1. There are significant differences between Romanian and Israeli teachers' perceptions regarding their personalized digital learning classroom practice.
H2. There are significant differences between Romanian and Israeli teachers' PDL usage according to their teaching environment.
H3. There are significant differences between Romanian and Israeli teachers' PDL usage according to their teaching level.
H4. There are significant differences between Romanian and Israeli teachers' PDL usage according to their academic background.

6. RESEARCH METHODOLOGY

6.1 Participants

This research focused on pre-university teachers from Romania and Israel who were asked to complete the online questionnaire. Data was gathered from 95 pre-university teachers from Romania and 102 teachers from mainly High Schools in Israel, both in urban and rural areas. The teachers' study subjects were diverse, encompassing all subjects in the educational system without focusing on a specific topic or content.

6.2 Sampling

In order to select the research participants, we used convenience sampling. Key teachers from both Romania and Israel were asked to distribute the online questionnaire through various social media teacher groups.

6.3 Method

Data gathering involved distributing the questionnaire online through the Google Forms application. The online survey method facilitated the data collection, allowing us to cover many teachers from different locations.

6.4 Instruments

The questionnaire used to gather data, which includes an informed consent section, demography items, and two other parts assessing teachers' practices in personalized digital learning, has been carefully adapted for this study (Johnson, 2023). It demonstrates robust psychometric properties, ensuring its reliability and validity. We used the Google Forms tool to create a questionnaire with closed questions about Personalized learning and using digital tools online in a virtual environment in class and outside school, with a 1-5 Likert scale rating. Teachers who confirmed using digital personalized systems used Google Classroom, MS Learning Classroom, and REVODUCATE (only in Israel) Personalized Digital Learning system, and the university or college used the Moodle learning platform.

6.5 Procedure

We used the Google Forms tool to create a questionnaire with closed questions about Personalized learning and using digital tools online in a virtual environment in class and outside school. The questionnaire was distributed and completed online with prior informed consent. The participation in the study was voluntary and anonymous. The collected data were analyzed using IBM SPSS statistical software.

7. RESULTS

The split file option, as shown in Table 1, was used to facilitate the comparison between the two groups of teachers in Israel and Romania. The table provides a comparative snapshot of the teaching demographics in these countries.

Table 1. Demographic characteristics - Ages

Country			Frequency	Percent	Valid Percent
Israel	Valid	under 25	40	39.2	39.2
		25-29	62	60.8	60.8
		Total	102	100	100
Romania	Valid	under 25	7	7.4	7.4
		25-29	30	31.6	31.6
		30-39	40	42.1	42.1
		40-49	18	18.9	18.9
		Total	95	100	100

The following Table 2 provides a detailed breakdown of the distribution of teaching environments by location, highlighting the proportion of educators working in urban, suburban, and rural settings.

Table 2. Demographic Characteristics – Teaching Environments Location

Country			Frequency	Percent	Valid Percent
Israel	Valid	Rural	58	56.9	56.9
		Urban	44	43.1	43.1
		Total	102	100	100
Romania	Valid	Rural	31	32.6	32.6
		Urban	64	67.4	67.4
		Total	95	100	100

Table 3. Demographic Characteristics – Grade level in schools

Country			Frequency	Percent	Valid Percent
Israel	Valid	Secondary	14	13.7	13.7
		High-School	88	86.3	86.3
		Total	102	100	100
Romania	Valid	Pre-School	33	34.7	34.7
		Primary	11	11.6	11.6
		Secondary	26	27.4	27.4
		High-School	23	24.2	24.2
		Vocational	2	2.1	2.1
		Total	95	100	100

Table 4 below presents a detailed comparison of teachers' academic backgrounds.

Table 4. Demographic Characteristics – Academic background

Country			Frequency	Percent	Valid Percent
Israel	Valid	Bachelor's Degree	69	67.6	67.6
		Master's Degree	33	32.4	32.4
		Total	102	100	100
Romania	Valid	High-School	3	3.2	3.2
		Bachelor's Degree	50	52.6	52.6
		Master's Degree	40	42.1	42.1
		Doctorate Degree	2	2.1	2.1
		Total	95	100	100

Table 5 below presents a detailed comparison of the nature of a teacher's employment status.

Table 5. Demographic Characteristics – employment status

Country			Frequency	Percent	Valid Percent
Israel	Valid	Temporary	6	5.9	5.9
		Permanent	96	94.1	94.1
		Total	102	100	100
Romania	Valid	Temporary	57	60	60
		Permanent	38	40	40
		Total	95	100	100

Table 6. examines the data through these descriptive measures, and we gain valuable context for interpreting trends, relationships, and potential implications within the dataset between the two groups.

Table 6. Descriptive statistics

Type	Country			Statistic	Std. Error
PL Overall	Israel	**Mean**		**3.7604**	0.03791
		95% Confidence Interval for Mean	Lower Bound	3.6852	
			Upper Bound	3.8356	
		5% Trimmed Mean		3.7652	
		Median		3.8125	
		Variance		0.147	
		Std. Deviation		0.38287	
		Minimum		2.75	
		Maximum		4.75	
		Range		2	
		Interquartile Range		0.52	
		Skewness		-0.308	0.239
		Kurtosis		-0.014	0.474
	Romania	**Mean**		**3.9336**	0.06077
		95% Confidence Interval for Mean	Lower Bound	3.8129	
			Upper Bound	4.0542	
		5% Trimmed Mean		3.9399	
		Median		3.875	
		Variance		0.351	
		Std. Deviation		0.59228	
		Minimum		2.13	
		Maximum		5	
		Range		2.88	
		Interquartile Range		0.63	
		Skewness		-0.037	0.247
		Kurtosis		-0.062	0.49

The results showed that the data did not meet the assumptions of normality, particularly for the Romanian group, where Shapiro-Wilk ($p = .020$) and Kolmogorov-Smirnov ($p = .008$) suggested deviation from a normal distribution. Consequently, a non-parametric Mann-Whitney U test was used to compare the two groups. This potentiatest, which does not rely on normality assumptions, was considered appropriate to provide a robust analysis of the differences between the two groups from the two countries (Romania and Israel).

This analysis showed significant differences in the rankings of Personalized Learning scores between the two groups ($U = 4064.000$; $Z = -1.956$; $p = .050$). The Romanian teachers' group demonstrated a higher mean rank ($M = 107.22$) than their Israeli colleagues ($M = 91.34$). The results suggest a slightly greater integration of personalized learning approaches by the Romanian teachers, who have achieved a mean overall PL score of 3.93 compared to their Israeli counterparts, who achieved a mean score of 3.76. Moreover, the results highlight that both teacher groups have a positive perception of PL environments, confidence in implementation, readiness to overcome challenges, and recognition of the benefits of PL environment usage.

To gain more insights into PDL practices, the further analysis aimed to identify significant differences between Romanian and Israeli teachers regarding their personalized learning practices based on various demographic variables exposed in the specific hypothesis.

Teaching Environment

The results showed a statistically significant difference in terms of PDL practices between the Romanian and Israeli teachers based in rural settings ($U = 495.00$, $Z = -3.486$, $p < .001$). Romanian teachers achieved a higher mean rank ($M = 58.03$) compared to their Israeli counterparts ($M = 38.03$), suggesting a greater emphasis on personalized learning practices in the rural settings of Romania. However, no significant difference was observed in urban settings ($U = 1392.00$, $Z = -0.100$, $p = .920$), indicating similar PDL practices among the teachers in the two groups from the urban environments.

Teaching Level

No statistically significant difference was found in the PDL practices of educators teaching at the secondary school level ($U = 143.00$, $Z = -1.109$, $p = .268$). Similarly, high school teachers showed no significant difference ($U = 990.00$, $Z = -0.160$, $p = .873$), indicating comparable perceptions and usage of personalized digital learning approaches between Romanian and Israeli teachers.

Academic Background

A significant difference among teachers with a Bachelor's degree ($U = 1361.5$, $Z = -1.960$, $p = .050$), with Romanian teachers ($M = 67.27$) reporting higher PDL usage compared to Israeli teachers ($M = 54.73$). However, no significant difference was found among teachers holding a Master's degree ($U = 619.0$, $Z = -0.455$, $p = .649$).

In conclusion, the findings underscore significant disparities in personalized digital learning practices in rural teaching environments. Notably, among teachers with a bachelor's degree, Romanian educators outperform their Israeli counterparts. These disparities may stem from contextual or systemic gaps, such as resource availability, professional development opportunities, or pedagogical priorities. However, these disparities were not observed in urban settings and among teachers with higher qualifications, suggesting a more equitable landscape.

8. CONCLUSION

The digital era brings technology skills and abilities to a higher level of learning with digital content resources, opportunities, and learning approaches. Integrating various digital resources and learning platforms is crucial for promoting and implementing personalized digital learning in Romania. This integration is crucial for creating adaptive and specially personalized digital learning approaches with great experiences that respond to the different needs of the students in every generation and country and become more detailed ahead of time. However, successful implementation in both countries requires continuous professional development and teacher support. A significant part of today's accelerating digital age directs starting with teachers in the training stage, emphasizing the potential to be derived from digital abilities and tools on a personal level and in the manner required as an integration and support envelope and implementation with students. This depends on more than just the abilities of each teacher but also on an unambiguous definition of the teacher's level of entry into the education system. Limitations in which a teacher would not be interested must be a condition. Otherwise, he will not be able to integrate into the education system, which does not exist today, in the view of the traditional concept that digital education is only a tool for enrichment. Today, teachers are both teachers and learners, required to learn and acquire digital skills to accompany students on their learning path because of the currently integrated resources. Digital learning allows teachers to be trained before they penetrate the education system, even if they are retraining from a profession they previously worked in. It also allows them to lead and control various technological tools, such as LMS platforms, adaptive tools, professional applications, and digital media. The teacher does not have to control them all since the operating principles are the same in all of them, and acquiring proficiency in several tools will enable the ability to deal with new tools and platforms each time, alongside the required training. Collaboration between countries will enable the acquisition and exchange of information on skills in which Israel is superior to Romania and vice versa in every professional field and interest. Digital tools today, except for specific ones developed in a specific country, are open to all users worldwide, and leadership is required to manage the change and the pedagogical approach to meaningful use of digital tools today. Today's teachers cannot teach the skills of tomorrow with the learning approaches they learned in the past. We are in an era of life-long learning. A teacher in the digital age serves as a facilitator. A facilitator who is not learning is a contradiction (Taylor, 2007).

Collaborations between teachers in the two countries, also possible in training and applications themselves in the education system, can take place in full Collaboration in the digital age in online meetings to transfer knowledge and training for acquiring skills. The application is also possible at the level of the systems themselves in virtual environments to present identical topics at the level of the platforms themselves (classroom next to classroom) while coordinating and leading the presentation of individual/group products between the countries without any need for travel and cumbersome logistics, as leaders of the digital learning approach, just as it takes place in international high-tech companies today, located in a variety of countries, under the limitations and localization required for coordination between them.

A key advantage in the current era is to teach, within the framework of personalized learning, tools that are suitable for any type of activity, such as research, questionnaire, data analysis, activity documentation, gamification, project management, use of a simulator, working in a learning platform, project presentation, self-presentation, product design, editing tools, online meetings, AI tools. For each of these topics mentioned, there are currently a variety of digital alternatives. The teacher is not required to master all of them but must be familiar with at least one of each and its potential and, within the framework of the personal learning path, encourage the student to use and promote the products that he presents in order to lead the student to learn and become familiar with the additional applications, which he will also present to his classmates at the first opportunity in class, as part of enrichment, research or teamwork. This enrichment can also occur among teachers in both countries, quite immediately, in light of any gaps that may arise, and generally as digital enrichment for a successful implementation that has been carried out and not only as part of enrichment within the framework of official educational conferences. As extra feedback, as Zmuda Allison describes, games insert players at their achievable challenge level and reward player effort and practice with acknowledgment of incremental goal progress (Zmuda et al., 2015), which will increase the student learning experience in the teacher's new goal. We are in the digital era, and advances in technology have transformed personalized learning (Walkington, 2020). That can shape and shift forward the teachers to a new and higher level from the beginning. The process through the stages of personalized learning as change management is crucial and not just to be familiar with. The last stage is learner-driven, with the teacher as a facilitator or mentor as a partner in learning (Bray, 2015). The use of personalized approaches, adaptive technologies, tools, and feedback helps create a learning environment tailored to each student's individual needs (Kerimbayev, 2023). We are facing an era of lifelong learning in which the teacher, for changing his role in class, also becomes a learner in the PL approach. For the teacher, as for the evolution process, personalized learning in terms of learning digital environment and approaches (individualized, differential, adaptive, blended, and more), the PL approach is the highest level (Peng, 2019). The personalized learning approach can be implemented as an immediate shift from the lower methods without collaboration through other methods or environments as an evolutionary process. Future studies should consider evaluating teacher performance using statistical inference techniques, a personalized learning approach combined with a collaborative qualitative research approach, and learning methods. The potential impact of future research to delve into the factors contributing to these disparities, particularly in rural/peripheral areas, and to evaluate the impact of educational policies on personalized digital learning practices is significant and promising.

9. LIMITATIONS

The main objective was to understand and compare teachers in digital environments from both countries' approaches to recognizing and using personalized learning and opinions and perceptions about the educational possibilities of augmented reality among high school teacher colleagues. The study compared Romania and Israel due to the opportunity provided. However, the educational systems are not necessarily equal in their PL approach. Also, only two countries are examined with educational systems; more is essential to have a complete and exhaustive picture. To address this study's limitations, future research should include more balanced and larger samples providing key demographic variables and also use a mixed methods approach, combining the self-reported data with observational, performance-based data, or qualitative methods. Further studies could specifically focus on subjects like STEM and languages (wording or vocabulary). However, the presented approach to personalized digital learning is suitable for all subjects.

ACKNOWLEDGEMENT

The authors would like to thank the collaboration between Romania and Israel on this essential issue, the educational state networks Amal and Ort in Israel, and the public pre-university schools in Romania. We also acknowledge the teachers and students involved in the questionnaire.

REFERENCES

Bitzer, D. L. (1961). *PLATO: Programmed Logic for Automatic Teaching Operations*. Educational Technology.

Bloom, B. S. (1956). *Taxonomy of Educational Objectives*. Longman.

Bray, B. and McClaskey, K. A., (2018). *Make Learning Personal. The What. Who. Wow. Where and Why.* Corwin.

CAST, (2024). *Universal Design for Learning Guidelines version 3.0.* Retrieved from https://udlguidelines.cast.org

Contrino, M. F. et al. 2024. Using an Adaptive Learning Tool to Improve Student Performance and Satisfaction in Online and Face-To-Face Education for a More Personalized Approach. *Smart Learning Environments, 5-11.*

Dewey, J. (1916). *Democracy and Education*. Macmillan.

Gardner, H. (1983). *Frames of Mind: The Theory of Multiple Intelligences*. Basic Books.

Johnson, L. et al. (2023). *Survey on Personalized Learning Approaches in K-12 Education*. Center for Digital Education.

Kerimbayev, N. et al. (2023). A Student-Centered Approach Using Modern Technologies in Distance Learning: A Systematic Review of the Literature. *Smart Learning Environment, 61.*

Montessori, M. (1912). *The Montessori Method.* Stokes.

O'Donoghue, (2010). *Technology-supported environments for personalized learning. Methods and case studies.* Information science reference.

Peng, H. et al. (2019). Personalized Adaptive Learning: An Emerging Pedagogical Approach Enabled by a Smart Learning Environment. *Smart Learning Environments, 6*(1), 1–14

Rose, T., (2013). The myth of average: Todd Rose TEDx Sonoma County. Retrieved 2013, from //youtu.be/4eBmyttcfU4.

Rousseau, J. J. (1762). *Émile, or On Education.* Basic Books.

Taylor, B. (2007). Learning for Tomorrow. Whole Person Learning. p.180–181. *The OASIS School of Human Relations.*

Walkington, C. and Bernacki, M. L. (2020). Appraising Research on Personalized Learning: Definitions, Theoretical Alignment, Advancements, and Future Directions. *Journal of Research on Technology in Education*, *52*(3), 235–252.

Watters, A., (2021). Teaching machines. The history of personalized learning. The MIT Press. Cambridge, Massachusetts, London, England.

Yilmaz, R. M. and Goktas, Y. (2022). Virtual Reality in Education. *Educational Technology Research and Development.*

Zmuda, A. et al. 2015. *Learning Personalized. The Evolution of the Contemporary Classroom.* Jossey-Bass, A Wiley Brand.

THE BENEFITS OF TRANSFORMING ENGINEERING EDUCATION AND TRAINING WITH METAVERSE TECHNOLOGIES

Veselina Nedeva, Snezhana Dineva and Zlatoeli Ducheva
Trakia University – Stara Zagora, Faculty of Technics and Technology
8600 Yambol, 38 Graf Ignatiev Str., Bulgaria

ABSTRACT

After analysing various publications and leveraging our direct experiences, we have identified the benefits and advantages of incorporating the metaverse. The Metaverse and related technologies such as Virtual Reality, Augmented Reality, and Artificial Intelligence offer innovative approaches to transforming engineering education. These technologies overcome the limitations of traditional methods by providing interactive and accessible learning opportunities.

This study integrates insights from a comprehensive bibliometric analysis of research publications for the period 2013–2024, an extensive content analysis of selected academic articles, and the practical experiences of the Faculty of Engineering and Technology. Our research is informed by professional engagements with e-learning platforms such as MOODLE and by observations from mobility exchanges at Karlsruhe Institute of Technology, where faculty members gained valuable insights into virtual and immersive education practices.

The data reveals significant growth in interest and impact in recent years, with a peak in publications and citations. The analysis highlights how Metaverse and immersive technologies enhance student engagement, foster better understanding of complex concepts, and enable safe, realistic simulations.

In addition to identifying opportunities for transforming traditional teaching methods, this study provides recommendations for integrating the Metaverse into engineering education. It also examines current technology trends and best practice applications, while addressing key challenges and outlining future prospects. By combining research insights with practical expertise, this paper underscores how Metaverse technologies can revolutionise engineering education and offer sustainable solutions to existing challenges.

KEYWORDS

Metaverse, Engineering Education, Virtual Reality, Bibliometric Analysis, Innovations in Learning

1. INTRODUCTION

Virtual Reality (VR) technologies have become affordable, portable, and realistic, and the use of VR for education has become a reality (Gomes et al., 2020), it has emerged as a promising tool for enhancing practical skills of students in engineering education (Yang et al., 2024). Similar to the development of the Internet, the Metaverse, also known as the immersive Internet, will take decades to build (Lee et al., 2022).

Engineering education plays a vital key role in developing modern technology and innovation. Hence, traditional teaching methods are often limited, especially in providing hands-on experience and motivating students (Schmidt & Ford, 2020). The Metaverse and related technologies, such as virtual reality (VR), augmented reality (AR), and artificial intelligence (AI), offer new opportunities to overcome these challenges by providing interactive and accessible learning (Johnson et al., 2021). Metaverse have expanded to create new opportunities for learning and education (Prakash et al., 2023). A Metaverse is a virtual environment in which users can interact both with each other and with various digital objects (Lee et al., 2022). Metaverse technologies enable the creation of realistic simulations that enable students to immerse themselves in hands-on experiences that would be difficult or expensive to implement in real-world settings (Brown & Green, 2023). This makes the Metaverse a powerful learning tool, providing opportunities for deeper understanding of engineering concepts and stimulating global collaboration (Wang & Smith, 2022).

This report explores the benefits of implementing Metaverse technologies in engineering education. By analysing current trends and challenges, it shows how these technologies can transform traditional teaching methods and increase the quality of learning.

2. RESEARCH METHOD

This research is based on the experiences of the academic staff at the Faculty of Technics and technologies (FTT) of Trakia University – Stara Zagora gained from working in virtual e-learning environments such as MOODLE (Trakia Electronic University, based on MOODLE, https://edu.uni-sz.bg/) and virtual communications, which inform our professional engagements and research. A significant portion of the analysis is based on personal observations from working in a virtual environment at the Karlsruhe Institute of Technology (KIT) in Karlsruhe, Germany, where two-thirds of the FTT academic staff participated in a mobility program lasting one to three months in 2023.

The literature review and content analysis were conducted through a targeted search of the academic databases Scopus and Web of Science, both of which are widely used in research. Studies released from 1997 to 2021 were meticulously screened using the specified keywords: "augmented," "virtual," "mixed," "reality," "education," "course," "learning," "training," "architecture," "engineering," and "construction," within the title, abstract, or keywords. To enhance search precision and ensure comprehensive results, the search criteria were applied as follows: ((augmented OR virtual OR mixed) AND reality) AND (education OR course OR learning OR training OR architecture OR engineering OR construction). A total of 36,612 studies were identified across both databases, with 20,662 from Web of Science and 15,950 from Scopus. Upon eliminating duplicate studies, 31,231 unique records remained. Subsequently, non-journal or conference papers (n = 5231) and non-AEC industry papers (n = 25,679) were excluded, yielding 321 articles for the initial screening. A thorough full-text screening process was then implemented to ensure the relevance of all retrieved articles to education and training within the AEC industry. Ultimately, 82 studies were selected for bibliometric analysis.

Table 1. Publications and Citations per Year

Years	Publications	Citations
2024	128	2480
2023	143	2631
2022	109	2294
2021	122	1450
2020	98	957
2019	93	676
2018	56	367
2017	62	197
2016	35	77
2015	24	52
2014	23	16
2013	20	3

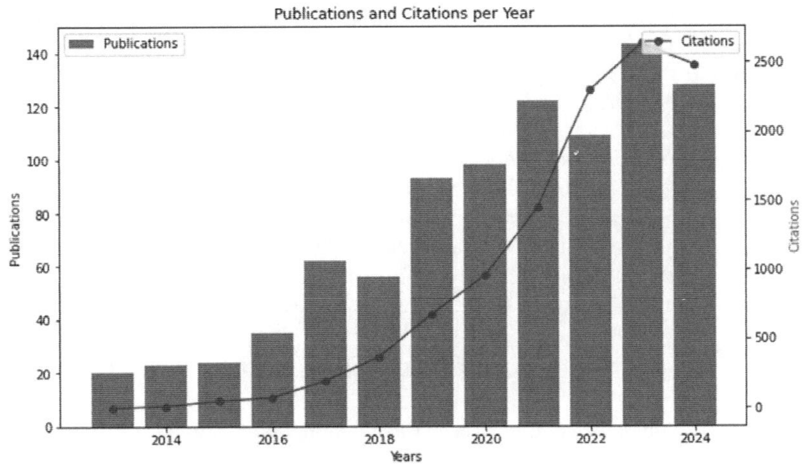

Figure 1. Publications and citations per year connecting to the Metaverse

During the period, there is a steady and consistent growth in the number of publications, starting from 20 in 2013 to 143 in 2023. For 2024, there are already 128 publications to date, indicating a trend towards maintaining high activity. After 2019, the number of publications increased significantly, possibly reflecting the growing interest in the use of the Metaverse, virtual reality (VR), augmented reality (AR), and other immersive technologies in engineering education. Citations also show significant growth, peaking in 2023 with 2,631 citations. This demonstrates the increasing impact of the topic on the scientific community. The growth in publications in recent years (2021-2023) has been accompanied by a dramatic increase in citations. This suggests that research related to the Metaverse and related technologies in engineering education is gaining popularity and making a significant impact. During the period 2019-2020, interest begins to grow, possibly due to the influence and development of the Metaverse and new technologies. In 2020 and 2021, there was a significant growth in both the number of publications (98 and 122) and citations (957 and 1450). The period from 2022 to 2024 marks a peak in the number of publications and citations, reflecting a significant increase in scientific interest and diffusion of these technologies in engineering education.

The table and diagram reflect the development of scientific output and influence on the topic "Benefits of transforming engineering education with Metaverse Technologies" by keywords: "(Metaverse OR (augmented OR virtual OR mixed) AND reality) AND engineering AND (education OR learning OR training) AND (benefits OR impact OR positive effects)" in the period 2013-2024. The data indicates a noticeable rise in interest and impact of immersive technologies like the Metaverse and VR/AR in engineering education. The volume of publications and citations has notably increased, particularly in the past five years. This subject is becoming increasingly prominent in scientific research, and this growth is anticipated to persist in the future, especially considering recent technological trends.

Out of 626 studies initially considered, 61 were carefully analysed. The results show that these technologies greatly improve student engagement by offering immersive and interactive learning experiences that connect theoretical knowledge with practical application. Additionally, their use has been found to enhance learning outcomes by fostering a better understanding of complex concepts and boosting student motivation.

3. RESULTS AND DISCUSSIONS

The concept of the Metaverse incorporates the benefits of e-learning while introducing new, more engaging features specific to online technology (Yang& Xia, 2023). By merging the physical world with digital virtual reality (Barteit& Beiersmann, 2021), an immersive 3D virtual environment is formed. This affords learners from any location with internet access the opportunity to engage in a diverse array of educational activities, including courses, quizzes, simulations, and experiments. (Dalgarno& Lee, 2010). By creating an environment where students can actively participate in their learning process, VR helps foster curiosity, critical thinking, and problem-solving skills (Vats& Joshi, 2024).

Although it does not claim to be exhaustive, this study represents a significant innovation in the field of education. It divides the benefits of the metaverse into four main strands.

1. The potential for immersion, outreach and interaction;
2. Accessibility and security in education;
3. Independent and collaborative knowledge building;
4. Reliability of knowledge assessment and access to resources.

The results show how the authors' observations and analyses, as well as the articles studied, highlight different aspects of the impact of the metaverse. Immersive technologies not only improve access to learning, but also provide new ways to simulate real-world situations that promote long-term retention and effective collaboration. These findings confirm the potential of the Metaverse to transform the educational process by providing a safer, more accessible and interactive learning environment.

3.1 The Potential for Immersion, Outreach and Interaction

The FTT analyses and evaluations of the metaverse educational environment are based on extensive research and practical experience. This includes observations of best practices and work in the CAVE virtual environment of the KIT, participation in seminars and analysis of thesis defences of students at the KIT, as well as literature reviews. These activities allowed us not only to gain in-depth impressions, but also to draw well-founded conclusions about the significant potential of the metaverse for enhancing the learning process.

- ***Increased immersion:*** Research shows that the metaverse overcomes the limitations of two-dimensional learning environments. Observations of simulations and exercises conducted by colleagues in Karlsruhe show how the combination of physical reality and digital virtuality creates a fully immersive 3D environment. In the experience of KIT educators, these immersive and interactive aspects enhance learner engagement and provide new learning opportunities.

- ***Futuristic appeal:*** The practices studied in the context of KIT and other authors prove that Metaverse offers innovative applications in the field of education. This environment is particularly attractive to students of the digital generation, as it integrates advanced technologies that change traditional learning methods. According to the literature, the Metaverse expands the possibilities for interactivity and accessibility in the learning process, which is of particular interest to educators and students seeking innovative approaches. Metaverse applications in education enhance interactivity and accessibility, appealing to both the digital generation and educators seeking innovative ways to engage learners and improve educational outcomes. (Prakash et al., 2023).

- ***Enhancing social learning:*** The Metaverse enhances the social aspects of learning by providing opportunities for the development of emotional intelligence and socialisation in the learning process. Observations of metaverse applications show that this technology can enhance the social aspects of learning. Opportunities to develop emotional intelligence and socialisation in the learning process are particularly valuable. For example, according to reports and analyses by colleagues at KIT, VR and AR technologies support the development of soft skills through telepresence, avatar interactions, and simulated social situations that promote more effective communication and teamwork. The Metaverse uses VR and AR to improve communication and interpersonal skills by addressing the lack of soft/transversal skills development. This is achieved through telepresence, avatar body language and precise facial expressions that help to practice and apply communication skills in a social environment. (Maloney, D, 2021).

3.2 Accessibility and Security in Education

The metaverse enhances access to education by offering equal learning opportunities across diverse locations and potentially reducing the costs associated with traditional methods. This perspective is informed by the FTT's experience with various forms of e-learning in a MOODLE-based virtual environment, complemented by personal observations of working with computer applications in the CAVE at KIT. These insights are further enriched by an in-depth analysis of relevant literature in this field. The teaching staff of the FTT appreciates the possibilities of the metaverse to improve access and security in education. These studies reveal key aspects that highlight the potential of the Metaverse to transform the learning process: The Educational Metaverse improves accessibility and equity by enabling immersive, interactive learning experiences from anywhere, potentially reducing the cost and time associated with traditional educational methods.

- ***Equal Education Opportunities***: Our experience with MOODLE shows that digital platforms provide greater opportunities for inclusion and equity. Similarly, access and equity are essential to promote educational equality and accessibility in the Metaverse, allowing learning from diverse locations to effectively participate in the learning process. Despite the potential of the Metaverse, some scholarly sources have raised concerns regarding its ability to fully support educational equity and inclusion for all students. Unequal access to educational resources has been identified as an important factor that can impact cognitive achievement, faster internet connections help students think and learn better, while slower connections do not provide much benefit (Pigultong 2022). The metaverse offers opportunities for educational equity and accessibility by enabling distance learning and potentially reducing costs, particularly useful in low- and middle-income and conflict-affected areas (Naqishbandi et al., 2023).

- ***Cost Savings***: Platforms such as MOODLE show that reducing the cost of physical resources is a realistic goal. In this context, the Metaverse offers new perspectives for cost optimisation through the integration of virtual laboratories and simulations. Metaverse-enabled learning spaces improve educational accessibility by providing immersive 3D environments that enable experiential learning from anywhere, potentially reducing the cost and time associated with traditional educational methods. Metaverse can reduce the costs associated with traditional assessment practices by eliminating the need for physical testing centres, the use of paper and printing, and reducing the cost of administering exams (Thango, 2024). It ensures equal access to assessment regardless of location or economic background. Metaverse environments offer cost savings to educational institutions by reducing the need for physical materials and resources such as textbooks and laboratory equipment, especially for subjects and systems that cannot be practised in laboratories. In addition, immersive environments can reduce the costs associated with travel and accommodation for students attending remote campuses or distance learning courses.

- ***Simulation of Dangerous Experiments***: Our observations of the use of simulation modules in MOODLE virtual courses support the ability of Metaverse to provide a safe environment for experimentation and learning without risk to users. The Metaverse provides a unique platform for simulating risky experimental scenarios, allowing experiments that do not physically endanger the user. This virtual environment uses advanced technology to create immersive experiences that can safely replicate real-world conditions. The Metaverse allows risky experimental scenarios to be simulated in experiments without physically endangering users. It supports scenario simulation in education, providing a safe space for learners to engage in complex problem solving without real-world consequences. Metaverse-enabled Learning Spaces facilitate the transfer of knowledge by enabling seamless navigation between conventional web-based platforms and immersive 3D environments. The Metaverse enables the creation of digital twins, allowing users to interact with virtual representations of real-world systems, which is crucial for testing and training in various fields (Cali et al., 2022). The flexibility of the Metaverse allows for the exploration of diverse scenarios, from industrial applications to educational settings, ensuring comprehensive risk assessments (Lee et al. 2022). In particular, students responded positively to the effectiveness of virtual world simulations, suggesting that these environments facilitate meaningful learning experiences, especially in complex or risky subjects.

- ***Ease of Transition***: Improved accessibility allows for quick and easy switching between virtual environments in the Metaverse. While Metaverse offers significant benefits for knowledge transfer, challenges such as technology access and user equity remain critical to its successful implementation in education. Metaverse enhances knowledge transfer through immersive, multi-sensory interactions, allowing users to engage in realistic simulations and collaborative learning experiences that mimic real-life activities (Wang et al., 2022). However, the depth of user engagement with virtual environments affects the degree of enhanced learning. Metaverse-enabled learning spaces facilitate knowledge transfer by enabling seamless navigation between traditional web-based platforms and immersive 3D environments. The metaverse offers extensive opportunities for knowledge dissemination. However, in order to fully realise its potential in education, it is imperative to address the challenges of technology accessibility, data security and user rights.

3.3 Independent and Collaborative Knowledge Building

Facilitating both independent and collaborative knowledge construction, the Metaverse serves as a transformative platform for individuals and groups to come together in virtual settings, engage in discussion, and collectively advance knowledge. This collaborative endeavour has the potential to generate innovative concepts and problem-solving approaches. The authors posit that there is a need to integrate the principles of constructivism with the tools of the Metaverse in order to provide a structured space for independent and cooperative knowledge construction. This facilitates the identification of efficacious methodologies for the creation of learning content that encourages active participation and interaction among learners. The principles of constructivism are employed in the assessment of applications within the Metaverse that facilitate active learning through simulations and personalised content. This enables educators to adapt materials to students' requirements, thereby facilitating effective learning.

- ***Constructivist Approach***: As defined by the authors of the paper, collaboration assessment encompasses the analysis of the extent of interaction within the Meta-Universe. This analysis considers factors such as participation in collaborative projects, the global availability of resources, and the ease of integration of customised curricula. One area of assessment is the evaluation of cooperative learning functionalities, such as virtual workspaces and shared resources. For instance, platforms that facilitate team projects and real-time interaction are rated highly according to the aforementioned criteria. The reconfiguration of traditional pedagogical approaches through the utilisation of collaborative learning represents a viable strategy within the Metaverse (Prakash et al., 2023; Damaševičius & Sidekerskienė, 2023). Our experience of undertaking collaborative projects in a variety of virtual contexts demonstrates that we have been able to successfully conduct such projects through the use of online communication and information sharing platforms. The educational Metaverse provides a platform for users to engage in project collaboration, idea exchange, global access to resources and virtual cooperative ventures (Akour et al., 2022; Damaševičius & Sidekerskienė, 2023; Onu et al., 2024; Kulkarni et al., 2024). The Metaverse, with its immersive environments, provides an ideal setting for both independent and collaborative knowledge building. Users are able to participate in a variety of interactive learning experiences and engage in the co-design of personalised learning programmes.

- ***Long-term Retention***: Virtual experiences, unlike written text, are encoded in the brain as vivid memories, thus significantly enhancing the process of learning and retention (Do& Moreland, 2014). The impact of 3D multimodal visualization and learning rehearsal on memory recall has been researched. The findings indicated that the training condition involving audio-visual modality is linked to the highest accuracy. The conditions involving visual and auditory modalities showed lower accuracy rates, while the no-training condition demonstrated minimal learning acquisition (Do & Moreland, 2014).

- ***Enhanced Collaboration***: The assessment of collaboration, according to the authors, includes criteria for analysing the degree of interaction in the meta-universe, measuring factors such as participation in collaborative projects, global availability of resources and ease of integration of customised curricula. One aspect is the evaluation of collaborative learning features such as virtual workspaces and shared resources. For example, platforms that provide opportunities for team projects and real-time interaction score highly on our criteria. Collaborative learning represents a viable strategy within the Metaverse for the reconfiguration of traditional pedagogical approaches (Prakash et al., 2023; Damaševičius & Sidekerskienė, 2023). Our experience in various forms of virtual collaboration shows that we successfully run collaborative projects using online communication and information sharing platforms such as Google Meet, Zoom, Microsoft Teams and Google Docs. We also use the Moodle plugin BigBlueButtonBN for virtual meetings and training. This includes participating in online training, webinars and projects with colleagues from different regions of the world, covering areas such as engineering, information systems and machine learning. The educational Metaverse provides a platform for users to engage in project collaboration, idea exchange, global resource access, and virtual cooperative endeavours (Akour et al., 2022; Damaševičius & Sidekerskienė, 2023; Onu et al., 2024; Kulkarni et al., 2024). Leveraging immersive environments, the Metaverse fosters both independent and collaborative knowledge construction, enabling users to partake in interactive learning experiences and co-develop personalized curricula.

- ***Transparent Accreditation***: The authors endorse the principle of transparent accreditation, offering a set of criteria for the evaluation of students' competencies and individual abilities. This enables institutions to develop programmes that meet transparent and objective standards, thereby enhancing confidence in the quality of educational services provided. Accreditation signifies that an educational establishment, institution of higher learning, or programme of study has been deemed to meet the requisite quality standards. Transparency is an essential element in the establishment of trust in the assessment of standards and the quality of education. Transparency entails the open disclosure of the procedures and criteria that must be fulfilled in order to attain accreditation, as well as the manner in which the fulfilment of these criteria will be evaluated. The integration of the Metaverse into the educational sector effectively applies the concept of "transparent accreditation," which considers competencies, learning techniques, skill sets, individual abilities, and learner interests. The technological features of the Metaverse facilitate sustained attention, thereby rendering learning engaging and enjoyable. Furthermore, they encourage active interaction with both peers and new learning content.

The benefits of transparent accreditation according to (Ryan & Sharkey, 1999) are:

- *Informed Choices*: Students and parents can make better decisions about where to study because they understand the accreditation process.
- *Accountability:* Schools know they must meet clear standards, which encourages them to improve and maintain quality.
- *Fairness:* Everyone is judged by the same rules, which helps ensure that all schools are held to high standards.

Figure 2 illustrates various ways (Lin et al., 2022) in which the Metaverse is transforming education, namely through Immersive Learning, Visualization, Collaborative Learning, Accessible Learning, Remote Learning, Personalized Learning, Promoting communication.

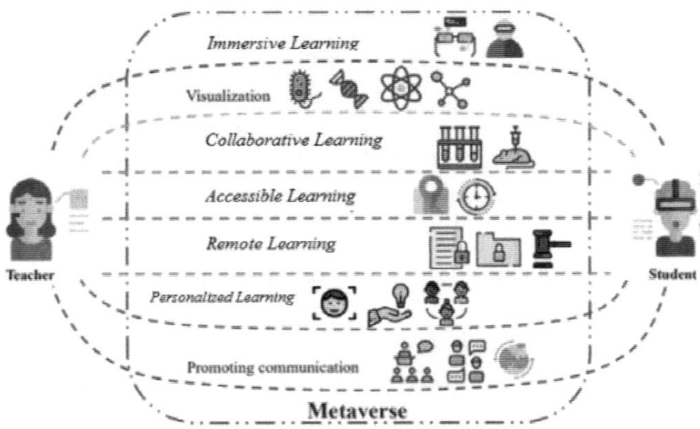

Figure 2. Ways that the Metaverse changes education (Lin et al., 2022)

The authors' proposal aims to provide tools for educators to adapt the metaverse to different learning scenarios by applying appropriate technology-enhanced educational methods. This includes the creation of personalised learning pathways and collaborative problem-solving projects.

3.4 Reliability of Knowledge Assessment and Access to Resources

Our experience with MOODLE and virtual communication includes the use of plugins such as Collaborative Submissions and Assignment Submission for collaborative assignments and their evaluation, as well as automatic code evaluation with tools such as Virtual Programming Lab and CodeRunner. These tools are essential for assessing student progress in programming. However, Metaverse takes these activities to a higher level by adding new assessment capabilities through innovations in learning and collaboration. Metaverse is on the cusp of revolutionising educational assessment by significantly increasing its reliability and transforming traditional assessment methods through the integration of compelling technologies and innovative frameworks. Metaverse offers entirely new possibilities for reliable knowledge assessment by integrating innovative technologies and advanced frameworks that transform traditional assessment methods. This framework analyses how these innovations can be effectively implemented to ensure greater objectivity and transparency in educational processes.

- ***Improved Evaluation Reliability:*** Through integrating virtual reality, augmented reality, and blockchain, the Metaverse can create a more trustworthy and equitable evaluation ecosystem and aids in advancing traditional evaluation methods (Zi & Cong, 2024; Rodzin et al., 2024). The Metaverse enhances traditional evaluation methods by creating interactive, immersive environments that foster engagement, collaboration (Jindal& Jindal, 2024; Jindal et al., 2024; Nguyen& Ngo, 2024). It can provide improved security and authenticity by incorporating biometric identification and real-time monitoring to prevent cheating and ensure accurate and reliable exam results (Thango, 2024). AI-assisted (AI – Artificial Intelligence) educational support system lies in providing educators with timely and accurate information regarding the learning statuses of students (Yang& Xia, 2023).

Metaverse enhances interaction, immersion, and collaborative learning, fostering innovative pedagogical activities that surpass traditional evaluation methods in education (Batalla& Pedrero, 2023). The current methods for evaluating teaching depend on exam results and the educator's teaching experience. In contrast, the Metaverse architecture relies on four-layer virtual entities built from event logs recorded in the Learning Management System (LMS). These entities are visualized as spatiotemporal digital profiles for students. In the spatial dimension, the profile can reflect a student's learning situation in various aspects, such as assignment completion, knowledge mastery, practical ability, and more (Liu et al., 2022).

- ***Global access to educational resources:*** The metaverse facilitates global access to virtual libraries, museums and experts. The framework assesses the capacity of platforms to provide a diverse range of educational resources, thereby guaranteeing the equality and calibre of learning. The metaverse has the potential to provide learners with access to high-quality educational resources and experts from any location worldwide (López-Belmonte et al., 2024). The utilisation of these resources has been observed to facilitate a more comprehensive comprehension of intricate concepts, largely attributed to the comprehensive contextualisation and innovative visualisation techniques.

- ***Increased engagement and motivation:*** The utilisation of AI technologies within the Metaverse facilitates the creation of adaptive content, which in turn serves to enhance student motivation and engagement within the learning process. These technologies facilitate progress tracking and the development of metacognitive skills (Yang & Xia, 2023). The framework assesses the efficacy of platforms that integrate AI with immersive environments to facilitate adaptive learning pathways. The Metaverse allows for immersive learning experiences and simulations, which can increase student engagement and achievement (López-Belmonte et al., 2024). By combining AI technologies with the Metaverse, educators can develop intelligent systems that personalize learning experiences, track student progress, and enhance metacognitive skills, thereby improving self-regulation and learning outcomes (Yang& Xia, 2023). AI can create adaptive content, enhancing student engagement and achievement through tailored educational interactions in immersive virtual environments (López-Belmonte et al., 2024).

- ***Real-time feedback***: The metaverse enables the provision of immediate feedback to students through interactive features and digital resources. This helps to identify knowledge gaps and improve self-regulation in the learning process. This aspect includes indicators to evaluate the platforms according to their ability to provide timely and useful feedback. Metaverse enables real-time feedback, helping students identify knowledge gaps and improve learning through interactive features and digital resources (Singh et al., 2022; Cai et al., 2022; Praherdhiono et al., 2022). AI in the Metaverse provides real-time feedback, and personalizes learning experiences (López-Belmonte et al., 2024).

4. CONCLUSION

The metaverse and related technologies, VR, AR, and AI, offer substantial potential for transforming engineering education. These technologies provide interactive and accessible solutions that effectively address the limitations of traditional teaching methods. The research highlights how they enhance student engagement, facilitate the comprehension of complex concepts, and create a safe environment for simulations.

An analysis of research publications from 2013 to 2024 indicates a steady rise in interest in the metaverse as a transformative tool for engineering education. The increasing number of publications and citations reflects the growing influence of these technologies within the academic community. Key benefits include the ability to simulate complex or hazardous experiments, ensure objective assessment, and improve long-term knowledge retention.

However, integrating the metaverse into education poses challenges, such as the high costs of creating quality experiences, the need for adequate technological infrastructure, and the necessity for teaching staff and student training. Additionally, potential physical and mental health risks require careful management.

For successful implementation, it is essential to develop effective teaching strategies, support a smooth transition for teaching staff and students, and invest in infrastructure and resources. Prioritizing data privacy and security, along with assessing the impact of these technologies on the learning process, is also crucial.

The metaverse presents a unique opportunity for global collaboration and adaptability in engineering education. With proper planning and execution, these technologies can revolutionize learning, enhancing its quality and effectiveness. Future research should focus on addressing technical challenges and adapting curricula to ensure a sustainable and meaningful contribution to the advancement of engineering education.

ACKNOWLEDGEMENT

The paper is part of a research project: Metaverse Approach for a New Generation of Engineering Education and Collaborative Learning (MAGURA), as the frame of Project No. BG-RRP-2.004-0006-C02 "Development of research and innovation at Trakia University in service of health and sustainable well-being".

REFERENCES

Akour, I. A., Al-Maroof, R. S., Alfaisal, R., & Salloum, S. A. (2022). 'A Conceptual Framework for Determining Metaverse Adoption in Higher Institutions of Gulf Area: An Empirical Study Using Hybrid SEM-ANN Approach'. Computers and Education: Artificial Intelligence, vol. 3, 2022, p. 100052. DOI.org (Crossref), https://doi.org/10.1016/j.caeai.2022.100052.

Al-kfairy M., M. Alzaabi, B. Snoh, H. Almarzooqi and W. Alnaqbi, (2024) 'Metaverse-Based Classroom: The Good and the Bad'. 2024 IEEE Global Engineering Education Conference (EDUCON), IEEE, 2024, pp. 1–7. DOI.org (Crossref), https://doi.org/10.1109/EDUCON60312.2024.10578570

Barteit, S., Lanfermann, L., Bärnighausen, T., Neuhann, F., & Beiersmann, C. (2021). 'Augmented, Mixed, and Virtual Reality-Based Head-Mounted Devices for Medical Education: Systematic Review'. JMIR Serious Games, vol. 9, no. 3, July 2021, p. e29080. DOI.org (Crossref), https://doi.org/10.2196/29080.

Batalla De Matías D, Pedrero Bueno AS. (2023). 'Metaverse to Foster Learning in Higher Education'. Metaverse, vol. 4, no. 1, June 2023, p. 16. DOI.org (Crossref), https://doi.org/10.54517/m.v4i1.2184.

Brown, T., & Green, D. (2023). The role of virtual simulations in enhancing practical skills in engineering education. Journal of Educational Technology Systems, 51(4), 369-389. https://doi.org/10.1177/00472395221100l8

Cai S., Jiao X., Song B. (2022). 'Open Another Door to Education—Applications, Challenges and Perspectives of the Educational Metaverse'. Metaverse, vol. 3, no. 1, Jan. 2022, p. 11. DOI.org (Crossref), https://doi.org/10.54517/met.v3i1.1798.

Cali U., M. Kuzlu, E. Karaarslan &V. Jovanovic (2022). 'Opportunities and Challenges in Metaverse for Industry 4.0 and Beyond Applications'. 2022 IEEE 1st Global Emerging Technology Blockchain Forum: Blockchain & Beyond (iGETblockchain), IEEE, 2022, pp. 1–6. DOI.org (Crossref), https://doi.org/10.1109/iGETblockchain56591.2022.10087104.

Dalgarno, B., & Lee, M. J. (2010). What are the learning affordances of 3-D virtual environments?. British journal of educational technology, 41(1), 10-32.

Damaševičius, R., & Sidekerskienė, T. (2024). Virtual Worlds for Learning in Metaverse: A Narrative Review. Sustainability, 16(5), 2032. https://doi.org/10.3390/su16052032

Do, P. T., & Moreland, J. R. (2014). 'Facilitating Role of 3D Multimodal Visualization and Learning Rehearsal in Memory Recall'. Psychological Reports, vol. 114, no. 2, Apr. 2014, pp. 541–56. DOI.org (Crossref), https://doi.org/10.2466/04.28.PR0.114k17w9.

Jindal, P., & Jindal, (2024). A. 'The Metaverse in Education: An Upcoming Future Trend'. Transforming Education with Virtual Reality, edited by Reena Malik et al., 1st ed., Wiley, 2024, pp. 127–43. DOI.org (Crossref), https://doi.org/10.1002/9781394200498.ch8.

Johnson, T., Smith, R., & Wang, X. (2021). Virtual reality, augmented reality, and artificial intelligence in education: Opportunities and challenges. Educational Technology Research and Development, 69(3), 543-562. https://doi.org/10.1007/s11423-021-10034-0.

Kulkarni, P., Gaddi, A., Ramona, B., Popescu, V., Hiremath, V., K., S., Shetty, S. K., & Kagawade, S. (2024). 'A Sustainable Approach on Metaverse in Education: A SCOPUS-Based Bibliometric Analysis to Test TMIOS'. Advances in Environmental Engineering and Green Technologies, edited by Sofia Idris, IGI Global, 2024, pp. 189–211. DOI.org (Crossref), https://doi.org/10.4018/979-8-3693-2845-3.ch011.

Lee, S., Kim, J., & Park, Y. (2022). Metaverse as a collaborative learning environment: New perspectives for engineering education. International Journal of STEM Education, 9(1), 112-127.

Lin, H., Wan, S., Gan, W., Chen, J., & Chao, H.-C. (2022). Metaverse in education: Vision, opportunities, and challenges. ArXiv Preprint. Retrieved from ArXiv:221114951

Liu, F., Zhang, Y., Zhao, L., Dai, Q., Liu, X., & Shi, X. (2022). A metaverse-based student's spatiotemporal digital profile for representing learning situation. In 2022 8th International Conference of the Immersive Learning Research Network (iLRN) (pp. 1–8). IEEE. https://doi.org/10.23919/iLRN55037.2022.9815985

López-Belmonte, J., Pozo-Sánchez, S., Moreno-Guerrero, AJ., Marín-Marín, JA. (2024). Metaverse Learning: A New Frontier for Education. In: Liu, D., Huang, R., Metwally, A.H.S., Tlili, A., Fan Lin, E. (eds) Application of the Metaverse in Education. Smart Computing and Intelligence. Springer, Singapore. https://doi.org/10.1007/978-981-97-1298-4_1.

Maloney, D. (2021). A youthful Metaverse: Towards designing safe, equitable, and emotionally fulfilling social virtual reality spaces for younger users. Proceedings of the ACM on Human-Computer Interaction, 5(CSCW2), Article 308. https://doi.org/10.1145/3479536.

Naqishbandi, T. A., Mohamed, E. S., & Veronese, G. (2023). Metaverse!: Possible Potential Opportunities and Trends in E-Healthcare and Education. *International Journal of E-Adoption (IJEA), 15*(2), 1-21. http://doi.org/10.4018/IJEA.316537.

Nguyen, HT., Ngo, QD. (2024). Benefits and Challenges of Metaverse in Education. In: Joby, P.P., Alencar, M.S., Falkowski-Gilski, P. (eds) IoT Based Control Networks and Intelligent Systems. ICICNIS 2023. Lecture Notes in Networks and Systems, vol 789. Springer, Singapore. https://doi.org/10.1007/978-981-99-6586-1_50.

Onu, P., Pradhan, A. & Mbohwa, C. (2024). Potential to use Metaverse for future teaching and learning. Educ Inf Technol 29, 8893–8924 https://doi.org/10.1007/s10639-023-12167-9.

Pigultong M., (2022). 'Cognitive Impacts of Using a Metaverse Embedded on Learning Management System for Students with Unequal Access to Learning Resources'. 2022 10th International Conference on Information and Education Technology (ICIET), IEEE, 2022, pp. 27–31. DOI.org (Crossref), https://doi.org/10.1109/ICIET55102.2022.9779045.

Praherdhiono H. et al. (2022). 'Synchronization of Virtual and Real Learning Patterns in E-Learning Systems with Metaverse Concept'. 2022 8th International Conference on Education and Technology (ICET), IEEE, 2022, pp. 185–89. DOI.org (Crossref), https://doi.org/10.1109/ICET56879.2022.9990891.

Prakash A, Haque A, Islam F, Sonal D. (2023). 'Exploring the Potential of Metaverse for Higher Education: Opportunities, Challenges, and Implications'. Metaverse Basic and Applied Research, vol. 2, Aug. 2023, p. 40. DOI.org (Crossref), https://doi.org/10.56294/mr202340.

Rodzin S. I., Bova V. V., Koniushenko S. M., Pechalova L. V., at al. (2024). *Theoretical and practical aspects of pedagogy and psychology*, 184. Чебоксары: PH "Sreda". https://doi.org/10.31483/a-10617.

Ryan M. D. &P. M. Sharkey, (1999). 'The Causal Surface and Its Effect on Distribution Transparency in a Distributed Virtual Environment'. IEEE SMC'99 Conference Proceedings. 1999 IEEE International Conference on Systems, Man, and Cybernetics (Cat. No.99CH37028), vol. 6, IEEE, 1999, pp. 75–80. DOI.org (Crossref), https://doi.org/10.1109/ICSMC.1999.816458.

Schmidt, A., & Ford, P. (2020). Enhancing student engagement in engineering education through active learning methods. Journal of Engineering Education.

Thango A., B. (2024). 'The Future of Education: Writing Exams in the Metaverse at South African Universities'. Business, Management and Economics, edited by Vito Bobek and Tatjana Horvat, vol. 14, IntechOpen, 2024. DOI.org (Crossref), https://doi.org/10.5772/intechopen.112003.

Vats, S., Joshi, R. (2024). 'The Impact of Virtual Reality in Education: A Comprehensive Research Study'. Transfer, Diffusion and Adoption of Next-Generation Digital Technologies, edited by Sujeet K. Sharma et al., vol. 699, Springer Nature Switzerland, 2024, pp. 126–36. DOI.org (Crossref), https://doi.org/10.1007/978-3-031-50204-0_11.

Wang, H., & Smith, L. (2022). Global collaboration in the Metaverse: Fostering deeper understanding of engineering concepts. Journal of Engineering Education, 111(1), 95-113.

Yang, C., Zhang, J., Hu, Y. *et al.* (2024). 'The Impact of Virtual Reality on Practical Skills for Students in Science and Engineering Education: A Meta-Analysis'. International Journal of STEM Education, vol. 11, no. 1, June 2024, p. 28. DOI.org (Crossref), https://doi.org/10.1186/s40594-024-00487-2.

Yang, Yanan, and Nan Xia, (2023). 'Enhancing Students' Metacognition via AI-Driven Educational Support Systems'. International Journal of Emerging Technologies in Learning (iJET), vol. 18, no. 24, Dec. 2023, pp. 133–48. DOI.org (Crossref), https://doi.org/10.3991/ijet.v18i24.45647.

Zi, Lingling, and Xin Cong. (2024). 'Metaverse Solutions for Educational Evaluation'. Electronics, vol. 13, no. 6, Mar. 2024, p. 1017. DOI.org (Crossref), https://doi.org/10.3390/electronics13061017

METASKILLS4TCLF ERASMUS+: DEVELOPMENT OF A VIRTUAL REALITY TECHNOLOGY FOR SKILLS DEVELOPMENT IN THE TEXTILE, CLOTHING, LEATHER AND FOOTWEAR INDUSTRIES

Irene Capecchi[1], Tommaso Borghini[1], Alessandro De Rosa[1], Iacopo Bernetti[2] and Rita Souto[3]
[1]PIN Foundation - Prato Campus of University of Florence. Piazza dell'Università 1 - 59100 Prato (PO) - Italy
[2]Department of Agriculture, Food, Environment and Forestry (DAGRI) University of Florence, Piazzale delle Cascine 18, Florence, Italy
[3]CTCP – Portuguese Footwear Technological Centre / Rua de Fundões – Devesa Velha, 3700-121 S. João da Madeira, Portugal

ABSTRACT

The METASKILLS4TCLF Erasmus+ project aims to revolutionize vocational education and training in the Textile, Clothing, Leather, and Footwear (TCLF) industries through the integration of Virtual Reality (VR) technology. This four-year initiative, involving 25 partners across 11 European countries, seeks to address skill gaps by developing an innovative e-learning platform and immersive educational resources. The project focuses on enhancing training in circular economy principles and digitalization within TCLF sectors. By employing advanced VR methodologies—such as 360° video-based scenes and 3D model simulations—METASKILLS4TCLF provides scalable, interactive, and multilingual learning experiences. The initial prototypes, featuring both immersive and non-immersive VR applications, demonstrate the potential of VR to improve skill acquisition, reduce training time, and promote sustainability. These tools are designed to be accessible, fostering industry-wide adoption and supporting TCLF's transition towards resilience and competitiveness. Preliminary results emphasize the effectiveness of VR in bridging theoretical knowledge with practical skills, setting a new standard for vocational training in these industries.

KEYWORDS

Virtual Reality Training, Textile, Clothing, Leather, and Footwear (TCLF) Industries, Circular Economy, Vocational Education and Training (VET), Immersive Learning Technologies

1. INTRODUCTION

METASKILLS4TCLF1 "Alliance for Cooperation on Digital Skills and the Circular Economy for the Textile Clothing, Leather and Footwear (TCLF) Sector" is a 4-year Erasmus+ project involving 25 partners from 11 European countries, started on September 2023.

The project is empowering Vocational Education and Training (VET) and Higher Education (HE) centers with innovative curricula focused on the circular economy and the digitalization of the fashion industry, accompanied by immersive educational resources. These resources include immersive virtual reality (VR) experiences that allow students to virtually explore TCLF factories, and the creation of a European Virtual Fashion Campus that will serve as an informative and educational hub for the TCLF industries.

Virtual Reality (VR) is emerging as a transformative technology in vocational training, offering significant advantages over traditional methods. VR enables the creation of immersive and interactive environments that facilitate hands-on learning, reducing the risks associated with real-world training scenarios. For instance, in the manufacturing sector, VR has been used effectively to train workers on complex machinery, allowing them to develop skills without the danger of accidents or equipment damage (Gonzalez-Franco & Lanier, 2017). Furthermore, VR supports customizable learning experiences, adapting to individual skill levels and learning paces, which enhances the effectiveness of training programs (Radianti et al., 2020).

The immersive nature of VR increases learner engagement and motivation, making the learning process more interactive and memorable (Makransky & Petersen, 2019). Studies have shown that VR-based training can reduce skill acquisition time by up to 75%, while simultaneously improving knowledge retention and learner confidence (Smith et al., 2022).

Building on these advantages, the "METASKILLS4TCLF project seeks to address the specific challenges of the TCLF sectors. The primary objectives of the project are:

1. Developing a comprehensive e-learning platform that integrates augmented and virtual reality content, VR courses accessible in both non-immersive (2D) and immersive formats (using head-mounted displays).
2. Optimizing skill development processes through interactive and engaging VR experiences, significantly reducing training time while ensuring high proficiency in critical, high-demand areas.
3. Creating scalable training solutions that are freely accessible, ensuring widespread adoption and addressing the global skills gap in TCLF industries.

This initiative represents an innovative approach to vocational education, fostering technological advancement and supporting the evolution of the TCLF industries into more resilient and competitive sectors.

2. METHODOLOGIES

2.1 The E-Learning VR Platforms

The METASKILLS4TCLF e-learning platform will be a comprehensive and user-friendly digital ecosystem designed to support advanced training in the Textile, Clothing, Leather, and Footwear (TCLF) industries, directly integrated into the broader concept of the Virtual Fashion Campus (developed under WP6). This future digital platform will host an array of innovative educational resources, such as interactive e-books, non-immersive Virtual Reality (VR)-enhanced courses and specialized training materials. All resources will be accessed for free. Emphasis will be on the creation of a platform that fosters innovation and "Edutainment" for TCLF digital and green skills.

The METASKILLS4TCLF Erasmus+ project employs two key approaches to Virtual Reality (VR) content development: 360° video-based scenes and 3D model-based environments. Each method offers distinct advantages and disadvantages, ensuring a well-rounded approach to vocational training in the Textile, Clothing, Leather, and Footwear (TCLF) industries.

METASKILL4TCLF is based on high-resolution 360° immersive video. 360° videos represent a powerful tool in vocational training, providing an immersive experience that allows learners to explore real-world environments from all angles. Filmed in ultra-high resolution, such as 5K, these videos enable users to observe workplaces, production processes, and industry practices with a level of detail and realism that traditional video formats cannot offer. The ability to freely adjust the viewpoint within the video enhances the learner's sense of presence, making the experience more engaging and interactive.

One of the main advantages of 360° videos in vocational training is their ability to capture and present authentic working environments, enabling learners to gain practical insights into complex workflows without requiring physical access to the locations. This approach is particularly valuable for industries where access to certain facilities or operations may be limited due to logistical, financial, or safety constraints. Furthermore, 360° videos can replicate hazardous or high-risk scenarios, allowing learners to explore and understand these environments safely and without exposure to real-world dangers.

Another key benefit is their accessibility. 360° videos can be viewed using a variety of devices, from head-mounted displays for immersive experiences to standard screens, making them adaptable to different learning contexts and resource availability. They also offer flexibility by incorporating interactive elements such as hotspots, which provide additional layers of information through text, images, or supplementary videos. This enhances the learning experience by allowing users to engage with specific details relevant to their training.

Overall, 360° videos combine realism, safety, and interactivity, bridging the gap between theoretical learning and hands-on practice. They offer a scalable and cost-effective solution for vocational training, particularly in sectors such as textile, clothing, leather, and footwear, where visualizing detailed processes and environments is critical for skills development.

3D models provide fully interactive experiences, enabling learners to engage with simulated environments and processes that are often inaccessible or impractical to observe in real life. For example, 3D models can simulate complex chemical reactions or offer detailed explorations of machinery interiors, providing unique opportunities for learners to gain insights into otherwise hidden or hazardous scenarios. However, these environments require significant resources for development, including advanced technical expertise and substantial time for creating realistic and accurate models. 3D models might be implemented inside the Metaskills Erasmus project.

2.2 Immersive and Non-Immersive VR Technologies

The project will deliver both immersive VR and non-immersive VR technologies, catering to diverse learning needs and resource constraints:

- Immersive VR involves the use of head-mounted displays (HMDs), which completely immerse the user in a virtual environment. This method enhances focus and engagement by isolating learners from external distractions and providing an unparalleled sense of presence. However, immersive VR often requires more expensive hardware and can cause motion sickness in some users.
- Non-Immersive VR leverages standard 2D screens, such as computers or tablets, to simulate a virtual environment. While less immersive, this method is more accessible and scalable, allowing broader adoption without the need for specialized equipment.

2.2.1 Collaborative Immersive VR (Multiplayer)

One of the project's most innovative features is the development of collaborative immersive VR, enabling multiple users to interact simultaneously within the same virtual environment. This multiplayer approach introduces two distinct roles: teacher and students, facilitating dynamic interaction between the instructor and the learners (Slavin 1980). In this setup, the teacher can guide, monitor, and interact with students in real-time, simulating classroom-like collaboration within the virtual space. This functionality not only fosters teamwork and communication skills but also allows for immediate feedback and adaptive instruction tailored to the learners' needs. In the study by Drey et al. (2022), symmetrical collaborative VR provided statistically significantly greater presence, immersion, player experience, and lower intrinsic cognitive load, all of which are important factors for learning.

By enabling these teacher-student interactions, the collaborative immersive VR environment supports active learning, problem-solving, and peer collaboration in ways that traditional training methods cannot replicate. Despite these advantages, collaborative immersive VR requires robust technical infrastructure to ensure seamless, synchronized interactions and an intuitive user experience (Capecchi et al. 2023).

2.2.2 Non-Immersive VR Platform

The non-immersive VR platform is designed to ensure accessibility and inclusivity, making virtual learning experiences available to a broad audience. This platform will feature explanations of the VR environments in all the languages of the participating countries, ensuring usability for diverse learners. To enhance interactivity, the platform will incorporate hotspots—interactive elements embedded within the 360° videos that provide additional content such as texts, images, and 2D videos. These hotspots allow learners to engage more deeply with the environment by exploring detailed information about specific aspects of the scene, creating a semi-immersive and engaging learning experience even without specialized VR equipment.

By integrating these complementary methods and technologies, the METASKILLS4TCLF project ensures that learners benefit from a rich, versatile, and effective training experience, addressing the specific needs of the TCLF sectors while leveraging the strengths of various VR modalities.

2.3 Topics and Storytelling

The development of the METASKILLS4TCLF Virtual Reality (VR) training project is organized into systematic phases to ensure the creation of effective, relevant, and engaging learning content tailored to the textile, clothing, leather, and footwear (TCLF) industries. Each phase addresses a specific step in the design and implementation process, from identifying training needs to deploying the final VR tools, ensuring alignment with industry goals and educational outcomes.

1. Identification and Vetting of VR Learning Needs: Analyze curricula and evaluate the suitability of VR for specific training topics.
2. Definition of Learning Outcomes and Contexts: Define clear learning objectives and contextual scenarios tied to industry practices.
3. Content Development: Create 3D models and 360° videos with interactive hotspots and multilingual support.
4. Collaborative Immersive VR Design: Develop multiplayer VR scenarios with teacher-student interaction for collaborative learning.
5. Testing and Piloting: Conduct pilot sessions to gather feedback and refine content and technical aspects.
6. Deployment and Evaluation: Launch the VR platform and assess its long-term impact on skills development and industry performance.

This structured methodology ensures a robust and well-targeted learning framework for the TCLF industries, addressing their evolving needs through innovative VR training solutions.

3. THE E-LEARNING VR PLATFORMS

3.1 Topics and Storytelling

The METASKILLS4TCLF project is currently in the process of developing storytelling-driven educational content, a critical component of its innovative approach to vocational training. This storytelling has been carefully designed with the active collaboration of all project partners, ensuring a diverse and comprehensive representation of the textile, clothing, leather, and footwear (TCLF) industries. For each educational topic, an innovative manufacture was identified in one or more of the 11 project countries in which to shoot the 360° videos.

The topics and scenes identified by the partners will enable storytelling to create narratives that address the different challenges and opportunities of the textile, clothing and leather industries. By grounding theoretical knowledge in realistic scenarios, the project aims to provide students with a practical understanding of sustainability, innovation and ethical practices, while highlighting the interconnectedness of these sectors.

3.1.1 Clothing and Footwear Sectors

Storytelling in the Clothing sector focuses on innovation and sustainable practices throughout the value chain:

• Traceability and transparency: The narratives describe the adoption of digital product passports and smart control systems based on blockchain. These tools ensure the integrity of garments, allowing students to understand how transparency promotes consumer trust and regulatory compliance.

• Zero-waste design: The storytelling process captures real-world examples of companies implementing zero-waste strategies, from conceptual design mapping to 3D simulation. Students explore how these practices minimize material waste while maintaining aesthetic and functional quality.

• Sustainable brand identity: The project explores how clothing brands develop marketing strategies that emphasize sustainability, documenting every step from material selection to production. Real-world examples show the role of certifications, digital platforms and effective storytelling in improving consumer perception.

• Durability and consumer engagement: Practical cases highlight methods to improve garment durability through innovative material treatments and consumer education on repairs, fostering a more circular approach to clothing consumption.

3.1.2 Textile Sector

The textile sector narrative addresses its central role in promoting circular economy practices and material innovation:

• Circularity and Recycling: Narratives focus on closed-loop systems, such as automated sorting lines and mechanical recycling processes, that reduce textile waste. Real case studies illustrate how supply chains adapt to support circularity by collecting, sorting and preparing materials for recycling.

• Materials innovation: Storytelling highlights alternative materials, such as bio-based and low-impact textiles, providing a comparative perspective with conventional materials. Learners can understand how these materials are developed, tested and integrated into sustainable textile production.

• Water-free and low-impact processes: Learners are exposed to advanced dyeing and surface treatment methods that drastically reduce the use of water and chemicals, addressing one of the most significant environmental impacts of the textile industry.

• Audits and quality assurance: Simulated company audits allow participants to step into the role of sustainability assessors, understanding the processes and parameters used to assess environmental performance and compliance with industry standards.

3.1.3 Leather Sector

In the leather sector, the narrative focuses on reducing environmental impact and improving traceability:

• Minimizing the impact of production: Stories document sustainable practices in leather production, including strategies to reduce waste and reuse by-products of cow and sheep leather processing. Participants explore case studies where companies successfully implement innovative waste management solutions.

• Water management: The project emphasizes the critical role of water in leather processing by recounting the adoption of closed-loop water systems on a pilot and semi-industrial scale. These cases demonstrate how companies can optimize water use and effectively treat wastewater, reducing their environmental footprint.

• Traceability systems: Students are confronted with detailed examples of traceability in leather production, from the sourcing of raw materials to the manufacture of the final product. These narratives highlight the integration of digital tools to trace materials, ensuring ethical and sustainable practices throughout the supply chain.

• Durability and circularity: Examples of durable leather articles and their recycling potential are presented, highlighting the role of long-lasting products in reducing overall consumption and waste.

3.1.4 Integrated Cross-Cutting Themes

In all three areas, the narrative approach emphasizes shared goals such as sustainability, resource optimization and ethical practices. Through real-world examples and business cases, learners are encouraged to identify synergies between the sectors, such as shared strategies for waste reduction, traceability and digital transformation. This integrated perspective fosters a holistic understanding of how TCLF industries contribute to broader sustainability goals.

3.2 Prototype of the App

As part of the METASKILLS4TCLF project's progress, prototypes of both the immersive VR app and the non-immersive VR app have been developed, focusing on the footwear manufacturing sector. These prototypes address two critical topics: traceability and eco-design/circular economy. Both topics leverage storytelling through immersive 360° 5K video content, providing a rich and engaging learning experience.

3.2.1 Immersive VR App

The initial scene serves to accustom the students to the 360 degree immersive environment (Figure 1). In these initial classroom, the teacher is free to choose from the teaching topics and within the topics select the teaching sequence of 360 degree immersive video scenes.

Figure 1. Initial classroom scenes

For each topic, the immersive VR app features three distinct 360° videos, offering a progressive narrative structure:

1. Introduction to the Topic (Figure 2.a): The first video is set at the "Politecnico Calzaturiero" in Veneto and follows an interview-style format. This video introduces the general concept of the topic, providing a foundational understanding of either traceability or eco-design/circular economy within the footwear industry.
2. Product Presentation (Figure 2.b): The second video takes place in the marketing office of an innovative footwear company. It focuses on explaining the product in detail, highlighting its unique features related to traceability or sustainable design, and linking these aspects to the broader market context.
3. Production Process (Figure 2.c): The third video is filmed on-site at a production facility, capturing and illustrating the key stages of the manufacturing process. This immersive footage provides learners with an in-depth view of how theoretical concepts are implemented in real-world production environments.

3.2.2 Non-Immersive VR App

The non-immersive prototype complements the immersive experience by offering accessibility through traditional devices such as computers or tablets. The storytelling content from the immersive app is adapted for this platform and is enriched with interactive hotspots (Figure 3), which provide additional layers of information. The hotspots include:

- Text descriptions elaborating on concepts introduced in the videos.
- Images that visually reinforce key points.
- 2D videos that further illustrate aspects of the process or product.

By combining immersive and non-immersive approaches, the prototype demonstrates how VR can cater to diverse learning needs, ensuring scalability and accessibility while maintaining a high level of engagement and educational value. This dual-platform design is a significant milestone in the development of the METASKILLS4TCLF VR learning tools.

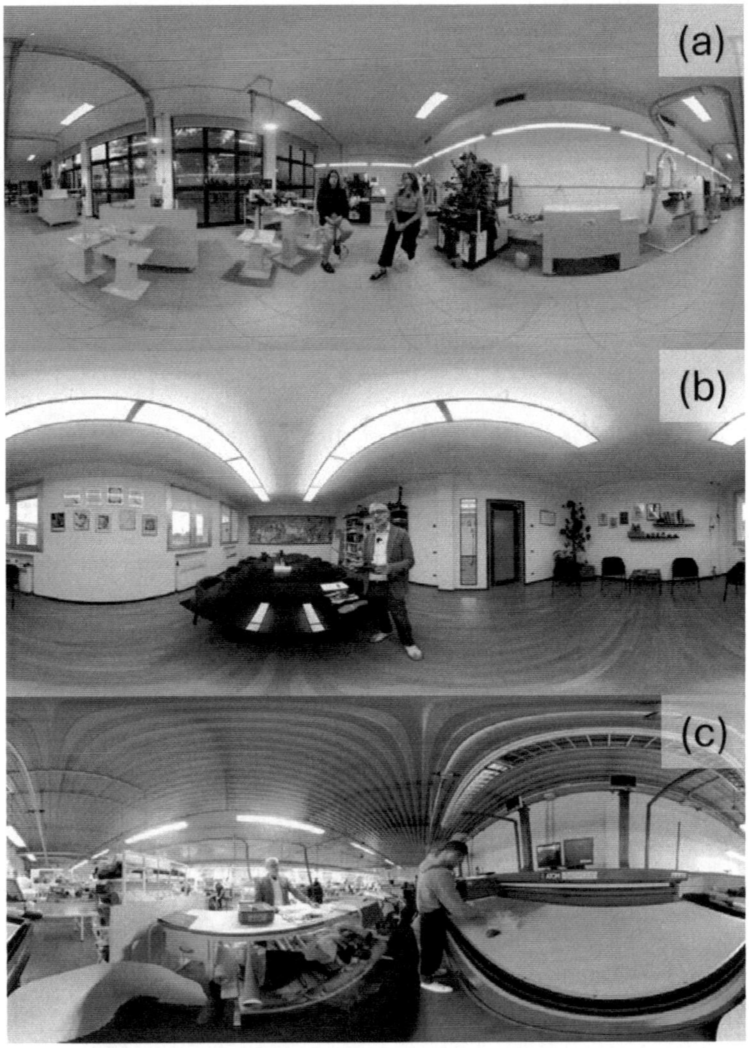

Figure 2. 360° video scenes: (a) Introduction to the Topic. (b) Product Presentation. (c) Production Process

Figure 3. Example of HotSpot

4. CONCLUSION

The METASKILLS4TCLF project has completed the development of initial prototypes for immersive and non-immersive VR applications, focusing on traceability and circular economy in the footwear manufacturing sector. These prototypes provide a basis for the next stages of the project, which will involve testing the tools with learners, collecting feedback to improve their design and usability, and extending the content to address additional industry needs. The upcoming phases aim to ensure the effectiveness and practicality of the VR tools in supporting skills development across the TCLF industries.

REFERENCES

Capecchi, I., Neri, F., Borghini, T., & Bernetti, I. (2023). Use of virtual reality technology in chainsaw operations, education and training. Forestry: An International Journal of Forest Research, 96(5), 718-732.

Dey, A., Piumsomboon, T., Lee, Y. and Billinghurst, M. 2017 Effects of sharing physiological states of players in a collaborative virtual reality gameplay. In Proceedings of the Conference on human factors in computing systems. Denver, CO, USA, pp. 4045-4056.

Gonzalez-Franco, M., & Lanier, J. (2017). Model of Illusions and Virtual Reality. Frontiers in Psychology, 8, 1125.

Radianti, J., Majchrzak, T. A., Fromm, J., & Wohlgenannt, I. (2020). A systematic review of immersive virtual reality applications for higher education: Design elements, lessons learned, and research agenda. Computers & Education, 147, 103778.

Makransky, G., & Petersen, G. B. (2019). Investigating the process of learning with simulation-based virtual reality: A structural equation modeling approach. Computers & Education, 136, 1-14.

Slavin, R. E. 1980 A review of peer tutoring and cooperative learning projects in twenty-eight schools. Rev. Educ. Res. 11, 315-342.

Smith, S., Jones, A., & Taylor, R. (2022). The effectiveness of virtual reality training in vocational education: A meta-analysis. Journal of Vocational Education and Training, 74(3), 401-421.

UNCOVERING TIME-RELATED STUDENTS' BEHAVIOURAL PATTERNS IN VIRTUAL LEARNING ENVIRONMENTS

Martin Drlík and Jozef Kapusta
Constantine the Philosopher University in Nitra
Tr. A. Hlinku 1, 949 74 Nitra, Slovakia

ABSTRACT

The e-learning courses became an ordinary part of the everyday life of the stakeholders participating in life-long learning programs. Their use and popularity vary from discipline to discipline. Different delivery forms of the courses have a significant impact on stakeholders' time management and financial sustainability, mainly tutor-led courses. Therefore, a better understanding of the time-related students' behavioral patterns can contribute to effectively utilizing personal, time, and financial resources. The paper aims to show how the analysis of time-related characteristics of students' activity in courses can uncover typical behavioral patterns of students and how they can be further analyzed. For this purpose, the data about student activity from the tutor-led e-learning course for learning foreign languages created in LMS Moodle was analyzed using TimeSeriesKMeans clustering method. As a result, two cases, with three and four clusters representing typical students' behavior, were examined. The differences in students' behavioral patterns confirmed the ability to find groups of students with interpretable behavioral patterns even though the performance metrics indicated the need for further analysis. These findings can be further utilized and used for continual improvement of the course structure and schedule, as well as for better planning of tutors' activities, students' assignments, and gamification to sustain the students' motivation.

KEYWORDS

Behavioral Patterns, LMS Moodle Logs, Machine Learning, Time Series Analysis

1. INTRODUCTION

The e-learning courses became an ordinary part of the everyday life of the stakeholders participating in life-long learning programs. Their popularity and effectiveness vary from discipline to discipline. Different delivery forms of the courses and the visibility of the tutor significantly impact the total number of students who successfully finished the course and received a certificate. Simultaneously, this delivery form directly influences the stakeholders' time management and financial sustainability, mainly in tutor-led courses. The longer the course lasts, the more exposed the students may be to various situations, which can negatively influence their motivation and engagement and decrease their overall learning progress. Therefore, a better understanding of the time-related students' behavioral patterns can contribute to more effective utilization of personal, time, and financial resources. At the same time, these patterns can be used for continual improvement of the course structure and schedule, as well as for better planning of tutors' activities, students' assignments, and gamification to sustain the students' motivation.

Therefore, the paper aims to show how analyzing time-related characteristics of students' activity in e-learning courses created in LMS can uncover typical behavioral patterns and how they can be further analyzed. The paper introduces a study in which log data about the students' activities in tutor-led e-learning courses extracted from the LMS will be pre-processed to the time series format and analyzed using suitable clustering methods. As the next section will show, even though this approach combining time series and clustering methods is not frequently used in the learning analytics domain, it has the potential to result in finding cluster models, which can, after thorough evaluation, confirm or uncover hidden patterns in online learners' behavior.

2. RELATED WORK

Several papers from the last decade described the application of clustering methods on log data. For example, the authors (Hooshyar et al., 2020) published a systematic review of clustering methods in the learning analytics domain. They proposed an evaluation approach that automatically compared several clustering methods using multiple internal and external performance measures on nine real-world educational datasets of different sizes. However, the review did not deal with the clustering of time series.

Other authors (DeFreitas and Bernard, 2015) focused on data stored in the learning management systems. They presented a case-based experiment to show the relative performance of clustering algorithms with Learning Management System log data. They compared partition-based (K-Means), density-based (DBSCAN), and hierarchical (BIRCH) methods to determine which technique to consider the most appropriate for performing clustering analysis within the LMS. They confirmed that the most appropriate methods are closely related to the quality and semantics of the analyzed dataset. Similarly, the authors (Li et al., 2021) proposed an unsupervised ensemble clustering framework to use student behavioral data stored in LMS to discover behavioral patterns. Three unsupervised learning models (BIRCH, DBSCAN, and GMM) were applied to identify distinct student clusters. Their further analysis revealed a strong correlation between student engagement and academic outcomes, with two high-risk clusters demonstrating the highest dropout rates (Pecuchova and Drlik, 2024). However, these studies did not pay extra attention to the temporal nature of the data.

Other authors considered the log data stored in LMS as time series and applied different machine and deep learning methods to predict students' performance in e-learning courses. As a result, they presented a new version of the ReaderBench framework, grounded in Cohesion Network Analysis. The Recurrent Neural Network with LSTM cells that combined global features, including participation and initiation indices, with a time series analysis on timeframes was used to predict student grades. At the same time, multiple sociograms were generated to observe interaction patterns (Dascalu et al., 2021). Another study by Chiang (Chiang et al., 2022) used deep learning techniques with Moodle log data to predict student performance in introductory computer programming courses. The results suggested that deep learning models are promising in predicting student performance and identifying low-performing students in the researched context.

As can be seen, predictive analytics in higher education using LMS activity data did not adequately accommodate student behaviors in the form of time series. However, as Chen and Cui showed in their study (Chen and Cui, 2020), using the deep learning approach, time series information about click frequencies successfully provided detection of at-risk students with moderate prediction accuracy. On the other hand, they did not apply time series analysis and clustering methods to log data.

The authors (Joseph and Abraham, 2023) showed how this combination of methods can be applied to log data. They used the students' rates of learning and grade points, along with the total learning time, calculated from the time series log data, to cluster the learners. The K-Means clustering approach was applied to group learners with similar performance without collecting a learner's previous academic records or demographic information. In the experimental evaluation, they identified slow, average, and advanced learners.

Another study examined the relationship between consistency in students' online work habits and academic performance in a blended course using the data from logs recorded in the LMS. The consistency was measured by using Data Time Warping (DTW) distance for two successive tasks as an appropriate measure to assess the similarity of the time series. As a result, meaningful clusters of students exhibited similar behavior, and three distinct consistency patterns were identified: highly consistent, incrementally consistent, and inconsistent users (Sher et al., 2020).

The studies confirmed that log data stored in LMS are suitable for students' behavioral pattern analysis using clustering machine learning methods. Simultaneously, they showed that considering the log data as a time series, which is input to the clustering algorithms, has often been analyzed, although they can potentially uncover temporal behavioral patterns of LMS stakeholders.

3. METHODS

As mentioned before, this study aims to identify potentially helpful behavioral patterns in students who decided to learn a new foreign language using a tutor-led e-learning course created in LMS Moodle. The logs about the student's activity in the e-learning course, active from September 2023 to July 2024, were selected as a data source for this study. At the beginning of the period, 667 students from different countries enrolled in this introductory language course. The course contained ten sections with thematically oriented study materials, quizzes, and assignments. The individual sections were open approximately every four weeks. The participants were asked to finish all quizzes and assignments before the deadlines. After completing all required activities, the students received a certificate at the end of the course in July 2024. Four tutors regularly monitored the course dynamics and helped students in their progress. Simultaneously, they provided regular feedback to the students.

3.1 Data Understanding and Pre-Processing

The information about all activities of individual students is stored in the form of logs stored in the LMS productional database. Simultaneously, this information is available for the teachers and managers in each e-learning course. The teacher can read, download, and further analyze this data.

The original input dataset contained 113120 records about the activity of 667 students. Figure 1 shows the total students' activity in individual weeks of the year (1a) and the distribution of the activity of individual students (1b). Figure 1a confirmed the expected decline in total activity of the group of online students over time. On the other hand, Figure 1b provides more insights into the behavior of individual students over the whole study period. However, this visualization does not uncover possible typical patterns in students' behavior, which could be further analyzed. The gap around week 20 represents the winter holidays.

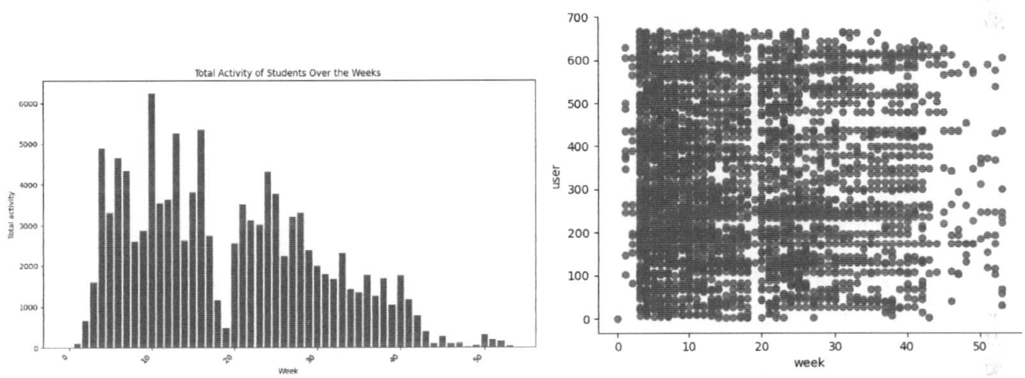

Figure 1. Total students' activity in individual weeks of the year (1a). The distribution of the activity of individual students over the observed study period (1b)

The downloaded dataset contains features such as timestamp, user full name, affected user, event context, component, event name, description, origin, and IP address. These columns follow the xAPI format, allowing standardized log data exchange or sharing. However, this dataset structure is not directly suitable for most reports or advanced analyses, and data must be pre-processed in the following pre-processing steps:

1. The data was anonymized to ensure all requirements, which are defined by the university's Ethical Committee, were met. All personal information was removed. The student's unique ID was replaced by an artificial one to ensure that it, together with the timestamp, allows the creation of a time series representation of the student's activity in the course over the observed period of approximately 10 months.
2. The obsolete columns (user full name, affected user, event context, component, event name, description, origin, and IP address) were removed.
3. While the online students were not usually active every day, the time series representation of their activity had different lengths and contained various numbers of items. Therefore, it was necessary to adjust the individual time series to the same length by adding zeros to all inactive dates.
4. As a consequence, the time series contained many zeros, which would potentially affect the clustering results. Therefore, a new column, "week," was calculated from the timestamp of each record.

5. To further shorten the time series, a new dataset was created, which contained the triple (user, week, sum of activities) for each user.
6. Finally, the time series representing the students with very low activity over the observed period of ten months were removed holistically to ensure that these low-frequency time series did not distort the interpretability of clustering results. As a result, the number of course participants decreased from 667 to only 76. This phenomenon will be discussed later in the discussion section.

The final dataset, which will be analyzed in the next section, can be represented by the matrix with three dimensions (student, week, and sum of activities) (76, 52, 1).

3.2 Data Modeling

Clustering methods belong to unsupervised machine learning methods. Many clustering algorithms require estimating the most suitable or expected number of clusters. The well-known elbow method is one of the methods that can help find this number and was used in this study. Considering the visualization of the relationships between the number of possible clusters and the Silhouette score shown in Figure 2, three and four clusters were further analyzed.

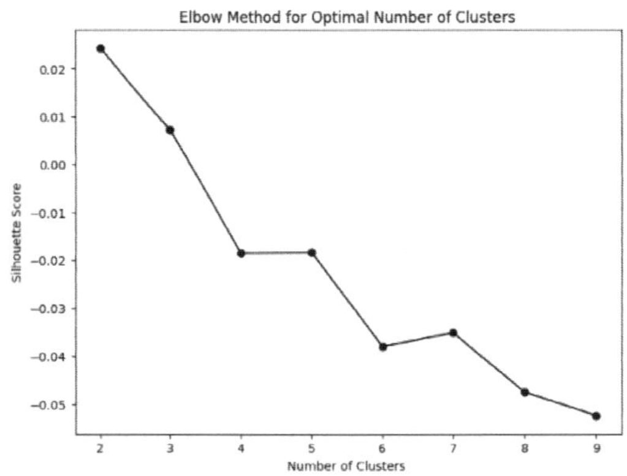

Figure 2. Calculation of the most suitable number of clusters using the elbow method

Subsequently, the clustering algorithm TimeSeriesKMeans, with a similarity measure Euclidean distance, was selected as the most appropriate algorithm to cluster time series data to the expected number of clusters. Table 1 shows the results of the Silhouette Score for different types of distances and numbers of clusters.

Table 1. The results of the Silhouette Score for different types of distances and number of clusters

Algorithm (Similarity Measure)	Silhouette Score 3 Clusters	Silhouette Score 4 Clusters
TimeSeriesKMeans (Euclidian)	0.0616	0.0498
TimeSeriesKMeans (DTW)	-0.0052	-0.0063
TimeSeriesKMeans (softdtw)	-0.0109	0.0029
KShape	-0.0085	-0.0201
KernelKMeans	-0.0123	-0.0255

After hyperparameter tuning, typical time series, which represent each type of student's behavior over time in the course, were visualized for three clusters (Figure 3). The identified time series confirmed the tutors' personal experience and general expectations and can be interpreted as follows:

1. Cluster 1 represents the active students who followed the course schedule, systematically and regularly visited the course activities, and submitted required assignments. They were active throughout the whole period and finished the course on time.
2. On the other hand, the time series identified in Cluster 2 represents the typical group of students who started the course but dropped out too early. However, it is interesting to note that the students from this cluster returned to study after a long period of inactivity and tried to pass the final exam, which opened around the 40th week.

3. The last Cluster 3 shows a similar behavior and activity of the students as Cluster 2, but it shows a longer period of slowly declining activity in contrast to Cluster 2.

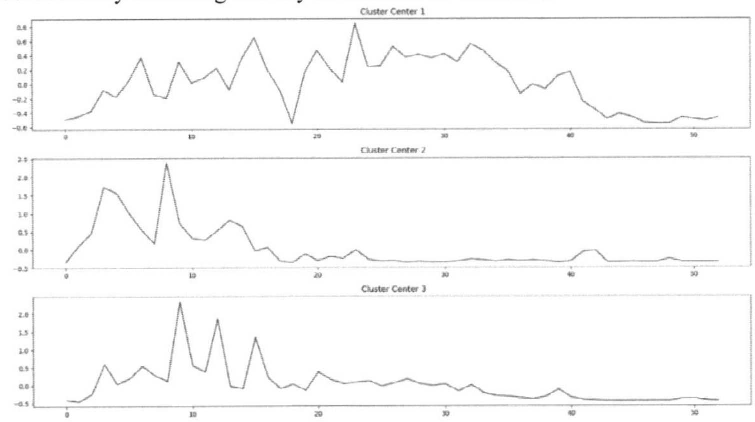

Figure 3. Identified typical time series in the case of three clusters, which represent each type of student's behavior over time in the course

Considering the possible inaccuracy in estimating the optimal number of clusters after applying the Silhouette Score calculation, the same approach was repeated for four clusters (Figure 4). The identified clusters can again be interpreted in line with the expected behavior of the student groups.

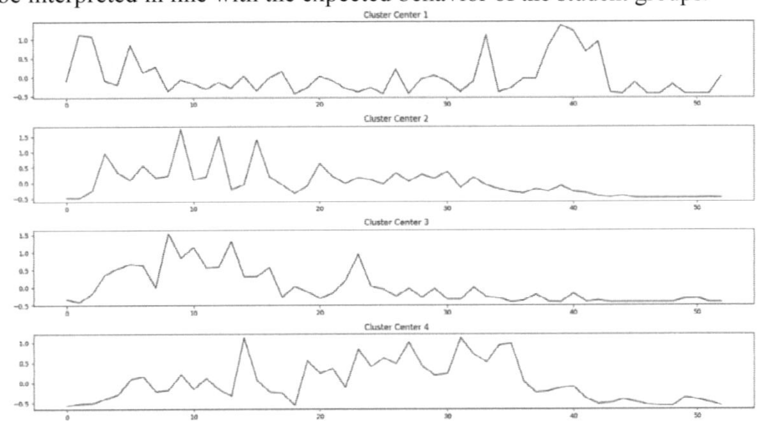

Figure 4. Identified typical time series in the case of four clusters, which represent each type of student's behavior over time in the course

It is necessary to emphasize that the order and number of the clusters do not correspond to the order of clusters identified before. However, the clusters can be interpreted as follows:

1. Cluster 1 represents a group of students who started studying intensively but then declined in activity. However, they finally increased their activity before the end of the course with the aim of successfully passing the exam and receiving a certificate.
2. Cluster 2 and Cluster 3 show similar activity with gradual decline. In addition to the students who were removed from the dataset in the pre-processing phase, these clusters represent students who lost their motivation or external circumstances prevented the successful completion of the course.
3. Cluster 4 shows interesting behavior, which was not identified in the case of three clusters. This cluster represents students whose activity started more slowly and increased over time.

3.3 Model Evaluation

Several performance metrics were analyzed to evaluate the clustering quality. Table 2 shows that even though the clusters were correctly identified, they contained borderline records, which means the typical behavioral patterns can be interpreted concerning this fact and require further analysis.

Table 2. The performance metrics for identified clusters

Metrics	3 Clusters	4 Clusters
Silhouette Score	-0.0161	-0.0099
Davies-Bouldin Index	7.0291	6.7311
Calinski-Harabasz Index	1.0288	1.1948

Other simple metrics can also be used to evaluate the internal structure of the identified clusters. For example, Figure 5 shows how equally individual items are distributed between the clusters. In the cases of the three identified clusters, this distribution did not uncover any cluster with significantly fewer items (Figure 5a). Therefore, it can be stated that the selected clustering methods created equally dense clusters, which are clearly different from each other. However, a lower number of the items assigned to the first cluster in the case of four identified clusters indicates that this student's behavioral pattern may not fully correspond to the real pattern of students who started studying intensively and came back to the course as the end of the course had been approaching (Figure 5b).

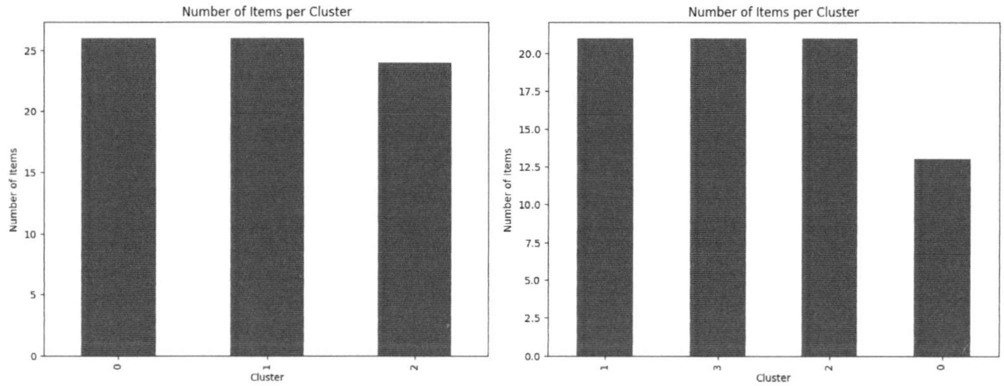

Figure 5. The distribution of individual time series items between identified three and four clusters

Similarly, Figure 6 visualizes the heatmap of the pairwise distances between cluster centers after performing time series clustering. The core of the similarity comparison is based on pairwise distance calculation, which is based on the calculation of the Euclidean distance between all pairs of cluster centers. The method iterates through each pair of clusters and computes the Euclidean norm (distance) between their respective centers. In this case, the Euclidean distance is a standard measure of dissimilarity between vectors.

The more considerable differences between the distances in the case of the three identified clusters confirmed that this clustering found clusters that represent different types of student behavioral patterns over the observed period, which are in line with the expectations (Figure 6a). On the other hand, a slight difference between the distances of the first cluster and the others in the case of four identified clusters confirmed the previous statement that the first cluster may not represent such a standalone behavioral pattern of students' activity as others.

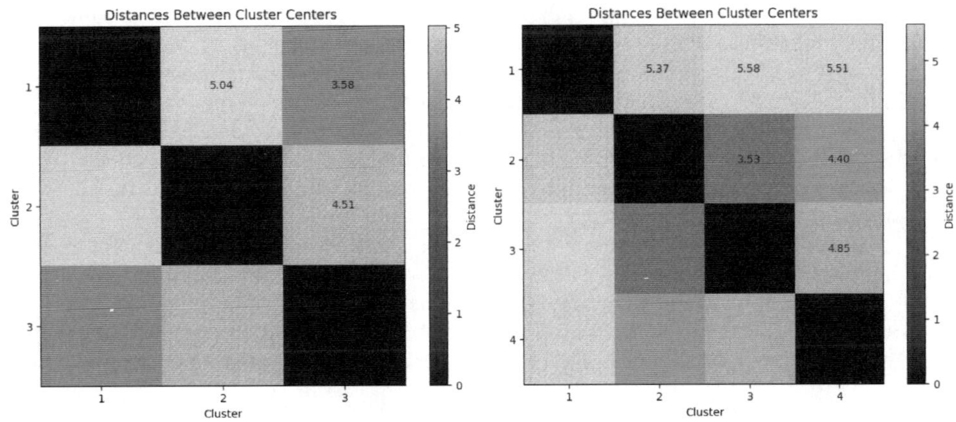

Figure 6. The heatmap of the pairwise Euclidean distances between cluster centers after performing time series clustering in the case of three (a) and four (b) clusters

4. DISCUSSION AND CONCLUSIONS

The study showed how clustering time-related data about students' activity in e-learning courses can uncover typical behavioral patterns. The paper presented a study in which log data about the students' activities in tutor-led e-learning courses extracted from the LMS was pre-processed to the time series format and analyzed using suitable clustering methods for time series. The dataset used in this study originated from the LMS log database. It contained digital traces of 667 unique students enrolled in the e-learning course. Although the number of records was sufficient for preprocessing and modeling using machine learning methods, the first sight of the data showed that the overall activity of the individual students was not high. The students focused mainly on mandatory activities like quizzes and assignments, supplemented by text and audio files. It can be assumed that enrichment of the course with more interactive activities, gamification, and targeted feedback could significantly contribute to the overall increase of the activity and possibly engage more students to be more active for a longer time. However, after removing students in the pre-processing phase, the dataset contained data about only 76 students, which reflected in a significant increase in average activity. It can be stated that this observation is consistent with the generally known fact about the approximate percentage of online students who continue learning after losing the initial effort and engagement.

The pre-processing phase summarized all evitable modifications of the input raw dataset, which were necessary for several reasons. Firstly, the large group of inactive students had to be removed because they would significantly influence the final shape of the found time series, which represents typical student behavior in a given cluster. Secondly, the temporal feature of the dataset was represented by the column week, which replaced the original timestamp field from the raw dataset. This modification was necessary to minimize the differences in the length of the individual time series, which represented individual students. As a result, TimeSeriesKMeans clustering with Euclidian distance outperformed the DTW distance, which usually reaches better results in the case of time series with different lengths. Simultaneously, this modification eliminated the large portion of dates with zero student activity, which could again negatively impact clustering results.

The application of clustering methods in the modeling phase uncovered typical temporal behavioral patterns based on students' activities. Based on the results of elbow methods, two cases with explicitly defined three and four clusters were examined. The already mentioned TimeSeriesKMeans algorithm was selected based on the Silhouette Score value. Even though the selected hyperparameters of this algorithm were tuned, it is possible that further hyperparameter tuning of other clustering algorithms for time series, like KShape or KernelKMeans could lead to more precise results. On the other hand, identified clusters represent typical behavior of the students' archetypes in online courses. These findings can be further utilized and used for continual improvement of the course structure and schedule, as well as for better planning of tutors' activities, students' assignments, and gamification to sustain the students' motivation. The evaluation phase confirms the correctness of these findings using the calculation of pairwise distances between the cluster centers and item distribution in individual clusters. The presented study has several limitations. First, data came only from one cycle of the course. Identification of typical time series representing student behavior from several cycles could significantly contribute to a better generalization of the findings. Secondly, as was mentioned before, the students did not visit the course regularly. As a result, the time series, which represents the student's activity in time, did not contain data from many dates. Therefore, these dates had to be added to the time series to be compared across all students. This modification created a time series with a high frequency of zero-value sequences. To overcome this issue, dates were replaced with weeks in this study. However, it could be interesting to focus more on these zero-value sequences, calculate their length, and use them as the data in a dataset for the time series clustering. A comparison of the clusters found using these two approaches could bring more light to further understanding of the students' behavioral patterns over time. Finally, the records about the students with low activity were removed from the dataset. The same approach could be applied to the students who showed very high activity. Removing these outliers could change the shape of the identified patterns. However, this step should be realized carefully to ensure that interesting behavioral patterns are not lost.

The study's results confirmed the application of machine learning methods to temporal characteristics of digital traces, which represent students' activity in LMS courses. This can confirm the subjective feelings of the teachers or managers involved in online learning and help better understand the behavior of typical student groups. Future improvements to the study will focus on eliminating the limitations and extending the research with more sophisticated time series methods.

ACKNOWLEDGEMENT

This work was supported in part by the Science Grant Agency of the Ministry of Education of the Slovak Republic under Grant VEGA 1/0490/22.

REFERENCES

Chen, F., Cui, Y., (2020). Utilizing Student Time Series Behaviour in Learning Management Systems for Early Prediction of Course Performance. J. Learn. Anal. 7, 1–17. https://doi.org/10.18608/jla.2020.72.1

Chiang, Y.V., Lin, Y.-R., Chen, N.-S., (2022). Using deep learning models to predict student performance in introductory computer programming courses, in: Chang, M., Chen, N.S., Dascalu, M., Sampson, D.G., Tlili, A., Trausan-Matu, S. (Eds.), 2022 INTERNATIONAL CONFERENCE ON ADVANCED LEARNING TECHNOLOGIES (ICALT 2022), IEEE International Conference on Advanced Learning Technologies. Presented at the 22nd IEEE International Conference on Advanced Learning Technologies (ICALT), IEEE, New York, pp. 180–182. https://doi.org/10.1109/ICALT55010.2022.00060

Dascalu, M.-D., Ruseti, S., Dascalu, M., McNamara, D.S., Carabas, M., Rebedea, T., Trausan-Matu, S., (2021). Before and during COVID-19: A Cohesion Network Analysis of students' online participation in Moodle courses. Comput. Hum. Behav. 121, 106780. https://doi.org/10.1016/j.chb.2021.106780

DeFreitas, K., Bernard, M., (2015). Comparative Performance Analysis of Clustering Techniques in Educational Data Mining. IADIS-Int. J. Comput. Sci. Inf. Syst. 10, 65–78.

Hooshyar, D., Yang, Y., Pedaste, M., Huang, Y.-M., (2020). Clustering Algorithms in an Educational Context: An Automatic Comparative Approach. IEEE Access 8, 146994–147014. https://doi.org/10.1109/ACCESS.2020.3014948

Joseph, B., Abraham, S., (2023). Identifying slow learners in an e-learning environment using k-means clustering approach. Knowl. Manag. E-Learn. 15, 539–553. https://doi.org/10.34105/j.kmel.2023.15.031

Li, X., Zhang, Y., Cheng, H., Zhou, F., Yin, B., (2021). An Unsupervised Ensemble Clustering Approach for the Analysis of Student Behavioral Patterns. IEEE Access 9, 7076–7091. https://doi.org/10.1109/ACCESS.2021.3049157

Pecuchova, J., Drlik, M., (2024). Enhancing the Early Student Dropout Prediction Model Through Clustering Analysis of Students' Digital Traces. IEEE Access 12, 159336–159367. https://doi.org/10.1109/ACCESS.2024.3486762

Sher, V., Hatala, M., Gasevic, D., (2020). Analyzing the consistency in within-activity learning patterns in blended learning, in: LAK20: The Tenth International Conference on Learning Analytics & Knowledge. Presented at the 10th International Conference on Learning Analytics and Knowledge (LAK), Assoc Computing Machinery, New York, pp. 1–10. https://doi.org/10.1145/3375462.3375470

CONTEMPORARY CHALLENGES AND PROSPECTS IN ENGINEERING EDUCATION IN THE CONTEXT OF INDUSTRY 5.0

Veselina Nedeva and Zlatoeli Ducheva
Trakia University – Stara Zagora, Faculty of Technics and Technology
8600 Yambol, 38 Graf Ignatiev Str., Bulgaria

ABSTRACT

The article presents a discussion of the significance of novel trends in engineering education in the context of the advancement of Industry 5.0. The article places emphasis on the integration of innovation into the learning process, highlighting the importance of customised products, human-robot (cobots) collaboration, and the transition to high-value, sustainable manufacturing. The research is based on an analysis of existing best practices and training methods, including internships and project-based learning (PBL). The importance of hands-on learning and university-industry collaboration is highlighted as key components in preparing students for future challenges in the industrial environment. The authors highlight the importance of project-based learning in engineering education as a crucial method for fostering professional and social skills essential for success in Industry 5.0. The paper presents practical guidance for the future evolution of engineering education, while examining existing best practices and proposed strategies for integrating new technologies and principles.

KEYWORDS

Industry 5.0, Engineering Education, Problem-Based Method, Project-Based Methods, Metaverse Technologies

1. INTRODUCTION

Over the past decade, the industrial sector has undergone substantial transformation, progressing from Industry 4.0 to the subsequent phase of technological and societal advancement, designated as Industry 5.0. While Industry 4.0 is characterised by a focus on automation, digitisation and the utilisation of technologies such as the Internet of Things (IoT), artificial intelligence (AI) and robotics, Industry 5.0 builds upon these concepts, emphasising the human factor, collaboration between people and smart technologies and sustainability. In this context, the objective of Industry 5.0 is to establish a harmonious relationship between humans and technology, with an emphasis on their mutual reinforcement.

The ongoing developments in industrial technology and the human-centric approach inherent to Industry 5.0 necessitate the adaptation of engineering education to align with the emerging requirements and equip future professionals with the requisite skills for success in this novel technological era.

The key characteristics of Industry 5.0, as identified by Breque et al. (2021), Fukuyama (2018) and Morawska-Jancelewicz (2021), include:

- Human-centricity: In Industry 5.0, the human element is of paramount importance. Technology is designed to augment human capabilities, rather than supplant them. This encompasses the provision of personalised solutions and the facilitation of collaboration between humans and intelligent machines.

- The collaboration of humans and robots is a significant aspect of Industry 5.0. The use of collaborative robots, or cobots, is a crucial element in this regard. Such automated systems operate in conjunction with human personnel, assuming the execution of arduous or repetitive tasks, thereby enabling human employees to concentrate on more imaginative and strategic endeavours.

- Sustainability - Industry 5.0 places a strong emphasis on sustainability and environmental responsibility, with the objective of optimising production processes and reducing waste.

- Personalised products – Technological advancements facilitate the mass customisation of products while maintaining high efficiency and meeting individual user requirements.

The principal aim of this report is to examine the challenges currently facing engineering education in the context of Industry 5.0, and to identify potential avenues for adapting the educational process to align with the emerging requirements. In order to meet the dynamic needs of modern industry, engineering education must integrate new approaches that incorporate interdisciplinary work, creativity and sustainability.

2. RESEARCH METHODS

(1) Database Selection: The Web of Science Core Collection (WoSCC) database were used for scientific research on the topic. After identifying the keywords essential to the subject through graphical visualization, additional keyword searches were conducted in Google Scholar.

(2) Search Strategy and data collection: The search strategy was based on keywords determined according to the authors' experience in the field, preliminary information on the topic, and the goals of the scientific publication. The search was conducted using the following keywords: a) WoSCC with this rules: industry 5.0 AND engineering AND (education OR training or training); b) industry 5.0 AND.characteristics; c) Some of the publications included in this study were initially gathered as part of literature searches conducted for my previous research projects. These searches were based on different keywords relevant to those studies, and as a result, certain publications may address topics that are slightly outside the current focus but still provide valuable context. Applies to the following keywords: metaverse, augmented reality, virtual reality, simulations. As a result, a list of 1642 publications was compiled.

(3) Inclusion and Exclusion Criteria: Publications were screened based on parameters such as language (only English), document type (articles, conference papers; open access), and publication year (from 2010 to June 2024); research areas (engineering education and research). Some earlier publications related to pedagogical approaches have been included. Although they are from previous years, they are typical of the field of traditional education and are essential for the comparative analysis. As a result, an additional 6 sources before 2000 year were identified, some of which were manually scanned and analyzed. The final number of analyzed and detailed scanned publications are 32.

3. CONTEMPORARY CHALLENGES IN ENGINEERING EDUCATION

The Faculty of Engineering and Technology (FTT), which is primarily concerned with the training of engineering personnel, is actively engaged in addressing the challenges posed by societal and industrial changes. The primary objective is the advancement of professional competencies among prospective engineers. In the context of the Innovative Research on Solar Energy Systems and Their Application in Project-Based Engineering Education project and in collaboration with employers, the competencies required for the successful professional realisation of engineers were analysed, and directions for changes in training were identified with the objective of enhancing the competitiveness of graduates in the labour market.

The adaptation of education to modern conditions encompasses the updating of curricula and the redesign of training programmes, with a shift in focus from predominantly theoretical training to practical skills and the integration of up-to-date and specialised knowledge. It is also crucial to cultivate a T-shaped professional, encompassing not only technical expertise but also social competencies such as team management, effective communication, and conflict resolution. Additionally, developing abilities in research and design, solving intricate production challenges, and other skillsets are vital.

The aforementioned alterations to academic activities will be implemented by the introduction of novel methodologies and the incorporation of interactive technologies into the training of prospective engineering and technical professionals, thereby equipping them with the requisite skills to meet the challenges of Industry 5.0.

The advent of Industry 5.0 is having a profound effect on engineering education, with the introduction of novel approaches and technologies that students must master. The principal impacts that inform our work are as follows:

An increased emphasis is being placed on the development of multidisciplinary skills amongst students. In addition to acquiring technical expertise, it is becoming increasingly important for them to also gain proficiency in creativity, teamwork and collaboration with intelligent systems.

The integration of new technologies: The utilisation of coding cobots, artificial intelligence and the analysis of large data sets have become integral elements of the engineering curriculum at the university level.

A further key area of focus is sustainability. Students are instructed in the design of sustainable systems that reduce waste, utilise renewable energy sources and minimise carbon footprints.

The concept of personalised learning is an important aspect of modern education. The advent of Industry 5.0 has brought with it a new generation of educational technologies that facilitate the customisation of learning pathways in accordance with the specific needs and interests of individual students.

The advent of new technologies inevitably has an impact on higher education. In this context, the new demands on institutions preparing engineering personnel, including FTT, require priority changes in activities and functions, as well as in the competencies of faculty and students. It is not sufficient for education to merely meet the social demands of society; it must also prepare engineers to be competitive in the future that will be shaped by Industry 5.0. The historical record of industrial revolutions demonstrates that institutions that fail to adapt to new paradigms risk losing their competitive advantage (Carayannis, EG, & Morawska-Jancelewicz, J. 2022).

The characteristics of Industry 5.0, in conjunction with technological advancements, necessitate a re-evaluation of educational methodologies and technologies to align them with the emerging demands. In this regard, the team responsible for the project is focusing its efforts on the integration of interactive technologies with the objective of:

The following areas require attention:

1. Active student engagement;
2. Development of learning and research skills, self-assessment;
3. Acquisition of practical competences that link education with real life;
4. Skills for continuous learning in a diverse environment.

The objective of engineering education is to combine human creativity with the precision of robots in order to achieve the goals of Industry 5.0, namely more efficient, sustainable and safe production. This necessitates the presence of engineers who have undergone comprehensive STEM (Science, Technology, Engineering And Math) education and possess expertise in emerging technologies, as well as the emergence of novel professional roles such as robotics manager and human-robot interaction specialist.

The incorporation of virtual technologies into the educational process not only serves to reduce costs but also to create more engaging and dynamic learning environments. The training of engineers in FTT encompasses not only the acquisition of professional skills but also the development of social and flexible competencies. This is achieved through project-based learning methods and the active resolution of real-world industrial problems. It is thus anticipated that students will be adequately prepared to adapt to the requirements of Industry 5.0 and to flourish in the global marketplace.

4. INTEGRATING NEW TECHNOLOGIES AND METHODS IN ENGINEERING EDUCATION

4.1 Implementation of Metaverse Technologies as Virtual Reality (VR), Augmented Reality (AR) and Simulations in The Learning Process

The utilisation of metaverse education technologies has been demonstrated to have a considerable effect on the enhancement of learning outcomes and student engagement. At the Faculty, we are engaged in the active implementation of digital and pedagogical technologies in the field of education. The results of the literature review align with the findings of Yamba-Yugsi M. et al. (2023), which indicate that these technologies facilitate dynamic and engaging learning environments that enhance motivation and promote long-term knowledge retention. Students are able to actively generate content, participate in group projects and access virtual learning resources, which makes the integration of the metaverse into education an extremely beneficial process (Flores-Castañeda, RO et al., 2024). This is of particular importance with regard to the improvement of educational equity and accessibility.

As posited by Yamba-Yugsi et al. (2023), the implementation of gamification within the metaverse has the potential to enhance student motivation, thereby fostering more productive learning environments. In the context of the aforementioned projects, we address issues pertaining to privacy and potential concerns regarding teacher interference in the context of utilising artificial intelligence (AI) (Yamba-Yugsi et al., 2023). It is imperative that educators undergo comprehensive training in order to ensure the successful implementation of these technologies (Pahmi, S. et al., 2023). Moreover, the incorporation of learning theories, such as embodied and experiential learning, can facilitate the creation of effective virtual reality learning environments within the metaverse (Kim, T. et al., 2023).

The metaverse presents a potential solution to the challenges of accessibility in education, particularly for students from underrepresented groups and those with disabilities. The utilisation of augmented and virtual reality facilitates the creation of immersive learning environments that enhance accessibility and interaction while promoting inclusivity (Zhang, CY & Chemnad, K. 2024; Pahmi, S. et al., 2024). As a result of these technological developments, students are able to engage in interactive learning, create materials and work together on a global scale, which encourages creativity and collaboration while ensuring accessibility for people with disabilities (Bernaschina, D. 2023; Flores-Castañeda, RO 2024).

The incorporation of new technologies, including artificial intelligence, cloud computing, and augmented reality, has significantly enhanced the accessibility of education, expanding learning opportunities and preparing students for a digital and continuously evolving world. The metaverse has the potential to transform education by facilitating more inclusive teaching methods, addressing obstacles related to privacy concerns and technological constraints (Meena, SD 2023).

The pervasive implementation of metaverse educational technologies is precipitating substantial alterations in pedagogical approaches and classroom dynamics. As posited by Pahmi, S. et al. (2023) and other researchers, the utilisation of metaverse technologies enhances interactivity, accessibility and engagement within the educational process. This is achieved through the creation of immersive learning environments that are adaptable to different learning styles. As demonstrated by applications such as Meta-STEM (Rachmadtullah et al., 2023), these technologies have the potential to enhance critical thinking and facilitate dynamic and easily accessible learning experiences that combine virtual and physical learning environments.

Nevertheless, integrating the metaverse into the educational process presents a number of challenges, including differences in levels of enthusiasm and concern among educators. This underscores the necessity for comprehensive research, educator training, and broader engagement to fully harness the potential of these technologies while addressing their limitations (Flores-Castañeda, RO et al., 2024).

4.2 The Role of Project-Based and Problem-Oriented Learning Methods

The revised model of engineering education integrates technical expertise with adaptable skills and professional practices. A student-centred approach fosters active learning through knowledge construction and problem-solving, with problem-based learning (PBL) gaining prominence in engineering education (Kolmos, 2009).

Modern engineering education in fields like Automation, Process Control, and Heat and Gas Supply emphasises independent student research and project development, grounded in competency-based and student-centred paradigms. Rooted in Dewey's instrumentalism and constructivism, PBL engages students in solving real problems through hypothesis formation, experimentation, and reflection, linking learning to immediate experiences. Other theorists like Lewin and Piaget further highlight the role of collaboration and cognitive development in this method.

PBL involves interdisciplinary, long-term activities where students plan, execute, and evaluate projects, producing tangible outputs such as prototypes or databases. Studies (ABET, 2001; SARTOR, 2024) affirm the need for such active approaches in engineering education, aligning with accreditation criteria. At FTT, academics and industry professionals collaborate on project-based assignments in automation, computer systems, and heat and gas supply, following phases outlined by Blumenfeld (1991):

1. Refining questions
2. Collecting and analysing data
3. Sharing and discussing ideas
4. Formulating hypotheses and conducting experiments
5. Creating artefacts

6. Summarising findings and presenting them
7. Posing new questions for further research

PBL integrates into Master's and PhD thesis projects, helping students address technical, financial, and human factors in real-world contexts. Teamwork, feedback, and competitive elements foster creativity and innovation while enhancing skills in analysis, synthesis, and decision-making.

Digital tools, such as design software, simulations, and Metaverse environments, are integral to PBL, enabling students to test models and simulate industrial processes. This method nurtures transferable skills like time management, effective communication, and technological proficiency. Faculty roles transition to facilitators, while students take responsibility for project goals and reflective evaluations.

For digital-native learners, PBL's emphasis on real-world relevance, hands-on experience, and prompt feedback boosts engagement. Recommended for advanced study years, PBL enhances metacognitive abilities, cultivates interests, and motivates sustained learning (Lantada A.D. et al., 2013).

4.3 Learning by Doing: The Importance of Internships and Collaboration with Industry

The expectation for engineers to possess knowledge and skills to address modern challenges has prompted engineering schools to prepare graduates capable of implementing innovations. Many graduates face the challenge of entering unfamiliar work environments. Evidence highlights the value of experiential learning, particularly internships, in providing real-world experience (Callewaert, JH 2019; Howell, J. et al. 2019; Van Hemelrijck, I. et al. 2016; Fowinkle, L. 2018).

Collaboration between academia and industry, a key goal of the European Commission's innovation agenda, offers students opportunities to develop essential competencies through internships in relevant companies. An internship is a learning experience in a real work environment aligned with a student's field of study. Programs like cooperative education in the U.S., internships in Germany, and the sandwich system in the U.K. exemplify this approach (Ocampo, ACG et al. 2020).

At FTT, the Student Internship Project, supported by Bulgaria's Ministry of Education and Science, enables practical, industry-focused education for students and doctoral candidates. Collaboration with industrial partners enhances this process, with companies providing internships and mentorships for summer and pre-graduate placements. Full-time students must complete annual 80-hour internships in relevant companies, fostering professional development through hands-on experience.

Internships not only benefit students but also employers and faculty. They help students acquire skills in job searching, self-presentation, and teamwork—crucial for the transition from academia to the professional world (Luperfoy, S. 2013). Interns learn to navigate team dynamics and organisational roles within engineering environments.

Given that students belong to digital-native generations, employers should support their integration by providing clear contexts, mentoring, and guidance on professional behaviours (Ferri-Reed, J., 2012). Millennials thrive when they understand the organisation's structure, goals, and their role within it. Interns also need support in adapting to workplace expectations, boundaries, and career-building behaviours.

Such practices act as "career success accelerators" (UPOP, September 2024), significantly enhancing the career readiness of engineering students specialising in automation, computer science, and energy.

5. PROSPECTS FOR THE DEVELOPMENT OF ENGINEERING EDUCATION IN THE CONTEXT OF INDUSTRY 5.0

The training of future engineers must take into account the principal functions and characteristics of Industry 5.0, which include:

- The bespoke production of highly personalised products, tailored to the specific requirements of the customer.
- The implementation of cobots (collaborative robots) represents a significant advancement in manufacturing technology. These robots are integrated with human ingenuity and creativity, enabling the production of highly personalized products.

- Human empowerment: as AI and robots assume responsibility for routine, repetitive, and potentially dangerous tasks, humans will be free to engage in activities that require unique human capabilities.

- Speed and quality: the implementation of new, accelerated production lines will facilitate the generation of superior quality products, as a consequence of technological innovations and the introduction of more professional human intervention.

- Respect for the environment: the utilisation of renewable energy sources and production chains that are adapted to the economical use of resources, with the objective of reducing emissions and waste, and the creation of more sustainable products.

In the context of engineering professions, the design process represents a fundamental aspect of the work undertaken. Engineering activities are typically associated with the design, implementation, or maintenance of projects, processes, and facilities. As Williams and Williams (1994) observe, the strategy and design of PBL (problem-solving learning) in engineering education bear a striking resemblance to the problem-solving process. The authors synthesise the analogous characteristics of these two approaches in several aspects, including the following:

- The differing phases of project work/problem solving.

- The process commences with the identification of a problem or situation that serves to guide the learning context.

- In the initial stages of the process, students are responsible for initiating observations and conducting investigations into the problem at hand. These activities serve as key indicators of the progress of learning.

- The attainment of success is contingent upon the demonstration of a high level of initiative, motivation and organisational skills.

- Reflection is an important aspect of both models, with students encouraged to evaluate their performance.

- Group work is a key component of the approach, facilitating the development of a range of skills, including social skills, planning, communication, and leadership.

- PBL is a suitable approach for long-term projects, but it can also be used for shorter periods of time.

- The option of selecting an outcome that aligns with their interests, following an appropriate research phase.

It is imperative that these perspectives be incorporated into engineering education in order to adequately prepare engineers for the advent of the new industrial era, while ensuring their ability to cope with the novel technological and social demands of Industry 5.0.

6. CONCLUSION

The advent of Industry 5.0 has brought about significant shifts in the landscape of engineering education, necessitating a reorientation of learning approaches to align with the evolving demands of technology and market dynamics. Applied methods, such as project-based learning (PBL) and internships in industrial environments, have been demonstrated to provide effective solutions for equipping students with the requisite skills to navigate the challenges of the future industrial environment. By fostering active collaboration between universities and industry, the opportunity arises for students to acquire the essential practical skills required for a successful career. It is of significant importance to note that the integration of innovation, in addition to the development of social and leadership skills, plays a pivotal role in the learning and preparation process of students. It is imperative that future developments focus on enhancing these methodologies through the integration of novel approaches and technologies, thereby ensuring optimal preparation for the evolving industrial landscape. It is clear that educational institutions will continue to play a pivotal role in equipping engineers with the requisite skills to thrive in the era of Industry 5.0. To this end, they must offer training that effectively integrates theoretical knowledge with practical experience, ensuring adaptability to the rapidly evolving technological and industrial landscape.

ACKNOWLEDGEMENT

The paper is part of the research project: “Innovative Research on Solar Energy Systems and Their Application in Project-Based Engineering Education” as the frame of Project No. BG-RRP-2.004-0006-C02 "Development of research and innovation at Trakia University in service of health and sustainable well-being".

REFERENCES

ABET, Criteria for Accrediting Engineering Programs. Engineering Accreditation Commission of the Accreditation Board of Engineering and Technology, Baltimore, Maryland, (2001). Available on-line at http://www.abet.org/criteria.html

Bernaschina, D. (2023). Art gamification (and digital/media arts) for special school: New thinking shifts for inclusive metaverse’s engineering. https://doi.org/10.54517/m.v4i2.2274

Blumenfeld, P. C., Soloway, E., Marx, R. W., Krajcik, J. S., Guzdial, M., & Palincsar, A. (1991) Motivating project-based learning: Sustaining the doing, supporting the learning. Educational Psychologist, Vol. 26, No. 3-4, 1991, 369-398.

Breque, M., De Nul, L., & Petridis, A. (2021). Industry 5.0, towards a sustainable, human-centric and resilient European industry. European Commission, Directorate-General for Research and Innovation.

Callewaert, J. H. (2019, June). Measuring the impact of experiential learning. Presented at the 2019 ASEE Annual Conference & Exposition. https://peer.asee.org/measuring-the-impact-of-experiential-learning

Carayannis, E. G., & Morawska-Jancelewicz, J. (2022). The futures of Europe: Society 5.0 and Industry 5.0 as driving forces of future universities. Journal of the Knowledge Economy, 13(4), 3445-3471. https://doi.org/10.1007/s13132-021-00854-2

de Los Rios, I., Cazorla, A., Díaz-Puente, J. M., & Yagüe, J. L. (2010). Project–based learning in engineering higher education: two decades of teaching competences in real environments. Procedia-Social and Behavioral Sciences, 2(2), 1368-1378.

Dewey, John. 2024, Democracy and Education: An Introduction to the Philosophy of Education. Columbia University Press.,

Ferri-Reed, J. (2012, April). Three ways leaders can help millennials succeed. The Journal for Quality and Participation, 35(2), 18–19.

Flores-Castañeda, R. O., Olaya-Cotera, S., & Iparraguirre-Villanueva, O. (2024). Benefits of metaverse application in education: A systematic review. International Journal of Engineering Pedagogy (iJEP). https://doi.org/10.3991/ijep.v14i1.42421

Fowinkle, L. (2018, August). Internship opportunities for millennial students. Presented at the 2018 ASEE Conferences - Conference for Industry and Education Collaboration. https://peer.asee.org/internship-opportunities-for-millennial-students

Fukuyama, M. (2018). Society 5.0: Aiming for a new human-centered society. Japan Spotlight, 1, 47–50

Howell, J., Ferekides, C. S., Moreno, W. A., Weller, T., & Takshi, A. (2019, June). Preparing engineering students for their profession: A novel curricular approach. Presented at the 2019 ASEE Annual Conference & Exposition. https://peer.asee.org/preparing-engineering-students-for-their-profession-a-novel-curricular-approach

Kim, T., Planey, J., & Lindgren, R. (2023). Theory-driven design in metaverse virtual reality learning environments: Two illustrative cases. IEEE Transactions on Learning Technologies. https://doi.org/10.1109/tlt.2023.3307211

Koehn, E., (1999) ABET program criteria for educating engineering students. International Conference on Engineering Education, ICEE'99, Paper 413, (1999). Available on-line at http://www.fs.vsb.cz/akce/1999/ICEE99/Proceedings/papers/413/413.htm

Lantada A. D., Morgado P. L., Munoz-Guijosa J. M., Sanz J. L. M., De la Guerra E., Otero J. E., Tanarro E. C., (2013) Towards Successful Project-Based Teaching-Learning Experiences in Engineering Education, International Journal of Engineering Education Vol 29, N 2, pp 1-15

Lewin, K. (1946). Action research and minority problems. Journal of social issues, 2(4), 34-46.

Luperfoy, S. (2013). An overview of MIT’s undergraduate practice opportunities program (UPOP). In Proceedings of the 2013 ASQ Advancing the STEM Agenda Conference, Grand Rapids, MI. http://rube.asq.org/edu/2013/04/career-development/

Meena, S. D., Mithesh, G. S. S., Panyam, R., Chowdary, M. S., Sadhu, V. S., & Sheela, J. (2023, June). Advancing education through metaverse: Components, applications, challenges, case studies and open issues. In 2023 International Conference on Sustainable Computing and Smart Systems (ICSCSS) (pp. 880-889). IEEE.

Morawska-Jancelewicz, J. (2021). The Role of Universities in Social Innovation Within Quadruple/Quintuple Helix Model: Practical Implications from Polish Experience. Journal of the Knowledge Economy. https://doi.org/10.1007/s13132-021-00804-y

Ocampo, A. C. G., Reyes, M. L., Chen, Y., Restubog, S. L. D., Chih, Y.-Y., Chua-Garcia, L., & Guan, P. (2020). The role of internship participation and conscientiousness in developing career adaptability: A five-wave growth mixture model analysis. Journal of Vocational Behavior, 120, 103426. https://doi.org/10.1016/j.jvb.2020.103426

Pahmi, S., Pradiftha, A. J., & Supriyadi, E. (2023). Exploring metaverse integration in education: A case study on vocational school teachers. Jurnal BELAINDIKA (Pembelajaran dan Inovasi Pendidikan). https://doi.org/10.52005/belaindika.v5i3.125

Piaget, Jean (1973). To understand is to invent: the future of education. New York: Penguin Books. Edited by Jean Piaget; ISBN: 0140043780 0670720348

Rachmadtullah, R., Setiawan, B., Jati, A., Wasesa, A., & Wicaksono, J. W. (2023). The utilization of metaverse technology applications based on science, technology, engineering and mathematics (Meta-STEM) to improve critical thinking skills. Journal of Education and E-Learning Research. https://doi.org/10.20448/jeelr.v10i4.5203

SARTOR, Standards and Routes to Registration: SARTOR (3rd ed), (2000). On-line from http://www.engc.org.uk/registration/sartor.asp

UPOP Undergraduate Practice Opportunities Program. (n.d.). About UPOP. Massachusetts Institute of Technology. http://upop.mit.edu/about/ Accessed at Sept. 2024

Van Hemelrijck, I., Londers, E., Burman, M., Suttels, C., & Berbers, Y. (2016, September 1). Enhancing employability: Internships and entrepreneurship at the Faculty of Engineering Science at KU Leuven.

Williams, A. & Williams, P.J., Problem based learning: An approach to teaching technology. In Ostwald, M. & Kingsland, A. (Eds.). Research and development in Problem Based Learning, Vol. 2, 1994: Reflection and Consolidation. Australian Problem Based Learning Network, University of Newcastle, NSW. 355-367, (1994).

Yamba-Yugsi, M., Contreras-Espinosa, R. S., Maldonado-Mahauad, J., & Eguia Gomez, J. L. (2023). Examining the opportunities of the metaverse and gamification in education: Benefits and constraints. https://doi.org/10.18817/vjshr.v2i2.32

Zhang, C. Y., & Chemnad, K. (2024). Is the metaverse accessible? An expert opinion. https://doi.org/10.54455/mcn2507.

DESIGNING AN ONLINE TRAINING MODULE TO DEVELOP VIRTUAL AND BLENDED INTERNATIONAL MODALITIES IN HIGHER EDUCATION

Alice Barana[1], Vasiliki Eirini Chatzea[2], Kelly Henao[3], Ania Maria Hildebrandt[4], Marina Marchisio Conte[1], Daniel Samoilovich[3], Georgios Triantafyllidis[4] and Nikolas Vidakis[2]
[1]Department of Molecular Biotechnology and Health Sciences, University of Turin, Piazza Nizza 44, 10153 Torino, Italy
[2]Department of Electrical & Computer Engineering, Hellenic Mediterranean University, Estavromenos, 71410 Heraklion, Greece
[3]Columbus Association, 1 rue Moillis 75015 Paris, France
[4]Department of Architecture, Design and Media Technology, Aalborg University, A. C. Meyers Vænge 152450 Copenhagen, Denmark

ABSTRACT

Virtual and blended international collaboration activities, including Collaborative Online International Learning and Blended Intensive Programmes, offer inclusive and sustainable alternatives to traditional mobility programmes. Effective training programmes for teachers and administrative staff are indispensable to enhance the higher education institutions' capability to implement similar activities. This paper introduces an online training module aimed at providing higher education teachers and staff with competencies to implement virtual and blended modalities of international collaboration. The module is designed according to the principles of the Self-Determination Theory and the Analysis, Design, Development, Implementation and Evaluation (ADDIE) model. The paper explores whether the design of the module is effective in creating a valuable learning experience and what its strengths and areas for improvement are. Results were derived from 150 responses to the final survey questions completed by participants who completed the online training module, analysed qualitatively and quantitatively. Findings show that the autonomy, structure, and involvement support were perceived as effective in achieving the desired learning outcomes. The results offer valuable insights into the design of training modules for higher education staff to develop international collaboration modalities.

KEYWORDS

ADDIE Model, Blended International Collaboration, Higher Education, Professional Development, Self-Determination Theory, Training Module, Virtual International Collaboration

1. INTRODUCTION

Internationalisation in higher education has emerged as a pivotal focus for institutions worldwide, reflecting the growing importance of integrating global perspectives into academic experiences. Defined by Knight (2008) as "the process of integrating an international, intercultural, or global dimension into the purpose, functions, and delivery of post-secondary education," this trend emphasises creating opportunities for students to engage with diverse cultures and ideas (Vahed and Rodriguez, 2021). Besides traditional physical mobility programmes, more inclusive and sustainable mobility forms have recently been introduced: among them, virtual and blended international collaboration modalities stand out. They are academic modalities that involve teachers and students from at least two different countries participating in collaborative academic activities (Garcés and O'Dowd, 2021; Perfölz and López-Varela, 2022). We refer to them as virtual international collaboration activities when they are shaped exclusively through online platforms and communication tools. The most famous form is Collaborative Online International Learning (COIL), where students engage in collaborative projects in a digital learning environment without leaving their home institutions (Hackett et al., 2024). We refer to them as blended international collaboration activities when they combine virtual interactions with face-to-face activities. A recent form of blended international collaboration activity is the Blended Intensive Programme (BIP), promoted by the EU Erasmus+ Programme (European Commission, 2023).

Examples of BIPs are described in a previous publication by the authors (Barana *et al.*, 2024). Designing and implementing virtual and blended collaboration modalities requires noticeable effort and collaboration by higher education teachers and staff. Based on interviews with experts, Barana and Marchisio Conte (2024) identified eight drivers for the implementation of similar international formats: among them, enhancing collaboration opportunities, training teachers and staff members, and activating practice communities stood out. There is little research in the literature on teacher training and faculty development in higher education on international activities and virtual mobility. According to O'Dowd and Dooly (2022), COIL activities are formative not only for students but also for teachers. Buchem et al. (2018) describes a learning hub aimed to provide students and teachers with competences to tackle virtual mobility experiences. They suggest that online courses can be an optimal format for training university staff since they offer flexibility. Still, there is a need for studies about the engagement of higher education staff in training programmes about the design of virtual or blended modalities of international collaboration.

The INVITE Erasmus+ Project aims to develop teaching and learning competencies for designing and implementing new virtual and blended modalities of international collaboration in European higher education institutions. The INVITE consortium, composed of Aalborg University (Denmark), Columbus Association (France), Hellenic Mediterranean University (Greece), and University of Turin (Italy), organised an online training module for teachers and institutional staff to prepare them to design and implement activities such as COILs and BIPs. This paper aims to present and discuss the structure of the training programme and show the effectiveness of the proposed activities in achieving their goals, according to the participants' perspectives. The paper is structured as follows: section 2 presents the theoretical framework on which the training module is built, namely, Self-Determination Theory, the Analysis, Design, Development, Implementation, Evaluation (ADDIE) model, and the INVITE Learning Design Framework. Section 3 presents the training module, its structures and the kinds of activities included. Section 4 provides details about the research method. In Section 5, the results of this study are presented and discussed. Lastly, Section 6 draws the conclusions of the study.

2. THEORETICAL FRAMEWORK

Self-determination Theory (SDT) is a theory of motivation and human development often used in the design of blended and virtual learning environments (Chen and Jang, 2010; Chiu, 2022). It proposes that all individuals have three innate psychological needs: the need for autonomy, the need for relatedness, and the need for competence. Autonomy is the need to feel in control of one's own life and to make one's own choices. Relatedness is the need to feel connected to others and to experience a sense of belonging. Competence is the need to feel capable of achieving one's goals and mastering new skills (Chen and Jang, 2010). SDT suggests that when these three needs are satisfied, individuals are more likely to be motivated, engaged, and successful in their endeavours. Conversely, when these needs are not satisfied, individuals are more likely to experience amotivation, disengagement, and failure (Chen and Jang, 2010). Teacher support influences students' motivation and engagement in online and blended learning. SDT distinguishes three dimensions of teacher support (Chiu, 2022): autonomy support, which enhances students' feeling of being in charge of their goals and behaviour; structure support, which enhances students' ability to accomplish tasks and experience mastery; and involvement support, which enhances students' relatedness and the sense of social belonging. Autonomy-supportive online learning environments will consider student perspectives, allow for choices around learning, give a rationale when choice is constrained, avoid controlling language, and reduce unnecessary stress and demands on the learners. The structure involves communicating clear expectations concerning student behaviour; in online learning, it takes the form of designing well-structured activities with demarcated boundaries, providing strong guidance and competence-relevant feedback, and delivering effective materials. Involvement pertains to the types of behaviour shown by teachers, including warmth, affection, and enjoyment, which have been shown to encourage a close and caring teacher-student relationship. In online learning, it can be carried out through collaborative learning and motivational support (Chiu, 2022).

The ADDIE model is a widely used framework for designing and developing online and blended courses, often used in digital education (Spatioti, Kazanidis and Pange, 2022). It includes five phases: Analysis, Design, Development, Implementation, and Evaluation (Peterson, 2003). These phases are used to systematically and cyclically approach instructional design, allowing for continuous improvement and refinement of instructional materials over time. The INVITE project's consortium, based on SDT and the ADDIE model, proposed a

Learning Design Framework (LDF) for designing and developing virtual or blended international collaboration activities. The LDF is based on six phases, which are in line with the ADDIE model, with the addition of an introduction phase. The six phases are the following: (0) Preparation phase: it includes the project ideation and partner identification; (1) Analysis phase: this phase includes assessing the international participants' needs and analysing the tasks by identifying learning objectives and outcomes. During this phase, the international and intercultural added value of the activity should be identified; (2) Design phase: this phase involves choosing active learning methodologies in accordance with SDT and selecting digital platforms and tools; (3) Development phase: it consists of creating culturally sensitive and relevant learning materials, selecting open educational resources, and integrating with digital technologies, with a focus on active learning; (4) Implementation phase: it includes mentorship, promoting intercultural collaboration, and monitoring students' progress; (5) Evaluation phase: it includes designing formative and summative assessment forms, collecting data about learning achievements and feedback on the activity, and adjusting accordingly.

3. THE INVITE TRAINING MODULE

The INVITE training module was designed based on the SDT and the ADDIE model. The primary goal of the module is to provide higher education teachers and staff with the competences to design and develop blended and virtual international collaboration activities in line with the INVITE LDF. The target of the module is composed of two distinct groups, which we call "Teachers" and "Staff". The teachers' group included all those interested in developing digital international teaching and learning activities. The staff group included all those interested in creating international bridges among institutions and supporting teachers and/or students in developing or implementing digital international activities. The learning outcomes of the module were, for teachers: identifying student needs, integrating active learning, using digital tools, diagnosing challenges, and assessing learning; formulating objectives, planning activities, fostering intercultural collaboration, utilising technology, and evaluating outcomes; adopting context-aware, intercultural strategies, choosing effective tools, and reflecting on teaching practices. For Staff: understanding activity design, active learning challenges, digital tools, student difficulties, and assessment methods; supporting teachers and students in planning, implementing, and utilising digital tools for international activities; addressing challenges; mentoring teachers, proposing improvements; and critically reflecting on practices.

The training module was fully online, self-paced, and asynchronous, and it was delivered through an online course hosted on the University of Turin's Moodle platform. It opened in April and closed in October 2024, lasting six months. The course was conceived as an interactive guide to designing virtual or blended activities of international collaboration, like COILs or BIPs, according to the INVITE LDF framework. The course included two paths, one for teachers and one for staff. The two paths shared the learning materials but differentiated in the tasks. Once reached the end of one path, participants achieved a Moodle badge and could download a certificate of attendance. The course's main content has a modular structure, with six sections, one for each of the six phases of the LDF. The access to a section was conditioned to completing the previous one. In each of the sections, participants could find:

- Two reflection questionnaires (one for teachers and one for staff) aimed at introducing the phase and making participants reflect on their experiences in that part of the process.
- A brief introductory video which highlights the main features of the phase.
- One or two slideshows on the main steps of each phase.
- A forum that participants could use to share doubts and reflections on the content.
- Additional resources and external links to deepen the contents.
- Two case studies, one about a virtual activity (a COIL) and one about a blended activity (a BIP) of international collaboration, which shows the theory applied to real cases.
- A quiz with automatically graded questions about the content.
- Two final tasks (one for teachers and one for staff) where they were asked to design a virtual or blended international activity (for teachers) or to identify their potential role in supporting the development of such activities (for staff), thus putting into practice what they learnt in the section. The tasks included a self-assessment form.

In the preparation phase, teachers could share a draft idea for an activity to create, and the other participants (including staff) could contact them to collaborate on developing the activity. The tasks were mainly conceived as individual work looking to achieve learning outcomes and foundational understanding; however, they could be completed collaboratively. The submissions were shared with all participants so that everyone could get inspiration from the other activities for their work. The ADDIE model and the SDT are both the training module's content and basis since they were used to develop and structure it. The activities were carefully designed to provide participants with the three dimensions of support (Chiu, 2022). Autonomy is fostered through the self-paced modality, the possibility of choosing the path, and the provision of materials to explore. Structure is fostered through the fixed structure of the sections and clear and concise materials. Involvement is fostered through active tasks, automatic assessment, and self-assessment, the possibility of collaboration, and forum discussions. The training module also included an initial and a final survey for all participants.

4. RESEARCH METHOD

The study aims to answer the following research questions (RQ): (RQ1) Were the online training module's autonomy, structure, and involvement support effective in creating a valuable learning experience? (RQ2) According to participants, what were the module's strengths and areas for improvement in terms of autonomy, structure, and involvement support?

To address the RQs, the answers to the final survey of the participants who completed the training module were collected and analysed. Of the 163 participants who completed the module and received a badge, 143 accepted that their survey answers were used for research purposes. The sample was then restricted to the answers of these participants. Considering that 7 participants followed both paths and completed the survey twice, one per path, the sample was composed of 150 answers, of which 108 were given by participants who followed the path for teachers and 42 by those who followed the path for staff. Both the answers to the questionnaires filled by participants who followed both paths were included since the paths were slightly different. The final survey consisted of 19 questions with a total of 80 items. Only the 18 items listed in Table 1 were considered for this study.

Table 1. Items of the final survey used in the study

Item	Question	Item text	Answers
Q1a	How much do you agree with the following statements?	This experience was relevant to my career and/or professional development.	1-5 scale (5=to a great extent)
Q1b		The module provided me with ideas that could be used in my teaching/professional activity.	1-5 scale (5=to a great extent)
Q1c		The course was an opportunity for personal enrichment.	1-5 scale (5=to a great extent)
Q1d		Participating in this training was a good investment of my time.	1-5 scale (5=to a great extent)
Q1e		The overall training experience was adequately interactive/engaging.	1-5 scale (5=to a great extent)
Q1f		I took advantage of the international interaction and collaboration with teachers and staff from other countries/institutions.	1-5 scale (5=to a great extent)
Q2	Did you achieve the learning outcomes of this module?		In an 80-100%/In a 50-70%/In a 30-50%/In a 10-20%/The activities were not consistent with the learning outcomes.
Q5a	To what extent do you think that the following methodologies were effective in helping you fulfil the module's outcomes?	Exploration of videos and resources	1-5 scale (5=to a great extent)
Q5b		Case study and application	1-5 scale (5=to a great extent)
Q5c		Learning materials and activities	1-5 scale (5=to a great extent)
Q5d		Project-based learning	1-5 scale (5=to a great extent)
Q5e		Interaction with other participants	1-5 scale (5=to a great extent)
Q5f		Collaboration with other participants	1-5 scale (5=to a great extent)
Q5g		Self-reflection	1-5 scale (5=to a great extent)
Q5h		Self-assessment	1-5 scale (5=to a great extent)
Q5i		Automatic assessment	1-5 scale (5=to a great extent)
Q17	What did you like the most about this experience?		Open answer
Q18	What frustrated you about the training module?		Open answer

To address the impact of autonomy, structure, and involvement (RQ1), the answers to items Q5a-i were considered: Q5a was related to autonomy support; Q5b, Q5c, and Q5d referred to structure support; Q5e, Q5f, Q5g, Q5h, and Q5i referred to involvement support. For structure and involvement support and each participant, the average of the answers to the items related to the support dimension was computed. This way, indexes of the effectiveness of the three support dimensions were created. Descriptive statistics were then computed, and the ANOVA test was run to verify the differences among the two groups (teachers and staff). Moreover, the involvement index was cross-checked with items Q1e and Q1f to verify if the interaction with others influenced the effectiveness of involvement support. Then, the autonomy, structure, and involvement support indexes were cross-checked with the participants' self-assessment rates about the achievement of the course learning outcomes, extracted from the answers to Q2. The answers were coded through numbers from 5 to 1, where 5 corresponds to the answer "In an 80-100%" and 1 to "The activities were not consistent with the learning outcomes" to have a numeric self-assessment rating of the achievement of the course learning outcomes. Pearson's correlation coefficients between this variable and the three indexes of the support dimensions were computed to understand if the support dimensions were correlated with the achievement of learning outcomes. Lastly, the answers to items Q1a-d from the final survey were examined to refine the analysis. They were used to create an index of appreciation of the module in relation to personal and professional development. The appreciation index was correlated with the autonomy, structure, and involvement support indexes to investigate if the perception of the effectiveness of support influenced the appreciation of the learning experience.

To investigate the strengths and weaknesses of the training module (RQ2), the open-ended items Q17 and Q18 were analysed. All answers were carefully read and labelled with "S", "A", or "I" if they referred to aspects of the structure support, autonomy support, and involvement support. Answers could be characterised with two or three labels if two or three dimensions of support were mentioned. The percentages of occurrence of the three support dimensions were then computed, and exemplifying responses were selected.

5. RESULTS

To address RQ1, descriptive statistics of the indexes of perceived effectiveness of the three support dimensions were computed. The results are listed in Table 2.

Table 2. Statistics of the items. The answers were given on a scale from 1 to 5, where 5 is the highest agreement value

Statistics	Autonomy	Structure	Involvement
Mean	4.40	4.27	3.89
Median	5	4.33	3.80
Standard deviation	0.74	0.60	0.72

The results show that all three dimensions of support included in the INVITE training module were considered effective in achieving the learning outcomes. The ANOVA test did not show any significant differences between the answers given by the teacher and the staff groups, meaning that the same support was perceived in both paths. The autonomy support, fostered through the possibility of autonomously exploring the learning materials in a self-paced way, was particularly appreciated by higher education teachers and staff, who usually have little time to dedicate to professional development due to many other commitments. At the same time, the appreciation of involvement structure is slightly lower than that of the other two dimensions, while it remains considerable. The reason is that many participants did not take the opportunity to interact with others and preferred to work autonomously. Indeed, 58% of participants gave a negative or neutral answer to item Q1f, "I took advantage of the international interaction and collaboration with teachers and staff from other countries/institutions". The analysis of the Pearson coefficient between the index of involvement and the participants' answers to item Q1f shows that the participants' perception of the effectiveness of the involvement support in achieving the course outcomes is aligned with their level of interaction with other participants in the course. The value of the Pearson coefficient is 0.499, with a p-value <0.001. This result indicates a good level of correlation between the two variables. However, 80% agreed or strongly agreed with item Q1e, "The overall training experience was adequately interactive/engaging". This means that involvement support was activated even if the level of interaction among the participants was not so high: in fact, active learning methodologies, such as self-assessment, self-reflection, and automatic assessment, contributed to its effect.

Almost all the participants declared that they had reached at least 50% of the learning outcomes through the course activities. In particular, out of the 150 participants, 67.3% rated to have achieved 80% to 100% of the learning outcomes, and 30% rated to have achieved 50% to 70%. Only 3 participants (2%) said to have reached 20% to 40%, and 1 participant (0.7%) 30% or below. No participants selected the answer "The activities were not consistent with the learning outcomes". These results indicate that the activities included in the training module allowed participants to achieve the learning outcomes. The participants' answers were translated into numbers from 1 to 5, where 5 is the highest achievement, and correlated with the indexes of perception of support. The Pearson coefficients obtained were 0.418 (p-value: <0.001) for autonomy, 0.411 (p-value: <0.001) for structure support, and 0.315 (p-value: <0.001) for involvement. These values indicate moderate to good levels of correlation between the perception of support and the achievement of learning outcomes. They show that the methodologies used in the online activities provided support that facilitated the achievement of learning outcomes.

Lastly, items Q1a-d were analysed to investigate the module's appreciation. Table 3 shows the percentage of answers to the four items and the statistics of the appreciation index, built by computing, for each participant, the mean of the answers to the four items. The answers are very high: participating in the module was considered a good investment of time and an occasion of personal and professional enrichment. For all items, neutral answers are below 10%, and there are no or hardly any negative responses. The appreciation index is very high, too, with mean and median equal to 4.5 on a scale from 1 to 5 and with a small standard deviation, indicating that the index values are concentrated between 4 and 5.

Table 3. Statistics of the appreciation items. The answers were given on a scale from 1 to 5, where 5 is the highest agreement value

Statistics	Q1a	Q1b	Q1c	Q1d	Appreciation
Mean	4.38	4.58	4.62	4.41	4.50
Median	4	5	5	4.5	4.5
Standard deviation	0.65	0.62	0.67	0.66	0.51
Percentage of 5	47.3%	63.8%	70.7%	50.0%	
Percentage of 4	43.3%	30.9%	22.0%	40.7%	
Percentage of 3	9.3%	4.7%	6.7%	9.3%	
Percentage of 2	0%	0.7%	0.7%	0%	
Percentage of 1	0%	0%	0%	0%	

The appreciation index was correlated with the indexes of perception of the effectiveness of autonomy, structure, and involvement support. Pearson's coefficients are statistically significant ($p<0.001$ in all three cases): 0.607 for structure, 0.461 for involvement, and 0.511 for autonomy. They show a moderate to high level of correlation. This result indicates that the more participants felt supported in structure, involvement, and autonomy, the more they appreciated the learning path, which thus was considered valuable.

To address RQ2, the participants' responses to Q17 and Q18 were qualitatively analysed. In Q17, among the most appreciated aspects of the training module, 71 participants (47.3%) referred to the structure support dimension, 21 participants (14%) referred to the autonomy support dimension, and 50 participants (33.3%) referred to the involvement dimension. 20% of answers to Q17 did not mention any aspects related to the support dimension, but other aspects related to their personal experience, such as learning new things, or were too general (e.g., "*everything*"). Comments on the structure support included the module's organisation, which reflected the content, the well-focused materials, rich examples, and clear explanations. Examples of answers to this question that mention the structure support are as follows: "*I liked the structure: it accompanies you in all steps, reflective questions and tasks foster creativity.*"; "*The quality and the variety of the instructional and supplementary materials. The tasks were small, affordable and connected to each other, so that they are relevant but not cumbersome.*" Positive comments on the autonomy support mainly referred to the asynchronous and flexible format that allowed participants to complete the module at their own pace. Examples of answers in this direction are: "*The asynchronous dimension of the class, which I suppose it helped most of us work at our own pace.*"; "*The flexibility of the online format, which gave me the freedom to manage my time while still participating actively in discussions and group projects.*" Strengths referring to the involvement dimension mainly mentioned the possibility of interacting with participants from other countries and institutions and the interactive tasks and activities which pushed participants to put into practice what they learnt. Examples of answers are: "*It was very interesting to have this learning experience in an international framework. I read about the concerns of others and thought about my own and various solutions. I browsed other project ideas/titles and found everything interesting and novel because the content surpassed community barriers and country/teaching system barriers*."; "*The possibility to collaborate with peers and colleagues in projecting a BIP on a topic very close to the one I teach in my courses, which rendered this experience very useful.*"; "*I like the quizzes since I had a chance to see if I really grasped the meaning of the intervention*."

Q18 provided us with insights into the improvement areas of the design of the training module according to the participants. Out of the 150 answers collected, 33 (22%) mentioned the structure support, 8 (5.3) mentioned the autonomy support, and 26 (17.3%) the involvement support. 86 answers (56.3%) did not mention any aspects related to support. Still, they said that nothing frustrated them or indicated other aspects related to their personal experiences, such as having too little time to dedicate to the module. Comments related to structure support mainly mentioned an excessive quantity of materials, which, in some cases, resulted in being repetitive. In many cases, similar comments refer to the additional materials or to eligible activities (such as posting in the forum), which were not mandatory to complete the course: probably, the distinction between mandatory and eligible activities was not clear. In some cases, participants expressed their preference for videos instead of slideshows to read. In contrast, others preferred the slideshows since they allowed them to move through the pages autonomously. Examples of answers mentioning the structure support are: "*I felt frustrated by the repeated prompts at the beginning of each new module asking for my personal experience, as they disrupted the flow of learning. While I understand the importance of reflection, a more streamlined approach could have allowed for deeper engagement with the content without constant interruptions*."; "*There was too much material to read, and the external resources were too long as well.*" Comments related to autonomy support mainly referred to the restrictions on access to activities based on the completion of previous ones and the impossibility of downloading the slideshows. Examples are: "*Sometimes, not being able to begin a new phase because of the condition imposed to finish all the activities of the previous stage*."; "*The fact that I could not download slides and videos provided on the platform. This could be very useful for teachers*." Comments related to involvement support mainly referred to the lack of synchronous sessions, which resulted in a lack of perception of human presence and little interaction between participants. This was due to the asynchronous format, which was appreciated as a source of autonomy support. Examples of answers are: "*I missed a part of synchronous interactions with the other participants*." and "*The low interaction in the forums*."

6. CONCLUSION

This study aimed to present the design of the INVITE training module, which is based on the ADDIE model and the SDT, and investigate its effectiveness in helping participants achieve learning outcomes. The data collected and analysed allowed us to answer the two research questions. Regarding RQ1 (Were the online training module's autonomy, structure, and involvement support effective in creating a valuable learning experience?), the quantitative and qualitative evidence showed that autonomy, structure, and involvement support were appreciated by participants, even if a relevant percentage did not avail themselves of the possibility of interaction with others, and that the perception of effectiveness of the three dimensions of support was positively correlated with the achievement of learning outcomes and with the appreciation of the training module as a valuable learning experience. In the various analyses, the statistics related to structure and autonomy support are slightly better than those related to involvement support, probably due to the fact that many participants did not actively interact with others. In designing the course, the choice was made to favour the self-paced and asynchronous mode over the collaborative mode, which would have necessitated a timetabling of the tasks and reduced the possibility of university teachers participating. Regarding RQ2 (According to participants, what were the module's strengths and areas for improvement in terms of autonomy, structure, and involvement support?), participants appreciated the asynchronous self-paced modality (autonomy support); the quality and variety of materials and the guidance provided by the structure (structure support); the possibility of interacting with colleagues worldwide and the active-learning approach (involvement support). Areas of improvement, based on comments by participants, are the presence of too rigid restrictions on accessing materials and the impossibility of downloading some materials, which hindered autonomy, lack of clarity in the distinction between compulsory and non-compulsory activities, which hindered structure support, and the low level of interaction, which hindered involvement. The INVITE consortium plans to revise the training module's materials and structure, considering the strengths and weaknesses identified, and transform it into an open online course. This study's main limitations include the fact that the data used are based on self-assessment, and the sample is not particularly wide. More refined analysis will be repeated using more reliable data from participants' activities and cross-checking them with other data. Moreover, a follow-up survey will be launched to investigate how the knowledge gained through the online module was used to design and implement virtual or blended international collaboration activities. This study can offer relevant insights to higher education institutions that desire to train teachers and staff to develop international collaboration activities, whose diffusion is increasingly relevant in the higher education landscape.

ACKNOWLEDGEMENT

The research is connected with the Erasmus+ Programme 2021-2027 Cooperation Partnerships Project "Developing Competencies for New Virtual and Blended Modalities of International Collaboration" (INVITE) n. 2021-1-DK01-KA220-HED-000031145.

REFERENCES

Barana, A. et al., (2024). Unpacking the three spheres of interest in a Blended Intensive Programme: Collaborative Learning, Blended Learning and Internationalisation. *Proceedings of the 21st International Conference on Cognition and Exploratory learning in the digital age*, IADIS Press, pp. 43-50. https://doi.org/10.33965/CELDA2024_202408L006.

Barana, A. and Marchisio Conte, M., (2024). Eight Sustainable Practices for Digital Activity Development: Drivers and Barriers in International Higher Education Collaboration. *In Computer*, Vol. 57, No. 3, pp. 117–122. https://doi.org/10.1109/MC.2023.3344236.

Buchem, I. et al., (2018). Designing a Collaborative Learning Hub for Virtual Mobility Skills - Insights from the European Project Open Virtual Mobility. In: Zaphiris, P., Ioannou, A. (eds) *Learning and Collaboration Technologies. Design, Development and Technological Innovation. LCT 2018*. Lecture Notes in Computer Science, Vol. 10924. Springer, Cham. https://doi.org/10.1007/978-3-319-91743-6_27

Chen, K.-C. and Jang, S.-J., (2010). Motivation in online learning: Testing a model of self-determination theory. *In Computers in Human Behavior*, Vol. 26, No. 4, pp. 741–752. https://doi.org/10.1016/j.chb.2010.01.011.

Chiu, T.K.F., (2022). Applying the self-determination theory (SDT) to explain student engagement in online learning during the COVID-19 pandemic. *In Journal of Research on Technology in Education*, Vol. 54(sup1), pp. S14–S30. https://doi.org/10.1080/15391523.2021.1891998.

European Commission, (2023). *Erasmus+ Programme Guide 2024*. Available at: https://erasmus-plus.ec.europa.eu/programme-guide/erasmusplus-programme-guide.

Garcés, P. and O'Dowd, R., (2021). Upscaling Virtual Exchange in University Education: Moving From Innovative Classroom Practice to Regional Governmental Policy. *In Journal of Studies in International Education*, Vol. 25, No. 3, pp. 283–300. https://doi.org/10.1177/1028315320932323.

Hackett, S. et al., (2024). Defining Collaborative Online International Learning (COIL) and Distinguishing it from Virtual Exchange. *In TechTrends*, Vol. 68, No. 6, pp. 1078–1094. https://doi.org/10.1007/s11528-024-01000-w.

Knight, J., (2008). *Higher Education in Turmoil: The Changing World of Internationalization*. Rotterdam Taipei: Sense Publishers. https://doi.org/10.1163/9789087905224.

O'Dowd, R. and Dooly, M., (2022). Exploring teachers' professional development through participation in virtual exchange. *In ReCALL*, Vol. 34, No. 1, pp. 21–36. https://doi.org/10.1017/S0958344021000215.

Perfölz, R. and López-Varela, A., (2022). Internationalisation of Teaching and Learning through Blended Mobility: Potentials of Joint International Blended Courses and Challenges in Their Implementation, *In Education Sciences*, Vol. 12, No. 1, p. 810. https://doi.org/10.3390/educsci12110810.

Peterson, C., (2003). Bringing ADDIE to Life: Instructional Design at Its Best. *In Journal of Educational Multimedia and Hypermedia*, Vol. 12, No. 3, pp. 227–241.

Spatioti, A.G., Kazanidis, I. and Pange, J., (2022). A Comparative Study of the ADDIE Instructional Design Model in Distance Education. *In Information*, Vol. 13, No. 9, p. 402. https://doi.org/10.3390/info13090402.

Vahed, A. and Rodriguez, K., (2021). Enriching students' engaged learning experiences through the collaborative online international learning project. *In Innovations in Education and Teaching International*, Vol. 58, No. 5, pp. 596–605. https://doi.org/10.1080/14703297.2020.1792331.

TWO SIDES OF THE SAME COIN: RISKS AND OPPORTUNITIES OF CHATGPT IN HIGHER EDUCATION

Eva Späthe[1], Philipp Danylak[1], Sebastian Lins[1] and Ali Sunyaev[2]
[1]*Karlsruhe Institute of Technology, Germany*
[2]*Technical University of Munich, Campus Heilbronn, Germany*

ABSTRACT

The introduction of ChatGPT has marked a new era in education, as Generative Artificial Intelligence can generate human-like text effortlessly. This study examines the divergent perspectives of academic staff and students towards ChatGPT, characterized by either high optimism or reluctance. Our research addresses the pressing need to synthesize recent debates on risks and opportunities associated with ChatGPT in educational settings due to the increasing amount of multidisciplinary and heterogeneous literature. We conducted a comprehensive literature review by identifying and analyzing 50 relevant articles. We highlight the nuances of integrating ChatGPT into educational practice, discuss technical capabilities and limitations, and uncover 31 risks and 18 opportunities on an individual, institutional, and societal level. The synthesis of these findings contributes to the ongoing discourse by providing a balanced perspective on ChatGPT's paradoxical nature in higher education.

KEYWORDS

ChatGPT, Generative Artificial Intelligence, Education, Risks, Opportunities

1. INTRODUCTION

Large Language Models (LLMs) have revolutionized the landscape of natural language processing and human-computer interaction. ChatGPT, one of the most advanced LLM-based chatbots to date, has democratized the ability to generate human-like texts in seconds (Kalla et al., 2023). Its public and free-of-charge introduction into the education sector has been disruptive, bringing LLM technology into daily educational practice (Naidu & Sevnarayan, 2023; Panagopoulou et al., 2023). We observe two tendencies of academic staff and students dealing with ChatGPT, either approaching it with high optimism or reluctance. On the one hand, ChatGPT has caused quite a sensation in universities, and individuals often believe that it will revolutionize education and bring about rapid change (Okaiyeto et al., 2023). For instance, academic staff can use ChatGPT to create better and more personalized assignments and grade them more objectively (Jukiewicz, 2023). On the other hand, ongoing discussions also revolve around risks, such as the threat to academic integrity (Wach et al., 2023) and academic staff being pressured to adapt traditional assignment formats that are becoming less relevant or obsolete (van Slyke et al., 2023). At the same time, academic staff face a lack of regulations and guidelines on AI usage (Perkins & Roe, 2023; Wang et al., 2023), leading to high uncertainty on how to deal with plagiarism, copyright, and issues of legal responsibility (Panagopoulou et al., 2023). A recent analysis of the top 100 universities in the US shows that most universities tend to approach the situation with careful consideration (Wang et al., 2023). These contrary views on ChatGPT are unfortunate as individuals either tend to overestimate ChatGPT's beneficial impact and may oversee potential adverse effects or tend to be reluctant to use ChatGPT due to uncertainties, preventing them from leveraging its full potential (Okaiyeto et al., 2023). Education stakeholders require a deeper understanding of both the risks and opportunities related to ChatGPT. Researchers thus call for public discussions and research to identify potential risks and benefits.

Given the practical relevancy of ChatGPT, related research on using ChatGPT in educational settings is ever-increasing. We identified four key research streams: (1) using ChatGPT for medical education (e.g., Draganic, 2023); (2) examining the application and performance of ChatGPT (e.g., Dobslaw & Bergh, 2023); (3) stakeholders' perception of ChatGPT (e.g., Ngo, 2023); and (4) discussing risks and opportunities (e.g., Hung & Chen, 2023). Despite providing valuable contributions, "the effects of ChatGPT on higher education and information systems education are unclear" (van Slyke et al., 2023, p. 2). Extant research faces three key problems. First, ChatGPT's public accessibility and being free of charge (Panagopoulou et al., 2023) have led to a rapid increase in research articles on using ChatGPT in education within a relatively short period. These articles vary greatly in terms of quality and content. Some research articles only list or name opportunities and risks, while others strongly argue and provide empirical evidence for their presence (e.g., Ibrahim et al., 2023; Tan et al., 2023). Second, the literature is spread among several disciplines due to the multidisciplinary character of this research topic (e.g., education studies, philosophy, or computer science). Each discipline has a different view of ChatGPT usage, hampering the comparison of research findings. This is especially problematic for information systems (IS) research because it is interdisciplinary and multifaceted, and influenced by different research streams including social and computer sciences. Third, related research examines different educational levels (e.g., early childhood education; Luo et al., 2024), each with specific requirements and boundary conditions. Focusing on different layers makes it challenging to compare the research results.

There is a need to review and synthesize the existing research articles to oppose the risks and opportunities of ChatGPT as a disruptive technology in higher education. This synthesis is essential to deal with the amount of research, increase our understanding of ChatGPT's impact, and formulate recommendations for future action. To answer recent calls (e.g., Perera & Lankathilaka, 2023) and maintain a balanced perspective between optimism (e.g., due to its opportunities) and reluctance (e.g., due to potential risks) (Okaiyeto et al., 2023), we ask: *What are the opportunities and risks of using ChatGPT in higher education?*

2. RESEARCH METHOD

We conducted a descriptive literature review to synthesize the large body of existing research by applying a keyword search combined with thematic analysis. We followed established guidance on conducting literature reviews. As the first step, we defined a search string that included the key elements of our research question: (ChatGPT OR chatbot OR "Large Language Model" OR "LLM" OR "generative AI" OR "generative artificial intelligence" OR "generative adversarial network" OR "GAN") AND (education OR teaching OR university OR school) AND (risk OR benefit OR chance OR opportunity OR effect OR implication OR impact OR consequence). We then applied the search string to four scientific databases, EBSCOhost, IEEE Xplore, ACM Digital Library, and AISeL, to identify relevant conference and journal articles. To complement this search and cope with the transdisciplinary nature of the topic, we also used Google Scholar as an additional search database. We limited the search to titles, abstracts, and keywords, yielding 775 articles.

Next, we checked the articles for relevancy. We excluded 618 papers based on their title and abstract because they were thematically not relevant (e.g., no educational context) (376), duplicates (75), not scientific articles (e.g., theses, newspaper article) (117), or not in English (25). We also excluded 25 literature reviews that lacked methodological rigor (i.e., rapid reviews), reviewed ChatGPT in general, or performed quantitative analyses (e.g., citation networks). After the first relevancy check, we had 157 potentially relevant papers left and looked into the full text to perform a second and more detailed relevancy check. We excluded 107 further articles because they did not fit with the scope of our research question (e.g., articles about early childhood education) (56), because they missed rigor (e.g., discussion articles, opaque or inconsistent methods) (42), or because we could not get access to the articles (9). This left us with a final set of 50 relevant articles.

Following, we started coding for opportunities and risks by applying the six steps of thematic analysis (Braun & Clarke, 2006). First, we *familiarized ourselves* with the data by reading the relevant articles and noting key characteristics. Articles originated from diverse scientific fields (e.g., computer science, law, education), particularly focused on ChatGPT as technology or Generative AI in general, and applied varying methods (e.g., surveys, interviews, case studies, experiments). Second, we *generated initial codes* looking for opportunities and risks in the articles. For this purpose, we went through the articles line by line and assigned labels to the opportunities and risks we identified. For example, we found the opportunity "improved efficiency and freeing time" (e.g., Mhlanga, 2023) across several articles and coded it as "saving time". Overall, we labeled 175 codes related to opportunities and 203 codes related to risks. Third, we started *searching for themes* in our data and codes. To find theme candidates, we analyzed the initial codes to find patterns and relations between them. By doing so, we identified 18 opportunity and 31 risk theme candidates. For example, we grouped the codes "time saving on preparation, interaction and feedback" and "save administration time and effort" to the theme candidate "time saving". Fourth, we moved on to *reviewing themes*. In this iterative phase, we extensively discussed the theme candidates within the author team. Our core criteria for themes were achieving internal homogeneity and external heterogeneity (Patton, 2014). For example, we aggregated the theme candidates "time saving", "workload", and "ease of use" to the higher-level theme "efficiency". After reviewing the themes, we ended up with six (higher-level) themes for opportunities and seven for risks, which are summarized in Table 1. Finally, we concluded the analysis by *defining and naming themes* and *producing the report*. Here, we wrote detailed descriptions of the themes based on the data.

3. OPPORTUNITIES AND RISKS OF CHATGPT

Table 1. Overview of risk and opportunity (sub-)themes

Risk Subtheme	Theme	Opportunity Subtheme
Inaccuracy (19), data bias (9), hallucinations (8), performance (33)	Technical Capabilities /Limitations (R:70, O:72)	Availability (4), generation of output (17), personalization (19), functional support (32)
Overreliance (3), technostress (2), human interaction (7), job loss academic staff (2), learning experience (2), AI policy (4), cost (4), dependence (2), discrimination (4), distrust in students (2), empathy (2), ethics (9)	Social and Educational Impact (R:44, O:48)	Teaching assistance (14), learning assistance (8), learning experience (16), motivation (6), costs (4)
Creativity (2), critical thinking (6), technology dependence (7), expertise (10), overreliance (2)	Adaption of Skills (R:27, O:10)	Critical thinking (4), new skills (6)
Time consuming (2)	Efficiency (R:2, O:28)	Time saving (17), workload (5), easy use (2)
Data bias (3), discrimination (1), inequality (7)	Fairness (R:11, O:16)	Inclusivity (4), objectivity (3), equality (9)
Cheating (14), detection (5), copyright (4), plagiarism (10)	Academic Integrity (R:38, O:1)	Promoting academic integrity (1)
Data protection (5), information security (4)	Privacy (R:11)	
Note: Some codes were assigned directly to the theme. The brackets refer to the number of times coded. R = Risks, O = Opportunities		

3.1 Technical Capabilities and Limitations

Our literature review reveals that ChatGPT's technical capabilities and inherent limitations are frequently discussed to explain how opportunities and risks manifest in the educational context. However, the terms are not used distinctly, so technical capabilities are described synonymously as opportunities and technical limitations as risks. We briefly summarize these.

Technical capabilities. ChatGPT brings several novel technical capabilities that can be leveraged in higher education, including the generation of content and a variety of further supportive functions as well as personalization options. Prior research emphasized the value of ChatGPT's 24/7 availability (Gill et al., 2023; Michel-Villarreal et al., 2023; Thu et al., 2023). One of the most frequently used functions of ChatGPT is the generation of human-like text for creating teaching and learning material. ChatGPT enables academic staff to generate and adapt practical problems for (legal) case studies and virtual laboratories, among others, while requiring low effort (Menekse, 2023). In addition, it can be used to assist people with little or no programming experience in performing simple coding (Atlas, 2023; Borger et al., 2023). ChatGPT offers further supportive functions. It can increase the quality of texts by improving readability and accessibility, for instance, by compressing, expanding, or changing vocabulary (Abbas et al., 2023; Borger et al., 2023; Nikolic et al., 2023). ChatGPT can also provide, organize (Fiialka et al., 2023; Tan et al., 2023), and, if necessary, directly translate information (Bakare et al., 2023), thus creating convenient access to specific topics for users. Especially for teaching, (mass) personalization is valued as a technical advantage because personalized tasks, guidance, and feedback (Kasneci et al., 2023; Naidu & Sevnarayan, 2023; Rasul et al., 2023) can be used to foster students' individual learning experience (Fiialka et al., 2023; Thu et al., 2023) and learning efficiency (Hung & Chen, 2023). While initially being offered as a chatbot, it has evolved into an online platform providing access to various tools harnessing ChatGPT's capabilities, like math tools, personal AI tutors, or language teachers. Also, it allows users to connect ChatGPT with other apps like Google Drive.

Technical limitations. ChatGPT comes with several technical limitations, such as inaccuracy, data bias, and hallucinations that lead to risks and impose restrictions on leveraging opportunities. ChatGPT's responses have been shown to suffer from biased, outdated, or incorrect training data (Fiialka et al., 2023; Rasul et al., 2023). Producing biased or offensive output (Baskara & Mukarto, 2023) also has ethical implications such as the risk of discrimination (Atlas, 2023; Rahman & Watanobe, 2023). As with other LLMs, ChatGPT can create hallucinations (Ji et al., 2023), which are inaccurate, falsified, and distorted output information. "It generates more extrinsic hallucinations – factual statements that cannot be verified from the source" (Bang et al., 2023, p. 2), mostly due to limitations of the model and training data or specific user queries (Jukiewicz, 2023).

Prior research has also acknowledged the diverse limitations of ChatGPT in general. It lacks human nuance and cultural awareness (Baskara & Mukarto, 2023; Kılınç, 2023), limited understanding of abstract concepts and complex contexts (Baskara & Mukarto, 2023), and limited domain knowledge in different fields (Mhlanga, 2023). It has problems with exact descriptions (Dobslaw & Bergh, 2023) and correct citation of sources (Ngo, 2023). The general performance also differs in language; for example, there are far more issues when processing Vietnamese than English (Thu et al., 2023). Inaccurate answers exhibited logical errors and contradictions, reduced the output quality, and caused reliability problems. Besides, there are weaknesses when particularly applied to educational contexts, including problems with mathematical formulas (Borger et al., 2023), reflective thinking, interpreting figures (Nikolic et al., 2023), and a lack of creativity (Bakare et al., 2023).

3.2 Risks for Higher Education

ChatGPT's negative social and educational impact. Prior research strongly emphasizes that the introduction of ChatGPT can lead to adverse effects – *representing one side of the coin.* Our synthesis reveals that risks relate to different layers. On an individual level, overdependence and overreliance on technology (Kılınç, 2023; Mhlanga, 2023) impact personal and skills development. Uncertainties on how to use ChatGPT due to, for instance, a deficiency in users' AI literacy (Walter, 2024) and a lack of regulation can lead to technostress in learning situations among users (Wach et al., 2023). Risks can also emerge at an institutional level, such as incorrect output information that jeopardizes the credibility of the educational experience (Gill et al., 2023), a general distrust in students by academic staff (Farazouli et al., 2023), or automation-related job losses at universities (Wach et al., 2023). On a societal level, concerns are about the ethical implications of ChatGPT (Borger et al., 2023; Gu & Ferdaous, 2023), particularly related to discrimination.

Loss of skills. The influence of ChatGPT on users' competencies is often discussed with regard to concerns about a loss of skills (van Slyke et al., 2023). In any case, students should be trained for the future and their later careers. Besides the loss of creativity and a potential homogenization of text styles (Alkaissi & McFarlane, 2023; Laato et al., 2023; Smolansky et al., 2023), research is mostly concerned about losing critical thinking skills. Not only could the development of critical thinking be hindered (Su & Liu, 2023), but students' abilities could also be decreased (Abbas et al., 2023). This can lead to an overreliance on generative AI (Rahman & Watanobe, 2023) and a greater dependency on technology (Fiialka et al., 2023; Mhlanga, 2023; Tan et al., 2023). Some researchers fear software could replace students' ability to learn, think, and reflect (Hung & Chen, 2023; Malinka et al., 2023).

Efficiency. Although using ChatGPT's technical features tends to improve efficiency, research also points to adverse effects that stakeholders should not underestimate. Personalization of teaching can lead to an increased examination load for academic staff (Dobslaw & Bergh, 2023). Potential system bias and errors can lead to an increased workload for academic staff in reviewing assessments and results (Fowler et al., 2023).

Fairness. Ethics is closely linked to ChatGPT's unfair effects, such as bias and inequality. Students' and academic staff's unequal access to technologies like ChatGPT exists globally and nationally. Infrastructural access requirements such as electricity and a stable internet connection are not available everywhere (Mhlanga, 2023), and even in high-income countries, not everyone has the necessary hardware. Applying ChatGPT in higher education should ensure equal access to technology in a university and across universities to prevent the disadvantages of individuals' limited technology access and ensure stakeholders can harness intended opportunities. Potential biases resulting from ChatGPT's technical limitations also threaten fairness, particularly when considering that research argues that data biases mainly affect already marginalized groups (Atlas, 2023; Kasneci et al., 2023; Su & Liu, 2023). ChatGPT is largely designed for and trained with data from Western cultures and languages. Technical limitations are much more evident and severe outside Western cultures (Thu et al., 2023). In addition, this data bias is also prevalent in research on Generative AI because studies in this research field are predominantly from countries in the global north (Gill et al., 2023). All these points contribute to global inequality in access to education.

Academic integrity. ChatGPT's threat to academic integrity was a central issue in almost every article examined. This includes any kind of misuse of ChatGPT, like cheating or plagiarism, but also questions related to AI detection and copyright. Especially when it comes to assignments and exams, research is strongly concerned about cheating students (Rahman & Watanobe, 2023; Smolansky et al., 2023), mainly because it is currently not possible to reliably detect students' use of AI. Although diverse verification software has recently been introduced (e.g., ZeroGPT), errors or mistakes can still occur (Chaudhry et al., 2023; Ibrahim et al., 2023).

Educational stakeholders also have high uncertainties about copyright and plagiarism related to AI-generated texts (Hung & Chen, 2023; Laato et al., 2023). To date, it is unclear whether AI-generated output qualifies as copyrighted work, for instance, whether ChatGPT performs a "creation" and can be considered as an author (Dalalah & Dalalah, 2023). Nevertheless, the use of AI-based tools always involves the potential risk of plagiarism because the training data may have provided copyrighted material without identifying the source. Given that safeguarding academic integrity is essential for universities, there is a high need for solutions such as the development of regulations and providing academic staff access to reliable AI detection methods.

Privacy. As in dealing with AI in general, the risks relating to privacy and data protection are frequently highlighted when using ChatGPT for higher education (Menekse, 2023). Protecting sensitive personal data and ensuring individuals' privacy when promoting and performing personalization becomes crucial when using ChatGPT (Wach et al., 2023). Data processing may not only relate to sensitive personal information (e.g., students' names) but may also comprise critical information about students that can impact their social and job status (e.g., their learning profiles). Further information security research is needed because there are neither technical nor organizational restrictions on the usage of content entered as text prompts or files at the moment (Borger et al., 2023; Thu et al., 2023). Privacy risks will even increase in the future once ChatGPT offers features for real-time voice and video conversation.

3.3 Opportunities for Higher Education

ChatGPT's positive social and educational impacts. *On the other side of the coin*, ChatGPT provides benefits for higher education at an individual, institutional, and societal level. As a learning and teaching assistant, it creates improvements on all three levels. It supports individuals in their learning, provides students with real-time feedback (Menekse, 2023), and can be used as a complementary learning resource (Michel-Villarreal et al., 2023). Language support (Mhlanga, 2023) also simplifies institutional and social communication processes. Academic staff can streamline and improve assessment and grading (Bakare et al., 2023), course content generation, and evaluation through automation (Kasneci et al., 2023).

Using ChatGPT as a learning and teaching assistant leads to an overall improvement in teaching quality and learning experience. Adaptive learning (Bakare et al., 2023) as well as flexible, personalized, and customized learning (Abbas et al., 2023; Mhlanga, 2023), can lead to increased motivation (Su & Liu, 2023; Tan et al., 2023) and decreased stress (Fiialka et al., 2023). Compared to expenditure on academic staff, the cost of using ChatGPT as teaching and learning support for higher education institutions is minor, a factor that is particularly important on a global level for countries with low income (Gu & Ferdaous, 2023; Mhlanga, 2023).

Developing of skills. In contrast to some authors who express concerns about the decrease in critical thinking by using ChatGPT (e.g., Abbas et al., 2023; Su & Liu, 2023), others propose ChatGPT as an opportunity to improve those skills (e.g., Tan et al., 2023). ChatGPT provides the option to implement, for instance, game-based learning in courses. Students can then explore and validate different problem-solving strategies, leading to more engagement and experience, and ultimately fostering problem-solving and critical thinking (Fiialka et al., 2023). In addition, it can promote autonomous and self-directed learning, as ChatGPT's personalized feedback and guidance allow students to identify their mistakes, learn at their own pace, and take responsibility for their learning process (Kılınç, 2023). ChatGPT's translation capabilities can lead to improved language and communication skills due to individualized teaching and learning (Michel-Villarreal et al., 2023). Eventually, transforming higher education institutions into places where the use of ChatGPT is common practicecan lead to the development of new skills to build AI literacy (Atlas, 2023), such as the competence to phrase prompts.

Efficiency. Technical capabilities such as automation and mass personalization have an overall positive effect on stakeholders' efficiency through time saving and ease of use. Outsourcing administrative and repetitive tasks such as preparation to ChatGPT frees up time for creative tasks (Borger et al., 2023; Su & Liu, 2023) and reduces the workload of students and academic staff (Abbas et al., 2023; Hung & Chen, 2023).

Fairness. Despite ChatGPT bearing the risk of discrimination and inequality, it also offers the chance to create more fairness in education. The technical capabilities of ChatGPT can compensate for disadvantages such as Dyslexia through writing support and promote inclusivity (Kasneci et al., 2023). Beyond empowering disabled students, features like personalized content can benefit everybody because they are designed for different needs and abilities (Su & Liu, 2023). Even though the prevalent data bias in ChatGPT does not provide true neutrality, machine-centered assessment reduces human bias, which can lead to greater objectivity in grading (Jukiewicz, 2023; Naidu & Sevnarayan, 2023). Ubiquitous access to information via ChatGPT and a reduced human bias through ChatGPT's objectivity can lead to a democratization of education and an improvement in equality, for instance, in terms of gender (Borger et al., 2023). In the global context, ChatGPT can help (developing) countries to share and supplement educational resources, which can be freely used and adapted due to the lack of copyright restrictions (Gu & Ferdaous, 2023).

Academic integrity. While nearly all authors see academic integrity at risk through ChatGPT, there are also positive propositions: By changing the way of accessing information, conducting research, and developing the critical thinking skills outlined above, ChatGPT can promote the use of reliable information for research, an important part of preserving academic integrity (Naidu & Sevnarayan, 2023).

4. DISCUSSION AND CONCLUSION

This study uncovered 31 risks and 18 opportunities (Table 1) of ChatGPT, aggregated them into seven themes, and provided descriptions and explanations related to their manifestation in higher education settings. Our findings show that risks and opportunities are two sides of the same coin, i.e., they are different ways of looking at or dealing with ChatGPT in higher education. With 203 coded risks to 175 coded opportunities, there is an overall tendency towards an increased awareness of ChatGPT's risks, which is not surprising, as "there has never been a lack of concerns from academic staff over the use of new technologies" (Hong, 2023, p. 38) when looking at the history of technological advancement in education. Grouping the codes into themes makes it particularly noticeable that most themes are considered both a risk and an opportunity (Table 1). Depending on the context, ChatGPT's impact on higher education not only differs. More importantly, our findings highlight that some risks and opportunities are interdependent. For example, although ChatGPT leads to less human bias in the assessment, the risks of data bias must be accounted for instead. While low costs positively impact equality on a global level, on an individual level, these costs can still act as a financial barrier for some students and lead to higher inequality. Lim et al. (2023) similarly highlight this as the paradoxical perspective of Generative AI: "Current discourse surrounding Generative AI and its impact on education tends to focus on the challenges [...] or the opportunities [...] [, that] highlight the inherently paradoxical nature of Generative AI and its role in education; it could destroy some education practices while at the same time supporting them" (Lim et al., 2023, p. 3). Depending on the theme, the risks and opportunities are relatively balanced. Themes related to the adaptation of skills, academic integrity, and privacy contain more or exclusively risks, while efficiency is dominated by opportunities. In the end, it depends on how the education sector deals with this new technology by balancing and simultaneously considering its risks and opportunities.

Reviewing the literature also revealed that most recommendations for future action involve stricter regulation, such as policies about ChatGPT (Michel-Villarreal et al., 2023), or are related to privacy, written exams, resp. assessment, and skills in dealing with AI. Due to the increasing relevance of generative AI at universities, guidelines for using AI-based tools are urgently needed to create binding rules for students and academic staff and to address current uncertainties (Fowler et al., 2023). Potential challenges such as academic integrity, inadequate regulation, privacy issues (Sullivan et al., 2023), or AI hallucinations (Alkaissi & McFarlane, 2023; Bang et al., 2023; Ji et al., 2023) require a holistic approach and mandatory guidelines. Such guidelines are available at numerous universities, but not yet at all (Moorhouse et al., 2023).

Consequently, universities should create guidelines, communicate them transparently, and make them easily accessible to provide educational stakeholders with more guidance (Fowler et al., 2023). Adapting teaching and assessment techniques (Michel-Villarreal et al., 2023) is also crucial to address changing conditions. Guidelines, examination regulations, and examination services that have become obsolete must be continuously revised and adapted to the current state of the art.

In addition, a key aspect is the development and promotion of AI skills (Menekse, 2023; Wang et al., 2023) to enable academic staff and students to critically approach generative AI and effectively use these tools without compromising academic integrity. However, no unambiguous advice on privacy could be identified in the literature. However, in the medium term, legal regulations or the use of university-owned and data-protection-friendly AI-based tools would be a possible alternative. Through adaptations in legal regulation, guidelines, and assessments, a balance between the use of AI-based tools, and the promotion of AI literacy, most of the effects currently described as both – opportunities and risks – can be turned into opportunities.

Notably, the education sector has faced many of these issues in the past: There has been a debate about the reliability of sources and the need to develop critical thinking skills in the context of Wikipedia. Likewise, ChatGPT's bias is rooted in the bias of training data as a consequence of real-life circumstances, which is also reflected in the discrimination of marginalized people in the academic world in the past and present. ChatGPT is nevertheless a disruptive technology that is leading to shifts in higher education. ChatGPT has abruptly created easy access to Generative AI, combines the functions and applications of numerous different tools, and has reached a new level of quality for functions such as text generation. The usage of ChatGPT acts as a catalyst for both opportunities and risks and is forcing negotiation, balancing, and adaptation processes in higher education. Higher education institutions are reacting slower to socio-technical changes than would be necessary with the technological development of AI. The resulting vacuum – the technology is already in use, but regulation and adaptation are still in their early stages – makes further research in this area necessary.

This study contributes to research and practice by conducting a multidisciplinary and open literature review. We synthesized findings from research articles from disciplines such as computer science, information systems, education, psychology, law, and management. We simultaneously considered ChatGPT's impact on students and the academic staff, in contrast to prior research that focused on specific stakeholders (e.g., Ngo, 2023). At the same time, we restricted our synthesis to higher education and carefully elaborated the applicability and relevancy of risks and opportunities discussed in prior research (e.g., Borger et al., 2023). Our findings thereby consider higher education's requirements and boundary conditions when using ChatGPT and how they impact risk and opportunities. Whereas prior research predominantly treated opportunities and risks in isolation, our study emphasizes their interwoven and paradoxical nature. We purposely grouped risks and opportunities under common themes to highlight, for instance, that ChatGPT not only results in a loss of skills (van Slyke et al., 2023) but can be harnessed to foster problem-solving and critical thinking (Fiialka et al., 2023). We strive to raise researchers' awareness to consider potential adverse effects when examining how to leverage ChatGPT's promising features, ultimately achieving a more integrated view on ChatGPT's impact on higher education.

Nevertheless, our study does not come without limitations. Our review has an inherent bias in the selection of the search string and the identification of relevant literature. We aimed to mitigate this bias by making our data collection and analysis as transparent as possible. We captured a broad set of 50 papers, which can, regardless, lack saturation. Although we reviewed empirical studies, our findings emerged from the literature and some of them may lack empirical validation. Future studies may use qualitative or quantitative research methods to extend our findings and examine potential solutions to mitigate risks. Further, our findings may be skewed toward the usage of ChatGPT in countries in the global north (Gill et al., 2023). Although the opportunities and risks of AI in education are comparable for the global south (Mhlanga, 2023), future research should examine differences and their impact on risk and opportunity manifestation. Finally, AI technology is developing rapidly, especially ChatGPT. While synthesizing the most recent debate in the education sector has been a driving force behind this literature review, the findings may need to be updated as AI technologies or education systems and their conditions have changed.

REFERENCES

Abbas, S. G. et al. (2023). Effects Of Chatgpt Integration As An Artificial Intelligence Tool For Education And Research: An Exploratory Survey At The University Level. *Palarch's Journal Of Archaeology Of Egypt/Egyptology*, *20*(2), 1993–2017.

Alkaissi, H. & McFarlane, S. I. (2023). Artificial hallucinations in ChatGPT: implications in scientific writing. *Cureus*, *15*(2), Article 2.

Atlas, S. (2023). *ChatGPT for Higher Education and Professional Development: A Guide to Conversational AI.*

Bakare, O. D. et al. (2023). ChatGPT and Other Generative Artificial Intelligence (AI) Tools in Teaching and Learning as Integrative Pathways to Contemporary University Education: In J. Keengwe (Ed.), *Advances in Educational Technologies and Instructional Design,* 168–180.

Bang, Y. et al. (2023). *A Multitask, Multilingual, Multimodal Evaluation of ChatGPT on Reasoning, Hallucination, and Interactivity* (Version 4).

Baskara, R., & Mukarto. (2023). Exploring the Implications of ChatGPT for Language Learning in Higher Education. *Indonesian Journal of English Language Teaching and Applied Linguistics*, *7*(2), 343–358.

Borger, J. G. et al. (2023). Exploring the capabilities and implications of ChatGPT and other AI-assisted technologies in scientific research and education. *Immunology & Cell Biology*, *101*(10), 923–935.

Braun, V. & Clarke, V. (2006). Using thematic analysis in psychology. *Qual. Research in Psychology*, *3*(2), 77–101.

Chaudhry, I. et al. (2023). Time to Revisit Existing Student's Performance Evaluation Approach in Higher Education Sector in a New Era of ChatGPT. *Cogent Education*, *10*(1).

Dalalah, D. & Dalalah, O. M. A. (2023). The false positives and false negatives of generative AI detection tools in education and academic research: The case of ChatGPT. *The Int. Journal of Management Education*, *21*(2), 1–13.

Dobslaw, F. & Bergh, P. (2023). Experiences with Remote Examination Formats in Light of GPT-4. *Proceedings of the 5th European Conference on Software Engineering Education*, 220–225.

Draganic, K. (2023). Artificial intelligence: Opportunities and challenges in NP education. *The Nurse Practitioner*, *48*(4), 6–6.

Farazouli, A. et al. (2023). An exploratory study of AI chatbots impact on university teachers' assessment practices. *Assessment & Evaluation in Higher Education*, 1–13.

Fiialka, S. et al. (2023). ChatGPT in Ukrainian Education: Problems and Prospects. *International Journal of Emerging Technologies in Learning (iJET)*, *18*(17), 236–250.

Fowler, S. et al. (2023). First 100 days of ChatGPT at Australian universities: An analysis of policy landscape and media discussions about the role of AI in higher education. *Learning Letters*, *1*.

Gill, S. S. et al. (2023). *Transformative Effects of ChatGPT on Modern Education: Emerging Era of AI Chatbots*.

Gu, Q. & Ferdaous, R. (2023). Will ChatGPT Make Education more Equitable in Developing Countries? *Advances in Education, Humanities and Social Science Research*, *7*(1), 379.

Hong, W. C. H. (2023). The impact of ChatGPT on foreign language teaching and learning: opportunities in education and research. *Journal of Educational Technology and Innovation*, *5*(1).

Hung, J. & Chen, J. (2023). The Benefits, Risks and Regulation of Using ChatGPT in Chinese Academia: A Content Analysis. *Social Sciences*, *12*(7), Article 7.

Ibrahim, H. et al. (2023). Rethinking Homework in the Age of Artificial Intelligence. *IEEE Intelligent Systems*, *38*(2), 24–27.

Ji, Z. et al. (2023). Survey of hallucination in natural language generation. *ACM Computing Surveys*, *55*(12), Article 12.

Jukiewicz, M. (2023). *The Future of Grading Programming Assignments in Education: The Role of ChatGPT in Automating the Assessment and Feedback Process.*

Kalla, D. et al. (2023). *Study and Analysis of Chat GPT and its Impact on Different Fields of Study.*

Kasneci, E. et al. (2023). ChatGPT for good? On opportunities and challenges of large language models for education. *Learning & Individual Differences*, *103*.

Kılınç, S. (2023). *Embracing the Future of Distance Science Education: Opportunities and Challenges of ChatGPT Integration.*

Laato, S. et al. (2023). *AI-assisted Learning with ChatGPT and Large Language Models: Implications for Higher Education.*

Lim, W. M. et al. (2023). Generative AI and the future of education: Ragnarök or reformation? *The International Journal of Management Education*, *21*(2), 1–13.

Luo, W. et al. (2024). Aladdin's Genie or Pandora's Box for Early Childhood Education? Experts Chat on the Roles, Challenges, and Developments of ChatGPT. *Early Education and Development*, *35*(1), 96–113.

Malinka, K. et al. (2023). On the Educational Impact of ChatGPT: Is Artificial Intelligence Ready to Obtain a University Degree? In *Proc. 2023 Conference on Innovation and Technology in Computer Science Education* (pp. 47–53).

Menekse, M. (2023). Envisioning the future of learning and teaching engineering in the artificial intelligence era: Opportunities and challenges. *Journal of Engineering Education*, *112*(3), 578–582.

Mhlanga, D. (2023). ChatGPT in Education: Exploring Opportunities for Emerging Economies to Improve Education with ChatGPT. *SSRN Electronic Journal*.

Michel-Villarreal, R. et al. (2023). Challenges and Opportunities of Generative AI for Higher Education as Explained by ChatGPT. *Education Sciences*, *13*(9).

Moorhouse, B. L. et al. (2023). Generative AI tools and assessment: Guidelines of the world's top-ranking universities. *Computers and Education Open*, *5*, 100151.

Naidu, K. & Sevnarayan, K. (2023). ChatGPT: An ever-increasing encroachment of artificial intelligence in online assessment in distance education. *Online Journal of Communication and Media Technologies*, *13*(3), e202336.

Ngo, T. T. A. (2023). The Perception by University Students of the Use of ChatGPT in Education. *International Journal of Emerging Technologies in Learning (iJET)*, *18*(17), 4–19.

Nikolic, S. et al. (2023). A multidisciplinary and multi-institutional benchmarking and analysis of this generative artificial intelligence tool to investigate assessment integrity. *European Journal of Engineering Education*, *48*(4), 559–614.

Okaiyeto, S. A. et al. (2023). Generative AI in education: To embrace it or not ? . *International Journal of Agricultural and Biological Engineering*, *16*(3), 285–286.

Panagopoulou, F. et al. (2023). *Legal and ethical considerations regarding the use of ChatGPT in education* (Version 1).

Patton, M. Q. (2014). *Qualitative Research & Evaluation Methods* (4th ed.). Sage Publications Ltd.

Perera, P., & Lankathilaka, M. (2023). AI in Higher Education: A Literature Review of ChatGPT and Guidelines for Responsible Implementation. *International Journal of Research and Innovation in Social Science*, *VII*(VI), 306–314.

Perkins, M. & Roe, J. (2023). Decoding Academic Integrity Policies: A Corpus Linguistics Investigation of AI and Other Technological Threats. *Higher Education Policy*, 1–21.

Rahman, Md. M. & Watanobe, Y. (2023). ChatGPT for Education and Research: Opportunities, Threats, and Strategies. *Applied Sciences*, *13*(9), 5783.

Rasul, T. et al. (2023). The role of ChatGPT in higher education: Benefits, challenges, and future research directions. *Journal of Applied Learning & Teaching*, *6*(1).

Smolansky, A. et al. (2023). Educator and Student Perspectives on the Impact of Generative AI on Assessments in Higher Education. *Proc. Tenth ACM Conference on Learning @ Scale*, 378–382.

Su, Y. & Liu, Z. (2023). A Study of ChatGPT Empowering College Students' Innovation and Entrepreneurship Education in the Context of China. *International Journal of New Developments in Education*, *5*(13), 1–7.

Sullivan, M. et al. (2023). ChatGPT in higher education: Considerations for academic integrity and student learning. *Journal of Applied Learning & Teaching*, *6*(1), Article 1.

Tan, J. et al. (2023). *ChatGPT: A disruptive blessing in disguise for higher education?*

Thu, C. H. et al. (2023). *Integrating ChatGPT into Online Education System in Vietnam: Opportunities and Challenges.*

van Slyke, C.et al. (2023). Generative Artificial Intelligence in Information Systems Education: Challenges, Consequences, and Responses. *Communications of the Association for Information Systems*, *53*(1), 1–21.

Wach, K. et al. (2023). The dark side of generative artificial intelligence: A critical analysis of controversies and risks of ChatGPT. *Entrepreneurial Business & Economics Review*, *11*(2), 7–30.

Walter, Y. (2024). The relevance of AI literacy, prompt engineering, and critical thinking in modern education. *International Journal of Educational Technology in Higher Education*, *21*(1), 15.

Wang, H. et al. (2023). *Generative AI in Higher Education: Seeing ChatGPT Through Universities' Policies, Resources, and Guidelines* (Version 2).

THE FERNSTUDENT - EXPERIENCES WITH AN AVATAR TO SUPPORT HYBRID TEACHING FROM TEACHERS AND STUDENTS PERSPECTIVE

Daniel Ullrich[1], Sarah Diefenbach[2], Lara Christoforakos[2] and Andreas Butz[1]
[1]LMU Munich, Department of Computer Science, Frauenlobstr. 7a, 80337 München, Germany
[2]LMU Munich, Department of Psychology, Leopoldstr. 13, 80802 München, Germany

ABSTRACT

Hybrid teaching, a necessity during the Covid-19 pandemic, has remained a common format in universities. Typically, a synchronous live session is joined by students either in the physical classroom or via a remote option with interaction through textual chat. While hybrid formats have many advantages in terms of inclusivity and sustainability, research also reveals impairments of wellbeing and educational quality, such as the added cognitive load for teachers, perceived differences in social presence between the two student groups (on-site and remote), and limited interaction opportunities for remote students. To address such issues, we developed the concept of the "Fernstudent". Borrowing from the idea of telepresence robots, a physical avatar represents remote students collectively in the classroom, creating a communication channel based on the same modalities as for on-site communication. The present paper summarizes experiences with the concept and its evaluation from the perspective of teachers, on-site students and remote students. Among others, this includes a field test of the prototype in two different lectures, also contrasting it to the baseline of hybrid teaching with a standard remote software. Overall, the pilot applications showed promising results for all groups involved, however, on different levels and regarding different qualities. While teachers mainly profited from the reduced cognitive load, the remote students became more socially present to on-site students and were more motivated to actively participate in the lecture, for example, by posing questions. Implications and planned further developments are discussed.

KEYWORDS

Hybrid Teaching, On-Site Students, Remote Students, Social Presence, Cognitive Load, Fernstudent

1. INTRODUCTION

Hybrid teaching has become a standard in many universities and comes with several advantages such as inclusion and sustainability. Individuals who, due to illness or other restrictions are not able to leave their homes, can attend lectures and unnecessary travels are reduced (e.g., Johannessen et al., 2023; Klunder, 2022). However, from the perspective of educational quality, and the experience of learning and teaching, consequences of hybrid teaching are mixed (Huizinga, 2022; Gamage, 2023; Lorenzo-Lledo, 2021). In fact, the literature reveals many critical points, including increased attention requirements for teachers, low motivation to participate among the remote students, and a lacking social integration of both groups of students (remote, on-site). While remote teaching had become a standard during the Covid-19 pandemic, nowadays, the question arises to what extent remote teaching concepts, should be maintained. More specifically, as on-site teaching is possible again, the question emerges to what degree hybrid teaching can and should be offered (or can be expected from students), and how the best of both worlds (on-site and digital teaching) might be combined. As it applies for all educational technologies (e.g., blended learning, see Henderson et al., 2017), the technical opportunity alone does not guarantee that it is actually applied in a beneficial way. Instead, a detailed understanding of the realities of teachers' and students' encounters with digital technology is needed, to sensibly design such artefacts.

In order to address these issues, we developed the concept of the Fernstudent, i.e., an avatar in the classroom, offering advanced presence and interaction opportunities for remote students, thereby reducing the cognitive demands for teachers and making the interaction among all parties more natural. In the following sections, we first describe the concept and rationales for its development, and then reflect on experiences with its practical use in the classroom in pilot applications within multiple lectures, considering different perspectives of teachers, on-site students and remote students. Based on an overarching analysis across the different data sources, we summarize next steps for research and future development of the concept.

2. RELATED WORK

2.1 Hybrid Teaching

Basically, hybrid teaching refers to a mix of on-site and remote lectures, based on some way of integrating technology in education (e.g., Singh et al., 2021; Wu et al., 2021). Though the term is not used consistently, most researchers use the term to refer to a combination of on-site and digital teaching in a synchronous live-session, where some students join the lecture in the physical classroom and others follow the lecture via video and audio channels using an online platform (e.g., Zoom, Jitsi), with the opportunity to pose questions or comments via textual or voice chat. One of the obvious benefits of hybrid teaching is its inclusive character: Individuals who cannot be present in the physical classroom for reason such as travelling, childcare, illness or infection risks, still have a chance to participate (e.g., Johannessen et al., 2023; Klunder et al., 2022; Newhart et al., 2016). Once this option is provided, other students might also make use of it, so that the ratio of remote and physically present students might change to 50:50, or remote students might even be the majority. While many universities introduced the first offers of hybrid teaching during the pandemic out of necessity, students have come to appreciate the flexibility to join lectures without spatial constraints. Also, in many other settings (e.g., business meetings, adult education, gym classes), hybrid options are increasingly available. Providing a hybrid option has become a sign of an inclusive, modern, digital society, where it is no longer acceptable that participation is limited to those who are able to attend physically. All the more, it is important to systematically explore challenges and advantages of hybrid teaching, in order to ensure that the vision of inclusion and active participation of all individuals in hybrid settings really plays out.

The research literature reports a number of challenges on the remote students' side, as also known from digital teaching in general, such as a decrease in motivation, a feeling of loneliness, less interaction with the teaching staff and other students (Lorenzo-Lledo et al., 2021), and, connected to the lower engagement in discussions, less practice of active learning, critical thinking, and the ability to debate (Gamage et al., 2023). More specifically, it shows that the behavior of both parties (remote and on-site) contributes to growing psychological distance and reduced interaction between the two settings. Remote students often engage in side-activities while attending their lecture and participate less actively than on-site students (Lorenzo-Lledó et al., 2021). The teachers, in turn, tend to focus their attention on the on-site students, and do this even more if questions or comments from remote students are rare (Huizinga, 2022). Actually, teachers have to develop a full set of new skills to successfully perform hybrid teaching, ranging from the practical handling of the technology to new teaching styles. For example, teachers need to state expectations and information more clearly due to a lack of implicit, non-verbal communication with the (often non-visible) remote students. In turn, it becomes more difficult for them to check students' understanding of the subject matter and progress in their learning process, and it gets harder to capture remote students' attention (e.g., Huizinga et al., 2022; Gamage et al., 2023; Lorenzo-Lledo et al., 2021). Another particular challenge of hybrid teaching is the split audience, i.e., two groups of students following the same lecture but with very different contexts and options. Even if they seek to distribute attention equally, teachers tend to focus on the larger group of students (Huizinga et al., 2022), and a real "blending" of the physical and digital classroom does not happen. In many cases, the focus of interaction remains in the physical classroom, whereas remote students are less present and less engaged. As also known from other types of hybrid meetings, remote participants often feel neglected and uninvolved and cannot find the right timing or modality to join an intense local discussion (Ma et al., 2023). Besides impairments in students' wellbeing, this lack of experiencing themselves as one unity of learners, and the resulting psychological distance is also problematic from a perspective of theoretical models on student engagement (e.g., Fredricks et al., 2004), exploratory learning (e.g., de Freitas & Neumann, 2009), or analyses of satisfying learning experiences in terms of transactional distance (Gallon et al., 2019; Moore, 1993). Therefore, a main task for the design of educational technology to support hybrid teaching is to support hybrid learning in a way that is physically distant but psychologically close (also see Boye & Ayet, 2021).

2.2 Technology for Remote Presence in Educational Settings

Borrowing from the idea of telepresence robots (TPRs) a straightforward approach to enhance the social presence of remote students in the classroom could be a physical avatar. Through its physical presence, it could serve as a prominent representation and reminder of the remote students. Being equipped with functionalities such as camera, microphone and loudspeaker, it could help remote participants to see and hear what is going on, and also become visible and audible themselves. Usually, a telepresence robot is a 1:1 representation of a remote person, typically displayed on a screen, through which the remote person can operate the camera angle to control their view at the on-site setting (for examples see https://telepresencerobots.com). TPRs have already been applied in diverse educational settings (e.g., Kwon 2010, Velinov 2021, Virkus 2023) with generally promising findings. A review of 28 studies about TPRs in education lends support for a better socialization, integration, and collaboration of remote students with their peers (Velinov et al., 2021). For example, TPRs for homebound school children helped these students to stay socially connected with their classmates and overcome feelings of isolation, while the anthropomorphic appearance helped the on-site students to see the robot as an actual student and initiated talk about the person returning after illness (Newhart et al., 2016). At the same time, researchers emphasize that the acceptance of TPRs for wider use is still challenged and typically characterized by technical issues such as audio problems (Velinov et al., 2021; Virkus et al., 2023). Besides the classical TPR, exploratory design concepts address particular challenges of hybrid formats (e.g., Grønbæk et al., 2021; Ma et al., 2023), e.g., an automatic memory function/light signal that indicates a lack of active participation of remote participants in hybrid meetings (Ma et al., 2023). As documented by studies in human robot interaction (e.g., Airenti, 2015; Araujo, 2018; Damiano & Dumouchel, 2018; Klopfenstein et al., 2017), interaction with anthropomorphic artefacts naturally becomes more "human" than with purely technical, non-anthropomorphic representations. In line with these findings, positioning such a technology among the on-site students could further support feelings of unity. Also, the on-site students would hear the voice of participating remote students coming from their midst, and not as a disembodied voice "from the off". This way remote students could be integrated as seamlessly as possible into the situation of face-to-face teaching, making both student groups appear as a unity, receiving the same attention from teachers.

3. THE EVOLUTION OF THE FERNSTUDENT: CONCEPT DEVELOPMENT AND DESIGN RATIONALES

The Fernstudent concept was developed along the principles of user centered design. This also included a detailed context analysis and interviews with the target groups, namely, students and teachers. More specifically, we conducted in-depth interviews about previous experiences with hybrid teaching with two university teachers: Peggy [P], 31 years, background in psychology and Tom [T], 44 years, background in media informatics (the names are pseudonyms). In addition, we explored issues of relevance from a student perspective by interviews with 57 students conducted in the context of a practical course on "Experience Design" as part of the Media Informatics Curriculum at our university. Detailed findings of the context analysis can be found in Ullrich et al. (2023).

In sum, the main categories of mentions about the current state of hybrid teaching referred to

- Hybrid teaching as one-directional communication and lacking social interaction
- Hybrid teaching as exhausting to manage, dividing the teacher's attention
- The split audience and lacking unity between the two separate groups of students
- Difficulties in moderating discussions, lacking interest and care for the remote students
- Hybrid teaching as a bad compromise, where establishing a remote live session creates a lot of stress, but the advantage of being live is not exploited

When thinking about wishes and improvements, the following categories were named

- Bringing both student groups on one level (in visibility, modality, social interaction, appearance in the room)
- Separate remote students from teacher's screen to make comments welcome (and not a disturbance)
- Loudspeaker for questions from remote students, camera that records on-site students

In order to meet such requirements and the issues identified in the literature, we envisioned the idea of an avatar sitting the classroom which represents the remote students at home in a more prominent way than standard ways of hybrid teaching (e.g., a notebook on the teacher's desk). Picking up the German word for someone studying at a remote university, we coined the concept of the avatar in the classroom the "Fernstudent". Compared to a telepresence robot, the Fernstudent is an adoption tailored to a typical university lecture. Instead of a 1:1-representation, all remote students are represented by one physical entity placed at a fixed spot among the physically present students (which seems more practical and more affordable in typical university structures than multiple mobile devices). In addition, with the Fernstudent concept, image and sound from the lecture hall are transmitted to the remote students, and images and sound from remote students are transmitted into the lecture hall. Remote students can indicate that they want to speak (e.g., by motor elements, "hand signals", light signals) and the number of remote students is displayed in real time. With these features, the concept of the Fernstudent addresses the main identified challenges of hybrid teaching: It reduces the cognitive demands for the teaching person by limiting the focus of attention to one spot and modality. Signals from the remote students become visible in the same space as those from the on-site students, which frees up the instructor's attention capacities for lecture content and interaction quality. Furthermore, it enhances the presence of remote students by a physical, anthropomorphic representation and places both student groups on a more equal level (in visibility, modality, and opportunities for social interaction). To practically test the concept, a number of prototypes was built, allowing for experimentation with different shapes, sizes, and technical configurations (for more details on the technical realization see Ullrich et al., 2024). Figure 1 shows design variants, the set-up of hardware components, and functional prototypes used during field tests.

4. EXPERIENCES IN PILOT APPLICATIONS

Once the concept of the Fernstudent and first prototypes were developed, we tested the Fernstudent in pilot applications, to evaluate its suitability for real teaching situations. Thereby, we combined different studies and perspectives:

A field test of the prototype in multiple sessions of two different lectures, accompanied by

- A survey filled out by on-site and remote students after each Fernstudent lecture (N = 94)
- A survey filled out by the two teachers after each Fernstudent lecture
- A "baseline"-survey, capturing the experiences of on-site and remote students in regular sessions of hybrid teaching using a standard meeting software (Jitsi) to connect remote students (N = 151)
- A baseline-survey filled out by the two teachers after each Jitsi lecture
- Retrospective in-depth-interviews with the two teachers reflecting on both Jitsi and Fernstudent sessions at the end of the semester

Students were free to decide whether they wanted to join the lecture on-site or remote. In both types of sessions (Fernstudent, Jitsi), the ratio of remote students was about double the ratio of on-site students (Fernstudent: 36% on-site; Jitsi: 32% on-site). Moreover, we also conducted a potential analysis, where we presented the concept to a wider sample of teachers from diverse departments (e.g., politics, literature, law, computer science, economics) and collected their spontaneous opinion about the potential of the concept (N = 21). The studies were approved by the institutional review board of the faculty for mathematics, computer science and statistics and performed in accordance with the APA (American Psychological Association) ethical guidelines for research with human subjects. Informed consent was collected from all participants. Statistical analyses were performed by IBM SPSS statistics version 29. Interview data and open questions were analyzed by qualitative content analysis. Detailed study procedures and single findings have already been published in Ullrich et al. (2023). In the following sections, we summarize insights from the different data sources from the perspectives of teachers, on-site students, and remote students, followed by an overarching discussion.

Figure 1. Design variants, technical set-up, and functional prototypes of the Fernstudent

4.1 The Teachers' Perspective

In the potential analysis, where the concept was presented to a larger sample of 21 teachers, being interviewed about their own teaching experiences and which potential they see in concepts such as the Fernstudent, it showed that there definitely is a need for innovations and most teachers are dissatisfied with the current standards of hybrid teaching. The majority of teachers described technical problems in hybrid teachings, mostly audio problems, which made it hard for remote students to follow the lecture. In addition, several teachers described they experienced remote students as less motivated, which they ascribed to the lacking social component. In sum, such findings might reflect a downward spiral, where the remote students show less initiative to participate in the lecture (e.g., pose questions, virtually raise their hand). As a consequence, teachers pay even less attention to the remote software and the remote students. "The main challenge is to keep track of the remote students" [P5], was a typical statement. As one teacher stated, "You quickly forget that there is a person behind the screen" [P4]. Another teacher described that it was often the on-site students who drew his attention to remote students' questions: "Of course the people on-site are much more present than those floating around somewhere in digital nirvana. Fortunately, I usually have students in the lecture hall who notice that there are still questions online and remind me that I have to consider them somehow – otherwise I think I would have forgotten about them completely. But that's probably what this robot is supposed to solve." [P14]. Furthermore, it appears that even if there is an active endeavor to integrate both groups, it is still hard to establish real interaction, given the different modalities. If the remote students cannot be heard in the classroom and can only react via chat which then the teacher must read aloud, the discussion will probably not be as dynamic as it can be on-site. "It's really tricky to initiate some kind of interaction between the remote students and on-site students and then moderate between both groups." [P8]. In conclusion, when being asked about their teaching preferences, on-site teaching was still the preferred format for the largest group of teachers. If there was a necessity for remote teaching, most teachers said they would prefer fully online lectures to hybrid lectures, so that there is only one group of audience to speak to. If given the option to use the Fernstudent in hybrid session, most teachers were positive that this could reduce the existing problems and would make hybrid teaching a more attractive option. However, they also wanted to try it out first, to experience how much it actually reduces their cognitive load and how it would feel to have a technical entity sitting in the lecture hall. For the teachers who tested the Fernstudent prototype during their lectures, the main advancements provided were the reduction of cognitive load and the stronger connection to the remote students. Regarding the regular hybrid sessions (using Jitsi), they often expressed that they could not do justice to the remote students' needs and admitted that they largely ignored what was going on the software interface. In contrast, according to their statements, the physical representation of the remote students through the Fernstudent avatar, felt like a relief. There was just one direction to gaze at, including on-site students and remote students at eye-level. They could just direct their gaze towards the on-site students. As one of the teachers explained: "The remote students are just as present as the others and can draw attention by themselves. And these signals are so salient that you notice them automatically and don't have to look for them explicitly. All the stress of switching between background tasks and presentation view is gone. A very relaxed situation." [T]. The reduced cognitive load through handling technology, in turn, allowed more capacities to focus on the lecture content and discussion with the students, and teachers could re-discover the long-missed feeling of competence as a teacher and holding a lecture according to their personal standards. As Peggy explained: " Finally, you can offer good hybrid teaching. Everybody expects that this is something that should be feasible - and now you can meet these expectations." [P]. Also, the teachers experienced the two groups of students more like a unity and the interaction with the remote students as more satisfying and more natural. Still, teachers also uttered that the interaction with the remote students could still be improved and more equal to the on-site interaction.

4.2 The On-Site Students' Perspective

For the on-site students, the main changes provided by the Fernstudent were the enhanced presence of the remote-students through the avatar. While in the Jitsi sessions, there was no clue at all about remote students joining the lecture, the Fernstudent served as a constant reminder. Furthermore, on-site students rated the perceived the interaction between teacher and remote students, and teacher and on-site students as more similar in the Fernstudent sessions, compared to the Jitsi sessions. However, regarding their own activity and behavior, the presence of the Fernstudent in the lecture hall didn't change didn't change much. In both types of sessions, Jitsi and Fernstudent, their participation in the lecture (here: hand-raising behavior) was on a similar level. The majority of students described the Fernstudent as rather neutral (e.g., "Quite neutral", "After a short time you become used to it and it becomes part of the usual environment"). Some students described its presence as positive (e.g., "An agreeable presence") or expressed interest in its features and reactions (e.g., "Interesting. I liked how it started glowing when one of the remote students wanted to say something"). Some also wished for even more interaction and a more active role of the Fernstudent on-site (e.g., "A bit disappointing. It didn't do much. I would have liked more interaction with the prototype"). When being asked to describe their impression of the Fernstudent with three adjectives, a high ratio of the on-site students picked descriptive attributes (e.g., large, angular), referred to its outer appearance or prototypical look (e.g., rough, crafted, unfinished) or pragmatic aspects (e.g., simple, easy). Also, a few students mentioned character traits (e.g., cute, harmless). In sum, the new entity in the classroom made a mainly neutral or pragmatic impression. Figure 2 visualizes the mentions in form of a word cloud (created with tagcrowd.com).

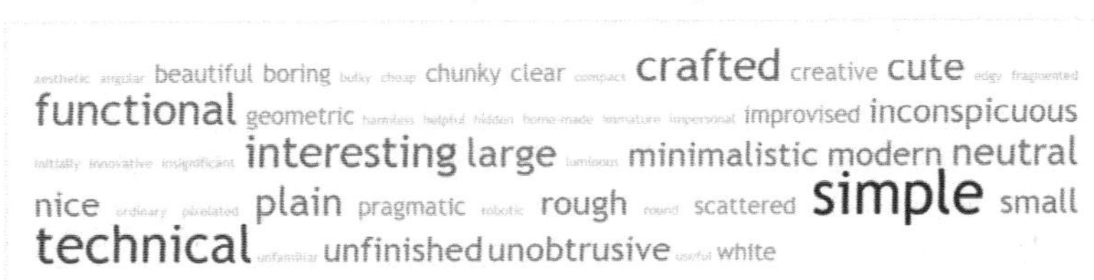

Figure 2. Student's characterization of Fernstudent by adjectives. Note: Text size visualizes frequency of mentions. Word cloud created with tagcrowd.com.

4.3 The Remote Students' Perspective

Regarding the remote students' perspective, the main changes initiated through the Fernstudent referred to their enhanced presence in the classroom, the enhanced affordances for active participation and enhanced modalities of interaction (participating in the discussion via speech, better hearing what the on-site students are saying). Being visually present through the avatar, it felt more natural for the remote students to engage in discussions. Also, according to their statements the fact that remote students could use the same modality as all others (i.e., speech, and being heard by their on-site classmates, their remote classmates and teachers alike) fostered a more intense involvement in the lectures. Consequently, compared to the Jitsi sessions, remote students reported a higher intention for active participation (raising their hand) in Fernstudent sessions, actually reaching up to the same level as the on-site students. Though our data do not allow for causal analyses, the combined findings indicate a positive spiral: through their constant visual presence, the remote students become more present. This enhanced their perceived appreciation as participants and contributors of the ongoing lecture. For example, through the LED panel which visualizes hand raises from the remote students at teachers' eye level, there is a lower risk that teachers might overlook questions posed by the remote students. Also, through the video channel, showing the remote students listening to the lecture, there is also a more natural, non-verbal feedback channel for teachers which directly communicates any irritations (if something was not understood) or also positive interest (e.g., head nodding, facial expressions of interest), and teachers can naturally adjust the ongoing lecture to all students' needs. At the same time, the enhanced social presence of remote students also stresses demands and their own responsibility to participate. As uttered by students interviewed in the context analysis phases, remote participation, especially when the camera is turned off, tempts them to engage in side activities ("If no one takes notice of what I am doing, I can also do something else".). The enhanced presence through the Fernstudent may reduce remote students' tendency to engage in side activities. Being more attentive to the lecture, in turn, makes it more interesting to listen, feeling more involved in the happening and more interested to participate, which is indicated by the increase in hand raising behavior in Fernstudent sessions compared to the Jitsi baseline. However, an important aspect for future developments is that the visibility of remote students in the classroom is also represented in what the remote students see on their screen at home. While remote students were physically represented by the avatar among on-site students and teachers, from their own perspective they only saw the composition image of lecture slides and a smaller video feed of the teacher. Thus, their mental model of participation was still "sitting at home" and not "being in the classroom".

5. CONCLUSION AND FUTURE DEVELOPMENT

In sum, the pilot applications of the Fernstudent showed benefits for all groups involved, however, on different levels and regarding different qualities. For future developments, main aspects of reflection for the three groups refer to (1) possible added benefits for the on-site students, (2) enhancing the remote students' awareness of their presence in the classroom, and (3) providing more information about the participating remote students to teachers. Besides, further developments should also address continuous technical improvements (e.g., audio quality) as well as the practical handling and mobility of the prototype. In the next section, we discuss first concrete ideas around such issues.

Referring to the on-site students (1), no special problems occurred. However, the innovative technical infrastructure could be seen as an invitation to reflect on what could still enhance dynamics of learning and interaction and how on-site students could benefit from this as well. For example, the LED matrix which in standard mode of the Fernstudent visualizes the remote students attending the lecture (e.g., each LED represents one student), could also serve to display interactive elements (e.g., poll results, quizzes) integrated in the lecture. Here, also the on-site students could be equipped with some type of interactive technology to affect what is shown on the matrix. One idea was to equip on-site students with "interactive dices", where the upper surface could represent their vote in a poll or a quiz. The remote students can answer the same polls/quizzes through their computer (or also have an according dice at home). The LED matrix then could display the combined results of both students' votes, which additionally emphasizes their unity as one group of students. In the end, of course, such decisions about additional features beyond the core concept also depend on the basic rationale and design philosophy: should the Fernstudent simulate the classical on-site lecture as much as possible, or do we aim for additional elements utilizing the digital and hybrid space (i.e., blended learning)?

Referring to the enhanced presence of remote students (2) in the classroom from their own perspective, the project team first discussed design solutions such as a 360-degrees field of view or adjustable camera angles, which however comes with privacy issues and uncertainties of who could be in charge of the camera angle (there are many remote students but only one adjustable angle). Other solutions addressed the conceptual understanding of remote students' own presence in the classroom. More precisely, one idea was in analogy to a seat reservation system (similar to choosing a seat in the theatre), where remote students see a seating plan of the lecture hall and remote students "pick their seat". Another idea was derived from computer games which sometimes begin with a perspective flight where you see a character from above and then you "fly" into its body, thereby attaining control. Such a fly-in sequence could be shown right after logging in where joining remote students see the lecture hall from above, flying into their robotic avatar and then changing to the normal view which shows the presentation slides and the lecturer. Both approaches could change the mental model of remote students in the desired direction, making them more aware of the situation and their place in the lecture. Of course, all such design ideas must be evaluated to test whether these are perceived as intended and actually lead to the aspired consequences in educational and experiential quality.

Finally, addressing the teachers' experience (3) and their wishes for more intense interaction with the remote students, one option could be to make remote students' "hand raises" less anonymous. In the current configuration, the Fernstudent shows the last remote student which actively used voice chat. While that was sufficient for many situations, teachers might like to know who the student is who initiated a new hand raise. Another improvement could be an indication of how many questions are in the queue. While the present concept works well in smaller groups, in larger groups, it could be helpful to have an idea about the number of students waiting to talk. Finally, in larger groups, where not all remote students can be simultaneously displayed with their camera picture on the screen, the shown camera pictures could randomly alternate. This would underline that the Fernstudent is no classical telepresence robot and represents not one but many individuals. Also, it would ensure that teachers perceive the diversity of joined remote students including the quiet ones who otherwise remain invisible.

In the end, it must be noted that the ideal configuration and features depend on the individual context, the size of lecture, how well students and teachers already know each other, the relevance of discussion and interactive learning for the particular lecture content, and many more. Further investigation is necessary to gain insights about how to integrate the Fernstudent in different settings, also considering the limitations of the present investigation. As main contributions we see the theoretically and empirically informed concept development and the systematic comparison of different perspectives, based on first insights from pilot applications. However, the concept still must be evaluated in more lectures, at different universities, with more diverse user groups, also considering potentially relevant person factors such as cultural background. Given this, we envision the Fernstudent as a basic solution with highly adaptable settings that can be adjusted to the current teaching situation. Starting from the positive experiences with introducing the Fernstudent at our own university, we hope to collect more experiences how it integrates and may support hybrid teaching in other countries, cultures, and teaching contexts, and are looking forward to collaborate with other researchers and educational institutions.

ACKNOWLEDGEMENT

Many thanks to Manuela Eska, Celina Lübben, Johanna Schlechter, Johanna Prinz, and Yara Turkmani for their support in setting up the functional prototype, conducting the field test and potential analysis and participating in workshops on further developments of the concept. Part of this research has been funded by the LMU Quality Teaching Fund (Fonds zur Förderung der guten Lehre) and the DFG-project PerforM—Personalities for Machinery in Personal Pervasive Smart Spaces (425412993) in the context of the Priority Program "Scalable Interaction Paradigms for Pervasive Computing Environments" (SPP 2199).

REFERENCES

Airenti, G. (2015). The cognitive bases of anthropomorphism: from relatedness to empathy. *International Journal of Social Robotics, 7*(1), 117-127.

Araujo, T. (2018). Living up to the chatbot hype: The influence of anthropomorphic design cues and communicative agency framing on conversational agent and company perceptions. *Computers in Human Behavior, 85*, 183-189.

Boye, T.& Eyet, J. (2021). *Fostering Inclusivitiy: Bridking the Gap Between In-Person and Online Student Learning.* Retrieved from https://share.vidyard.com/watch/b9o8hHQrLc55DXGn12ssMW (last access 17/12/2024).

Damiano, L., & Dumouchel, P. (2018). Anthropomorphism in human–robot co-evolution. *Frontiers in psychology* 9, 468.

De Freitas, S., & Neumann, T. (2009). The use of 'exploratory learning' for supporting immersive learning in virtual environments. *Computers & Education, 52*(2), 343-352.

Fredricks, J. A., Blumenfeld, P. C., & Paris, A. H. (2004). School Engagement: Potential of the Concept, State of the Evidence. *Review of Educational Research, 74*(1), 59–109. https://doi.org/10.3102/ 00346543074001059.

Gallon, L., Abénia, A., Dubergey, F., & Negui, M. (2019). Using a Telepresence Robot in an Educational Contex. In *15th Int'l Conf on Frontiers in Education: Computer Science and Computer Engineering* (FECS 2019).

Gamage, K. A., Jeyachandran, K., Dehideniya, S. C., Lambert, C. G., & Rennie, A. E. (2023). Online and Hybrid Teaching Effects on Graduate Attributes: Opportunity or Cause for Concern?. *Education Sciences, 13*(2), 221.

Grønbæk, J. E., Saatçi, B., Griggio, C. F., & Klokmose, C. N. (2021). MirrorBlender: Supporting hybrid meetings with a malleable video-conferencing system. In *Proceedings of the 2021 CHI* (pp. 1-13).

Henderson, M., Selwyn, N., & Aston, R. (2017). What works and why? Student perceptions of 'useful'digital technology in university teaching and learning. Studies in higher education 42(8), 1567-1579.

Huizinga, T., Lohuis, A., Zwerver-Bergman, J., & van der Meer, R. (2022). Student and teacher perceptions of community of inquiry in hybrid virtual classrooms. *Heliyon, 8(*12).

Johannessen, L. E., Rasmussen, E. B., & Haldar, M. (2023). Student at a distance: exploring the potential and prerequisites of using telepresence robots in schools. *Oxford Review of Education, 49*(2), 153-170.

Klopfenstein, L. C., Delpriori, S., Malatini, S., & Bogliolo, A. (2017). The rise of bots: A survey of conversational interfaces, patterns, and paradigms. In *Proceedings of the 2017 Conference on Designing Interactive Systems*, 555-565.

Klunder, S., Saab, N., & Admiraal, W. (2022). A teacher perspective on using a hybrid virtual classroom for students with a chronic illness in mainstream primary and secondary schools. *Technology, Pedagogy and Education, 31*(4), 493-508.

Kwon, O. H., Koo, S. Y., Kim, Y. G., & Kwon, D. S. (2010). Telepresence robot system for English tutoring. In *2010 ieee workshop on advanced robotics and its social impacts* (pp. 152-155).

Lorenzo-Lledó, A., Lledó, A., Gilabert-Cerdá, A., & Lorenzo, G. (2021). The pedagogical model of hybrid teaching: Difficulties of university students in the context of COVID-19. *European Journal of Investigation in Health, Psychology and Education, 11*(4), 1320-1332.

Ma, S., Hu, Q., Chen, Y., Zhao, Z., & Li, H. (2023). Social Bots that Bring a Strong Presence to Remote Participants in Hybrid Meetings. In *Companion of the 2023 ACM/IEEE International Conference on Human-Robot Interaction* (pp. 853-856). https://doi.org/10.1145/3568294.3580200

Moore, M. G. (1993). Theory of transactional distance. *Theoretical principles of distance education, 1*, 22-38.

Newhart, V. A., Warschauer, M., & Sender, L. (2016). Virtual inclusion via telepresence robots in the classroom: An exploratory case study. *The International Journal of Technologies in Learning, 23*(4), 9-25.

Singh, J., Steele, K., & Singh, L. (2021). Combining the best of online and face-to-face learning: Hybrid and blended learning approach for COVID-19, post vaccine, & post-pandemic world. *Journal of Educational Technology Systems, 50*(2), 140-171.

Ullrich, D., Butz, A., & Diefenbach, S. (2023). The "Fernstudent". Enhancing The Potential Of Hybrid Teaching Based On User-Centered Design. In *Proceedings of the 20th International Conference on Cognition and Exploratory Learning in Digital Age (CELDA)* 2023. https://www.iadisportal.org/digital-library/the-fernstudent-enhancing-the-potential-of-hybrid-teaching-based-on-user-centered-design

Ullrich, D., Butz, A., & Diefenbach, S. (2024). The Fernstudent. A User-Centered Design Case Study on Improvements of Hybrid Teaching Through A Physical Avatar in the Classroom. Fernstudent Case Study. In *Proceedings of the 2024 CHI Conference on Human Factors in Computing Systems*, Article No.: 534, doi: 10.1145/3613905.3637144

Velinov, A., Koceski, S., & Koceska, N. (2021). A review of the usage of telepresence robots in education. Balkan *Journal of Applied Mathematics and Informatics, 4*(1), 27-40.

Virkus, S., Leoste, J., Marmor, K., Kasuk, T., & Talisainen, A. (2023). Telepresence robots from the perspective of psychology and educational sciences. *Information and Learning Sciences, 124*(1/2), 48-69.

Wu, G., Zheng, J., & Zhai, J. (2021). Individualized learning evaluation model based on hybrid teaching. *The International Journal of Electrical Engineering & Education*, 60 (1), 0020720920983999.

ENHANCING STUDENT ENGAGEMENT AND PERFORMANCE THROUGH LMS-INTEGRATED PODCASTING AND SOCIAL MEDIA TOOLS IN HIGHER EDUCATION

Yasser Omar Abdallah[1] and Souheil Nassour[2]
[1]*Greenwich Business School, London, UK*
[2]*Emeritus, Dubai, UAE*

ABSTRACT

The integration of digital technologies in higher education, particularly through Learning Management Systems (LMS) like Canvas, has transformed student engagement, accessibility, and learning outcomes. This study investigates the impact of LMS-integrated podcasting and social media features on student engagement, perceived feedback effectiveness, and academic performance. Using a sample of 200 undergraduate students in a 10-week experimental study, participants were divided into an experimental group (utilising podcasting and social media tools within Canvas) and a control group (using traditional LMS features without interactive tools). Results indicate that the experimental group reported higher engagement levels (M = 4.12, SD = 0.78) compared to the control group (M = 3.45, SD = 0.85), alongside improved academic performance (M = 85.3%, SD = 8.2) versus the control group (M = 74.6%, SD = 9.1). Pearson's correlation further revealed a strong positive relationship between engagement and academic performance ($r = 0.63$, $p < 0.01$). These findings suggest that LMS tools, particularly podcasting and social media features, significantly enhance student engagement and learning outcomes, providing a practical and accessible framework for digital learning. Implications for institutional policies to support interactive learning environments are discussed, with recommendations on effective LMS integration to foster an engaging and interactive educational setting.

KEYWORDS

Learning Management System, Social Media Education, Higher Education, Student Engagement

1. INTRODUCTION

Digital transformation in higher education has brought significant advancements in how educational content is delivered, especially through the adoption of Learning Management Systems (LMS) like Canvas, Blackboard, and Moodle. LMS platforms are not only central to online and blended learning but have also evolved to support active, student-centred engagement (Al-Fraihat, Joy, & Sinclair, 2020; Gillet-Swan, 2017). Initially, LMS platforms served primarily as organisational tools for content management, yet recent developments have equipped them with interactive and social features, enabling educators to implement constructivist learning approaches and cater to varied student needs (Kintu, Zhu, & Kagambe, 2017).

Among the LMS interactive features, podcasting and social media functionalities are particularly beneficial for fostering self-regulated learning behaviours. Podcasting allows students flexible access to lecture content and instructor feedback, enabling them to revisit and reflect on complex topics at their convenience (Kay, 2012). Research underscores the accessibility and adaptability of podcast-based learning, particularly for supporting different learning preferences and enhancing engagement (O'Bannon et al., 2011; Heilesen, 2010). Social media-like tools embedded within LMS platforms, such as discussion boards and peer comments, promote collaboration and a sense of community among students, which has been shown to increase both engagement and learning outcomes (Junco et al., 2011; Dabbagh & Kitsantas, 2012).

Recent studies highlight the potential of LMS-integrated tools in enhancing student participation, motivation, and academic performance, but empirical research on the combined impact of LMS tools is limited (Al-Fraihat et al., 2020; Kintu et al., 2017). Most research to date has examined the LMS tools in isolation rather than their synergistic potential when integrated within a cohesive LMS environment. This study aims to address this gap by investigating how the combined use of LMS-integrated podcasting and social media features within Canvas influences student engagement, perceived feedback effectiveness, and academic performance. By focusing on Canvas as the LMS, this research provides insights into how educators and institutions can maximise LMS functionalities to create an engaging, student-centred learning environment that supports diverse educational needs.

2. LITERATURE REVIEW

2.1 Theoretical Foundations of Student Engagement

Student engagement is a multidimensional construct encompassing behavioural, emotional, and cognitive components (Fredricks, Blumenfeld, & Paris, 2004). Behavioural engagement includes students' participation in academic tasks and interactions; emotional engagement pertains to their feelings of interest, enjoyment, and sense of belonging; and cognitive engagement involves their investment in learning and willingness to go beyond basic requirements. These dimensions are essential for understanding how digital tools within an LMS can impact learning, as they allow educators to design experiences that target each engagement type (Appleton et al., 2008).

Constructivist and social learning theories also underpin many digital engagement strategies, emphasising that students actively construct knowledge through interaction with content and peers (Vygotsky, 1978). These frameworks support the idea that LMS-integrated tools such as podcasting and social media features can foster active learning by allowing students to interact with course materials and engage collaboratively.

Understanding student engagement by highlighting its social dimension and its impact on overall life experiences beyond academic settings. This broader perspective underscores the importance of fostering a sense of community and belonging among students, which can be facilitated through collaborative tools and interactive learning environments (Trowler, 2024).

2.2 LMS as a Digital Hub in Higher Education

Learning Management Systems have become centralised platforms that support various aspects of online and hybrid learning, including content delivery, feedback, assessment, and interaction. Studies indicate that LMS platforms like Canvas provide a unified environment that can support both the cognitive and social dimensions of learning (Beatty & Ulasewicz, 2006). Integrating LMS with interactive tools such as discussion forums, quizzes, and multimedia resources can enhance learning experiences by making them more cohesive and accessible (Chickering & Ehrmann, 1996).

LMS platforms are also recognised for their role in promoting self-regulated learning, as they provide features like notifications, progress tracking, and instant feedback, which allow students to monitor and adapt their learning behaviours (Zimmerman, 2002). By leveraging these tools, educators can encourage active participation and engagement within the digital learning environment.

2.3 Podcasting as a Tool for Content Delivery and Feedback

Podcasting has emerged as a valuable tool for content delivery and providing feedback in higher education. The flexibility of podcasting allows students to access lectures and personalised feedback at their convenience, catering to diverse learning needs and preferences (Kay, 2012). Research shows that students who use podcasts for content review or feedback often experience improved comprehension and retention, as podcasts enable them to revisit complex topics and clarify misunderstandings (Heilesen, 2010).

Podcasting is also useful for providing audio feedback on assignments, which many students find more personal and clearer than traditional text-based feedback. O'Bannon et al. (2011) found that students appreciated the accessibility of audio feedback, as it allowed them to receive insights in a conversational manner that felt more connected to their learning experience. Studies suggest that using podcasting within an

LMS framework can further enhance these benefits by making audio feedback more accessible and integrated within the course structure.

Also, podcasting has gained widespread recognition as an effective tool for content delivery and feedback in higher education. Its ability to offer flexibility and accessibility makes it particularly suited for modern learners who prefer on-demand learning experiences. According to Kang and Shin (2019), podcasts provide an engaging platform for delivering lectures, summaries, and additional resources, enabling students to revisit materials at their convenience. This flexibility accommodates diverse learning styles and fosters self-paced learning, which is crucial for improving comprehension and retention. Moreover, the multimodal nature of podcasts (audio combined with visual or text-based supplements) has been shown to enhance cognitive engagement by catering to different sensory preferences.

Another key advantage of podcasting is its utility in providing personalized feedback. Berk et al. (2021) found that audio feedback delivered through podcasts not only improved students' understanding of their performance but also created a sense of instructor presence and connection. This conversational and humanized form of feedback was highly valued by students, as it allowed for a deeper understanding of expectations and areas for improvement. When integrated into Learning Management Systems (LMS), podcasting further amplifies these benefits by embedding feedback directly into the course framework, creating a seamless and supportive learning environment. As such, podcasting is emerging as a versatile tool for both content delivery and fostering meaningful student-instructor interactions.

2.4 Social Media Features within LMS and Peer Interaction

The integration of social media functionalities within LMS platforms has shown promise in fostering peer-to-peer interaction, collaborative learning, and a sense of community among students. Discussion forums, instant messaging, and peer-to-peer sharing tools offer avenues for students to engage with one another, exchange ideas, and develop social connections that support learning (Junco et al., 2011). These social media-like features align with social learning theories, which posit that learning is a socially mediated process where students benefit from observing, discussing, and reflecting on others' perspectives.

Dabbagh and Kitsantas (2012) found that LMS-integrated social media tools promote self-regulated learning by enabling students to set goals, seek peer feedback, and reflect on their progress through discussions and collaborative tasks. Additionally, these tools can help foster a supportive environment that encourages students to ask questions and actively participate in the learning process, which has been linked to increased academic achievement and satisfaction (Moran et al., 2011).

Social media functionalities integrated within Learning Management Systems (LMS) have proven effective in enhancing peer interaction and fostering collaborative learning in higher education. These features, such as discussion forums, instant messaging, and content-sharing tools, create opportunities for students to connect, share ideas, and engage in collaborative problem-solving. According to Al-Rahmi et al. (2018), the integration of social media features within LMS significantly enhances communication and interaction among students, fostering a sense of community and belonging. Their study highlights that such features promote active participation and peer support, which are key to improving learning outcomes.

Additionally, Luo et al. (2020) emphasize the importance of LMS-integrated social media tools in promoting self-regulated learning and collaborative engagement. Their research found that students who actively used social media functionalities within LMS platforms were more likely to participate in group discussions, seek peer feedback, and reflect on their learning progress. These interactions align with social constructivist principles, which posit that learning is most effective when it is socially mediated and collaborative. By incorporating social media features, LMS platforms can bridge the gap between traditional and digital learning environments, offering a richer and more interactive learning experience.

2.5 Comparative Studies on LMS-Based and Traditional Learning Approaches

Comparative studies have been conducted to examine the impact of LMS-based tools on student engagement and performance relative to traditional learning approaches. Kay (2012) reviewed studies on video podcasting and found that students in LMS-supported environments reported higher engagement, particularly when video content was supplemented with discussion boards or quizzes. Similarly, Mayer and Moreno (2003) highlighted that multimedia learning tools, such as video podcasts within an LMS, help students better organise and process information, leading to improved learning outcomes.

Moreover, Beatty and Ulasewicz (2006) observed that moving from traditional LMS features to platforms with integrated social media tools resulted in improved engagement and peer interactions, particularly in blended learning settings. These studies indicate that LMS platforms that support multimedia and social functionalities can better cater to contemporary students' learning preferences, making them effective alternatives to traditional lecture-based or text-heavy LMS models.

Cidral et al. (2018) conducted a study examining the effects of LMS on student satisfaction and academic performance in higher education. The findings revealed that students utilizing LMS tools reported greater satisfaction and perceived improved learning outcomes compared to those who did not. This highlights the importance of integrating LMS, as it not only enhances engagement but also supports academic achievement and offers a more tailored learning experience. A significant contributor to the effectiveness of LMS-based learning environments was the capability to monitor progress and receive instant feedback (Cidral et al., 2018).

Recent research underscores the importance of gamification and interactive multimedia features in LMS environments, which have been shown to enhance student engagement and motivation. For example, Anderson and Rainie (2020) discovered that incorporating gamified elements in LMS platforms led to higher motivation and improved performance, indicating that competitive and game-like features can significantly increase student participation. Likewise, Chen et al. (2018) highlighted that interactive and adaptive LMS platforms, which offer personalized learning experiences, play a crucial role in boosting student engagement and academic success in higher education.

Additionally, recent studies have investigated obstacles to LMS adoption. Perez et al. (2020) found that faculty are often hesitant to fully adopt LMS-integrated tools due to concerns over increased workload and technological difficulties.

The research emphasizes the significant impact of LMS-integrated tools, such as podcasting and social media, in improving student engagement and academic achievement in higher education. These tools facilitate multiple dimensions of learning, including content delivery, collaborative peer interaction, and self-directed learning, which are vital for creating an interactive and engaging educational environment. Nevertheless, issues such as unequal access to technology and the necessity for faculty training remain critical barriers to their effective implementation. As educational institutions increasingly adopt and enhance LMS platforms, it is essential to address the changing needs of both students and educators to maximize the potential of these digital tools and improve the overall learning experience.

3. METHODOLOGY

3.1 Research Design

This study employed a quantitative, experimental design to measure the effects of LMS-integrated podcasting and social media tools on student engagement and academic performance. The study was conducted over a 10-week academic semester period, involving two groups of undergraduate students: an experimental group (using podcasting and social media tools embedded within the Canvas LMS) and a control group (following traditional LMS usage without these additional tools).

3.2 Participants

A sample of participants consisted of 200 undergraduate students was randomly assigned to ensure unbiased group assignments. to either the experimental group (n=100) or the control group (n=100). Participants were enrolled across various disciplines to control subject-specific biases. The sample was balanced in terms of gender and academic performance history, and field of study to avoid confounding variables.

3.3 Data Collection Instrument: Questionnaire

To assess student engagement and perceived effectiveness of LMS-integrated tools, a questionnaire was developed based on validated scales from previous studies on digital engagement (Fredricks et al., 2004; covering behavioral, emotional, and cognitive dimensions. Example item: "I actively participate in online discussions related to course material.", and Junco et al., 2011; Example item: "Receiving feedback through podcasts improved my understanding of the material."). The questionnaire consisted of 15 items rated on a 5-point Likert scale, with responses ranging from "Strongly Disagree" to "Strongly Agree."

3.4 Data Analysis

Data from the questionnaire were analyzed using SPSS to perform descriptive and inferential statistical tests. The analysis included:

- **Descriptive Statistics:** Means and standard deviations for each item to understand general trends in responses.
- **Independent Sample T-Tests:** To compare engagement levels between the experimental and control groups.
- **Pearson's Correlation Coefficient:** To assess the relationship between perceived engagement and academic performance within the experimental group.

4. RESULTS

The analysis indicates that these differences significantly impacted student engagement, perceived effectiveness of feedback, and academic performance.

4.1 Descriptive Statistics

Engagement Scores:

The experimental group reported higher engagement levels with a mean score of 4.12 (SD = 0.78), while the control group had a mean engagement score of 3.45 (SD = 0.85). This difference suggests that podcasting and social media tools within Canvas may foster a more immersive learning experience, encouraging students to interact with content and peers more frequently than traditional methods.

Perceived Effectiveness:

The mean perceived effectiveness score for the experimental group was 4.05 (SD = 0.83), compared to 3.20 (SD = 0.79) for the control group. Approximately 78% of the students in the experimental group agreed that podcasted feedback improved their understanding of course material, whereas only 52% of the control group reported similar benefits from traditional feedback.

Academic Performance:

Final assessment scores reflected a marked improvement in the experimental group, with a mean score of 85.3% (SD = 8.2) compared to 74.6% (SD = 9.1) in the control group. This improvement aligns with previous findings that digital tools like podcasting and discussion forums can enhance learning outcomes by reinforcing material and offering varied means of content interaction (Kay, 2012; O'Bannon et al., 2011).

4.2 T-Test Analysis

An independent samples t-test showed a statistically significant difference in engagement levels between the two groups, $t(198) = 6.47$, $p < 0.001$, suggesting that the interactive features in Canvas contribute positively to student motivation and participation.

4.3 Correlation Analysis

Pearson's correlation analysis revealed a strong, positive relationship between engagement and academic performance for the experimental group ($r = 0.63$, $p < 0.01$). This correlation suggests that students who felt more engaged due to the LMS tools also tended to perform better academically, underscoring the practical impact of enhanced engagement on student learning outcomes (Junco et al., 2011; Heilesen, 2010).

5. CONCLUSION

The results of this study have both theoretical and practical implications for the field of educational technology, especially concerning LMS-integrated digital tools in higher education.

5.1 Theoretical Implications

The study contributes to constructivist theories of learning, which advocate for active, student-centered engagement as a pathway to deeper learning (Vygotsky, 1978). By providing tools for discussion, peer feedback, and flexible content access, LMS platforms like Canvas can foster a constructivist environment where students are actively involved in constructing knowledge rather than passively receiving information. The positive correlation between engagement and academic performance reinforces theories suggesting that increased interaction with content and peers enhances learning (Fredricks et al., 2004).

Additionally, the findings align with social learning theories, which highlight the importance of collaborative learning and peer interaction. The social media tools embedded in Canvas create opportunities for peer-to-peer support and shared learning experiences, allowing students to benefit from each other's insights, experiences, and understanding. This study thus supports the expansion of social learning concepts within the context of digital education.

5.2 Practical Implications

For Educators and Institutions:

The data highlights the potential of LMS-integrated podcasting and social media tools to enhance student engagement and academic outcomes, offering practical insights for educators seeking to maximize the impact of their teaching methods. Incorporating podcast-based feedback allows instructors to deliver personalized insights without the constraints of traditional text-based feedback. Such feedback can be more accessible, enabling students to listen and review at their own pace, which enhances comprehension and retention (Kay, 2012).

Educational institutions may consider prioritizing LMS platforms with comprehensive social media tools to improve student motivation and support. The results suggest that LMS tools providing collaborative spaces (discussion boards, peer feedback) can enhance students' sense of community, especially in online or blended courses where face-to-face interaction is limited. By leveraging these tools, institutions can foster a more cohesive and interactive learning environment.

For Students:

For students, the study underscores the value of actively engaging with digital tools within an LMS. Engagement is shown not only to improve understanding but also to correlate with higher academic performance. As educational settings increasingly adopt hybrid and online formats, students can use LMS tools to take ownership of their learning process, building support networks through peer interaction and using podcasts for self-paced learning.

5.3 Limitations and Future Research

While the findings are significant, this study is limited by its relatively short duration (10 weeks) and the self-reported nature of engagement measures. Future research could explore longitudinal studies to assess the long-term impact of LMS tools on engagement and performance. Additionally, exploring how specific types of feedback—audio, video, or text-based—affect learning outcomes could provide further insights into optimizing LMS-integrated digital tools.

REFERENCES

Appleton, J. J., Christenson, S. L., & Furlong, M. J., (2008). Student engagement with school: Critical conceptual and methodological issues of the construct. *Psychology in the Schools*, *45*(5), pp. 369-386. https://doi.org/10.1002/pits.20303.

Beatty, B. J. & Ulasewicz, C., (2006). Faculty perspectives on moving from Blackboard to the Moodle learning management system. *TechTrends*, *50*(4), pp.36-45. https://doi.org/10.1007/s11528-006-0036-y.

Chickering, A. W. & Ehrmann, S. C., (1996). Implementing the seven principles: Technology as lever. *AAHE Bulletin*, *49*(2), pp.3-6.

Cidral, W. A., Oliveira, T., Felice, M. D. & Aparicio, M., (2018). E-learning success determinants: Brazilian empirical study. *Computers & Education*, *122*, pp.273-290. https://doi.org/10.1016/j.compedu.2017.12.001.

Dabbagh, N. & Kitsantas, A., (2012). Personal learning environments, social media, and self-regulated learning: A natural formula for connecting formal and informal learning. *The Internet and Higher Education*, *15*(1), pp. 3-8. https://doi.org/10.1016/j.iheduc.2011.06.002.

Fredricks, J.A., Blumenfeld, P.C. & Paris, A.H., (2004). School engagement: Potential of the concept, state of the evidence. *Review of Educational Research*, *74*(1), pp.59-109. https://doi.org/10.3102/00346543074001059.

Garrison, D.R. & Vaughan, N.D., (2008). Blended learning in higher education: Framework, principles, and guidelines. John Wiley & Sons.

Gillet-Swan, J., (2017). The challenges of online learning: Supporting and engaging the isolated learner. *Journal of Learning Design*, *10*(1), pp.20-30. https://doi.org/10.5204/jld.v9i3.293.

Hattie, J. & Timperley, H., (2007). The power of feedback. *Review of Educational Research*, *77*(1), pp. 81-112. https://doi.org/10.3102/003465430298487.

Heilesen, S.B., (2010). What is the academic efficacy of podcasting? *Computers & Education*, *55*(3), pp. 1063-1068. https://doi.org/10.1016/j.compedu.2010.05.002.

Junco, R., Heiberger, G. & Loken, E., (2011). The effect of Twitter on college student engagement and grades. *Journal of Computer Assisted Learning*, *27*(2), pp. 119-132. https://doi.org/10.1111/j.1365-2729.2010.00387.x.

Kay, R.H., (2012). Exploring the use of video podcasts in education: A comprehensive review of the literature. *Computers in Human Behavior*, *28*(3), pp. 820-831. https://doi.org/10.1016/j.chb.2012.01.011.

Kintu, M.J., Zhu, C. & Kagambe, E., (2017). Blended learning effectiveness: The relationship between student characteristics, design features, and outcomes. *International Journal of Educational Technology in Higher Education*, *14*(7), pp. 1-20. https://doi.org/10.1186/s41239-017-0043-4.

Mayer, R.E. & Moreno, R., (2003). Nine ways to reduce cognitive load in multimedia learning. *Educational Psychologist*, *38*(1), pp. 43-52. https://doi.org/10.1207/S15326985EP3801_6.

Moran, M., Seaman, J. & Tinti-Kane, H., (2011). Teaching, learning, and sharing: How today's higher education faculty use social media. Pearson Learning Solutions.

O'Bannon, B., Lubke, J., Beard, J. & Britt, V., (2011). Using podcasts to replace lecture: Effects on student achievement. *Computers & Education*, *57*(3), pp. 1885-1892. https://doi.org/10.1016/j.compedu.2011.04.001.

Vygotsky, L.S., (1978). Mind in society: The development of higher psychological processes. Harvard University Press.

Wdowik, S., (2014). Using a blended learning approach to support women returning to work in the United Arab Emirates. *Open Learning: The Journal of Open, Distance and e-Learning*, *29*(1), pp. 36-52. https://doi.org/10.1080/02680513.2014.908746.

Zimmerman, B.J., (2002). Becoming a self-regulated learner: An overview. *Theory into Practice*, *41*(2), pp. 64-70. https://doi.org/10.1207/s15430421tip4102_2.

Trowler, V., (2024). Toward a unified framework: The intellectual lineage of student engagement. *Higher Education Research & Development*, *43*(1), pp.1-14. https://doi.org/10.1080/2331186X.2024.2369002.

Kang, M. & Shin, W.S., (2019). An empirical investigation of student satisfaction and perceived learning outcomes with podcasting. *The International Review of Research in Open and Distributed Learning*, *20*(1), pp. 75-91. https://doi.org/10.19173/irrodl.v20i1.3938.

Berk, R.A., Olsen, T. & Chen, Y., (2021). Enhancing learning with audio feedback through podcasting: Benefits and challenges in higher education. *Educational Technology Research and Development*, *69*(2), pp. 543-562. https://doi.org/10.1007/s11423-021-09962-8.

Al-Rahmi, W.M., Alias, N., Othman, M.S., Marin, V.I. & Tur, G., (2018). A model of factors affecting learning performance through the use of social media in Malaysian higher education. *Computers & Education*, *121*, pp. 59-72. https://doi.org/10.1016/j.compedu.2018.02.010.

Luo, T., Shah, S. & Crompton, H., (2020). Designing collaborative learning in online courses: A review of the literature. *British Journal of Educational Technology*, *51*(4), pp. 1251-1264. https://doi.org/10.1111/bjet.12906.

Cidral, W.A., Oliveira, T., Felice, M.D. & Aparicio, M., (2018). E-learning success determinants: Brazilian empirical study. *Computers & Education*, *122*, pp.273-290. https://doi.org/10.1016/j.compedu.2017.12.001.

Anderson, C.A. & Rainie, L., (2020). The role of gamification in education: A literature review. The Pew Research Center. https://www.pewinternet.org/.

Chen, X., Yang, Y. & Zhang, J., (2018). Interactive multimedia learning systems in higher education: An exploration of their effects on engagement and performance. Educational Technology Research and Development, *66*(3), pp. 567-585. https://doi.org/10.1007/s11423-018-9581-3.

Perez, R., Shrestha, P. & Majumdar, M., (2020). Faculty adoption of LMS-integrated tools: Challenges and opportunities. Journal of Educational Technology Development and Exchange, *13*(2), pp. 15-30. https://doi.org/10.1007/s12345-020-4567.

SWOT ANALYSIS OF DISTANCE EDUCATION TECHNOLOGY: INDIGENOUS PERSPECTIVES INFORM PRACTICE

Paul Tauiliili[1,*], Deborah Zuercher[1,*] and Ivy Yeung[2]
[1]*University of Hawaii at Manoa, Professor and PACMED Executive Director*
[2]*University of Hawaii at Manoa, Assistant Specialist Faculty*
1777 University Avenue, Everly Hall 224, Honolulu, HI 96833, United States
[*]*Dr*

ABSTRACT

This qualitative study examined place-based program coordinators' perspectives of the strengths, weaknesses, opportunities, and threats (SWOT) of the trailblazing University of Hawai`i PACMED culturally responsive distance education program for Indigenous master's degree candidates across eight Pacific regions. Through triangulated data from qualitative focus group interviews, survey responses, and artifact analysis, emergent themes about the critical role of instituting on-island support systems—local Indigenous bilingual program coordinators, readers, and teaching assistants—who provide culturally responsive guidance, facilitate communication with off-island instructors and foster community engagement among Indigenous graduate candidates. This study uniquely contributes to the body of knowledge on place-based Indigenous education in the Pacific, particularly in an innovative graduate degree program that hires place-based Indigenous coordinators to support candidate retention. Participants emphasized that place-based support is vital for mentoring, technical support, and effective course delivery. The distance education (DE) program's online flexibility enabled PACMED candidates to remain on their home islands, balance education with work and community obligations, and reduce financial stress. This place-based model allows candidates to preserve their educational positions and enables them to apply new pedagogical strategies, strengthening local educational systems. However, the online program was perceived by coordinators to have the threat of infrastructure challenges, including frequent power outages, unreliable Internet connectivity, and inadequate technological resources. These barriers impede candidates' participation and engagement, highlighting the need for interventions to improve technological access and support. This self-study research underscores the importance of hiring place-based support and seeking opportunities for infrastructure improvements to sustain the success of distance education initiatives in remote regions.

KEYWORDS

Distance Education, Web-Based Communities, SWOT-Analysis, Place-Based, Culturally-Responsive

1. INTRODUCTION

The Pacific-Focused Masters in Education (PACMED) Master's Degree Program at the University of Hawai`i at Manoa (UH) is in its seventh year since its inception. The mission and vision of the PACMED program align with the College of Education's mission to envision a place of learning and teaching sustained by a collaborative community of educators who provide innovative research, teaching, leadership, and community engagement. The program offers most of its courses via DE in eight Pacific Islands. PACMED serves graduate-level educators residing in the Hawaiian Islands, the Republic of the Marshall Islands (RMI), American Samoa, the Republic of Palau, Hawaii, and the four states of the Federated States of Micronesia (FSM): Kosrae, Chuuk, Yap, and Pohnpei. Candidates from each island begin coursework as a cohort and complete their coursework together across five semesters. The program has successfully graduated 11 cohorts with nearly one hundred percent retention rates and foresees 15 graduating cohorts by the summer of 2025. PACMED graduates have earned a nationally accredited 30-credit master's degree from UH Manoa, focusing on Science, Technology, Engineering, and Mathematics (STEM) and Place-Based Education (PBE). Candidates consist of classroom teachers, school administrators, specialists, and program managers participating in online courses from their home islands. During the spring and fall semesters, when local K-12 schools are in session on the home islands, PACMED master's candidates gather in the evening as groups or work individually in a chosen location with Internet access and use DE communication software tools such as Zoom to participate synchronously in course discussions. Therefore, DE is a vital part of the program; it enables students to participate in class discussions, communicate with instructors and colleagues, complete assignments, present their final projects, and meet for advising. In the program's first semester, candidates learn how to use Google Suite applications and Zoom video conferencing software to better equip themselves with the technology aspects of the course delivery. The DE tools also enable candidates to complete the program on their islands rather than leaving their home country to attend the University of Hawai`i at Manoa campus. Several PACMED cohorts have candidates situated in remote outer island locations, and dependable Internet connections, updated laptops, and headsets are needed to facilitate their coursework. Each cohort is supported by a place-based Indigenous cohort coordinator who helps with technology issues such as setting up Zoom locations where candidates can meet to support them with Internet connectivity, laptop updates, Zoom etiquette, and Google Suite applications. The importance of place-based technological support in a distance education program's effective operation is a cornerstone to the success of the pioneer PACMED program.

The graduation requirement for the PACMED program is an ePortfolio, both a scholarly and practical project that documents evidence on how each candidate meets their local Department of Education's professional teaching standards (PTS). The ePortfolio uses Google Suite applications such as Google Docs and Google Folders to create a narrative of scholarly research that showcases evidence of each candidate's proficiency in meeting professional standards. Each candidate's ePortfolio contains hyperlinks to exemplars such as lesson plans, professional development certificates, STEM projects, field trips, and images of classroom work. The ePortfolio is used to meet university academic requirements and is a practical electronic document showcasing candidates' master-level proficiency in educational pedagogy, culturally responsive teaching, and professionalism. Following graduation, the ePortfolio is a valuable tool for performance evaluation, accreditation, and career advancement opportunities. Candidates complete, present, and submit their ePortfolio in the final semester entirely online as their final graduation requirement.

Candidates are supported by a team of on-island instructors, cohort coordinators, teaching assistants, home-based readers, and ePortfolio coordinators who assist with logistics such as DE in admissions, place-based course facilitation, setting up classrooms for class meetings, completing graduation applications, and assisting with computer and software issues. The instructional support team also assists with teaching, collaborating with off-island instructors, assisting with culture and language issues, mentorship, and administration tasks. Hiring on-island support from local Indigenous educators has proven to be a vital component in supporting the candidates. The PACMED program utilizes a "grow your own" philosophy and often hires graduates to serve on the place-based instructional team. The on-island support staff and facilitators use their experience of the many challenges and strengths they faced in this DE model to advise off-island faculty about the relevant issues and offer timely suggestions for continued success.

2. THEORETICAL FRAMEWORK

DE technology is an essential tool in providing higher education degrees to Indigenous educators in some of the most remote and underserved regions in the Pacific. In a Master's in Education degree program involving practical and theoretical applications of culturally responsive and relevant, place-based STEM education, technology connects instructors with their students and equips students with 21st-century skills. While technology presents immense opportunities, it also involves potential obstacles that affect the implementation and success of programs. An overview of the insights into the strengths, weaknesses, opportunities, and threats in the existing literature about DE is provided.

2.1 Importance of Distance Education Technology in the Pacific

The Pacific has a geographically dispersed population spread across many small islands. Access to quality education, especially at the graduate level, is often limited by logistical barriers (Whelan, 2008; Wardhani et al., 2018). DE technology has, therefore, become a key enabler in bringing higher education, including Master's in Education programs, to individuals who would otherwise have no access due to their location.

Distance learning platforms allow educational institutions to reach wider audiences and provide equitable access to learning materials, helping to overcome geographical and infrastructural challenges (Moore, 2014). DE in the Pacific region allows local educators and administrators to pursue higher education degrees while remaining at home and serving their communities and local schools (Kara et al., 2019; Zuercher et al., 2020). For educators in the Pacific islands, this reduces the need for costly travel and time spent away from their families. Allowing graduate candidates the opportunity to stay on their island and continue their jobs enables them to apply learning in their local communities, creating meaningful relationships between their graduate studies and their K-20 students.

2.2 What is Distance Education?

DE can be defined as formal education where the learning community is separated, and a telecommunications system is needed to connect each other to the learning material and instructors (Schlosser & Simonson, 2009). There are two different approaches to DE, which are synchronous and asynchronous coursework, as both have separations between instructors and students; however, in the latter, learners are also separated by time (Lou et al., 2006; Shahabadi & Uplane, 2015). Sometimes, a mixture of both asynchronous and synchronous instruction is employed. A significant advantage of DE courses is the convenience of bringing education to the location where learners live and work (Pontes et al., 2010). Furthermore, distance learning classes increase place utility, allowing learners to use a more convenient location for their learning. Consequently, students who have difficulty commuting to the face-to-face class location are likely to prefer DE. These courses also give students more flexibility in class schedules, especially those with work and family demands (Pontes et al., 2010). Several higher education institutions have strived to work toward providing DE opportunities to eliminate barriers and promote inclusive education for its learners (Schweighart et al., 2024). Further, Schweighart et al. (2024) state that DE in higher education has seen rapid growth since the 2020 pandemic, which has almost tripled from 11 million in 2017 to 27 million in 2023 and is expected to be five times greater by 2028. DE will likely continue as a mainstay and become an increasingly important component of formal higher education vs. face-to-face learning (Stewart et al., 2023).

2.3 Weaknesses and Threats of Distance Education

COVID-19 has revolutionized DE and traditional education as technological advancements allow more learners to have a to-go approach that will likely have lasting effects on educational environments (Pregowska et al., 2021). While DE technology has several advantages, innumerable challenges can halt its successful implementation. A place-based Master's in Education program in the Pacific region depends not only on technology but also on innovative staffing, infrastructure, digital literacy, and cultural appropriateness.

Although several challenges occur in online learning communities that lack funding and adequate infrastructure, it is the instructors' self-efficacy that is often the tool that allows them to overcome infrastructure challenges such as Internet connectivity, power outages, and lack of adequate devices (Kundu & Bej, 2021; Pokhrel & Chhetri, 2021). However, these barriers can continue to limit the effectiveness of online learning platforms such as Zoom, making it difficult for learners to listen and participate in discussions or lectures, understand course materials, and engage in meaningful talks (Almendingen et al., 2021; Yeh & Tsai, 2022). This causes severe learning disruptions and may cause frustration among learners and instructors. Learners in a DE community face several categories of external challenges, such as job-related challenges, including workload, lack of employer support, conflicts in schedules, financial problems, and time limitations for study (Kara et al., 2019). Furthermore, there are family-related issues, such as having an inconducive home environment for study and a lack of family support. Kara et al. (2019) also state that program-related challenges can include a lack of instructor or coordinator support, limited interaction with instructors, missing interaction with their colleagues, and feelings of isolation (Almendingen et al., 2021). Institutional barriers can exist, including a lack of online learning hardware and software support and offering a demanding program that limits online learners' success rate (Dutton & Dutton, 2005; Kara et al., 2019). Another challenge is that learners and instructors must adapt to DE's teaching and learning strategies, which are significantly different from those used in traditional face-to-face courses (Stewart et al., 2023). Also, when learners spend too much time on Zoom class sessions, they may face fatigue (Yeh & Tsai, 2022). Online learning facilitators often naively assume that students come with independence, self-motivation, and time management skills that enable them to succeed in DE (Means et al., 2014). Other challenges, such as a lack of digital literacy skills, may create a digital divide, compounding these challenges and making it more difficult for learners (Yeh & Tsai, 2022).

2.4 Strengths and Opportunities of Distance Education

The flexibility offered by DE is vital for educators in the Pacific, where there is a shortage of classroom teachers, and taking time off for extended study could negatively impact local schools (Tanaka & Sondergaard, 2023). Online platforms allow students to pursue graduate studies without leaving their jobs or communities for extended periods (Stewart et al., 2023). With the increase in international students who might face travel challenges and the need for educational needs in teacher training and professional development, DE is deemed a financially viable program that will benefit university stakeholders (Stewart et al., 2023; Ameri et al., 2023). DE learner's success can be linked to the program design that addresses individual learners' contextualized needs and the subsequent development of skills needed to adapt to DE (Schweighart et al., 2024).

One significant strength of DE is its cultural responsiveness, which allows for the incorporation of local traditions, values, and contexts into the curriculum, making education more relevant and respectful of learners' diverse backgrounds (Ameri et al., 2023). In addition, DE enhances access to qualified faculty who may otherwise be geographically distant. Furthermore, it often includes extensive support systems, such as academic advising, technical assistance, and peer networks, all of which are crucial for learners who might face challenges such as limited access to resources or physical campuses (Ameri et al., 2023). These systems help bridge the gap for students in remote areas and ensure they receive the academic and personal support they need to succeed.

Additionally, DE may promote cultural learning, as learners are exposed to diverse perspectives and educational practices from peers and instructors in different parts of the world while still maintaining a strong connection to their own cultural identities (Holmes & Gardner 2006). Another advantage is the financial benefit that distance education offers. Learners in the Pacific often face high costs associated with relocating to attend universities abroad, but DE eliminates these expenses, making advanced education more accessible to

individuals from lower-income backgrounds (Kezar, 2009). Finally, it strengthens the learner-instructor relationship by providing more consistent access to instructors through digital platforms. This ease of communication ensures timely feedback and support, which is vital for student success, especially in an online environment (Ameri et al., 2023).

DE technology has already changed the landscape of the PACMED Master's Education program delivery in the Pacific by providing educational access, levels of flexibility, professional development, increasing the local capacity of education leaders, and career advancement opportunities. The continued success of such programs will depend on addressing critical issues, including infrastructure limitations and opportunities, increasing obstacles with digital literacy, cultural responsiveness, and maintaining effective communication between instructors and learners. Overcoming these challenges will require careful planning, ongoing feedback, and suggestions from learners and instructors on successes and challenges to ensure that the technology used in the program is functional and maintains the rigor expected in higher education. With reflective and strategic practices, DE can continue to offer opportunities to educators residing on remote islands spread across the Pacific Ocean, transforming and improving the educational outcomes in the region.

3. METHODOLOGY

SWOT analysis is a qualitative research tool that helps institutions self-assess strengths, weaknesses, opportunities, and threats. The qualitative nature of SWOT analysis uses phenomenological or content analysis, allowing researchers to gather insights from program coordinators charged with problem-solving DE issues in their diverse cultural contexts (Sen et al., 2023; Dinçer & Şenkal, 2012). Creswell (2014) suggested that researchers use qualitative methods to unmask the meaning that individuals ascribe to a particular circumstance. This method is vital for the pioneer PACMED online master's degree program, which serves graduate Indigenous students in remote regions of the Hawaiian Islands, the Federated States of Micronesia, the Republic of Marshall Islands, American Samoa, and the Republic of Palau. New programs must intentionally engage in a feedback loop with stakeholders to continuously improve practice when there are no exact models to follow. By strategically examining local coordinators' perceptions of the program's strengths, weaknesses, opportunities, and threats, SWOT analysis provides a framework for identifying potential areas of program improvement (Leiber et al., 2018; Ustabulut, 2021). Using SWOT analysis as a lens enables decision-makers to maximize opportunities in unique cases and minimize organizational threats (Gable et al.,

2007; Vindača et al., 2021; Zhu & Mugenyi, 2015). Guest et al. (2006) suggest data saturation is reached when between six and twelve participants are interviewed in a qualitative study. Participants were eight local place-based administrators coordinating PACMED cohorts of graduate candidates on their home islands. These eight participants were purposively selected based on their knowledge of the online PACMED program and their experiences coordinating DE coursework. First, these eight participants completed a confidential Google Form survey. Second, participants engaged in confidential, open-ended focus group interviews to share perspectives in a culturally responsive oral tradition of mo`olelo or story-telling. Turner (2010) identified three qualitative interview methods: The Informal Conversational Interview, the General Interview Guide Approach, and the Standardized Open-Ended Interview. This self-study used the Standardized Open-Ended Interview. Ritchie and Lewis (2003) suggest focus groups are more appropriate when researchers desire an understanding of the group process; this was appropriate for the group/cohort model utilized in the PACMED program. Third, artifact analysis of graduate candidates' assignments was used to cross-check coordinators' perspectives with candidate outcomes. Data was triangulated through the confidential online survey, Zoom focus group interview, and artifact analysis of candidates' assignments. Typological analysis of the triangulated qualitative data was used to code emergent themes using the SWOT analysis as the guiding framework to categorize participants' perspectives of the program's strengths, weaknesses, opportunities, and threats. This self-study provided PACMED directors with valuable participant input for reflection on ways to move forward to capitalize on opportunities and continue to maintain the program's strengths. A strategic look at weaknesses and threats helped illuminate areas for growth and improvement.

4. RESULTS

A qualitative SWOT analysis of place-based Indigenous coordinators' perspectives of the PACMED Distance Education (DE) program resulted in emergent themes about the perceived strengths, weaknesses, opportunities, and threats associated with the pioneer program. The analysis provided valuable insights that can inform ongoing improvements to the program. The following typological categories emerged from the SWOT data.

4.1 Emergent Theme: Strengths

Table 1 displays the emergent themes that place-based PACMED coordinators perceived as the program's strengths. Seven themes became visible, describing the program's place-based, culturally responsive, and contextualized features. The master's degree program is not prepackaged and delivered to the Pacific region; it is co-designed and co-instructed with local stakeholders.

Table 1. Strengths

Emergent Theme	Characteristics
Place-Based Support Systems	Place-based on-island coordinators, teaching assistants, ePortfolio readers, and faculty members provide crucial technical and programmatic support, helping students address challenges and maintain engagement.
Flexible Learning Design	The program's flexibility enables candidates to remain on their home islands while continuing to work, fulfill cultural obligations, care for children and extended family, and avoid time away from their families. This flexibility contributes significantly to participants' ability to balance academic and personal responsibilities

Emergent Theme	Characteristics
Culturally Responsive Pedagogy	The PACMED program is tailored to be culturally responsive, incorporating a STEAM (Science, Technology, Engineering, Arts, and Mathematics) focus and place-based education that reflects the local context and Indigenous knowledge systems.
Financial Benefits	Participants can pursue higher education without the financial burden of housing, airfare, or living expenses typically associated with traditional university settings. Additionally, local stakeholders often provide third-party financial support for tuition.
Knowledgeable and Accessible Instructors	Co-instructors (place-based and online paired instructors) demonstrate sensitivity to the unique challenges online learners face, such as balancing academic requirements with family, work, and cultural responsibilities. This accessibility contributes to students' ability to navigate the program successfully.
Access to Education	The program offers learners access to higher education and professional development opportunities that are otherwise unavailable in their local communities, contributing to educational advancement in the region.
Program is Adapted to the Context	Co-instructors (place-based and online paired instructors) offer continuous feedback and adapt course content and structure to be culturally responsive and meet students' individual needs, enhancing the likelihood of success in the DE learning environment.

4.2 Emergent Theme: Weaknesses

Table 2 displays the emergent themes that place-based PACMED coordinators perceived as the program's weaknesses. Three themes became visible, describing the challenges in time zone differences, time management, and internet and equipment access. Identifying perceived weaknesses enables PACMED directors to strategically plan interventions to improve these areas. For example, PACMED can purchase and distribute technology equipment and is investigating the purchase of Starlink to provide more reliable Internet access.

Table 2. Weaknesses

Emergent Theme	Characteristics
Time Zone Difference	Coordinating communication and collaboration between faculty and students across different time zones presents challenges, particularly in aligning live sessions and cohort interactions.
Time Management	Balancing the demands of work, family, cultural obligations, and academic responsibilities remains a significant challenge for graduate-level participants.
Internet Access and Equipment Access	Internet access is unreliable, and DE equipment (e.g., laptops and headsets) are unavailable in remote locations.

4.3 Emergent Theme Opportunities

Table 3 displays the emergent themes that place-based PACMED coordinators perceived as the program's opportunities. Six themes became visible, describing the program's opportunities to provide professional development, impact the workforce, provide candidates with new technological tools, allow candidates to share cultural knowledge, create networking opportunities, and research opportunities in Internet infrastructure through Starlink. PACMED is a pioneer program that values feedback from stakeholders on their perspectives of opportunities to improve service continuously.

Table 3. Opportunities

Emergent Theme	Characteristics
Professional Development Demand	There is a growing need for higher education degrees within underserved international Indigenous communities, presenting an opportunity for the PACMED program to expand its impact by meeting this demand.
Workforce Impact	Equipped with advanced degrees, graduates of the PACMED program have the potential to build local educational capacity and serve as leaders within their communities, strengthening the educational infrastructure on their home islands.
Technology Tools	The program introduces candidates to digital tools and innovative teaching strategies that can be applied in local schools, contributing to the broader development of educational technology skills.
Cultural Learning	The sharing of cultural experiences and stories in the online classroom facilitates the integration of Indigenous ways of knowing into course content and discussions, enriching the learning experience for all participants.
Networking Opportunities	Students within each cohort share everyday cultural, familial, and professional experiences, creating opportunities for networking and collaboration. This sense of community among peers can enhance both academic and professional growth. Alumni workshops. Expanding degree offerings (e.g., social work, public health, economics)
Starlink Internet	PACMED is investigating the purchase of the Starlink satellite Internet constellation to provide global mobile broadband to at least one central location for synchronous course connection.

4.4 Threats

Table 4 displays the emergent themes that place-based PACMED coordinators perceived as the program's threats. Three themes became visible, describing the program's threats in lack of inadequate infrastructure affecting internet connectivity, financial hardships related to purchasing hardware and software for DE, and hiring policies restricting hiring local place-based instructors for both instructional and DE support.

Table 4. Threats

Emergent Theme	Characteristics
Lack of Adequate Infrastructure	Persistent infrastructure challenges, such as unreliable Internet connectivity, low bandwidth, power outages, and inadequate or outdated hardware (e.g., laptops), create significant barriers to participation and academic success.
Financial Hardships	The costs associated with maintaining Internet access, purchasing necessary technological devices (e.g., laptops), and commuting to locations with suitable Internet connectivity are significant financial burdens for many students, particularly in remote areas.
Hiring Policies	Restrictive university hiring policies threaten the ability to hire place-based support.

5. DISCUSSION

The success of the UH PACMED master's in education program for candidates in the Pacific region relies heavily on critical elements such as local support, flexibility, and the infrastructure that enables access to learning. This document explores the crucial role of on-island support, the flexibility of the DE model, and the infrastructure challenges that threaten its effectiveness. The findings emphasize how local coordinators, teaching assistants, and the program's flexibility contribute to student's academic success and satisfaction while addressing the barriers posed by limited infrastructure in remote island settings. The importance of these factors cannot be overstated, as they are integral to sustaining the program's growth and ensuring that candidates can access quality education while remaining in their home communities.

5.1 Importance of On-Island Support For DE

The findings highlight the indispensable role that local UH PACMED program coordinators, readers, and teaching assistants play in the success of the distance education program for master's degree candidates region. Candidates enrolled in courses benefit greatly from on-island staff familiar with their local context and accessible for real-time instructional, logistical, and technical assistance. This place-based support system provides tailored guidance to students and effectively bridges communication between students and off-island instructors. Participants noted that these local facilitators were critical for maintaining engagement, ensuring students could overcome technical challenges, and fostering community within the program. The data suggest altering this support system would risk undermining the program's success. Candidates and stakeholders repeatedly emphasized that local staff are crucial for timely troubleshooting, personalized mentoring, and efficient facilitation of online coursework. Additionally, the local team's role is to assist off-island instructors with communication and technical support, which helps streamline course delivery and address any issues. By supporting students in this manner, the local staff contributes to academic achievement and the candidates' overall satisfaction and confidence in their distance learning experience. Maintaining and possibly strengthening this on-island support structure is thus essential for the continued success and growth of the program in the region.

5.2 Flexibility of DE for Candidates and Personalization

The flexibility of the UH PACMED master's in education program is critical to its success for candidates in the Pacific region. This flexibility enables candidates to remain on their home islands while completing their courses, preserving their ability to work, support their families, and engage in community and cultural activities. Unlike traditional university settings that often require relocation, the online nature of the program allows candidates to maintain their income and fulfill responsibilities such as child-rearing, which enhances their overall quality of life. This model also significantly reduces the financial burden on candidates by eliminating travel and lodging expenses, making advanced education more accessible and economically feasible for many.

An additional advantage of the program's flexible structure is its positive impact on local educational ecosystems. By allowing candidates to continue teaching while enrolled in the program, the PACMED initiative ensures that valuable teaching positions are not vacated, thus preventing additional strain on local education departments already managing teacher shortages. This concurrent work-study model benefits both the candidates and their schools, as educators can immediately apply new pedagogical strategies learned through their courses, enhancing the quality of instruction provided to students. Keeping skilled educators within their communities while supporting professional development contributes to a more robust, resilient local educational framework.

Moreover, the program's adaptability extends beyond logistics. It includes recorded Zoom sessions that candidates can access to review lessons or catch up when personal or professional commitments prevent them from attending live. This feature, combined with the responsiveness of local coordinators and off-island instructors to students' needs, ensures that learning remains flexible and supportive. The program's capacity to adjust elective courses to align with the needs of candidates and the objectives of each Department of Education further demonstrates its commitment to meeting the evolving requirements of students and stakeholders. This level of customization and accommodation fosters a supportive educational environment that aligns with candidates' personal, professional, and cultural realities, contributing to the program's overall success.

5.3 Infrastructure Threats

The success of the UH PACMED master's in education program for candidates in the Pacific region faces threats due to persistent infrastructure challenges. One of the most pressing issues is frequent power outages, which disrupt the ability of students to participate in live Zoom sessions or complete assignments on time. Additionally, limited and unreliable Internet connectivity poses a significant barrier for candidates residing on remote islands. Even when Internet access is available, the high cost of maintaining connections at home or school further strains candidates, making it difficult for them to afford consistent, high-quality service. These connectivity issues are compounded by the challenges candidates face in accessing support from coordinators, particularly those living far from main island hubs where more assistance might be available. Compounding these challenges is the inadequate quality of personal equipment; many candidates do not have access to updated laptops with the latest software or sufficient capabilities to handle video streaming and sound during live sessions. This technological shortfall results in disrupted audio and visual quality, negatively affecting the candidates' ability to comprehend and engage with course content, so the PACMED program provides new laptops to all candidates. These infrastructure challenges—power outages, limited and costly Internet access, remote living conditions, and outdated technological tools—threaten the program's effectiveness. Addressing these issues is essential for ensuring that DE remains a viable and equitable option for candidates in the region.

6. CONCLUSION

In summary, the findings of this qualitative SWOT analysis highlighted the critical elements that contribute to the effectiveness of the PACMED DE program for master's degree candidates in its cohorts across its eight Pacific locations. The pivotal role of on-island support systems of coordinators, teaching assistants, and ePortfolio readers cannot be overstated, as they provide essential resources and foster a sense of community that enhances student engagement and success. The program's inherent flexibility further allows candidates to integrate their educational pursuits with personal and professional responsibilities, promoting overall well-being and accessibility. However, persistent infrastructure challenges present obstacles that must be addressed to ensure the program's sustainability and effectiveness. Moving forward, stakeholders must prioritize developing reliable technological resources and support systems. By investing in local support structures and necessary infrastructure improvements, the university can create a more equitable and effective DE experience that meets the unique needs of candidates in remote regions. This approach will benefit current students and pave the way for future educational initiatives in similar contexts.

REFERENCES

Almendingen, K., Morseth, M. S., Gjølstad, E., Brevik, A., & Tørris, C. (2021). Student's experiences with online teaching following COVID-19 lockdown: A mixed methods explorative study. *PloS One*, *16*(8), e0250378–e0250378. https://doi.org/10.1371/journal.pone.0250378

Ameri, H., Mahami-Oskouei, M., Sharafi, S., Saadatjoo, S., Miri, M., & Arab-Zozani, M. (2023). Investigating the strengths and weaknesses of online education during the COVID-19 pandemic from the perspective of professors and students of medical universities and proposing solutions: A qualitative study. *Biochemistry and Molecular Biology Education*, *51*(1), 94–102. https://doi.org/10.1002/bmb.21691

Bailenson, J. N. (2021). Nonverbal overload: A theoretical argument for the causes of Zoom fatigue. *Technology, Mind, and Behavior*, *2*(1). https://doi.org/10.1037/tmb0000030

Creswell, J. W. (2014). Research design: Qualitative, qualitative, and mixed methods approaches. Thousand Oaks, CA: SAGE Publications, Inc.

Dinçer, S. & Şenkal, (2012). Transforming traditional classes into e-learning platforms: A model study. *eLearning & Software for Education, 2*. https://doi.org/10.5682/2066-026X-12-112

Dutton, J., & Dutton, M. (2005). Characteristics and performance of students in an online section of business statistics. *Journal of Statistics Education*, *13*(3). https://doi.org/10.1080/10691898.2005.11910564

Gable, G. G., Lee, J., Kwahk, K., & Green, P. (2007). Administrative placement of the information systems academic discipline: A comparative SWOT analysis. *Communications of the Association for Information Systems 21*(8), 137-165. https://eprints.qut.edu.au/14026/1/14026.pdf

Guest, G., Bunce, A., & Johnson, L. (2006). How many interviews are enough? An experiment with data saturation and variability. *Field Methods*, *18*, 59–82.

Holmes, B., & Gardner, J. *E-Learning: Concepts and Practice*. 1st ed., SAGE Publications, Limited, 2006, https://doi.org/10.4135/9781446212585.

Kara, M., Erdoğdu, F., Kokoç, M. & Cagiltay, K. (2019). Challenges faced by adult learners in online distance education: A literature review. *Open Praxis, 11*(1), 5-22. *International Council for Open and Distance Education*. Retrieved October 21, 2024, from https://www-learntechlib-org.eres.library.manoa.hawaii.edu/p/208075

Kezar, A. (2009). Increasing access for low-income students and making financial education a priority for higher education. *Liberal Education*, *95*(3), 38.

Kundu, A., & Bej, T. (2021). We have efficacy but lack infrastructure: Teachers' views on online teaching learning during COVID-19. *Quality Assurance in Education, 29*(4), 344–372. https://doi.org/10.1108/QAE-05-2020-0058

Lane, L. M. (2009). Insidious pedagogy: How course management systems affect teaching. First Monday, 14. Retrieved September 2, 2024 from https://firstmonday.org/ojs/index.php/fm/article/download/2530/2303

Leiber, T., Stensaker, B., & Harvey, L. C. (2018). Bridging theory and practice of impact evaluation of quality management in higher education institutions: A SWOT analysis. *European Journal of Higher Education, 8*(3), 351-365. https://doi.org/10.1080/21568235.2018.1474782

Lou, Y., Bernard, R., & Abrami, P. (2006). Media and pedagogy in undergraduate distance education: A theory-based meta-analysis of empirical literature. *Educational Technology Research and Development, 54*(2), 141-76. https://doi.org/http://dx.doi.org/10.1007/s11423-006-8252-x

Means, B., Bakia, M., & Murphy, R. (2014). Learning online: What research tells us about whether, when and how. Routledge.

Moore, R. L. (2014). Importance of developing community in distance education courses. *TechTrends: For Leaders in Education & Training*, *58*(2), 20–24. https://doi.org/10.1007/s11528-014-0733-x

Pokhrel, S., & Chhetri, R. (2021). A literature review on impact of COVID-19 pandemic on teaching and learning. *Higher Education for the Future, 8*(1), 133-141. https://doi.org/10.1177/2347631120983481

Pontes, M. C., Hasit, C., Pontes, N. M., Lewis, P. A., & Siefring, K. T. (2010). Variables related to undergraduate students' preference for distance education classes. *Online Journal of Distance Learning Administration*, *13*(2), 8.

Pregowska, A., Masztalerz, K., Garlińska, M., & Osial, M. (2021). A worldwide journey through distance education—from the post office to virtual, augmented and mixed realities, and education during the COVID-19 pandemic. *Education Sciences, 11*(3). https://doi.org/10.3390/educsci11030118

Ritchie, J., & Lewis, J. (2003). *Qualitative research practice: A guide for social science students and researchers.* Thousand Oaks, CA: SAGE Publications Inc.

Schlosser, L.A.; Simonson, M. (2009). *Distance education: Definition and glossary of terms*; 3rd ed. Information Age Publishing: Charlotte, NC, USA, 2009.

Schweighart, R., Hast, M., Pampel, A. M., Rebien, J. A., & Trautwein, C. (2024). Transition into distance education: A scoping review. *Education Sciences*, *14*(10). https://doi.org/10.3390/educsci14101130

Sen, S., Taş, E., & Mert, H. (2023). An education faculty example in the evaluation of the distance education process: SWOT analysis. *International e-Journal of Educational Studies, 7*(14), 343-358. https://doi.org/10.31458/iejes.1254443

Shahabadi, M.M.; Uplane, M. (2015). Synchronous and asynchronous e-learning styles and academic performance of e-learners. *Procedia Social Behavioral Science, 176*(2), 125–138. https://doi.org/10.1016/j.sbspro.2015.01.453

Smyth, R. (2005). Broadband videoconferencing as a tool for learner-centered distance learning in higher education. *British Journal of Educational Technology*, *36*(5), 805–820. https://doi-org.eres.library.manoa.hawaii.edu/10.1111/j.1467-8535.2005.00499.x

Stewart, W. H., Lowenthal, P. R., & Richter, D. (2023). A model of remote teaching and learning under emergency and sustained crisis conditions: A description of novel distance education contexts and manifestations. *Turkish Online Journal of Distance Education, 24*(2), 183–201. https://doi.org/10.17718/Tojde.1090810

Tanaka, N., & Sondergaard, L. (2023). Analysis of teacher stock versus flow in primary education in East Asia and the Pacific middle-income countries: A simple model and results from simulation between 2020 and 2030. *The World Bank Policy Research Working Paper,* 10479. https://openknowledge.worldbank.org/server/api/core/bitstreams/9bb3e9af-42dd-460c-9bca-9267c0eb567b/content

Turner, D. W. (2010). Qualitative interview design: A practical guide for novice investigators. *The Qualitative Report, 15*(3), 754-760.

Wardhani, B., Dugis, V., & Saad, M. S. (2018). On the digital divide: Role of the University of the South Pacific in enhancing education in the Pacific countries. *World Transactions on Engineering and Technology Education*, *16*(1), 36-41. Retrieved November 1, 2024, from http://www.wiete.com.au/journals/WTE&TE/Pages/Vol.16,%20No.1%20(2018)/06-Wardhani-B.pdf

Whelan, R. (2008). Use of ICT in education in the South Pacific: Findings of the Pacific eLearning observatory. *Distance Education*, *29*(1), 53–70. https://doi.org/10.1080/01587910802004845

Ustabulut, M. Y. (2021). SWOT analysis for the distance education process of lecturers teaching Turkish as a foreign language. *Educational Policy Analysis and Strategic Research, 16(*1), 139-152. https://doi.org/10.29329/epasr.2020.334.8

Vindača, O., Ļubkina, V., Abuže, A., & Ušča, S. (2021). Life with COVID-19: SWOT analyses for transformative digital learning in educators' perspective. *Society, Integration, Education, 5*, 249-259. https://doi.org/10.17770/sie2021vol5.6199

Yeh, C.Y., & Tsai, C.C. (2022). Massive distance education: barriers and challenges in shifting to a complete online learning environment. *Frontiers in Psychology*, *13*, 928717–928717. https://doi.org/10.3389/fpsyg.2022.928717

Zhu, C., & Mugenyi, K. J. (2015). A SWOT analysis of the integration of e-learning at a university in Uganda and a university in Tanzania. *Technology Pedagogy and Education, 24*(5), 585-603. https://doi.org/10.1080/1475939X.2015.1093537

Zuercher, D.K., Nakano, G., Anjain, J. & Yeung, I. (2020). STEM education in the Pacific Islands. IATED Digital Library. Valencia, Spain: INTED2020 Proceedings, 7527- 7535. https://doi.org/10.21125/inted.2020.2014

THE IMPACT OF POPULAR COMMERCIAL-OFF-THE-SHELF GAME INTEGRATION IN JAPANESE SCHOOL EDUCATION: A CASE STUDY OF MOMOTARO DENTETSU: EDUCATION EDITION

Toru Fujimoto
Interfaculty Initiative in Information Studies, The University of Tokyo
7-3-1 Hongo, Bunkyo-ku, Tokyo,113-0033, Japan

ABSTRACT

Efforts to integrate game-based learning into school education have been undertaken worldwide for various purposes and audiences. In Japan, such practices have a long history and have maintained ongoing interest, though these initiatives have not been extensively examined within the international context of research on game-based learning. This study aims to understand the social impact of integrating "Momotaro Dentetsu: Education Edition," a notable recent example of large-scale game-based learning integration in Japan. By adopting a case study approach, the study investigated the developers' intentions, the reactions of educators who incorporated the game into their lessons, and the reactions from the general public since the game's release. The findings highlight the game's potential to address previously identified challenges in using commercial off-the-shelf games for educational purposes and offer valuable suggestions for future research in this field.

KEYWORDS

Game-based Learning, Edutainment, Serious Games, Gamification, COTS Games in Education, Japanese School Education

1. INTRODUCTION

Efforts to integrate game-based learning into school education have been undertaken worldwide for various purposes and audiences. Historically, board games were used for educational purposes even during the era of analog games. A well-known early example of edutainment is "The Landlord's Game," the precursor to Monopoly (Bogost, 2007). In Japan, the traditional board game Sugoroku was used for informal education for centuries (National Diet Library, 2013). Due to its simple and understandable format, Sugoroku became widely popular across various themes.

With the advent of computers, educational game software was introduced for home and school learning, forming the edutainment market. Examples from the US include "The Oregon Trail" and "Where in the World is Carmen Sandiego?" among others, highlighting the edutainment industry. However, the edutainment market experienced a rapid contraction (Shuler, 2012), partly due to the overly high expectations placed on immature learning games at the time. Additionally, various barriers to the educational use of games were identified, further contributing to the challenges faced by the edutainment market (Klopfer, et al., 2009).

In Japan, the global success of brain-training games on the Nintendo DS extended the formation of the edutainment market, which later spread to smartphone apps (Fujimoto, et al., 2024). Interest in game-based learning in schools has persisted, though many initiatives remained small-scale experiments. Recently, the educational version of Minecraft has gained significant attention in Japan, with increasing integration into classrooms (Ministry of Education, Culture, Sports, Science and Technology, 2024).

Other than the diffusion of Minecraft education, one of the most significant and latest developments in Japan is the introduction of "Momotaro Dentetsu: Education Edition" (hereinafter Momotetsu Education) to the school education (Figure 1). The game is the modified version of "Momotaro Dentetsu" (Momotaro Electric

Railway, commonly known as "Momotetsu"), a popular board game-style video game series produced by Konami Digital Entertainment (Konami Digital Entertainment, 2022). In the game, players act as presidents of railway companies, traveling across Japan to purchase properties, with the player holding the most assets at the end of the predetermined number of years emerging as the winner. Since the release of its original version in 1988, it has been played by a wide range of ages for over 30 years. In 2020, "Momotaro Dentetsu: Showa, Heisei, Reiwa mo Teiban!" was released, and it surpassed 4 million units in cumulative sales by December 2023. The franchise continued its success with the release of "Momotaro Dentetsu World: The Earth Spins with Hope!" in 2023, which has sold over 1 million units. This latest installment features 366 cities around the world as property stations, allowing players to learn about global specialties, industries, cultures, and geographies through gameplay.

Figure 1. Momotaro Dentetsu: Educational Edition ©Akira Sakuma & Konami Digital Entertainment

Momotetsu Education has released in 2023 for Japanese educational institutions for free. The game has seen significant adoption in Japanese schools, with over 7,000 schools registered to use the game as of March 2024. Of these, 4,000 are elementary schools, accounting for approximately 20% of all elementary schools nationwide (Konami Digital Entertainment, 2024). The game is part of a successful series that has captivated audiences for decades. Additionally, the educational impact of the series is supported by related products aimed at elementary school students, such as kanji and math drill books, as well as geography quiz reference books. These supplementary materials enhance the educational value of the game, making it a comprehensive tool for learning. This widespread acceptance and integration into educational settings underscore the potential of Momotetsu Education as an innovative educational tool, providing a unique blend of entertainment and education.

Given the background described above, this study aims to understand the social impact of integrating Momotetsu Education into school education. By adopting a case study approach, the research involved collecting data from publicly available online articles, user comments, and an online survey for educators. Through the analysis of game design and collected data, the study investigated the developers' intentions, the reactions of educators who incorporated the game into their lessons, and the overall impact on the school environment since the game's release.

2. LITERATURE REVIEW

2.1 Historical Background of Game-Based Learning in Japan

The integration of games into education has a long history in Japan, dating back to traditional games like E-sugoroku (illustrated sugoroku) and Karuta (card game). These games have been used as educational tools for centuries, traced back to the Edo era (Flickinger et al., 2010; Japan Karuta Culture Museum, 2023). E-sugoroku typically involves a board with a path that players follow by rolling dice, with each illustrated space representing different events or information. This game's structure helps in reinforcing memory and learning through repeated exposure to educational content in a playful manner. Similarly, Karuta involves matching cards based on poems, proverbs, or historical facts, thus fostering literacy and cultural knowledge. The key characteristics of E-sugoroku-type games include their narrative-driven gameplay and visual appeal, which help in engaging players and facilitating learning. These games are designed to be both entertaining and educational, with the primary educational value lying in their ability to make learning enjoyable and memorable. By embedding educational content within the game's narrative, players learn as they progress through the game, making the process of learning more interactive and less monotonous.

In a sense, Momotetsu Education builds on this rich tradition of educational gaming in Japan and takes these traditional concepts further by leveraging digital technology and interactive elements, which makes it more engaging for contemporary students. Similar to E-sugoroku, it uses a board game format where players travel across Japan, learning about geography, history, and economics. The game's design incorporates educational content seamlessly into the gameplay, ensuring that players are learning while they play. It also provides a structured yet flexible approach to learning, allowing teachers to integrate the game into various subjects and lessons. This connection highlights the continuity and evolution of educational games in Japan, showing how traditional educational values can be preserved and enhanced through modern game design.

2.2 Teaching with Commercial-Off-the-Shelf Game

Alongside the use of games developed specifically for educational purposes, research and practice on the educational use of commercial off-the-shelf (COTS) games have been continually explored. An early large-scale investigation of this nature is exemplified by the Teaching with Games (TWG) Project conducted by Futurelab in the UK (Sandford, 2006). The TWG report provides valuable insights into the integration of COTS games into educational settings, highlighting both potential benefits and challenges.

Unlike games developed specifically for educational purposes, the practice of modifying COTS games for educational use, though not common, has notable examples. One prominent case is the development and dissemination of SimCityEDU by GlassLab, established by Electronic Arts and the Institute of Play (Electronic Arts, 2013). SimCityEDU: Pollution Challenge, an educational adaptation of SimCity, aimed to teach students about energy management and environmental issues through in-game missions and concept maps. Despite initial gameplay challenges and a steep learning curve, the game engaged students and encouraged collaborative learning. It also highlighted the importance of data tracking for educational outcomes. Although resources from the project are no longer available following its closure, it garnered significant interest at the time (Wan, 2013).

These studies align with the exploration of Momotetsu Education in Japanese schools, where similar themes of engagement, technical barriers, and curriculum adaptation are evident. Understanding the broader context of game-based learning, as discussed in these previous studies, helps to frame the specific case of this study and its impact on Japanese education.

3. METHODOLOGY

This study is in its preliminary stages and aims to gain an overall understanding of how Momotetsu Education has been received by referencing a diverse range of data sources. Using a case study approach, the research analyzed online articles, classroom practice materials, public reactions on Twitter, and the results of an online survey targeting school teachers. By collecting and analyzing these varied sources, the case study method allows for an in-depth examination of the implementation and reception of Momotetsu Education, providing a comprehensive view of its educational impact and societal acceptance.

Data was gathered using several methods. First, online articles from publishers' announcements, educational websites, news outlets, and game-related publications were reviewed. These articles provided information on how Momotetsu Education is being used in schools, its educational benefits, and the challenges faced during implementation. Second, classroom practice materials, including conference materials and reflective reports by educators online, were analyzed. These materials illustrated how educators are integrating the game into their teaching practices and the responses from students. Twitter reactions from educators, students, and the general public were also examined to gauge the broader audience's perception of Momotetsu

Education, capturing both positive feedback and criticisms. To understand the context of the data, the researcher conducted game design analysis in terms of the game mechanics, and the educational and technical considerations taken in the game.

The study utilized purposive sampling to select relevant online articles, classroom practice materials, and Twitter reactions, ensuring the inclusion of diverse perspectives from various stakeholders involved with or commenting on Momotetsu Education. The data referenced in this analysis were articles and materials published online after the announcement of Momotetsu Education's planned release in September 2022, collected from May to July 2024. Given that most articles and comments were in Japanese, the study involved translating the data into English during the analysis process. The collected data were analyzed using qualitative content analysis techniques. Thematic analysis was employed to code and categorize the data, identifying key themes and patterns such as engagement, learning outcomes, challenges, and public perception. These themes were explored in detail to understand the initial impacts of Momotetsu Education. Ethical considerations included anonymizing direct quotes from Twitter to respect individuals' privacy and adhering to ethical guidelines for internet research, ensuring responsible data collection and analysis. The table below shows the examples of categories (Table 1).

Table 1. Collected Data

Media	Collected data
Official websites and news releases	7 articles
News media articles	25 articles (as of 2024/7/20)
YouTube video posts	24 video posts
X (Twitter)	More than 1700 tweets (during 2022/9/22-2024/7/20)
Other relevant data collected	Personal blogs, summary websites

Based on insights gained from the initial data analysis, an online survey was conducted to understand the actual usage conditions in schools, targeting school teachers who have registered to use the Momotaro Dentetsu: Education Edition. This survey was carried out between July and August 2024, with a total of 218 respondents. The age of the respondents ranged from 22 to 75, with an average age of 39.01. Regarding gender distribution, there were 159 men (72.9%) and 44 women (20.2%). By region, the highest number of responses came from the Kanto area, with 77 respondents (47.8%), followed by the Kinki area with 31 (19.3%), Tokai with 30 (18.6%), and Kyushu with 23 (14.3%), demonstrating a wide national distribution of responses. In terms of occupation, the majority were elementary school teachers, with 95 respondents (49.2%), and junior high school teachers, with 76 respondents (39.4%), primarily representing teachers in the compulsory education stages. Additionally, there were 9 special needs school teachers (4.7%), 3 university educators (1.6%), and 10 respondents classified as "other" (5.2%). This survey has provided diverse perspectives from the educational field regarding the use of the Momotaro Dentetsu: Education Edition.

4. RESULTS

4.1 Game Design Analysis

4.1.1 Game Mechanics and Educational Features

As mentioned, Momotetsu Education retains the core mechanics of the original "Momotaro Dentetsu" series. Players assume the role of a railway company president, navigating a virtual board game that represents the map of Japan. The goal is to travel to different cities, purchase properties, and accumulate assets over a predetermined period. The game uses a turn-based system where players roll dice to move across the board. Along the way, they encounter various events and challenges that can affect their financial standing.

The game includes several educational features that enhance its use as a teaching tool in schools. One of the key features is the ability to customize regions and playtime according to curriculum needs. Teachers can select specific regions of Japan, from Hokkaido to Kyushu/Okinawa, allowing for a focused learning experience on particular areas. This customization ensures that the game can fit within the standard class period, making it practical for school schedules.

Another significant feature is the geographical information display. When players stop at a station, the game provides basic information about the station and the prefecture. Additionally, a magnifying glass feature offers detailed information on various buildings, specialties, tourist attractions, and historical sites displayed on the map. This makes learning interactive and engaging, enhancing students' knowledge about different regions of Japan. The image shows players managing properties in Shibuya. The sidebar provides educational information about the area, including historical and cultural highlights (Figure 2).

Furthermore, the gameplay elements have been rebalanced to prioritize educational purposes. Competitive features that could lead to conflicts among students, such as blocking other players with attack cards, have been removed. Excessive fluctuations in game funds are also prevented. Notably, the "Binbo-gami" character, which negatively impacts a player's progress, has been excluded to maintain a positive and constructive learning environment. These adjustments ensure that the game remains educational and engaging without causing unnecessary frustration or competition among students.

Figure 2. Screenshot of 'Momotaro Dentetsu: Education Edition' gameplay ©Akira Sakuma & Konami Digital Entertainment

4.1.2 Technical Considerations

Momotetsu Education is designed to be accessible on multiple devices including Windows PCs, Chromebooks, and iPads. The game can be played using both keyboard and touch panel inputs, accommodating various types of devices used in educational institutions. It supports 1 to 4 players in a local multiplayer setting, but does not include online play functionality. This design choice ensures that the game can be easily integrated into classroom activities without requiring robust network infrastructure.

The game is provided as a browser-based application to ensure compatibility with the range of devices deployed in schools under the Ministry of Education, Culture, Sports, Science, and Technology's GIGA School Initiative (Government of Japan, 2021). This initiative has equipped schools nationwide with individual devices for each student. However, many schools still face challenges with network environments and maintenance capabilities. By offering Momotetsu Education as a simplified browser-based version, it ensures that even schools with lower-spec devices and limited ICT support can run the game smoothly. This approach has significantly contributed to the high adoption rate of the game in educational settings.

To extend its accessibility to younger students, including those in lower elementary grades, Momotetsu Education includes a new feature that displays furigana (phonetic readings) above kanji characters. This feature was added in response to user feedback following the game's initial release. It aims to support early literacy development and ensure that the educational content is comprehensible to a broader age range, enhancing the game's educational value across different grade levels.

4.2 Findings in Relation to the Research Purposes

4.2.1 Developers' Intentions and Reception by General Public

The development of Momotetsu Education was driven by a combination of educational and commercial objectives. Hidekazu Shoto, an elementary school teacher, played a crucial role in shaping the game's educational aspects. His insights ensured the game was pedagogically sound and engaging for students. Additionally, the creators had long been interested in the educational value of the game. They saw benefits in contributing to society through educational initiatives while simultaneously enhancing their brand and gaining insights that could inform their mainline game development efforts (Nippon Foundation, 2023). By continuously adding new features to the game based on educational needs, the project garnered media attention, creating a positive feedback loop that recognized the initiative's value.

The general public has responded favorably to Momotetsu Education. Tweets expressing anticipation and interest in the game highlight its widespread appeal. Users have shared their learning experiences, indicating that the game conveys educational content to players in an enjoyable manner. While there were some concerns about elements that could incite conflict among children, the educational adjustments made to remove such elements received high praise. Additionally, reactions to lessons where students presented to game developers in Hirakata City showed significant empathy, with many commenting that they wished they had such opportunities during their own childhoods (Togetter, 2024). Overall, the public perception has been largely positive, with many recognizing the game's potential to make learning more interactive and fun.

4.2.2 Reception by Educators

The reception of Momotetsu Education in schools has been positive. Educators have formed communities to share best practices and lesson plans, enhancing the game's educational impact. For example, Hirakata City has been proactive in incorporating the game into its curriculum, demonstrating a structured approach to integrating game-based learning. Educators have reported increased student engagement and motivation, advocating the game's potential as an educational tool (OVO, 2024). However, the number of practical reports available is limited, so the actual implementation in classrooms is not fully understood.

Focusing on respondents who have actually used the game in their classes, educators rate Momotetsu Education highly as an effective teaching tool for educational settings. As motivations for its adoption, 96.6% of educators feel it is "appealing as a teaching material," and 97.2% believe it "engages students' interest." Additionally, 85.3% find it "effective in supporting retention of learning content," and 80.7% regard it as beneficial for "enhancing teamwork and communication skills." These adoption motivations reveal that educators see significant educational potential in this game. Furthermore, regarding specific educational effectiveness, 66.9% of educators rate it as effective for "teaching new content," while 76.2% find it valuable for "reinforcing previously learned content." Notably, for enhancing learning motivation, 94.0% of educators rated it as effective, with 72.8% expressing it as "very effective." This shows that Momotetsu Education is widely recognized as a tool that boosts student motivation and supports educational activities (Figure 3).

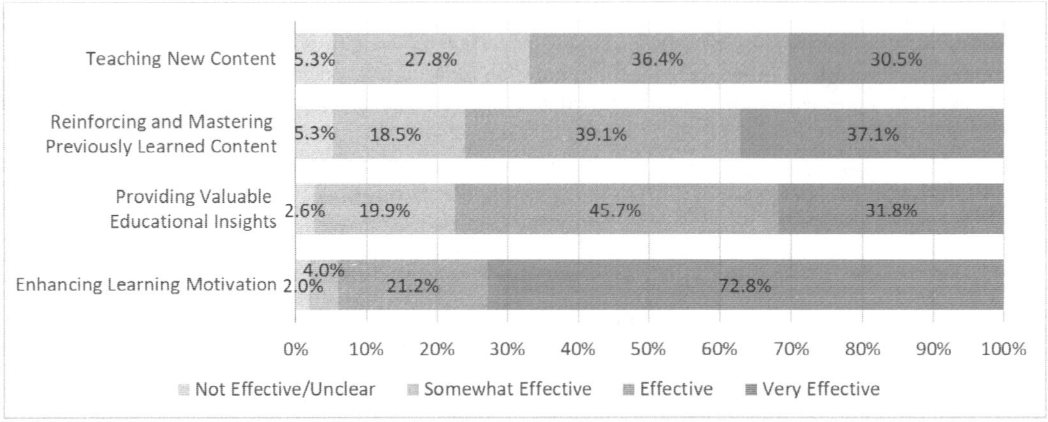

Figure 3. Educators' Perspectives on the Educational Effectiveness of Momotetsu Education

Regarding recommendations, 23.4% of respondents rated it a "10 out of 10" (strongly recommend), with an overall average score of 8.17. Overall, educators endorse this game as an excellent tool that can captivate student interest while aiding content retention and increasing motivation, signaling its promising impact for effective use in educational environments.

5. CONCLUSION

This study explored the implementation and reception of Momotetsu Education in Japanese schools. Key findings indicate that the game has been positively received by both educators and the general public. Educators reported increased student engagement and motivation, while the public showed favorable support for the game's educational value.

While definitive results have yet to be established, Momotetsu Education shows potential to contribute significantly to the field of educational game-based learning. The game addresses previously identified challenges and barriers in using commercial off-the-shelf (COTS) games for educational purposes. By integrating educational content seamlessly with gameplay, Momotetsu Education provides concrete suggestions for overcoming these obstacles and improving educational outcomes. Moreover, policymakers have begun to recognize the educational potential of this game, viewing it as an advanced example of using games for digital skills development. This recognition may lead to broader acceptance and support for educational games in school curricula, highlighting the game's potential as a tool for fostering essential skills in students (Ministry of Economy, Trade and Industry, 2024).

In terms of the limitations of this study, it is based on preliminary data and limited online resources. Detailed investigations and further research are needed to fully understand the game's implementation and impact in educational settings. Future research should include comprehensive surveys for educators and field studies in classrooms to gain a deeper understanding of how Momotetsu Education is being used and its effects on student learning. Such studies would provide more robust data to inform best practices and further development of educational games.

ACKNOWLEDGEMENT

This research was conducted as part of a collaborative research project with and funded by Konami Digital Entertainment Co., Ltd. We would like to express our gratitude for their support and cooperation throughout this project.

REFERENCES

Bogost, I. (2007). Persuasive games: The expressive power of videogames. MIT Press.

Electronic Arts. (2013). GlassLab launches SimCityEDU. Retrieved July 1, 2024, from https://www.ea.com/news/glasslab-launches-simcityedu

Flickinger, S., Podkowka, B., & Snyder, L. (2010). A window into modern Japan: Using Sugoroku games to promote the ideal Japanese subject in the early 20th century. University of Colorado Boulder. Retrieved from https://www.colorado.edu/ptea-curriculum/becoming-modern/window-modern-japan-using-sugoroku-games-promote-ideal-japanese-subject-early-20th

Fujimoto, T., Ikejiri, R., Fukuyama, Y., Furuichi, S., Matsukuma, H., & Ono, N. (2024). Serious games (Media technology series). Corona-sha.

Government of Japan. (2021). ICT in schools equips students with life skills for digital era. Retrieved July 10, 2024, from https://www.japan.go.jp/kizuna/2021/04/ict_in_schools.html

Japan Karuta Culture Museum. (2023). 'Hyakunin Isshu Karuta' as a teaching material for the education of the common people. Retrieved July 1, 2024, from https://japanplayingcardmuseum.com/5-5-4-6-hyakuninisshucarta-commonmaterial-education/

Klopfer, E., Osterweil, S., & Salen, K. (2009). Moving learning games forward: Obstacles, opportunities & openness. MIT The Education Arcade.

Konami Digital Entertainment. (2022). “Momotaro Dentetsu: Education Edition” announcement: Free to play for schools and educational institutions nationwide starting this winter. Retrieved July 10, 2024, from https://www.konami.com/games/corporate/en/news/release/20220915/

Konami Digital Entertainment. (2024). Momotetsu educational edition surpasses 7,000 schools in the first year; provided to 4,000 elementary schools nationwide, covering 20% of all schools. PR TIMES. Retrieved July 1, 2024, from https://prtimes.jp/main/html/rd/p/000000896.000050711.html

Ministry of Economy, Trade and Industry. (2024). Gamification for human resource development: Regional digital human resource development and securement promotion project report for fiscal year 2023. Retrieved July 10, 2024, from https://www.meti.go.jp/policy/mono_info_service/contents/downloadfiles/report/2024_gamification-jinzai.pdf

Ministry of Education, Culture, Sports, Science and Technology. (n.d.). Programming education portal focusing on elementary schools: Information on educational materials: Minecraft: Education Edition. Retrieved July 1, 2024, from https://www.mext.go.jp/miraino_manabi/content/376.html

National Diet Library, Japan. (2013). Famous places, people, and social customs on paper—Sugoroku board games from the Edo period. Retrieved July 1, 2024, from https://www.ndl.go.jp/kaleido/e/entry/12/

Nippon Foundation. (2023). The timeless classic game “Momotetsu” becomes educational material! What is “Edutainment”? Nippon Foundation Journal. Retrieved July 10, 2024, from https://www.nippon-foundation.or.jp/journal/2023/89006/education

OVO. (2024). “Please add Hirakata City to Momotetsu”: Sixth graders from Ogura Elementary School in Hirakata City present to the game director. Retrieved July 10, 2024, from https://ovo.kyodo.co.jp/ch/humhum/a-1945708

Sandford, R., Ulicsak, M., Facer, K., & Rudd, T. (2006). Teaching with games. Future Lab.

Shuler, C. (2012). What in the world happened to Carmen Sandiego? The edutainment era: Debunking myths and sharing lessons learned. The Joan Ganz Cooney Center at Sesame Workshop.

Togetter. (2024). “Please add Hirakata City to Momotetsu”: Sixth graders from Ogura Elementary School in Hirakata City present to the game director. Retrieved July 10, 2024, from https://togetter.com/li/2319884

Wan, T. (2013). Review: Going to town on SimCityEDU. EdSurge. Retrieved July 1, 2024, from https://www.edsurge.com/news/2013-11-24-review-going-to-town-on-simcityedu

INNOVATIVE EXPERIENTIAL LEARNING THROUGH THE IMPLEMENTATION OF OUTCOME-BASED EDUCATION

Aidrina Sofiadin
International Islamic University Malaysia, 53100 Kuala Lumpur, Malaysia

ABSTRACT

The increasing popularity of augmented reality in education can be attributed to its ability to captivate and engage students in ways traditional teaching methods often fail to do. This technology bridges the gap between the real and virtual worlds, providing students with the opportunity to experience learning in an interactive and immersive environment that enhances their understanding of complex concepts. This study addresses the research questions; (1) How extended reality technology leads on high achievement of student's outcomes (CLO)? and (2) How extended reality technology promotes experiential learning that improve students' grades? The answers were obtained through online survey from a total of 117 undergraduate students. The findings have enlightened the use of extended reality technologies in promoting experiential learning in a Business Fundamentals course.

KEYWORDS

Experiential Learning, Outcome-Based Education, Extended Reality, Innovative Education

1. INTRODUCTION

Experiential learning and Outcome-based education (OBE) have emerged as complementary approaches in modern pedagogical frameworks, offering valuable insights into enhancing student engagement and achieving desired learning outcomes. Experiential education emphasizes the importance of hands-on experiences, collaborative learning, and reflective practices to facilitate deeper understanding and skill development. On the other hand, OBE provides a structured framework to ensure that students achieve the intended learning outcomes. Educators can design learning activities and assessments that align with the desired outcomes, ensuring that students demonstrate the expected competencies.

Outcome-based education has been a subject of significant interest and discussion in the academic community for several decades, as educators and policymakers seek to develop educational systems that better align with the evolving needs of students and the workforce (Boschee and Baron, 1994). Broadly speaking, outcome-based education is a learner-centered approach that focuses on defining and measuring specific learning outcomes, rather than the traditional emphasis on content delivery and input-based measures (Rao, 2020).

Experiential learning has emerged as a prominent educational approach that emphasizes the importance of direct experience and active engagement in the learning process. Experiential learning offers opportunities for students to work collaboratively with peers and engage in reflection to achieve desired learning outcomes. This learning is designed to engage students in direct experiences tied to real-world problems and situations, where they analyse what they know, what they do not know, and how to learn it (Dernova, 2015; Rubin, 2000). This method of instruction moves away from traditional didactic or rote learning, instead focusing on immersing learners in authentic experiences that foster the development of new skills, attitudes, and ways of thinking (Gleason et al. 2011). Moreover, the strong motivation to learn provided by experiential learning can enhance student engagement and lead to meaningful learning experiences (Dernova, 2015).

The integration of extended reality technologies, encompassing virtual reality, augmented reality, and mixed reality, has gained significant attention in the realm of education (Ortega-Rodriguez, 2021; Jagatheesaperumal et al. 2024; Brooks, 2021). These emerging technologies have the potential to transform teaching and learning by creating immersive, interactive, and engaging learning experiences for students. The implementation of OBE can significantly strengthen students' entrepreneurship and business skills, as well as their entrepreneurial mindset. By incorporating an explicit learning outcome that concentrates on developing business and entrepreneurial skills, OBE can equip students with the necessary tools to navigate the dynamic and competitive business landscape, fostering their ability to identify opportunities, think creatively, and effectively manage resources.

2. EXPERIENTIAL LEARNING, OUTCOME-BASED EDUCATION, AND EXTENDED REALITY TECHNOLOGY

2.1 Experiential Learning

Experiential learning has emerged as a prominent educational approach that emphasizes the importance of direct experience and active engagement in the learning process. This method of instruction moves away from traditional learning, instead focusing on immersing learners in authentic experiences that foster the development of new skills, attitudes, and ways of thinking(Gleason et al. 2011).

Experiential learning was introduced early on by renowned educational theorists such as John Dewey, Jean Piaget, and Lev Vygotsky, who recognized the value of learner-centered, hands-on approaches (Nath, 2016). More recently, this philosophy of education has gained significant traction, shifting from the periphery to the center of educational practice (Lewis and Williams, 1994).

One of the key factors driving this shift is a changing conception of learning itself. Whereas previous models emphasized the passive acquisition of content, contemporary perspectives recognize the importance of active engagement, reflection, and the application of knowledge to real-world situations. As such, experiential learning is considered fundamental to meaningful and impactful learning (Lewis and Williams, 1994). The benefits of experiential learning are multifaceted. Its proponents argue that this approach is more easily applied to real-world scenarios and does not rely on extrinsic motivations such as grades (Hamilton, 1994). However, experiential learning is also acknowledged to be less efficient and less generalizable than highly symbolic classroom learning, necessitating its integration within a broader educational framework(Hamilton, 1994).

2.2 Outcome-Based Education

Outcome-based education (OBE) has been a subject of significant interest and discussion in the academic community for several decades, as educators and policymakers seek to develop educational systems that better align with the evolving needs of students and the workforce (Boschee and Baron, 1994). OBE is a learner-centered approach that focuses on defining and measuring specific learning outcomes, rather than the traditional emphasis on content delivery and input-based measures (Rao, 2020). The foundational principles of OBE were established by William Spady in the 1990s, who advocated for a shift in educational focus from "what is taught" to "what is learned." (Rao, 2020; Shyamalaprasanna et al. 2021). Spady argued that the goal of education should be to equip students with the knowledge, competencies, and orientations needed for success after leaving the institution, rather than merely exposing them to a predetermined curriculum (Pantao, 2021).

The shift towards OBE has been recognized as a critical component of the knowledge-based economy, as it aims to equip students with the skills and competencies needed to thrive in an increasingly complex and rapidly evolving global landscape (OECD, 2019; World Economic Forum, 2017). One of the key advantages of OBE is its ability to bridge the gap between academic theory and practical application. As such, the adoption and implementation of OBE models have been the subject of extensive research and debate within the academic literature.

2.3 Extended Reality Technology

The integration of extended reality technologies, encompassing virtual reality, augmented reality, and mixed reality, has gained significant attention in the realm of education (Ortega-Rodriguez, 2021; Jagatheesaperumal et al. 2024; Brooks, 2021). These emerging technologies have the potential to transform teaching and learning by creating immersive, interactive, and engaging learning experiences for students. Research has shown that these technologies not only enhance learners' motivation and engagement but also support collaborative and situated learning, enabling students to connect with content in ways that traditional methods may not facilitate (Yang, Zhou, and Radu, 2020). Moreover, the literature indicates that extended reality can foster the development of critical skills, such as collaboration, communication, and critical thinking, which are essential for student success in today's educational landscape (Yang, Zhou, and Radu, 2020; Trindade, Ferreira, and Pereira, 2023; Maas and Hughes, 2020).

Augmented reality has been a particularly prominent focus in the educational literature. Augmented reality allows users to interact with virtual objects that are seamlessly integrated into the real world, offering a unique learning experience. Research (Ortega-Rodriguez, 202; Brooks, 2021; Yang, Zhou, and Radu, 2020; Trindade, Ferreira, and Pereira, 2023; Alzahrani, 2020; Ersözlü, Karakuş, and Clark, 2019) has explored the various learning strategies that have been implemented using augmented reality, such as gamification, mobile learning, and ubiquitous learning. The meta-analysis by Hanid, Said, and Yahaya (Hanid, Said, and Yahaya, 2020) highlights the potential of augmented reality to enhance learning, with the technology enabling students to engage with digital information embedded within their physical environment.

Virtual reality, on the other hand, immerses users in a fully digital environment, allowing for simulated experiences and the exploration of virtual worlds. This technology has been shown to improve engagement and motivation among students, as well as support experiential learning through simulations that would otherwise be impractical or impossible in a traditional classroom setting, fostering critical thinking and collaboration skills in learners (Yang, Zhou, and Radu, 2020). Furthermore, mixed reality combines elements of both augmented and virtual reality to create enriched learning environments where the physical and digital worlds coexist, offering unique opportunities for learner interaction and engagement. While the distinct benefits of each technology are evident, the literature also suggests that their integration can lead to more robust educational outcomes, particularly as educators seek to leverage these tools for enhanced student-centered learning experiences and deeper comprehension of complex concepts (Yang, Zhou, and Radu, 2020; Maas and Hughes, 2020).

3. RESEARCH METHODS

Online surveys have become an increasingly popular tool for academic researchers in recent years, offering a range of benefits that have transformed the way data is collected and analyzed. This study used online survey due to their ability to streamline the data collection process, allowing researchers to gather responses from a larger and more diverse sample in a shorter amount of time than traditional methods would permit (Putranto, 2019). Moreover, the flexibility afforded by online surveys enables respondents to complete the surveys at their convenience, which can lead to increased participation rates and richer data, all while minimizing resource expenditure and the need for physical materials traditionally required in survey research (Putranto, 2019; Gosling and Mason, 2015). In addition to these logistical benefits, online surveys can incorporate dynamic features, such as automatic checks for item completion and adaptive questioning, which enhance the respondent's experience and improve the quality of the collected data, thereby making the research process more efficient and effective (Gosling and Mason, 2015).

This study will address the research questions;

1. How extended reality technology support high achievement of student's outcomes (CLO)?
2. How extended reality technology promotes experiential learning that improve students' grades?

Thus, to address this research question; online survey (N=117) was used to examine students' perspectives on using extended reality technology to promote experiential learning through outcome-based education, i.e. virtual tour and augmented reality. The online survey contained 10 questions asking students to provide their agreement on the use of extended reality technology in their outcome-based education course.

3.1 Participants

In this study, the 117 participants are students from the International Islamic University Malaysia, who are undertaking Bachelor Degree in Information Technology (BIT) and Bachelor Degree in Computer Science(BCS), enrolled in Business Fundamentals course. It was noted that Bachelor Degree is an important role in the exchange of knowledge, skills and experience via the practical assessment tasks.

3.2 Assessment Tasks

The assessment tasks for the Business Fundamentals course are: individual assessment task (30%), group project on business proposal and presentation (40%), and final exam (30%). These assessment tasks have been designed based on the university graduate attributes and Malaysia's education plans. The use of extended reality technology such as virtual tour and augmented reality application were utilized to assist students understanding in course topics. Virtual tours were given using virtual reality devices to allow students to experience the real-world practices and scenarios in Information Technology (IT) workplaces, e.g. Google Data Centre, Tesla Factory, BMW iFactory, and Cyber Security Lab. In addition, augmented reality apps such as virtual post-it notes and AR quiz were used.

4. FINDINGS AND DISCUSSION

The online survey was conducted during the middle of the semester. The survey results are presented and discussed in this section, see Table 1. Students were asked about their level of agreement through a five-Likert scale, 1-Strongly Disagree (SD), 2-Disagree (D), 3-Neither agree or disagree (N), 4- Agree (A), and 5-Strongly Agree (SA). The online survey was analysed using SPSS software.

Table 1. Students' Perspectives on Extended Reality (Xr) Towards Experiential Learning

Statements	SD	D	N	A	SA	Mean	Std. Deviation
I believe the extended reality improve my understanding on the topics and the application of the business theories.	0	2	13	33	69	4.44	.76
The extended reality technology has improved my self-esteem.	1	6	15	64	31	4.01	.83
The use of extended reality technology motivates me to attend the class.	0	1	11	61	44	4.27	.66
I believe the extended reality technology enriches my learning outcomes.	0	3	9	67	38	4.20	.69
The use of extended reality technology promotes experiential learning.	0	5	13	56	43	4.17	.79
The use of extended reality technology has improved my assessments' grades.	2	9	21	67	18	3.77	.86
The virtual tour has improved my learning experiences.	0	3	15	61	38	4.15	.73
The augmented reality app has improved my knowledge and understanding.	1	1	18	57	40	4.15	.77
The use of extended reality technology is not only improve my knowledge, but also my value.	2	5	17	54	39	4.05	.90
The use of extended reality technology allows me to experiences different culture and IT practices.	0	0	16	53	48	4.27	.69

Based on the results shown in Table 1, most participants agreed on the benefits of using extended reality technology. At the higher education level, the literature indicates that the educational technology discipline has been a particularly active area of research in the field of augmented reality (Ersözlü, Karakuş, and Clark, 2019). The result has highlighted the use of extended reality technologies in enhancing student understanding, motivation, and learning outcomes. Based on Table 1, where the average of standard deviation is 0.8 and the mean is 4.1 for the 5-Likert scale, this indicates that the responses are alternatively closely clustered around the mean value (Sullivan and Artino, 2013; Redmiles et al. 2017; Bao, 2020). This pattern may indicate a high level of agreement or consistency among the survey participants in their ratings of the survey questionnaires (Sullivan and Artino, 2013). It also noted that there is only one statement with the mean below value of 4, which is on the ability on XR to improve assessments' grades. This may due to lack of capturing and measuring rubrics on XR activities for assessment marks.

Furthermore, the findings indicated that the extended reality technologies has been complimented for its potential to improve student learning outcomes, enhance instructional quality, and better achievement on of student's outcomes and grades. However, some participants were disagreed on the use of extended reality technology. This is due to their preference in traditional learning rather than using virtual reality devices.

Additionally, the most participants agreed that augmented reality it enables them to visualize and interact with educational content in a manner that promotes better retention and encourages active participation in the learning process, ultimately making lessons more enjoyable and impactful for learners. They also believed that the integration of augmented reality applications enhances the educational experience by allowing for personalized learning, which caters to different learning styles and paces, thereby this findings aligns with study by Pal and Ade (Pal and Ade, 2022) in 2022.

Based on the findings, virtual tours have emerged as a powerful tool in the educational landscape, offering students a unique and immersive experience that can significantly impact their learning outcomes and personal values. By simulating real-world environments through 360-degree imagery and multimedia elements, virtual tours engage students in a manner that enhances their motivation and engagement, subsequently fostering a deeper understanding of the subject matter being explored.

5. CONCLUSION

Outcome-based education has emerged as a revolutionary approach in the field of education, emphasizing the importance of clearly defined learning outcomes and the implementation of innovative teaching and learning strategies to achieve those outcomes. OBE emphasizes the importance of equipping students with the necessary knowledge, skills, and competencies that are directly aligned with the demands of the workforce and industry. By focusing on the desired learning outcomes, educators can design and implement innovative experiential learning opportunities that allow students to apply their knowledge and skills in authentic settings, such as internships, project-based learning, and simulations. Thus, by aligning educational practices with industry-relevant learning outcomes, OBE ensures that graduates are well-prepared to meet the evolving needs of the job market, which could enhance their employability and career prospects.

As evidenced by the findings presented in this paper, the use of XR can lead to innovative and engaging experiential learning and engaging experiential learning opportunities, bridging the gap between theory and practice, and strengthening students' entrepreneurial and business skills through OBE. While the literature and this study findings presents a largely positive outlook on the integration of extended reality in education, it is essential to consider the practical challenges and limitations. Factors such as the availability of resources, teacher training, and the seamless integration of the technology into the curriculum must be addressed to ensure successful implementation. As the field of extended reality in education continues to evolve, there is a need for further research to explore new applications, refine the technology, and develop effective strategies for integrating these innovative tools into various educational contexts.

ACKNOWLEDGEMENT

The author would like to thank the Ministry of Higher Education Malaysia, for the research grant (FRGS-EC/1/2024/ICT09/UIAM/03/1) that supports this study.

REFERENCES

Alzahrani, N. M., (2020). Augmented Reality: A Systematic Review of Its Benefits and Challenges in E-learning Contexts. *Multidisciplinary Digital Publishing Institute*, Vol.10, No.16, pp, 5660-5660.

Boa, X. (2020). Green packaging use willingness factor scale development. *IOP Conference Series Materials Science and Engineering.* IOP Publishing. Vol. 768, p. 52084, viewed 17 November 2024, https://iopscience.iop.org/article/10.1088/1757-899X/768/5/052084

Boschee, F. and Baron, M. A. (1994). *OBE: Some Answers for the Uninitiated.* Taylor & Francis, Vol. 67, No.4, pp.193-196.

Brooks, A. L. (2021). *Gaming, VR, and Immersive Technologies for Education/Training*. Springer Nature, 17-29.

Dernova, M. (2015). Experiential Learning Theory As One of the Foundations of Adult Learning Practice Worldwide. *Comparative Professional Pedagogy,* Vol. 5, Iss. 2, p. 52-57, viewed 18 October 2024, https://doi.org/10.1515/rpp-2015-0040

Ersözlü, A., Karakuş, M., and Clark, A. C. (2019). *Augmented Reality Research in Education: A Bibliometric Study*. Modestum Limited, Vol.15, No.10.

for Economic Co-operation and Development, viewed 3 September 2024, <https://www.oecd.org/education/2030-project/teaching-and-learning/learning/learning-compass-2030/OECD_Learning_Compass_2030_Concept_Note_Series.pdf>.

Gleason, B. L. et al., (2011). *An Active-Learning Strategies Primer for Achieving Ability-Based Educational Outcomes*. Elsevier BV, Vol.75, No.9, pp.186-186.

Gosling, S. D., and Mason, W. (2015). *Internet Research in Psychology*. Annual Reviews, Vol.1, pp.877-902.

Hamilton, S. F. 1994. *Experiential Learning Programs for Youth*.University of Chicago, Vol.88, No.2, pp.179-215.

Hanid, M. F. A., Said, M. N. H. M. and Yahaya, N. (2020). *Learning Strategies Using Augmented Reality Technology in Education: Meta-Analysis*. Horizon Research Publishing, Vol.8(5A), pp. 51-56.

Jagatheesaperumal, S. K., Ahmad, K., Al-Fuqaha, A., and Qadir, J. (2024). *Advancing Education Through Extended Reality and Internet of Everything Enabled Metaverses: Applications, Challenges, and Open Issues*. Cornell University.

Lewis, L. H. and Williams, C. (1994). *Experiential learning: Past and present*. Wiley, pp.5-16.

Maas, M. J. and Hughes, J. (2020). *Virtual, augmented and mixed reality in K–12 education: a review of the literature*.Taylor & Francis, Vol.29, No.2, pp.231-249.

Nath, S. (2016). Instructional Programme on Experiential Learning in Science Education: Appraising its Impact through Students' Reflections. Vol.7, No.1, pp.2238-2246. viewed 11 October 2024 <https://doi.org/10.20533/licej.2040.2589.2016.0296>.

OECD, (2019). *Future of Education and Skills 2030. OECD Learning Compass 2030.* Organisation

Ortega-Rodriguez, P. J. (2021). From broad reality to the Metaverse: Critical reflection on the contribution of education. *Metaverse.* Vol.2, No.2, pp. 1-12.

Pal, R. A. B., and Ade, M. (2022). Applications and Challenges of Augmente Reality in Education Sector: A Report. *International Journal for Research in Applied Science and Engineering Technology.* viewed 29 August 2024, < https://doi.org/10.22214/ijraset.2022.45183>.

Pantao, J. (2021).Crisscrossing Textbook Writing Tasks and Core Values of Education Students in an Outcomes-Based Education Platform. *Proceedings of the 6th UPI International Conference on TVET 2020.* Vol. 520, pp. 357-364.

Putranto, L. S. (2019). *The use of an online survey to speed up the data collection process*. IOP Publishing, Vol.508, pp.012013-012013.

Rao, N. (2020). *Outcome-based Education: An Outline*. SAGE Publishing, Vol.7, No.1, pp. 5-21.

Redmiles, E. M., Acar, Y., Fahl, S., and Mazurek, M. L. (2017). A Summary of Survey Methodology Best Practices for Security and Privacy Researchers. viewed 17 November 2024, https://drum.lib.umd.edu/items/683d78b0-a0e3-4fae-9c93-b75aae4ad11b

Rubin, S. G. (2000). *Developing Community Through Experiential Education*. In New Directions for Higher Education. Wiley, Vol. 2000, Iss. 109, p. 43-50.

Shyamalaprasanna, A., Velnath, R., Pousia, S. and Kumar, M. (2021). *Survey of an Effective Outcome Based Teaching Learning Taxonomy in Professional Undergraduate Courses*. IOP Publishing, Vol.1084, No.1, pp.012098-012098.

Sullivan, G. M., and Artino, A. R. (2013). Analyzing and Interpreting Data From Likert-Type Scales. *Journal of Graduate Medical Education,* Vol. 5, no. 4,p. 541-542.

Trindade, N.V., Ferreira, A. and Pereira, J., (2023). Beyond the Screen: *Reshaping the Workplace with Virtual and Augmented Reality*. Cornell University. viewed 9 September 2024 < https://doi.org/10.48550/arxiv.2312.00408>

World Economic Forum, (2017). *Realizing Human Potential in the Fourth Industrial Revolution,* viewed 16 September 2024,<http://www3.weforum.org/docs/WEF_EGW_Whitepaper.pdf>

Yang, K., Zhou, X., and Radu, I. (2020). *XR-Ed Framework: Designing Instruction-driven andLearner-centered Extended Reality Systems for Education*.. Cornell University. viewed 11 September 2024 < https://doi.org/10.48550/arxiv.2010.13779>

INVESTIGATING THE DEVELOPMENT OF INTERCULTURAL COMPETENCES THROUGH BLENDED INTENSIVE PROGRAMMES

Alice Barana[1], Antonino Cambria[1,2], Marina Marchisio Conte[1] and Enrico Spinello[3]
[1]*Department of Molecular Biotechnology and Health Sciences, University of Turin, Piazza Nizza 44, 10153 Torino, Italy*
[2]*High Defence Study Centre, Piazza della Rovere, 83, 00165 Roma, Italy*
[3]*Army Officers School, Via Arsenale 22, 10121 Torino, Italy*

ABSTRACT

The increasing use of concepts such as globalisation, hyper-connected world, and cultural aggregations cannot be separated from a progressive process of innovation in the field of education, especially in Higher Education (HE). The HE environment is studded with thousands of activities where people can approach different realities from which they absorb competences and skills. As far as multicultural activities are concerned, it is necessary to find that inspiration that allows students to develop intercultural competences based on abilities and tendencies that constitute the multicultural personality in order to be ready and well-equipped at the moment of interaction in our hyper-connected world. At the University of Turin, precisely at the SUISS (University Interdepartmental School of Strategic Sciences) and the Army Officers School, seven Blended Intensive Programmes (BIP) on interdisciplinary subjects are held every year with the participation of 290 civilian, military and international students. The paper tries to measure the development of multicultural effectiveness during the attendance of the seven BIPs, with the intent to trace how it can be useful for all learners. Almost 2900 responses are the data collected with a questionnaire delivered at the beginning and the end of the BIPs over two academic years (2023 and 2024). The results were compared and analysed through descriptive and bivariate statistic tools. The results support the international orientation importance of the intensive programmes, and highlight the fact that these are an optimal field of experimentation for the students. These international activities are safe laboratories where it is possible to nurture the intercultural competences that will be fundamental for the near future.

KEYWORDS

Blended Intensive Programme, Higher Education, Intercultural Competences, Internationalization, Multicultural Personality

1. INTRODUCTION

In today's global and hyperconnected world, the job market, the higher education environment, and society are becoming more international in orientation. Increasingly, people, whether students or employees, have to be able to relate to foreign cultures at school, in the workplace, or even on their way around the cities (Tushar and Sooraska, 2023). To flow smoothly in this complex environment rich in various cultures, people need a tool bag with skills and competences that offer them advantages in international orientation. People need to be aware of the intercultural differences that arise in such an environment, which can consist of different perceptions regarding facts or approaches to problem solving and a variety of cultures that coexist simultaneously. Indeed, nowadays, this variety originates in a multicultural environment (Deardorf & Jones, 2012). The starting point for being aware of all connections and intercultural relationships as well as clashes is to understand what a culture is. A culture may be defined as a pattern of behaviors, customs, and traditions that are acquired and transferred through symbols, language, actions, and interactions that are commonly shared and accepted within a group and serve as a cognitive map or a blueprint for future behavior (Kluckhohn and Kroeberg, 1952; Van Der Zee and Van Oudenhoven, 2000). Besides technical skills, students should also be exposed to soft skills such as critical thinking, empathy, problem solving, creativity and social communication (Schulz, 2008). Once these soft skills are introduced in an international environment of education, where there is multiculturality and a global orientation, the aim of internationalisation is to ensure Higher Education (HE)

Institutions produce global-ready personnel who have acquired the intercultural competences to be able to address issues associated with global developments and challenges (Deardorf & Jones, 2012). These competences include attributes that can be considered aspects of a personality, such as respect, openness, curiosity, cultural knowledge, and skills, such as the ability to observe, listen, evaluate, and interpret (Deardorf, 2006; Hackett 2023). Intercultural competences refer to skills and items based on psychological well-being, satisfaction, relationships, empathy, sociality, reflexing, and so on (Van Der Zee and Van Oudenhoven, 2000). These allow people to enter the new environment, ready for the inputs coming from all actors and interrelationships. Multicultural effectiveness shows itself through the implementation of intercultural competences. A new course format called the Blended Intensive Programme (BIP) is a good place where intercultural competences may be developed. BIPs are short international and intensive mobility experiences that consist of an online part and a residential part. The online phase takes place in a digital learning environment where students work collectively and simultaneously on specific assignments. The residential phase takes place face-to-face at the institution promoting the programme. Three or more institutions need to participate in this short-exchange mobility. The duration of the physical component of a blended intensive programme, combining lectures and working groups, must be between 5 and 30 days for learners (EU 2021; EU 2023). The paper aims to understand if the BIPs contribute to enhancing the intercultural competences of the students and to measure efficiently the multicultural personality aspects, considering that students and teachers are immersed in an international experience generating a great number of inputs among all participants. The multicultural personality aspects, once played in the situations, are expressions of multicultural effectiveness, which not only encompasses successful interaction within a new cultural environment or "the capacity to make things work", but also concerns a feeling of psychological well-being in that environment (Van Der Zee and Van Oudenhoven, 2000). In the field of Security and Defence Education, it is particularly important to develop intercultural competencies, as officers are required to work alongside counterparts from other countries during operations, missions, and discussion panels throughout their careers. Since 2013, the SUISS and the Army Officers School have begun an internationalization process by introducing International Modules, which were short, one-week residential courses for both Italian and foreign student officers (Marchisio and Spinello, 2021). They have adopted a virtual learning environment for the entire training (Marchisio et al., 2017), as key and winning tool for internationalization, and have helped instructors develop digital skills (Marchisio Conte et al., 2024). The context of this study is 7 Blended Intensive Programmes organized at the University of Turin SUISS (University Interdepartmental School of Strategic Sciences) and the Army Officers School. They can be defined as safe laboratories where students can be helped to gain experience from their mistakes and as fertile soil for evaluating and gathering data to create future models (Cambria et al., 2023a; Barana et al., 2024a). The SUISS BIPs saw the implementation of other tools on the digital platform, such as forums and web conferences, which allowed the students to contact each other. During the residential phase, various opportunities were implemented to let students interact among themselves, accomplishing the tasks assigned during working group sessions. The BIPs were implemented for the first time during the academic year 2022/2023 and redesigned the next academic year to include some gamification and role-play activities in an immersive scenario. At the end of the BIPs, a final test was administered to the students to assess the achievement of learning outcomes (Cambria et al. 2023b).

The following section reports the theoretical framework on the topics, defining the most important terms of the research and describing them for subsequent use in the practical research process. The third section highlights the research question and explains the various phases that, step by step, have brought the coding and merge process, trying to recognize possible methodological gaps and explicitly setting out the research question. In the fourth part, the results section, the data are analyzed quantitatively by consolidating a matrix to analyze data. Starting from the analysis, graphs are created and discussed in the fifth part. Lastly, conclusions are drawn, answering the research question and highlighting possible future research programmes, using this paper as a stepping stone for future research and contribution to other papers.

2. THEORETICAL FRAMEWORK

It can be stated that new multicultural activities in the educational landscape must employ collaborative learning, blended learning, and internationalisation as key elements (Barana et al. 2024b). It has been seen that the merging of these elements enhances the interaction and engagement of students in the field of learning and teaching, especially in the field of military education (Namyssova 2019; Barana et al. 2024b). Creating courses that apply the spheres mentioned above produces challenges that course designers, teachers and students should bear in mind. The immersion in a multicultural environment, the necessity to work closely together, and the use of digital tools generate different types of inputs from the past. Culturally mixed group work has become a common mode of assessment in higher education to encourage students from different cultural and linguistic backgrounds to learn from and work with each other (Liang and Schartner, 2022). Culture is a sphere at the base of all interconnection between people. The result of Lantz-Deaton and Golubeva (2020) defines culture as "Everything that you are and everything you can potentially become". Comparing this with the first definition, we can say that the first part of the statement concerns the section regarding all the patterns and behaviours of a group of people, while the final part of the statement, which regards what people can potentially become, refers to the idea of translation and inheritance by others in contact. This idea of movement and evolution means that there are competences that allow one to interconnect cultures. Another definition provided by Spencer-Oatey (2000) can help identify culture as "a fuzzy set of attitudes, believes, behavioral norms, and basic assumptions and values that are shared by a group of people and that influence each member's behavior and their interpretation of the meaning of other people's behavior". Intercultural competences allow people to understand, respect, and communicate effectively across different cultures. Intercultural competences are fundamental for the global workplace and are not only based on academic knowledge, which is composed of many elements - hard and technical skills (these refer to the specific skills and capabilities that one might have and will need in order to fulfil a certain role; they are often technical and can be proven and even measured, because are entirely learnable and developed due to knowledge, training or some kind of experience in a specific area: i.e. the specific knowledge of the topic, the capacity and the experience to conduct a task being aware of the causes and origins of the phenomena). It is necessary to put into practice interpersonal and intercultural competences that act as a strong glue that makes the knowledge and skills coherent and cohesive when they need to be applied. There is a vast range of definitions and conceptualizations regarding what intercultural competences are. Deardorf (2006) define intercultural competence as "the ability to communicate effectively and appropriately in intercultural situations based on one's intercultural knowledge, skills and attitudes" (Hackett, 2023; Deardorf 2006, p.247). According to Friedman and Antal (2005), intercultural competence is the ability to recognize and use cultural differences as a resource for learning and for generating effective responses in a specific context. According to Liang and Schartner, intercultural competence is "a complex of abilities needed to perform effectively and appropriately when interacting with others who are linguistically and culturally different from oneself" (Liang and Schartner, 2022; Fantini & Tirmizi, 2006). From all the definitions and assumptions available in the literature, we can deduce that there is not a clear agreement on the components of intercultural competence. Still, there is a need for a comprehensive model that includes attitudes, skills, tendencies, and knowledge. Reproducing the concepts of multiculturality (multicultural environment) and intercultural competences on a Cartesian chart, we could say that the former is represented by a horizontal segment and the latter by one vertical. The intersection between these two components is the capability to interact efficiently in the context faced at that moment. This heterogeneous composition can impact the behaviour and communication between people. There are indeed a lot of challenges and hidden endpoints that can derail the ongoing activities held in the course. For example, students may prefer to collaborate with peers of a similar cultural background rather than engage with those they perceive as different, or for example, local students may think that their international counterparts/peers are not interested in working or interacting with them and vice versa (Liang and Schartenr, 2020). Linguistic barriers may also hinder communication and the expression of intent, or there could be psychological blocks at the moment of the real activity (De Hei et al. 2020). For this reason, course designers and teachers need to incorporate not only inspiration and desire into multicultural activities but also a concrete and solid orientation, in addition to the expectations that students have before starting the activity. The idea is to use collaborative learning to build a strong commitment and a higher enthusiasm for diversity concerning solving a common task and the assignments provided to the groups. Engaging students in good-quality collaboration may contribute to several learning outcomes (De Hei et al., 2020). Besides definitions, some assumptions can be expressed. According to Cabrera et al. (2002), Collaborative Learning increases openness to diversity; according to Vahed, A., & Rodriguez, K. (2020), Collaborative Online International Learning positively influenced intercultural awareness with the consequential stimulation for students to be globally involved; according to Kayumova, A. R., & Sadykova, G. V. (2016), diversity in communication styles may hinder successful learning experiences; according to De Hei M. et al (2020) and Liang and Schartenr (2020), students who have collaborated in group work, specifically in multicultural teams in the physical classroom, have developed intercultural competences.

Understanding the rationale and purpose of the group activities regarding intercultural development could enhance students' experiences of working in multicultural groups, leading to real intercultural learning in the classroom (Liang and Schartenr 2020). The possibility of enhancing and developing intercultural competences is strictly related to the multicultural aspects of the personality and its effectiveness. Multicultural effectiveness is defined as "success in the fields of professional effectiveness, personal adjustment and intercultural interactions" (Hacket et al 2023). Multicultural effectiveness is composed of five areas distributed in this way: three abilities, one tendency and one attitude. The personal attributes are Cultural Empathy, Flexibility, Social Initiative, Open-mindedness, and Emotional Stability. Cultural Empathy is the ability to empathize with the feelings, thoughts, and behaviours of members from different cultural groups. Flexibility is the ability to switch easily from one behavioural strategy to another. Social Initiative is the tendency to actively approach and interact in social situations, initiating conversation instead of taking a back seat. Open-mindedness is an open and unprejudiced attitude towards people from different cultures or cultural norms and values. Emotional Stability is the ability to remain calm in stressful situations versus a tendency to show strong emotional reactions under stressful circumstances (V. D. Zee and V. Oudenhoven, 2001). These five personal attributes are good indicators of the multicultural effectiveness of learners immersed in international groups.

3. METHODOLOGY

The research question we want to investigate in this paper is the following: **RQ: Which aspects of multicultural effectiveness have been developed during the Blended Intensive Programme?**

This study lays on a process of investigation composed of different steps. The five components of multicultural effectiveness identified by Van Der Zee and Van Oudenhoven (Hacket et al 2023) were used to build a questionnaire. The questionnaire was administrated to the students participating in 7 BIPs held at the SUISS during the 2022/2023 and 2023/2024 academic years: two editions of "Biosafety and Bioterrorism" (B&B); two editions of "Problem solving and Critical Thinking" (PSCT), two editions of "Law of Armed Conflict" (LOAC) and one edition of "Common Security and Defence Policy" (CSDP). In total, the BIPs were attended by 290 students, of which: 40% international and 60% local students; 35% civilian and 65% military personnel, 41% female and 59% male students. We collected 290 questionnaires with a different allocation of answers. One of the first tasks was to fill out an initial questionnaire (IQ). The residential phase lasts five days, from Monday to Friday. Here, the students are divided into groups and need to solve and complete the assigned tasks related to the lessons they attended. Generally, problem-solving tasks, discussions, and public presentations are the tasks assigned to the students. In the academic year 2023/2024 an immersive scenario was introduced in order to stimulate and enhance the engagement of the students. The created groups were mixed and balanced with the same number of civilians, military and international students. A balance based on gender was attempted as well. At the end of the experience, after a final test to assess the knowledge gained and a final feedback questionnaire (FQ), 3ECTS and a certificate of attendance are provided to the students. These programmes are introduced through the Erasmus+ project (EU 2021; EU 2023). In particular, the questions and the answers analysed were taken from the initial and final feedback questionnaire and the items inside the questions of reference are shown in Table 1. The answers are given through a 4-point Likert Scale, where the value 1 refers to "not at all", the value 2 refers to "very little", the value 3 to "somewhat", and the value 4 to "to a great extent". The questionnaire also included the "not applicable" (N/A) answer, to be selected if they did not understand the question.

Table 1. Items analyzed to investigate multicultural effectiveness.

Component name	Text of the item
Cultural Empathy	To what extent did you improve Empathy during this experience?
Flexibility	To what extent did you improve Flexibility and adaptation to different contexts and situations during this experience?
Social Initiative	To what extent did you improve Team and collaborative work during this experience?
Social Initiative	To what extent did you improve communication in social settings during this experience?
Social Initiative	To what extent did you improve creativity during this experience?
Open-mindedness	To what extent did you improve tolerance and respect for others during this experience?
Emotional Stabilit	To what extent did you improve being reflexive during this experience?

The Social Initiative component included three items: for each student, the mean of the answers to the three items was computed and the result rounded to the nearest integer. All the data were collected in an Excel matrix and analysed through descriptive and bivariate statistical tests such as the Student's t-test and the ANOVA test. The results were integrated with the notes and qualitative elements jotted down during the observing participation in the residential phase.

4. RESULTS

After the collection of data, there was a phase to pair the students' answers amid the initial and final questionnaires and eliminate the cases in which at least one of the questionnaires was an empty or N/A answer. Out of 2900 answers in total, considering the initial and the final questionnaire for all the ten items considered, 159 responses were not usable, namely only 5,4 %. Table 2 shows the number and percentage of answers to the selected items. To build this table, we considered only those records where both the initial and the final response from the student were visible.

Table 2. Results collected and analysed.

Type	Component name	Responses collected	Average	4 N	%	3 N	%	2 N	%	1 N	%
IQ	Cultural Empathy	262	3.458	147	50.6%	92	31.7%	19	6.5%	4	1.3%
FQ	Cultural Empathy	262	3.488	156	53%	83	28.6%	18	6.2%	5	1.7%
IQ	Flexibility	265	3.524	150	51.7%	106	36.5%	7	2.4%	2	0.6%
FQ	Flexibility	265	3.633	178	61%	79	27%	6	2%	2	0.6%
IQ	Social Initiative	269	3.414	138	47.5	114	39.5	15	5%	2	0.6%
FQ	Social Initiative	269	3.529	156	53.7%	101	34.8%	11	3.7%	1	0.3%
IQ	Open-mindedness	260	3.707	189	65%	66	22.5%	5	1.5%	0	0%
FQ	Open-mindedness	260	3.634	180	62%	67	23.1%	11	3.7%	2	0.6%
IQ	Emotional Stability	265	3.503	143	49.3%	110	38%	11	4%	0	0%
FQ	Emotional Stability	265	3.538	155	53%	97	33.4%	11	3.8%	1	0.3%

For Cultural Empathy the final average increased. The number of students who answered with 2 and 3 decreased, while 4 increased by 9 points, meaning 2,4% more than at the beginning. For flexibility, the final average increased. The number of students who answered with 2 and 3 decreased, and those who answered with 4 increased by 28 points, and the percentage increased by 10 points. For Social Initiative, the final average increased. The number of answers reporting 1, 2 and 3 decreased and those indicating 4 increased by 18 points. For openness, the final average, despite the pattern of improvement of the other items, decreased. The responses indicated by 1, 2 and 3 increased by 9 points and the value of 4 decreased by 9 points. For emotional stability, the final average increased. The responses indicating the value of 1 and 3 decreased, and the value of 4 increased by 12 points. Figure 1 shows how the samples evolved after the activity was held.

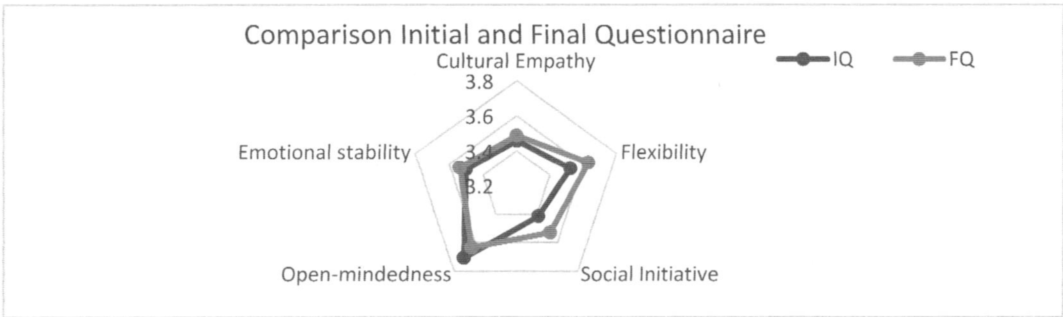

Figure 1. Means of students' answers in the five components of multicultural effectiveness

The pairwise Student's t-test was conducted to compare the students' answers in the five components of the initial and final questionnaire. Table 3 shows the results. Negative differences indicate increases in the FQ with respect to the IQ.

Table 3. Results of the pairwise Student's t-test.

Pair	Component name	Difference Mean	Standard Dev.	T-index	p-value
IQ - FQ	Cultural Empathy	-0.031	0.737	-0.671	0.252
IQ – FQ	Flexibility	-0.109	0.707	-2.521	0.006
IQ - FQ	Social Initiative	-0.11512	0.624	-3.024	0.001
IQ - FQ	Open-mindedness	0.073	0.651	1.811	0.036
IQ - FQ	Emotional Stability	-0.038	0.669	-0.920	0.179

The Student's t-test shows a significant increase in the means between IQ and FQ for flexibility and social interaction, a significant decrease for openness, and nonsignificant increases for empathy and emotional stability. Lastly, the analysis of variance (ANOVA) was run to identify differences in the students' answers to the final questionnaire between the two academic years. Results are shown in Table 4. An increase in all the five components of multicultural effectiveness emerges in 2023/2024 compared to the previous year. The growth is significant for cultural empathy and social interaction, while it is slightly below the statistical significance threshold for flexibility, open-mindedness, and emotional stability. These are moderate increases.

Table 4. Results of the ANOVA test

Year		Cultural Empathy	Flexibility	Social Interaction	Open-mindedness	Emotional Stability
2022/2023	Mean	3.31	3.56	3.43	3.55	3.45
	N	111	112	111	109	110
	Standard dev.	0.760	0.550	0.580	0.616	0.599
2023/2024	Mean	3.62	3.69	3.60	3.69	3.59
	N	173	175	175	172	175
	Standard dev.	.622	0.564	0.530	0.586	0.599
	F	14.81	3.69	6.03	3.74	3.86
	p-value	<0.001	0.057	0.15	0.054	0.051

5. DISCUSSION AND CONCLUSION

The first element to consider in this analysis is that while mixed cultural group work is complementary to developing and improving certain competences, such as empathy and open-mindedness, it can also have decreasing results. The experience can contribute to various positive and negative feelings towards the students after the sojourn. Compared to the work of Liang and Schartner (2022), our work has found the same decrease in open-mindedness and tolerance towards international students. This intriguing result can be derived from the fact that during the online phase and before the residential phase, the students' expectations can be very high. They may think they are ready to include and integrate with another culture. However, when they get in contact with it for the first time, or after some hours spent together, no matter how nice the interaction may be, the first moment may be considered a moment of reflection to absorb the cultural shock and achieve the same level of cultural empathy. However, the decrease is moderate. Cultural empathy and emotional stability moderately increase, even if not significantly: this could be due to a ceiling effect since the initial level is generally high, that is, the phenomenon that when starting from high results, it is difficult to improve them. It should be considered that the BIP is a short experience, and for this reason, we cannot expect huge changes in the results. At the beginning of the residential phase, it was possible to observe that students distributed themselves sitting in groups of the same nationalities. Interaction speeded up their relationships after the teachers intervened in redistributing the students. From dialogues with students, the observer and the tutors reported that initially some students, especially the local ones, felt a sense of exclusion or found some problems with the vehicular language. In this case, teachers take on the role of cultural mediator and guide for everyone. On the other hand, the indicator that reflected a higher rate of increase was social interaction, which was composed of social communication, creativity, and teamwork. The nature of the programmes leads towards this direction, thanks to the assignments of tasks that shall be completed to achieve the course, characterised by the students' immersions in groups with a heterogeneous composition. In these two years, different methodological approaches have been used. Indeed, the implementation of new methodologies (such as the combination of immersive scenarios, gamification, planning of the didactic in a specific way to make the period more inclusive) impacted the development of intercultural competences. In relation to this, the link in achieving the goal is to create an inclusive, immersive, experience-based environment. Considering the final values of the five components in Table 3, it is noted that in the 2024 editions, all the values are higher than in 2023. The increase is significant for cultural empathy, social interaction and openness. However, generally speaking, these are moderate increases. Very often, multiculturality and interculturality are synonymous, but this practice is not correct because the two spheres imply different situations. They are both connected and interdependent. Multiculturality is the soil, the sphere where different cultures coexist. The point of view is horizontal, and in the group, everyone has an equal status (Friedman and Antal, 2005). Interculturality is an extension of multiculturality. Indeed, this area focuses on the dialogue among the cultures inside the group. It can be considered more as an oriented process instead of describing a particular state that occurs in a multicultural environment. Interculturality also means having skills that allow one to communicate in this multicultural environment. People, in general, and in particular here, students, should possess the following skills: knowledge, tolerance, social interaction, stability, awareness, flexibility, open-mindedness, self-reflection, and empathy. These indicators allow the students to be ready to enter another more heterogeneous reality without judging others or having biases that may hinder the interaction. These are the intercultural competences, and considering the results, it is possible to say that these elements can help have a positive intercultural experience. The most important element in these activities is still the human being and the interactions that originate from the group composed of human beings. Considering that some data increase and others decrease means that students were in new situations for them and experimenting with those skills. New situations are important moments where students can learn. This is the true impact of the BIP: learning *from* a culture is more important than learning *about* a culture. In this way, students start negotiating a common reality and, in this way, they achieve the goal of learning from a specific situation by generating the necessary cultural knowledge and intercultural competences needed for an efficient strategy of action and reaction to the surrounding environment's inputs. In order to answer our RQ, in line with the considerations done, it is important to underline that intercultural competences may not be needed at the same time, but they can help students achieve new ways of seeing and interacting that boost the learning process from a culture. The dialogue is necessary to negotiate reality and create an efficient response, action and reaction to the situation. Negotiating reality implies critically inquiring into people's interests, goals, and values. For these reasons, in order for students to get along with their colleagues and achieve a positive experience, they need to experiment with new attitudes and new skills to be prepared and aware of the context they are in (Friedman and Antal, 2005). The future steps are to administer the questionnaire for the 4 BIPs held in the academic year 2024/2025. The intention is to shape the course in consideration of the feedback and, with those collected in the future, understand and figure out the trends that originated during the years.

REFERENCES

Barana, A., et al., (2024a). Detecting blended learning, collaborative learning and internazionalization in military education: a systematic literature review, *Proceedings of 18th International Conference on e-Learning and Digital Learning 2024 and Sustainability, Technology and Education 2024*. Budapest, Hungary, 137-144.

Barana, A., et al., (2024b). Unpacking the Three Spheres of Interest in a Blended Intensive Programme: Collaborative Learning, Blended Learning and Internazionalization. *Proceedings of the 21th International Conference on Cognition And Exploratory Learning In The Digital Age.* Zagreb, Croatia, 43-50.

Cabrera, A. F., Crissman, J. L., Bernal, E. M., Nora, A., Terenzini, P. T., & Pascarella, E. T. (2002). Collaborative learning: Its impact on college students' development and diversity. *Journal of College Student Development*, 43(1), 20–34.

Cambria, A., et al., 2023a. Higher Education training activities in international environments for developing skills of civil-military cooperation. *Proceedings of the 20th International Conference on Cognition and Exploratory Learning in The Digital Age.* Madeira Island, Portugal, 402-406.

Cambria, A. et al. (2023b). Blended Intensive Programs for Fostering Collaboration and Knowledge Exchange in Security and Defence Education. *Proceedings of 16th International Conference of Education, Research and Innovation (iCERI),* Sevilla, Spain, 9441-9448.

De Hei, M. et al., (2020). Developing Intercultural Competence Through Collaborative Learning in International Higher Education, *Journal of Studies in International Education*, Vol. 24(2), 190-211.

Deardorf, D. K., (2006). Identification and assessment of intercultural competence as a student outcome of internazionalization. *Journal of Studies in International Education*, 10(3), 241–266. https://doi.org/10.1177/1028315306287002.

Deardorf, D. K., and Jones, E., (2012). Intercultural competence: An Emerging Focus in International Higher education. In D. K. Deardorf, H. De Wit, J. D. Heyl, & T. Adams (Eds.), *The SAGE Handbook of International Higher Education* (pp. 283–304). SAGE Publications, Inc. https://doi.org/10.4135/9781452218397.n16.

European Commission. Directorate General for Education, Youth, Sport and Culture., Blended learning for high quality and inclusive primary and secondary education: handbook. Luxembourg: Publications Office, (2021).

European Commission, Erasmus+ Programme Guide 2024. Disponibile su: https://erasmus-plus.ec.europa.eu/programme-guide/erasmusplus-programme-guide.

Fantini, A. E., & Tirmizi, A. (2006). Exploring and assessing intercultural competence. http:// digitalcollections.sit.edu/worldlearning_publications/1

Friedman, V. J., & Antal, A. B. (2005). Negotiating Reality: A Theory of Action Approach to Intercultural Competence. Management Learning, 36(1), 69–86. https://doi.org/10.1177/1350507605049904

Kayumova, A. R., & Sadykova, G. V. (2016). Online collaborative cross-cultural learning: Students' perspectives. *Journal of Organizational Culture, Communications and Confict*, 20, 248–255.

Kluckhohn, C. and Kroeberg, A., (1952). *Culture, a critical Review of concept and definitions*. Vintage, New York.

Hackett et al., (2023). The effectiveness of Collaborative Online International Learning (COIL) on intercultural competence development in higher education, *Int J Educ Technol High Educ* 20:5 https://doi.org/10.1186/s41239-022-00373-3.

Lantz-Deaton, C., Golubeva, I. (2020). What Is Culture?. In: Intercultural Competence for College and University Students. *Springer*, Cham. https://doi.org/10.1007/978-3-030-57446-8_2

Liang, Y. And Schartner, A., (2022). Culturally Mixed Group Work and the Development of Students' Intercultural Competence, *Journal of Studies in International Education,* Vol. 26(1), 44-60.

Marchisio, M. et Al., Advanced e-learning for it-army officers through virtual learning environments, Journal of E-Learning and Knowledge Society, (2017), 13(3), pp. 59–70.

Marchisio Conte, M., et Al., Development of Digital Competencies in Education Through Staff Training Events and International Schools Proceedings – 2024 IEEE 48th Annual Computers, Software, and Applications Conference, COMPSAC (2024), 103–108.

Marchisio, M., Spinello, E., Internationalization for enhancing the European Security and Defence Higher Education, 15th International Conference e-Learning, EL 2021 - Held at the 15th Multi-Conference on Computer Science and Information Systems, MCCSIS 2021, (2021), 99–106.

Namyssova, G., et al., (2019). Challenges and benefits of blended learning in higher education, *International Journal of Technology in Education*, Vol. II, No. 1, pp. 22-31.

Schulz, B. (2008). The importance of soft skills: Education beyond academic knowledge, *Nawa Journal of Communication*, vol. 2, no. 1, 146– 154.

Spencer-Oatey, H. (2000). *Culturally speaking. Managing rapport through talk across cultures,* London/ New York: Continuum, Language in Australia and New Zealand, https://www.degruyter.com/database/AUSBIB/entry/ausbib.key-3248/html. Accessed 2024-11-16.

Tushar, H., Sooraska, N. (2023). Global employability skills in the 21st century workplace: A semi-systematic literature review, *Heliyon*, Volume 9, Issue 11, ISSN 2405-8440, https://doi.org/10.1016/j.heliyon.2023.e21023.

Vahed, A., & Rodriguez, K. (2020). Enriching students' engaged learning experiences through the collaborative online international learning project. *Innovations in Education and Teaching International*, 596-605.

Van Der Zee, K. I. and Van Oudenhoven, J. P., (2000). The Multicultural Personality Questionnaire: A Multidimensional Instrument of Multicultural Effectiveness, *European Journal of Personality* Eur. J. Pers. 14, 291-309.

Van Der Zee, K. I. and Van Oudenhoven, J. P., (2001). The Multicultural Personality Questionnaire: Reliability and Validity of Self- and Other Ratings of Multicultural Effectiveness, *European Journal of Personality* Eur. J. Pers. 35, 278-288.

RAPID GUESSING BEHAVIOUR IDENTIFICATION IN PROGRAMMING COURSES

Ján Skalka, Matúš Valko and Martin Drlík
Department of Informatics, Faculty of Natural Sciences and Informatics, Constantine the Philosopher University in Nitra, Slovakia

ABSTRACT

The article examines rapid guessing behavior (RGB) in a microlearning environment for an introductory Python programming course for 207 first-year students. The study found a positive correlation between general academic readiness and midterm and end-of-year programming test performance. Students exhibiting RGB, identified using the CUMP-UP and NT10 methods, had lower accuracy rates and shorter response times, indicating potential disengagement or lack of comprehension. These findings suggest that monitoring RGB in microlearning platforms can help identify students at risk of underperformance and allow educators to provide targeted support and improve learning outcomes.

KEYWORDS

Rapid Guessing Behavior, Microlearning, Introductory Programming Courses, E-Learning

1. INTRODUCTION

The behavior of first-year students represents an exciting area of higher education research, as many challenges and opportunities mark this transitional phase. The initial year of study is a critical period during which students must transition to a new educational framework, adapt to the demands of higher education, and confirm that their chosen career path is correct and appropriate for them. The success of this transition often depends on factors such as the adequacy of their prior educational preparation, their readiness for independent learning, and the suitability of their chosen field of study.

Researching students' behavior during the first weeks of study provides valuable insights into potential risks and opportunities for academic success. By examining specific behaviors, patterns, and characteristics, educators and education system administrators can predict whether a student is likely to encounter problems, is already struggling, or has untapped potential that requires appropriate intervention. These observations are significant in technical fields such as information technology, where the complexity of the curriculum presents unique challenges.

In IT education, an introductory programming course is often a deciding factor in whether students continue their studies. Although it is commonly believed that programming skills come naturally to beginning IT students, evidence from numerous studies suggests otherwise. Introductory programming courses represent a significant barrier that often leads to an early dropout from IT degree programs. Identifying students who face challenges in this area and providing targeted support measures is thus essential to help them overcome this critical period and remain in the IT field.

This study examines first-year IT students' behavior in introductory programming courses, identifying variables correlating with their academic performance. In addition to assessing the knowledge and skills students bring from their prior education, the study emphasizes analyzing their approach to studying a microlearning course on Python programming, mainly through the lens of rapid guessing.

2. RAPID GUESSING

Rapid guessing is a test-taking behavior that can be identified through response time analysis. When test takers engage in rapid guessing, their reaction times are unusually short, indicating that they have not taken the time to meaningfully engage with the question (Wise, 2017), (Finn, 2015). This behavior undermines the validity of the test because rapid guesses do not provide accurate information about the test taker's knowledge, skills, or abilities (Guo *et al.*, 2016), (Wise and DeMars, 2010).

Rapid guessing typically occurs when test takers answer questions much faster than the expected time required to understand and think through a response (Alfian *et al.*, 2023). It often involves bypassing the process of thoroughly reading the question or carefully evaluating the answer options (Lindner, Lüdtke, and Nagy, 2019), (Wise, 2017). This lack of effort can stem from factors such as fatigue, disengagement, or time pressure during the test.

The term "rapid guessing" means that the test taker is not making an effort and instead selects answers at random (Wise, 2017), (Wise, 2019). However, research suggests that the selection process is not always purely random, even when response times are very short. Instead, rapid guessers may use a rapid heuristic approach, scanning the response options and relying on a "gut feeling" to select the most likely option, even when they do not fully understand the question or have not delved deeply into the problem. This nuanced understanding of rapid guessing behavior highlights the need to address such tendencies in test design and analysis to maintain the integrity of assessments.

Rapid guessing behavior (RGB) was first identified and studied in the context of standardized tests designed to assess student performance (Wise and DeMars, 2005). A typical example of RGB behavior occurs when test takers are pressed for time and attempt to answer as many questions as possible without carefully considering each one (Wise, Pastor, and Kong, 2009), (DeMars and Wise, 2010), (Wise, 2017).

A common visual characteristic of RGB is the appearance of a bimodal distribution in response times with two distinct peaks or modes (the visualization can also reflect the correctness of the response and the speed of its entry). These peaks (Figure 1) indicate the values where the response times are most concentrated. Unlike the unimodal distribution, which has a single peak representing a single cluster of data, a bimodal distribution reveals the presence of two groups with different behavior patterns. One peak corresponds to students who spent a reasonable amount of time answering the questions, indicating thoughtful responses. The other peak represents much shorter response times, indicating potential rapid guessing behavior. These two peaks separate students who were meaningfully engaged in the questions from those who responded too quickly to consider their answers carefully.

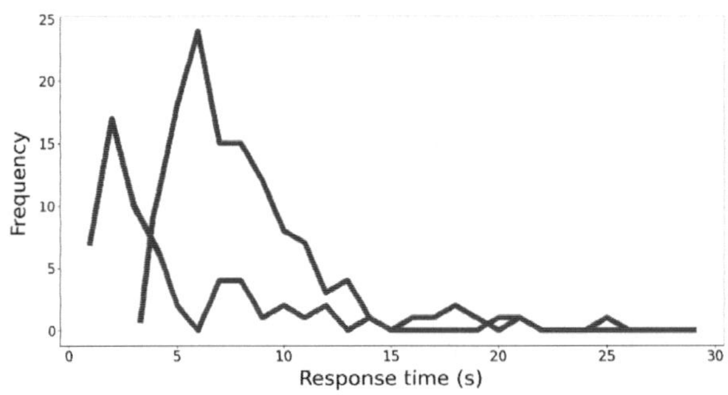

Figure 1. Bimodal distribution of responses. The red curve represents the distribution of rapid guessing answers over time (some correct, many incorrect); the green curve represents the solution behavior with the majority of correct answers (Skalka and Valko, 2024)

This visual distinction helps researchers identify and analyze contrasting behavior within a single data set, but it is not a rule that occurs on every task. A response time threshold (RTT) is used to distinguish between RGB and solution behavior, which considers responses taking less than the RTT time to be RGB and responses taking more than the RTT for thorough. The RTT typically falls between the two peaks in a bimodal response time distribution.

RGB is often associated with high-stakes testing, where test scores significantly impact students' academic trajectories or opportunities. Conversely, in low-stakes tests, where scores do not have immediate or significant consequences for a student's academic standing, RGB is more often associated with a lack of motivation, a lack of understanding of the content or question, or engagement with the test (Anaya and Zamarro, 2024), (Finn, 2015).

Applying methods typically used to identify RGB in high-stakes testing to microlearning environments can provide valuable insights into student engagement and motivation during the course. However, the unique context of microlearning requires consideration of these methods to account for several key differences (Skalka and Valko, 2024):

- Different question objectives – unlike standardized tests, which aim to assess mastery, microlearning questions are often designed to reinforce content immediately after it is presented. This fundamental difference in purpose can affect the frequency and characteristics of RGB, making it challenging to identify.
- Different levels of motivation – in microlearning, students benefit from immediate feedback and opportunities for remediation. While this promotes a supportive learning environment, it can also lower the stakes and reduce motivation compared to high-stakes testing, where results directly affect grades and future opportunities.
- Question quality and statistical validity – questions in a microlearning environment may not have undergone the rigorous validation processes typical of standardized tests. Poorly worded or unclear questions can bias RGB identification, necessitating methods to evaluate and mitigate the impact of question quality on RGB detection.
- Impact of question difficulty – the question difficulty level directly affects the probability of correct answers and can significantly influence RGB patterns. A deeper understanding of how question difficulty affects guessing behavior is essential for refining detection methods.
- Temporal distribution of responses – microlearning courses typically take more extended time frames, often weeks, than the single-session format of standard tests. This extended engagement introduces variables such as fatigue, mood swings, and fluctuating performance that must be considered when analyzing RGB in the microlearning context.

As part of the research (Skalka and Valko, 2024), the following methods were used to identify RGB in the environment of a micro-learning course.

- CUMP (Cumulative proportional method) was proposed by Guo et al. (Guo *et al.*, 2016) and incorporates response accuracy by analyzing the cumulative number of correct answers over time intervals. The RTT is the response time at which the cumulative number of correct answers from the start (time zero) up to the current interval exceeds the level expected by chance. At this point, RTT is set to the value of the previous interval. The method CUMP-UP evaluates responses cumulatively from interval 1 upwards. An RTT is identified in the first interval when the cumulative number of correct responses from interval 1 exceeds the chance level.
- NT10 is the method that does not consider response accuracy – it is one of the first attempts to identify RGB. The used RTT is set to 10% of the average student response time, with a maximum threshold value set at 10 seconds (Wise and Ma, 2012).

We will use these results in our research dataset to identify variables indicative of poorer results in the programming course.

3. STUDENTS BEHAVIOUR CHARACTERISTICS

To determine whether it is possible to identify at-risk students based on their initial characteristics and course behavior, we analyzed quantified data from 207 first-year students enrolled in the Applied Computer Science program during the 2022/23 and 2023/24 academic years. In a microlearning environment, these students participated in a Python course via the Priscilla system (Skalka and Drlik, 2018).

The data included the following variables:

- High school performance (*HSP*) is measured on a 0–40 scale based on high school grade point average. A grade of 1.0 corresponded to 40 points, while a grade of 4.0 corresponded to 0 points.

- The General academic prerequisites test (*GAPT*) was administered during the introductory week, assessing reading comprehension and essential logical thinking.
- The semester test scores (*T1*, *T2*) consisted of the scores from mid-term and end-of-semester tests. Each test required students to solve 10 programming problems within 90 minutes, with a maximum score of 500 points per test. These scores reflected students' success in completing the Programming course.

For this research, three types of tasks used in the course were analyzed:

- Type 1 – content lessons that provide students with the necessary information to complete subsequent tasks.
- Type 2 – open-ended questions that typically require a one-word answer or the result of a program activity, with 50 such tasks included in the course.
- Type 3 – multiple-choice questions that require students to select one correct answer from several options, with 66 tasks. This task type allows for the identification of rapid guessing behavior.

While Type 3 tasks focus on RGB detection, the other task types and their accuracy provide additional context to understand student behavior better. The following parameters were used to represent student behavior during the course with an emphasis on RGB:

- *Contl_T* – time taken to read a normalized number of characters (100) in the content activity.
- *Cor3_T* – time taken to answer a multiple-choice question correctly, normalized to 100 characters.
- *Perc_2* – a percentage of correct answers to type 2 questions given on the first attempt.
- *Perc_3* – a percentage of correct answers to type 3 questions given on the first attempt.
- *Done_to_all* – total number of correct answers in the course on the first attempt.
- *RGB CUMP-UP* – number of RGB behaviors of students identified using the CUMP-UP method.
- *RGB NT10* – the number of RGB behaviors identified using the NT10 method.
- *Avg_time* – average time taken to answer a type 3 question.
- *Avg_corr_time* – the average time taken to answer a type 3 question correctly.

Both categories of parameters were integrated to examine potential correlations between different aspects of student behavior and performance during the course. The results of the correlation analysis are summarized in Table 1, which presents the correlation matrix for the monitored parameters.

Table 1. Correlation matrix for students' knowledge and behavior groups

	HSP	GAPT	T1	T2	Contl_T	Cor3_T	Perc_2	Perc_3	Done_to_all	RGB CUMP-UP	RGB NT10	Avg_time	Avg_corr_time
HSP	1.00	0.02	0.12	0.23	0.08	0.11	0.15	0.19	-0.24	-0.25	-0.24	0.11	0.17
GAPT		1.00	**0.35**	**0.30**	-0.03	0.04	0.15	0.30	0.18	-0.14	-0.11	0.04	0.17
T1			1.00	**0.66**	-0.07	0.03	**0.36**	**0.43**	**0.34**	-0.13	-0.05	0.03	0.21
T2				1.00	0.13	0.16	0.20	**0.42**	**0.29**	-0.13	-0.09	0.16	**0.33**
Contl_T					1.00	0.22	0.01	0.23	-0.05	-0.14	-0.17	0.22	0.28
Cor3_T						1.00	0.02	0.32	0.20	-0.35	**-0.42**	1.00	**0.89**
Perc_2							1.00	**0.41**	0.00	-0.15	-0.06	0.02	0.18
Perc_3								1.00	0.24	**-0.49**	**-0.39**	0.32	**0.68**
Done_to_all									1.00	0.14	0.15	0.20	0.26
RGB CUMP-UP										1.00	**0.78**	**-0.35**	**-0.46**
RGB NT10											1.00	**-0.42**	**-0.48**
Avg_time												1.00	**0.89**
Avg_corr_time													1.00

Within the correlation table (Table 1), several correlations were identified between the individual pairs of variables. The following pairs of variables represent correlations with moderate to strong relationships:

Academic Performance Measures

- The *GAPT* and *T1* correlate at +0.35, indicating that higher general academic prerequisites test is moderately associated with better performance on the midterm test. However, the *GAPT* and *T2* correlated at only 0.30, indicating that general problem-solving ability is no longer sufficient or does not correlate strongly with success in mastering more demanding areas in the Python language.
- The results of the *T1* and *T2* tests show a strong positive correlation of +0.66, indicating that students who perform well on the midterm test tend to perform well on the end-of-term test.

Test Scores, Accuracy, and Course Completion

- *Perc_3* (the proportion of correct answers on the first attempt in multiple-choice questions) and *T1* correlate at +0.43, which means that students who answer correctly on the first attempt in multiple-choice questions tend to do well on the midterm test. Similarly, *Perc_3* also correlated with their second test (T2) results with a correlation of 0.42.
- *T1* and *Done_to_all* correlate with +0.34, suggesting that a responsible coursework approach leads to better performance on the first test. In the case of *T2*, the correlation is slightly lower at 0.29.
- *Perc_3* and *Perc_2* correlate at the level of 0.41, which expresses a medium correlation between the success of multiple-choice and short free-answer questions. This result indicates a relationship between the similarity of students' behavior (thinking) when formulating answers. However, only a medium dependence simultaneously says that some students may behave differently in free-answer and the case of multiple-choice questions.
- *T2* and *Avg_corr_time* correlate at +0.33, meaning that if students spend enough time answering the multiple-choice question, they will likely do well on the second test.

The above correlations link student performance and behavior and are perhaps the most important information in the analysis. Other correlations that describe the relationships between the parameters defining the behavior are not directly linked to the success of completing the course. Nevertheless, they explain some consequences of the students' behavior.

Time-based parameters

- *Cor3_T* and *Avg_corr_time* are strongly correlated at +0.89, representing that the more a student spends solving a type 3 task, the higher the chance he will answer correctly.
- *Perc_3* and *Avg_time show* a slight positive correlation of +0.32, which indicates that students who often answer multiple-choice questions correctly on the first attempt also tend to spend slightly more time on these questions overall.
- *Perc_3* is strongly correlated with *Avg_corr_time* (0.68), meaning those with higher accuracy take more time to answer.
- *Avg_time* and *Avg_corr_time* correlate +0.89, confirming that as the average total time per multiple-choice question increases, the average time to answer correctly increases.

Rapid Guessing

- *RGB CUMP-UP* and *RGB NT10* alone have a strong positive correlation of +0.78, reflecting that both methods measure quick guessing differently.
- *Cor3_T* (time to answer multiple choice questions correctly) and *RGB CUMP-UP* have a slight negative correlation of -0.35, while *Cor3_T* and *RGB NT10* are at -0.42. These results suggest that students who answer questions quickly (and correctly) are less likely to exhibit rapid guessing. *RGB_NT10* has a stronger negative relationship with *Cor3_T* than *CUMP-UP*, which means that the *NT10_RGB* detection method is more sensitive to fast-responding students.
- *Perc_3* (first-attempt accuracy on type 3) shows a slight negative correlation with *RGB CUMP-UP* (-0.49) and *RGB NT10* (-0.39). Higher first-attempt accuracy is associated with fewer rapid guessing responses. The negative correlation of -0.49 between *Perc_3* and *RGB_CUMP-UP* suggests a moderately strong relationship, with more accurate students guessing less. *RGB_NT10* (-0.39) has a weaker but still significant relationship, indicating that first-attempt accuracy is an important predictor of less rapid guessing behavior.
- The negative correlations between time and identification of the rapid guessing methods indicate that rapid guessers spend less time on questions. *Avg_corr_time* has a stronger relationship with *RGB_NT10* (-0.48) than with *CUMP-UP* (-0.46), suggesting that the NT10 method better captures true rapid guessers based on their answers. *RGB_NT10* vs. *Avg_time* (-0.42) shows that average response time is also relevant for capturing guessing but less so than for correct answers. Since *Avg_time* and *Avg_corr_time* are strongly correlated (0.89), this means that when RGB behavior is frequent, students spend less time on all questions, not just correct answers.

4. DISCUSSION AND CONCLUSION

Correlation analysis provides meaningful insight into the relationship between student behavior, academic performance, and rapid guessing in the context of a Python programming microlearning course. The findings contribute to understanding how course behavior influences student outcomes and inform potential interventions to improve engagement and performance.

A key finding from this study is that high school performance (*HSP*) and the General academic prerequisites test (*GAPT*) did not correlate with rapid guessing or performance in a programming course. These findings suggest that prior academic achievement does not necessarily predict success in microlearning-based technical education.

Instead, the analysis shows that *GAPT* scores positively correlate with semester test scores (*T1*, *T2*), suggesting that students with stronger reading comprehension and logical reasoning skills tend to perform better in programming courses. These findings highlight the importance of logical reasoning and reading comprehension for students entering technical fields. Educators could use *GAPT* scores to identify students needing additional support in developing these essential cognitive skills.

The study confirms the inverse association between quick guessing and lower academic performance. Negative correlations between rapid guessing metrics (*RGB_CUMP-UP* and *RGB_NT10*) and accuracy (*Perc_3*) and time spent on questions (*Avg_time*, *Avg_corr_time*) indicate that students who engage in rapid guessing behaviors are less likely to answer questions correctly and tend to spend less time on the task. This pattern suggests that quick guessing may reflect disengagement, lack of motivation, or poor understanding of the content, consistent with previous research in low-stakes testing environments. Given this, educators should consider implementing strategies to mitigate rapid guessing, especially in microlearning environments where engagement levels may vary.

These findings have important practical implications. By monitoring student behavior and identifying rapid guessers, instructors can implement targeted interventions such as additional explanations, structured engagement techniques, and motivational strategies to promote active learning. Early support measures could help students move from passive guessing to meaningful engagement with learning materials, ultimately improving their learning outcomes.

Despite its contributions, this study has several limitations. The research focuses on a single Python programming course with a relatively small sample size, which may limit the generalizability of the results. Future studies should examine rapid guessing behavior across different programming languages, course structures, and learning environments to confirm the findings. In addition, examining the underlying psychological and motivational factors that lead to rapid guessing, such as anxiety levels, self-confidence, or engagement strategies, could provide deeper insight into how to design interventions that effectively address disengagement in microlearning environments.

This study underscores the importance of understanding student response behavior and cognitive engagement in microlearning. By recognizing rapid guessing patterns and their implications, educators can better refine teaching methodologies to support student success in programming education.

ACKNOWLEDGEMENT

This work was supported in part by research Science Grant Agency of the Ministry of Education of the Slovak Republic under Grant 1/0490/22: Design and Evaluation of Selected Learning Analytics Methods for Understanding and Improving the Learning Process and Virtual Learning Environment and by the European Commission under the ERASMUS+ Programme 2021, KA2 under Grant 2021-1-SK01-KA220-HED-000032095: Future IT Professionals Education in Artificial Intelligence.

REFERENCES

Alfian, M. *et al.* (2023) 'Correction of Threshold Determination in Rapid-Guessing Behaviour Detection', *Information (Switzerland)*, 14(7). doi: 10.3390/info14070422.

Anaya, L. M. and Zamarro, G. (2024) 'The role of student effort on performance in PISA: Revisiting the gender gap in achievement', *Oxford Economic Papers*, 76(2). doi: 10.1093/oep/gpad018.

DeMars, C. E. and Wise, S. L. (2010) 'Can differential rapid-guessing behavior lead to differential item functioning?', *International Journal of Testing*, 10(3). doi: 10.1080/15305058.2010.496347.

Finn, B. (2015) 'Measuring Motivation in Low-Stakes Assessments', *ETS Research Report Series*, 2015(2). doi: 10.1002/ets2.12067.

Guo, H. *et al.* (2016) 'A New Procedure for Detection of Students' Rapid Guessing Responses Using Response Time', *Applied Measurement in Education*, 29(3), pp. 173–183. doi: 10.1080/08957347.2016.1171766.

Lindner, M. A., Lüdtke, O. and Nagy, G. (2019) 'The Onset of Rapid-Guessing Behavior Over the Course of Testing Time: A Matter of Motivation and Cognitive Resources', *Frontiers in Psychology*, 10, pp. 1–15. doi: 10.3389/fpsyg.2019.01533.

Skalka, J. and Drlik, M. (2018) 'Priscilla - Proposal of System Architecture for Programming Learning and Teaching Environment', *IEEE International Conference on Application of Information and Communication Technologies*. Available at: https://publons.com/publon/27387754/.

Skalka, J. and Valko, M. (2024)' Rapid Guessing Behavior Detection in Microlearning: Insights into Student Performance, Engagement, and Response Accuracy', *IEEE Access*, 12.

Wise, S. L. (2017) 'Rapid-Guessing Behavior: Its Identification, Interpretation, and Implications', *Educational Measurement: Issues and Practice*, 36(4), pp. 52–61. doi: 10.1111/emip.12165.

Wise, S. L. (2019) 'Controlling construct-irrelevant factors through computer-based testing: disengagement, anxiety, & cheating', *Education Inquiry*, 10(1). doi: 10.1080/20004508.2018.1490127.

Wise, S. L. and DeMars, C. E. (2005) 'Low examinee effort in low-stakes assessment: Problems and potential solutions', *Educational Assessment*, 10(1), pp. 1–17. doi: 10.1207/s15326977ea1001_1.

Wise, S. L. and DeMars, C. E. (2010) 'Examinee noneffort and the validity of program assessment results', *Educational Assessment*, 15(1), pp. 27–41. doi: 10.1080/10627191003673216.

Wise, S. L. and Ma, L. (2012) 'Setting response time thresholds for a CAT item pool: the normative threshold method', in *Paper presented at the 2012 annual meeting of the National Council on Measurement in Education*, pp. 1–24.

Wise, S. L., Pastor, D. A. and Kong, X. J. (2009) 'Correlates of rapid-guessing behavior in low-stakes testing: implications for test development and measurement practice', *Applied Measurement in Education*, 22(2), pp. 185–205. doi: 10.1080/08957340902754650.

INTEGRATING BOTS AND ARTIFICIAL INTELLIGENCE IN SECONDARY SCHOOL: THE NEW FRONTIER IN EDUCATION

Alessandro Barca
Pegaso Telematic University, Italy

ABSTRACT

The paper explores the impact of artificial intelligence in the context of secondary education, focusing on benefits and emerging issues. The examination is conducted by means of a literature review and a questionnaire survey addressed to teachers, with the aim of drawing a detailed picture of their training needs. From the analysis of the teachers' responses and the academic literature, it is clear that artificial intelligence deploys extensive opportunities, such as personalising learning, optimising access to teaching resources and reducing the teaching load for teachers. These potentials are positively received in classrooms, especially by students although, on the part of teachers, there is a clear awareness of the underlying criticalities, such as technological dependence, data security issues, the risk of plagiarism and the reduction of the capacity for autonomous and creative thinking. However, the specific training deficit for teachers and the limited familiarity with the latest technological developments in artificial intelligence emerge as major critical issues. Therefore, a fruitful integration of artificial intelligence in education requires a holistic approach, capable of proactively responding to the training needs of each actor involved.

KEYWORDS

AIED, Artificial Intelligence, Teacher Training

1. INTRODUCTION

In a constantly evolving society, technology is an indispensable element that has profoundly transformed the way we communicate, interact, work and learn, influencing every aspect of existence. The advent of Artificial Intelligence (AI) marked the beginning of a new era characterised by significant changes in many areas. As a driving force of innovation, AI is also having a major impact on educational systems; the interaction between AI-based technologies and teaching methodologies is redefining pedagogical strategies, learning environments and the entire educational experience, offering new opportunities to improve the teaching and learning process (Barca, Carruba, 2023). Digital has now established itself in school contexts of all levels, albeit with still heterogeneous modalities, timing and approaches (Carruba, 2020). In schools, where the needs of students are increasingly diverse and complex, the introduction of AI has ushered in a specific line of educational research (AIED) (Panciroli et al., 2020), which suggests that it offers numerous benefits, from timely feedback to automated assessment and the creation of tailor-made educational content. This essay explores the paradigm shift that is taking place in educational systems catalysed by AI in secondary education and teachers' perceptions of how these technologies can support professional development, improve teaching practices and enhance student learning. The research, which is still in progress, adopts a qualitative approach, based on a literature review and on the analysis of data retrieved from a questionnaire administered to a sample of primary and secondary school teachers at the end of the qualifying course envisaged by the Prime Ministerial Decree 4/08/2023.

2. LITERATURE REVIEW

The literature review involved the analysis of academic articles, research reports and case studies on the use of AI in education, found in the ERIC database, obtained with the following string: (AIED) OR ((AI OR 'artificial intelligence' OR chatbot OR bot OR chatgpt) AND (education OR learn* OR student OR didactics)). The search included articles from 2024, in order to see the most recent developments and reflections. We identified 88 articles, from which duplicates and articles not related to the research question were excluded: at the end of the screening we included 59 articles in the review. The articles were analysed with the aim of identifying the benefits and critical issues related to the use of artificial intelligence in education (Tables 1-2)[1].

Table 1. Bibliographic references on the benefits of AI in education divided by topic

BENEFITS	AUTHOR, YEAR
Accessibility	Julien, 2024; Betancourt Ramirez, Fuentes Esparrell, 2024; Nguyen et al., 2024; Sihag, Vibha, 2024; Gökçearslan et al., 2024; Abdelaal, Al Sawi, 2024; Solak, 2024; Barrera Castro et al., 2024; Otermans et al., 2024; Kaya, Kutluca, 2024; Jantakun et al., 2024
Customisation and individualisation	Julien, 2024; Bobula, 2024; Frazier, 2024; Alasgarova, Rzayev, 2024; Abdelaal, Al Sawi, 2024; Solak, 2024; Barrera Castro et al., 2024; Duran, 2024; Mcguire et al., 2024; Van den Berg, 2024; Guler et al., 2024; Noroozi et al., 2024
Performance enhancement	Julien et al., 2024; Noroozi et al., 2024; Hussim et al., 2024; Otermans et al., 2024
Motivation, interest and involvement	Julien, 2024; Betancourt Ramirez, Fuentes Esparrell, 2024; Gökçearslan et al., 2024; Nguyen et al., 2024; Alasgarova, Rzayev, 2024; Miralay, 2024; Solak, 2024; Barrera Castro et al., 2024; Noroozi et al., 2024; Kaya, Kutluca, 2024; Hussim et al., 2024; Chen, Liu, 2024
Digital competence and digital readiness	Hazari, 2024; Nayir et al., 2024; Magrill, Magrill, 2024; Hussim et al., 2024
Teacher-student interaction	Hazari, 2024
Problem solving and critical thinking	Betancourt Ramirez, Fuentes Esparrell, 2024; Bobula, 2024; Estaiteyeh, McQuirter, 2024; Nayir et al, 2024; Humble et al., 2024; Van den Berg, 2024; Coskun, Alper, 2024; Csaszar, Curry, 2024
Information understanding and management	Betancourt Ramirez, Fuentes Esparrell, 2024; Nguyen et al., 2024; Bennett, Abusalem, 2024; Humble et al., 2024; Abdelaal, Al Sawi, 2024; Chambers, Owen, 2024; Duran, 2024; Achinewhu-Nworgu, 2024
Immediacy of responses	Gökçearslan et al., 2024; Nguyen et al., 2024; Alasgarova, Rzayev, 2024
Reduction of teacher workload	Gökçearslan et al., 2024; Abdelaal, Al Sawi, 2024; Csaszar, Curry, 2024
Development of language skills	Gökçearslan et al., 2024; Noroozi et al., 2024; Van den Berg, 2024; Muslimin et al., 2024; Kramar et al., 2024
Creation of learning content	Bobula, 2024; Nguyen et al., 2024; Durak, Cankaya, 2024
Creativity	Miralay, 2024; Torres Carceller, 2024
Evaluation	Barrera Castro et al., 2024; Blegur et al., 2024
Autonomous learning	Achinewhu-Nworgu, 2024; Mcguire et al., 2024; Dilekli, Boyraz, 2024; Coskun, Alper, 2024; Kanont et al., 2024

[1] For an in-depth literature review, you can access the resources at the following link with the results of the ERIC database search.

Table 2. Bibliographic references on the critical issues related to the use of AI in education divided by topics

CRITICALITY	AUTHOR, YEAR
Dependence	Julien, 2024; Swindell et al., 2024; Gökçearslan et al., 2024; Bobula, 2024; Estaiteyeh, McQuirter, 2024; Alasgarova, Rzayev, 2024; Humble et al., 2024; Firincioglulari, 2024; Guler et al., 2024; Dilekli, Boyraz, 2024; Mcguire et al., 2024
Uneven accessibility	Julien, 2024; Betancourt Ramirez, Fuentes Esparrell, 2024; Frazier, 2024; Lowe 2024; Kanont et al., 2024; Jantakun et al., 2024
Technical difficulties	Julien, 2024; Swindell et al., 2024
Limited databases	Julien, 2024
Lack of specific skills/training for teachers	Hazari, 2024; Estaiteyeh, McQuirter, 2024; Frazier, 2024; Miralay, 2024; Abdelaal, Al Sawi, 2024; Firincioglulari, 2024; Grotrian et al., 2024
Privacy and security	Bai et al., 2024; Bennett, Abusalem, 2024; Bobula, 2024; Frazier, 2024; Abdelaal, Al Sawi, 2024; Lowe, 2024; Grotrian et al., 2024; Alexander et al., 2024
Complex or deficient regulations	Bai et al., 2024; Bobula, 2024
Ethical and pedagogical implications	Swindell et al., 2024; Eaton, 2024; Mcguire et al., 2024;
Reduction of the teacher's role	Duran, 2024; Abdelaal, Al Sawi, 2024;Torres Carceller, 2024; Betancourt Ramirez, Fuentes Esparrell, 2024; Achinewhu-Nworgu, 2024
Dehumanisation and lack of empathic interaction	Bennett, Abusalem, 2024; Gökçearslan et al., 2024; Nayir et al., 2024; Abdelaal, Al Sawi, 2024; Brunner, Tao, 2024; Solak, 2024; Duran, 2024
Resistance	Bennett, Abusalem, 2024; Grotrian et al., 2024; Magrill, Magrill, 2024; Sihag, Vibha, 2024
Inaccurate responses	Gökçearslan et al., 2024; Noroozi et al., 2024; Rodríguez Illera, 2024; Van den Berg, 2024;
Plagiarism	Gökçearslan et al., 2024; Bobula, 2024; Nguyen et al., 2024; Humble et al., 2024; Eaton, 2024; Achinewhu-Nworgu, 2024; Firth et al., 2024
Academic dishonesty	Bobula, 2024; Nguyen et al., 2024; Alasgarova, Rzayev, 2024; Ihekweazu et al., 2024; Beynen, 2024; Kramar et al., 2024; Durak, Cankaya, 2024
Reduction of autonomous thinking/critical reflection	Nguyen et al., 2024; Alasgarova, Rzayev, 2024; Humble et al., 2024; Durak, Cankaya, 2024; Dilekli, Boyraz, 2024; Duran, 2024
Reduction in creativity	Miralay, 2024
Costs	Abdelaal, Al Sawi, 2024; Jantakun et al., 2024

From a benefits perspective, much of the existing literature focuses on the use of AI for improving the efficiency of educational processes by providing greater support to both students and teachers. Among the most frequently cited benefits are the reduction of teachers' workload (Gökçearslan et al., 2024; Abdelaal, Al Sawi, 2024), thanks to the possibility of automating repetitive tasks such as assessment (Barrera Castro et al., 2024), and the ability to provide rapid and personalised feedback to students (Gökçearslan et al., 2024; Nguyen et al., 2024) through the use of tools such as chatbots and virtual assistants (Julien, 2024). The focus on personalisation of learning is a major theme, with a wide range of studies exploring how AI can provide solutions tailored to the individual needs of learners (Julien, 2024; Abdelaal, Al Sawi, 2024; Bobula, 2024; Barrera Castro et al., 2024; Van den Berg, 2024). Personalisation is often presented as one of the most promising aspects for improving learning effectiveness and increasing engagement and motivation (Julien, 2024; Nguyen et al., 2024; Miralay, 2024; Barrera Castro et al., 2024; Gökçearslan et al., 2024), thus leading to an overall improvement in school performance (Julien, 2024). Another significant benefit is accessibility (Julien, 2024; Nguyen et al., 2024; Abdelaal, Al Sawi, 2024; Barrera Castro et al., 2024; Gökçearslan et al., 2024): many of the articles reviewed emphasise how AI can democratise access to education, allowing students from all over the world to access high-quality educational resources (Van den Berg, 2024). The benefits brought about by the use of artificial intelligence in education also extend to the development of language skills (Van den Berg, 2024) and the promotion of digital literacy (Hazari, 2024; Magrill, Magrill, 2024), enabling students to be ready for an increasingly digitised labour market and world.

In the context of teacher education, the literature highlights how AI can facilitate professional development by supporting teachers in learning new skills and managing classroom dynamics more effectively (Eaton, 2024). The latter two aspects, i.e. teacher accessibility and professional development, also seem to be the most critical issues noted in the literature. In fact, the risk of reducing teachers' decision-making autonomy emerges in several studies, with AI that could, in some cases, overlap with educators' professional competences, compromising their ability to act creatively and personalise their teaching or even significantly limiting their role, leading to concerns regarding the possible reduction of jobs and the future of the professional figure of the teacher (Abdelaal, Al Sawi, 2024). Among the factors limiting the use of artificial intelligence in the classroom, in addition to complex and deficient regulations and legislation (Bobula, 2024), are the resistance of institutions and teachers themselves (Magrill, Magrill, 2024), who are often aware that they do not yet have the necessary skills to guide students in the responsible and effective use of AI (Hazari, 2024; Miralay, 2024; Abdelaal, Al Sawi, 2024). Precisely in connection with this, the urgent need to include courses on AI in initial teacher training also emerges in many articles (Hazari, 2024). The question of accessibility is also important, because although AI technology is becoming more intuitive and accessible every day, making the use of certain educational resources more inclusive, it is also true that not everyone has access to technology and connection, and therefore implementing AI in the classroom could exacerbate marginalisation dynamics and the gap that already exists between those who have access to education and those who do not (Julien, 2024).

A recurring theme is the ethical issue related to the use of AI, particularly with regard to student privacy, data management and the risk of algorithmic bias (Bobula, 2024; Abdelaal, Al Sawi, 2024), making the attempt to strike a balance between the automation of processes and the preservation of human intervention paramount (Gökçearslan et al., 2024). Another very relevant critical factor concerns technological dependency (Julien, 2024; Gökçearslan et al., 2024; Bobula, 2024; Dilekli, Boyraz, 2024), not only because of the risk of accepting inaccurate information and answers, but also because the continuous use of artificial intelligence tools may lead to a reduction in users' critical thinking skills, autonomous learning and critical reflection (Nguyen et al, 2024; Dilekli, Boyraz, 2024), to the point of degenerating into plagiarism (Gökçearslan et al., 2024; Bobula, 2024; Nguyen et al., 2024; Eaton, 2024) and more generally academic dishonesty (Bobula, 2024; Nguyen et al., 2024).

The literature therefore suggests that artificial intelligence has significant potential to transform the field of education by improving the efficiency of processes, personalising learning and providing new educational opportunities, but critical issues related to ethics, privacy and technological dependence cannot be overlooked and require careful consideration by researchers and educators, creating spaces and moments of critical reflection that make students aware of how the use of AI may affect their cognitive skills and abilities (Dilekli, Boyraz, 2024), while at the same time developing educational policies that allow for ethical oversight to respect academic integrity and ensure fair and democratic access to these new resources (Van den Berg, 2024). For these technologies to truly transform the educational experience, it is essential to accompany the design with critical reflection and to adopt a holistic approach that takes into account the needs and challenges of all stakeholders in order to shape a future in which education is truly inclusive, engaging and adaptive.

3. TEACHERS' EXPECTATIONS AND TRAINING NEEDS FOR EFFECTIVE USE OF AI IN THE CLASSROOM: QUESTIONNAIRE ANALYSIS

The literature analysed has highlighted some fundamental guidelines regarding the educational and didactic benefits of using artificial intelligence-based technologies. However, does not lack elements of difficulty or criticality, including resistance on the part of educators, teachers, students and institutions (Magrill, Magrill, 2024). It is therefore appropriate to investigate the perception and experience of Italian teachers regarding AI in the school context, with the aim of gaining a clear view of teachers' expectations and training needs.

Participants

The exploratory research was carried out in the context of the qualifying courses envisaged by the Prime Ministerial Decree of 4/08/2023 and involves a sample of 150 teachers belonging to the A001 competition class (Drawing and History of Art), of whom - for this contribution - only those belonging to the secondary school were considered (N=50). The gender is predominantly female (47 women, 3 men). The geographical location is mainly in southern Italy, particularly Apulia, Sicily and Calabria. All the teachers are employed on fixed-term contracts and have gained teaching experience mainly through occasional supply teaching, and teaching experience varies from a minimum of 3 years to a maximum of 6 years. In the current school year, all of them teach on a common place and do not have additional assignments.

Tools

A qualitative questionnaire was administered to the teachers involved, with exploratory intent, concerning the use of ICT and Artificial Intelligence and teaching methodologies, with also questions pertaining to training experiences. The questionnaire, administered via Google forms, contained:

1. A section on biographical data (age, gender, origin, work experience);
2. A section on the use of ICT, in which teachers were asked to express how and when they use technology in the classroom, the type of training and skills they have acquired, and to express on a 6-point Likert value scale how useful they consider it to be in promoting student interest, motivation, school performance and the development of transversal skills. The teachers were also asked to specify which platform they used most;
3. A section on the inclusion aspect. Specifically, the questionnaire asked whether or not technologies could promote inclusion and under what conditions;
4. A section more specifically dedicated to the latest developments in AI (immersive teaching, virtual reality, chatbots) and their use in the classroom;
5. Finally, a section on the training received. In this section, the teachers had to express whether or not they had participated in specific training courses and whether or not they considered the training received more or less adequate.

4. RESULTS AND DISCUSSION

All participants stated that they possessed good (86%) or at least adequate (10%) digital skills, acquired through training courses at the schools where they taught (96%). 57% of teachers attended courses mainly offered by the Area Network (73%), (2%) by universities and 25% by private training centers. With regard to the use of technology, daily use of digital applications by both teachers and students was noted. The most frequently cited tools include, Word Wall, Quizzes, Mindomo, Kahoot, Socrative, Learning Apps, Padlet, Book Creator, Canva and the Google platforms provided by schools. Lessons integrated with the use of digital tools take place once or twice a week, depending on the class schedule. When asked about the positive impact of ICT on teaching and learning, all participants gave the highest score, indicating a unanimous consensus on the added value that technologies bring in terms of motivation, engagement and student achievement. A significant aspect that emerged was the perceived importance of inclusion. Teachers emphasised that the use of ICT can benefit all students, as long as families are supported in acquiring appropriate devices such as computers and tablets. This data highlights a need for educational policies aimed at reducing the digital divide, ensuring equal access to technological resources.

With regard to the questions concerning the use of artificial intelligence in the classroom, no teachers have ever used visors or immersive teaching in the classroom or participated in specific training courses. However, most teachers (74%) have used AI in the classroom, mainly to create three-dimensional images and to show students how works of art, paintings and sculptures look in reality. In this regard, it is important to note that some teachers (35%) claim to be self-taught in the use of applications that allow them to create avatars and customised digital content. This fact, together with the fact that none of the participants have attended specific training courses on immersive teaching or on the use of visors, and that 40% of the participants consider the training they have received to be inadequate, suggests a significant area for improvement and the need for more training on emerging technologies in order to further broaden the range of digital and methodological skills of teachers.

5. CONCLUSION

The results presented form the basis of an ongoing research that aims to understand the potentials and criticalities of the use of Artificial Intelligence (AI) in education, and to address the training needs of teachers for the appropriate implementation of pedagogical and methodological innovations in the structuring of initial training course curricula. The analysis conducted highlights the significant impact of digital technologies, and in particular AI, on contemporary educational systems. Although the sample analyzed focuses on drawing and art history teachers working in secondary schools, the implications of the findings can be extended to a broader educational landscape, revealing opportunities and challenges that characterize the integration of AI in education. The survey shows an overall positive attitude towards digital technologies, with a unanimous consensus on their added value as evidence that digital transformation is already having a positive impact on the educational landscape, improving student motivation, participation and achievement. In addition, the introduction of AI is opening up new educational scenarios, with applications ranging from the creation of personalized content to the three-dimensional visualization of works of art.

These applications not only enrich the teaching-learning process, but also promote the development of critical and creative skills in students (Luckin et al., 2016). The ability of AI to personalize educational experiences is proving to be crucial in promoting differentiated learning and effectively addressing the diverse educational needs of students (Johnson et al., 2016). However, a lack of specific training in AI and immersive technologies has emerged, with 40 percent of participants complaining of inadequate training support. This highlights a significant gap that needs to be filled to ensure that faculty have the necessary skills to fully utilize these innovative tools to enable more effective and engaging instruction (Schleicher, 2018).

The autonomy demonstrated by a portion of the sample in learning new digital skills reflects a marked proactivity and growing interest in innovative technologies. This enthusiasm is a powerful ally in driving educational change, although institutional support through targeted training is essential. It is crucial that education systems respond to these needs by providing teachers with adequate resources for continuous learning. Indeed, a critical and creative approach to the use of emerging technologies can significantly improve the quality of education (Selwyn, 2017).

The integration of AI into the curriculum requires not only an update of technical skills, but also a cultural evolution in the way education is conceived and enjoyed. There is a need to structure educational programs that incorporate AI and digital elements in an application-relevant context. Such integration is critical to preparing learners not only for educational challenges, but also for 21st century professional challenges by fostering a school culture that values flexibility, resilience, and critical thinking skills (Anderson, 2019).

Research also supports the importance of structuring comprehensive and contemporary educational programs that adequately address modern needs. Such programs must not only integrate emerging technologies into educational practice, but do so in a way that enhances their direct applicability, ensuring a comprehensive preparation that embraces technological innovation in all its nuances (Fullan, 2013).

REFERENCES

Abdelaal, N.M., & Al Sawi, I. (2024). Perceptions, challenges, and prospects: University professors' use of artificial intelligence in education. *Australian Journal of Applied Linguistics*, 7(1), 1-24.

Anderson, T. (2019). Challenges and opportunities for digital education in the 21st century. Open Learning: The Journal of Open, *Distance and e-Learning*, 34(2), 180-190.

Barca, A., & Carruba, M.C. (2023). App come ambienti di apprendimento inclusivi: buone prassi per un approccio pedagogico. *Personae,* 2(2), 23-34.

Barrera Castro, G. P., Chiappe, A., Becerra Rodríguez, D. F., & Sepulveda, F. G. (2024). Harnessing AI for Education 4.0: Drivers of personalized learning. *Electronic Journal of e-Learning*, 22(5), 1-14.

Bobula, M. (2024). Generative artificial intelligence (AI) in higher education: A comprehensive review of challenges, opportunities, and implications. *Journal of Learning Development in Higher Education*, 30, 1-27.

Carruba, M. C. (2020). Carruba, M. C. (2020). *Back to school e tecnologie: per una "domotica educativa"* inclusiva. In L. D'Alonzo (Ed.), Back To school. #Iotornoascuola: un contesto per accogliere e includere. Pearson.

Dilekli, Y., & Boyraz, S. (2024). From "Can AI think?" to "Can AI help thinking deeper?": Is use of ChatGPT in higher education a tool of transformation or fraud? *International Journal of Modern Education Studies*, 8(1), 49–71.

Eaton, S. E. (2024). Pre-service teacher education in a postplagiarism world: Incorporating GenAI into teacher training. *Brock Education Journal*, 33(3), 11–16.

Fullan, M. (2013). *The New Meaning of Educational Change*. New York: Teachers College Press.

Gökçearslan, S., Tosun, C., & Erdemir, Z. G. (2024). Benefits, challenges, and methods of artificial intelligence (AI) chatbots in education: A systematic literature review. *International Journal of Technology in Education*, 7(1), 19-39.

Hazari, S. (2024). Justification and roadmap for artificial intelligence (AI) literacy courses in higher education. *Journal of Educational Research and Practice*, 14(1), 106-118.

Johnson, L., Becker, S. A., Cummins, M., & Estrada, V. (2016). NMC Horizon Report: 2016 Higher Education Edition. *The New Media Consortium.*

Julien, G. (2024). How artificial intelligence (AI) impacts inclusive education. *Educational Research and Reviews*, 19(6), 95-103.

Luckin, R., Holmes, W., Griffiths, M., & Forcier, L. B. (2016). *Intelligence Unleashed: An Argument for AI in Education.* Pearson.

Magrill, J., & Magrill, B. (2024). Preparing educators and students at higher education institutions for an AI-driven world. *Teaching & Learning Inquiry*, 12.

Miralay, F. (2024). Use of artificial intelligence and augmented reality tools in art education course. *Pegem Journal of Education and Instruction,* 14(3), 44–50.

Nguyen, T. N. T., Lai, N. V., & Nguyen, Q. T. (2024). Artificial intelligence (AI) in education: A case study on ChatGPT's influence on student learning behaviors. *Educational Process International Journal*, 13(2), 105-121.

Panciroli, C., Rivoltella, P. C., Gabbrielli, M., & Zawacki Richter, O. (2020). Artificial Intelligence and education: new research perspectives. Form@re - *Open Journal Per La Formazione in Rete*, 20(3), 1–12.

Schleicher, A. (2018). *Teaching and Learning International Survey (TALIS) 2018: Insights and Interpretations*. OECD Publishing.

Selwyn, N. (2017). *Education and Technology: Key Issues and Debates*. Bloomsbury Publishing.

Van den Berg, G. (2024). *Generative AI and educators: Partnering in using open digital content for transforming education*. Open Praxis, 16(2), 130–141.

Short Papers

DIGITAL TRANSFORMATION PROCESS IN TUTOR TRAINING: FROM FACE-TO-FACE TRAINING TO THE VIRTUAL ESCAPE ROOM FOR ENHANCING TEACHING COMPETENCIES

Michelle Pippig and Sabrina Hänsel
Dresden University of Technology
Center for Interdisciplinary Learning and Teaching, Mommsenstraße 6
01069 Dresden, Germany

ABSTRACT

This paper presents the digital transformation process of a face-to-face training programme at the Technical University of Dresden into mobile learning solutions aimed at improving the teaching skills of student tutors in higher education. It explores the development of a 360-degree learning environment that enables student tutors to access training content flexibly and independently of location. Furthermore, it demonstrates how this learning environment is extended through the development of a virtual escape room. By incorporating elements of gamification and artificial intelligence, the virtual escape room is designed to provide an immersive and customisable learning environment that specifically fosters competencies such as critical thinking, problem solving and collaboration. This approach addresses challenges such as accessibility, motivation, and skills development, while supporting the broader goals of digital transformation in higher education. The paper highlights the potential of mobile technologies for the sustainable development of tutor training.

KEYWORDS

Student Tutor Training, Gamification, AI, Virtual Learning Environment

1. INTRODUCTION

The digital transformation of higher education presents both significant challenges and opportunities to rethink traditional learning and teaching methods. In this evolving landscape, tutorial work plays a central role, with student tutors acting as key facilitators of learning. At the Technical University of Dresden (TUD), around 600 student tutors contribute to tutorials, exercises and practicals each semester, representing around 40 per cent of the teaching staff (TUD, 2022). These tutors are particularly important during the critical introductory phase of a student's academic journey, where they provide guidance, ensure continuity in teaching, and help to ensure the quality of teaching (Netzwerk Tutorienarbeit an Hochschulen, 2018; Zitzelsberger, 2015).

However, traditional methods of training tutors often lack the flexibility, scalability, and effectiveness needed to meet the demands of modern education. They are often time-consuming and limited in scope, leaving tutors unprepared for challenges such as hybrid teaching environments, technical issues, and the diverse needs of students.

Recent advances in game-based learning have demonstrated significant potential for improving educational outcomes. Escape rooms, in particular, have been shown to be effective in increasing motivation, fostering problem-solving skills, and developing critical thinking (Pais et al., 2023). These methods also encourage creativity and promote digital literacy by integrating tools and technologies that are increasingly relevant in virtual teaching environments.

This paper examines the transformation of a training programme for student tutors into mobile learning solutions. It focuses on the development phase of mobile training formats, highlighting the concept, theoretical foundations, and technological innovations – such as gamification and artificial intelligence – of a virtual escape room.

2. CONTEXT AND GOALS

2.1 Original Programme: Room of Horrors

In order to qualify the tutors at the TUD for their teaching activities, several training formats for student tutors are offered. These include the face-to-face qualification programme *Room of Horrors*, which is based on a medical simulation training method and uses a realistic and interactive training environment to sensitise participants to sources of error and risks in this environment. The concept has been adapted for further education in the context of tutor qualification to simulate typical challenges in the preparation of hybrid teaching-learning scenarios. The student tutors collaborate in small groups to identify and resolve prepared *traps* in a seminar room, such as locked laptops, misplaced cables, or documents containing sensitive data. The training focuses on developing skills such as structured communication, collaboration, time management and problem solving. During the setting, tutors are observed and evaluated by another group of participants, with feedback provided based on a structured evaluation framework (Figure 1).

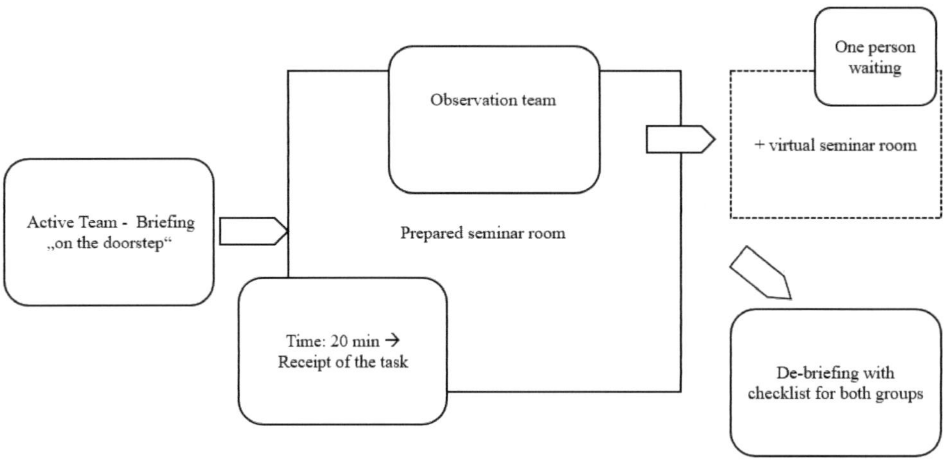

Figure 1. The setting – organization and structure of the *room of horrors* (own illustration)

In a survey (n=18) about the experience of the *room of horrors*, the participating tutors emphasized that it was a "*very well thought out concept and a learning effect could be seen*". "*Read carefully and stay calm*", "*read instructions better*", "*read first and then act*" were the main elements that participants took away from the experience.

The importance of a structured approach and clear communication within the team were key lessons learned: "*good consultation with each other makes teamwork easier*", "*organisation, structure and setting priorities*", "*structure is essential*".

The feedback shows that the participants identified the core competencies to be addressed – such as teamwork, structured communication and prioritisation – as key takeaways from the experience. This confirms the success of the approach in effectively targeting and fostering these skills, providing a strong basis for further development.

2.2 Motivation for Mobile Learning Solutions

In order to gain insights into the needs, challenges and working conditions of student tutors, a survey was conducted among active student tutors at the TUD in June 2024 (Schlegel & Ludwig, 2022; TU Dresden, 2025). The results will be used to derive specific training programmes and strategic recommendations for action to improve satisfaction. A total of 90 tutors from different faculties participated in the survey, mainly from the fields of mechanical engineering and educational science. In terms of training needs, the majority of respondents (68 per cent) were keen to take advantage of flexible training opportunities, with only 23 per cent stating that they had no specific needs. Figure 2 summarises the subject areas that respondents felt should be the focus of training. Particular emphasis was placed on topics such as facilitation and counselling, dealing with difficult students, organisation and didactic design of a course and personal development / soft skills.

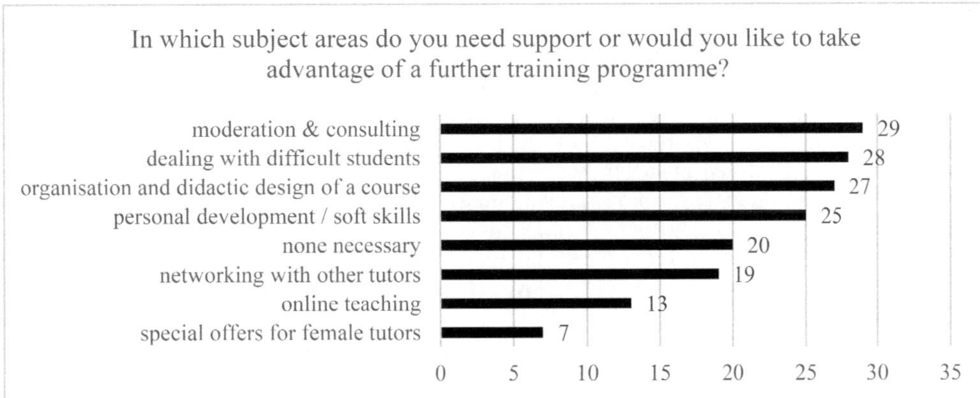

Figure 2. Topic requests for further training in frequencies (own illustration)

The majority of respondents (73 per cent) expressed a willingness to spend one or more days per semester on training, with a preference for flexible training formats. To meet the growing demand for flexible learning, the *room of horrors* has been transformed into a mobile-friendly, interactive 360-degree room. Using immersive technologies, student tutors can be prepared for the above challenges by virtually navigating through a simulated classroom, highlighting and identifying sources of error with the click of a mouse (Figure 3). This format increased accessibility and allowed tutors to participate asynchronously, overcoming the time constraints of traditional training.

Figure 3. Insight into the 360-degree room, developed with the Matterport software (picture TUTORING hybrid)

While the continuous availability of the 360-degree application minimizes the time required to set up in-person training, it does not allow for collaboration with other participants and error detection is only partially simulated. In order to address these limitations and remedy the deficits identified in the study, the existing programme is being extended through the development of a virtual escape room as a playful implementation format. This extension will provide a realistic yet engaging learning experience tailored to the needs of the target group.

3. PEDAGOGICAL APPROACH AND TECHNOLOGICAL INNOVATIONS OF THE VIRTUAL ESCAPE ROOM

Based on the results of the needs analysis and the implementation of the 360-degree virtual learning environment, the development of the virtual escape room is currently underway. The 360-degree application, designed as an immersive but asynchronous learning format, provided a flexible way for tutors to engage with the training content. However, it lacked the collaborative and interactive depth required to fully address real-world challenges. To fill these gaps, the virtual escape room is currently being developed to foster teamwork, critical thinking, and problem-solving skills through a gamified and adaptive learning experience tailored to the needs identified in the earlier phases. The development of the virtual escape room at TUD follows a structured and iterative approach, integrating research-based methods, pedagogical principles, and technological innovations.

3.1 Pedagogical Approach and Theoretical Foundations

The virtual escape room is based on problem-based learning and constructivist theories. These approaches promote critical thinking, problem solving and collaboration among tutors by simulating real teaching situations they encounter in their roles. The escape room is designed as an interactive, practical learning environment that encourages tutors to construct knowledge through active problem solving (Savery & Duffy, 1995; Gee, 2003).

From a media-didactic perspective, the virtual escape room combines the flexibility of digital educational offerings with problem-based and collaborative learning methods. By incorporating different media formats (text, audio, video), the escape room accommodates different learning styles and makes complex content more accessible (Mayer, 2001). This multimodal design ensures inclusivity for all participants. The escape room also encourages collaborative learning through the use of digital tools, which improves teamwork and communication (Johnson & Johnson, 1999).

In addition, the anonymity provided in a digital space may encourage creative behaviour and encourage unconventional problem solving, similar to Zimbardo's Deviance in the Dark experiment (Zimbardo, 1969). Tutors acting through avatars or anonymously may feel less constrained by social norms and more willing to take risks and experiment with new approaches (Joinson, 2001).

With the use of AI-powered chatbots, tutors receive personalised, real-time feedback during the training process, making learning more efficient and flexible. The virtual escape room thus provides a safe and motivating environment in which tutors can engage in practical and innovative learning (Labadze et al., 2023).

3.2 Technological Innovations

Building on the 360-degree environment, the virtual escape room adds further levels of gamification, interactivity and collaboration. The scenarios are designed to simulate real-life challenges in teaching situations. This promotes core competences such as stress resistance, creative problem solving and communication skills.

The platform will be compatible with smartphones, tablets and laptops, allowing teachers to participate in the training anytime, anywhere. This flexibility meets the growing trend towards mobile learning and the needs of modern tutors who require asynchronous, self-paced learning options. The use of 360-degree panoramas and interactive virtual spaces promotes a sense of spatial and social presence comparable to that of traditional virtual reality environments (Dyrna et al., 2022). This immersion allows tutors to engage intensively with the content, improving their teaching skills. In addition, the 360-degree environment provides a safe space for tutors to experiment with teaching strategies without fear of failure. AI-powered feedback through a chatbot allows participants to reflect on their performance and adjust their approach, fostering the development of both technical and interpersonal skills. This virtual assistant provides real-time guidance and personalised hints, and adapts to the level of difficulty of the tasks to achieve meaningful and individualised learning outcomes. To extend the reach of the virtual escape room beyond the local context, the platform supports multiple languages, making it accessible to international tutors. This promotes inclusion and accessibility for different student tutor groups.

4. CONCLUSION AND OUTLOOK

Tutor training formats at TUD will continue to evolve to address the challenges identified in the 2024 survey. The ongoing development of the virtual escape room specifically aims to address existing gaps in training, such as the need for better accessibility, flexible learning opportunities, and the development of interpersonal and technical skills. A detailed concept for the virtual escape room has been developed, outlining learning objectives, narrative structures, and task designs that are tailored to real-world teaching scenarios. This escape room will provide an initial qualification for the preparation of barrier-free seminar rooms, enabling tutors to effectively support inclusive teaching environments. By integrating playful elements, the escape room ensures that training is engaging and time-efficient, taking into account the limited time availability of student tutors.

Currently, the immediate focus is on building a working prototype and conducting beta testing with a small group of tutors. This testing phase will gather feedback to refine the platform's features and ensure an optimal user experience. Subsequent iterations will expand the scope of the virtual escape room by incorporating more advanced AI-driven features, such as adaptive feedback mechanisms and complex problem-solving scenarios. In addition, scalability remains a key objective, with the aim of adapting the virtual escape room for wider use across higher education institutions.

The virtual escape room currently being developed at the TUD is a promising innovation in tutor training. Through the use of gamification, AI and mobile learning technologies, the virtual escape room offers a flexible and engaging solution to the challenges facing tutor training today. While the project is still in the development phase, it has great potential to improve tutors' technical and interpersonal skills to better meet the demands of modern higher education.

As digital transformation continues to reshape higher education, the virtual escape room is an example of how innovative approaches can prepare tutors for future challenges. Further development will focus on expanding its capabilities and enhancing AI components, ultimately creating a scalable and impactful global learning platform for tutors.

REFERENCES

Dyrna, J., Stöhr, K., & Pippig, M., (2022). Do learners experience spatial and social presence in interactive environments based on 360-degree panoramas? A pilot study and future research agenda. *Communities in New Media. Digitality and Diversity Overcoming Barriers with Digital Transformation,* Dresden. https://doi.org/10.25368/2023.77

Gee, J. P., (2003). *What Video Games Have to Teach Us About Learning and Literacy*. Palgrave Macmillan. New York, USA.

Johnson, D.W. and Johnson, R.T., (1999). *Learning Together and Alone: Cooperative, Competitive, and Individualistic Learning*. Allyn and Bacon, Boston, USA.

Joinson, A.N., (2001). Self-disclosure in computer-mediated communication: The role of self-awareness and visual anonymity. *European Journal of Social Psychology*, Vol. 31, No. 2, pp. 177-192.

Labadze, L. et al., (2023). Role of AI chatbots in education: Systematic literature review. *International Journal of Educational Technology in Higher Education*, Vol. 56, pp. 1-19.

Mayer, R. E., (2001). *Multimedia learning*. Cambridge University Press, Cambridge, UK.

Netzwerk Tutorienarbeit an Hochschulen, (2018). *Zukunft der Tutorienarbeit an Hochschulen*. Positionspapier.

Pais, S. et al., (2023). Using an escape room activity to enhance the motivation of undergraduate life science students in mathematics classes: A case study. *Proceedings of the 17th European Conference on Game-Based Learning*, Brighton, UK, pp. 78-87.

Savery, J. R., & Duffy, T. M., (1995). *Problem-based learning: An instructional model and its constructivist framework.* Educational Technology, Vol. 35, No. 5, pp. 31-38.

Schlegel, B. and Ludwig, M., (2022). *Umfrage zur Situation von Fachtutor:innen der TU Dresden*. Technische Universität Dresden, Dresden, Germany.

Technische Universität Dresden, (2022). *Statistischer Jahresbericht 2022*. Technische Universität Dresden, Dresden, Germany.

Technische Universität Dresden, (2025). *TUTORING@TUD 2024: Herausforderungen und Chancen in Arbeits- und Weiterbildungsstrukturen für studentische Lehrende*. Technische Universität Dresden, Dresden, Germany. In Print.

Zimbardo, P.G., (1969). The human choice: Individuation, reason, and order versus deindividuation, impulse, and chaos. *Nebraska Symposium on Motivation*, Vol. 17, pp. 237-307.

Zitzelsberger, Olga (Hrsg.), (2015). Neue Wege in der tutoriellen Lehre in der Studieneingangsphase. Dokumentation der gleichnamigen Tagung im März 2014 an der TU Darmstadt. *Schriften zur allgemeinen Hochschuldidaktik*, Münster, Germany, WTM.

MOBILE LEARNING AND 3D IN PRIMARY SCHOOL TEACHER TRAINING

Barbara Bruschi and Melania Talarico
University of Turin, Italy

ABSTRACT

The study explores innovative methods in teacher training at the University of Turin, focusing on mobile learning and 3D content manipulation to enhance active and participatory learning. Through a course on Instructional Technologies and Learning, second-year students in the Primary Education program were tasked with designing augmented teaching lessons using mobile devices and 3D objects. This approach integrates gamification and constructivist principles to foster creativity, critical thinking, and technical skills. A total of 122 augmented lessons were created, with themes ranging from ancient history to science. Results showed significant student engagement, creativity, and alignment with instructional design principles. This experience underscores the potential of combining mobile and 3D learning to enhance digital skills, preparing future educators for modern, technologically enriched classrooms. Further analysis will be conducted to assess this teaching method's pedagogical outcomes and effectiveness.

KEYWORDS

Augmented Teaching, Digital Skills, Mobile Learning Students of University, 3D Technologies

1. INTRODUCTION

Educators must critically engage with the methods and tools that promote active and participatory learning in today's increasingly complex world. However, contemporary pedagogical discourse also highlights the importance of considering the sustainability of technological approaches (Szymkowiak et al., 2021), emphasizing using technologies not merely as tools for entertainment but as valuable educational resources (Haleem et al., 2022). In Italy, as in many other countries, there are ongoing debates about using smartphones and mobile devices in educational settings, including those reflected in school regulations.

Scientific research underscores the benefits of digital education and the integration of mobile devices within school environments, noting improvements in student participation, motivation, and critical engagement with digital tools (Criollo et al., 2021). Nonetheless, there remains considerable skepticism about the use of mobile devices, particularly within the framework of "Bring Your Device" (BYOD) policies, which some view as obstacles to effective and constructive education. These concerns often center on issues related to policy and privacy (Richard et al., 2022). However, at the European level, educational policymakers are increasingly encouraged to foster integrated learning environments (Bruschi, 2021) in order to enhance digital competencies, as outlined in the Digital Education Action Plan and Agenda 2030.

Given this context, engaging with students—particularly at the university level, as discussed in this contribution—is crucial to promoting a digital culture transcending mere technological literacy. For some time, the concept of "augmented teaching" has embraced various approaches and tools, increasingly geared toward this goal (Sansone, Ritella, 2020). Such a digital culture must be founded on a reflective and dynamic approach. It is evident that mobile learning, combined with emerging technologies such as augmented reality (AR), 3D content manipulation, and gamification, is exerting a profound influence on education. There is a growing awareness that mobile learning can be an effective pedagogical tool when integrated with constructivist or constructionist approaches (Garzón, 2021). This perspective also extends to the use of 3D technologies and gamification.

On the one hand, gamified learning activities have significantly enhanced student engagement and motivation (Khaldi et al., 2023; Zeybek & Saygı, 2024). For example, as Kao and colleagues (2023) demonstrate, gamification can be successfully applied in mobile learning contexts to boost participation and academic performance. Mobile devices provide an ideal platform for embedding game mechanics, such as levels, challenges, rewards, and instant feedback, which make the learning process more dynamic and interactive.

On the other hand, integrating these technological elements creates opportunities to explore additional pedagogical strategies, such as incorporating 3D models into instructional practices. The rising interest in mobile learning and 3D content manipulation opens new possibilities for active and participatory learning (Lisana & Suciadi, 2021). In particular, combining 3D technologies with constructivist or constructionist approaches represents a significant advancement in educational practice. By utilizing 3D technologies—often in conjunction with augmented reality—students can engage with complex concepts in an immersive and hands-on manner, facilitating a deeper and more meaningful understanding than traditional methods allow. The ability to manipulate three-dimensional models enables learners to explore structures or systems from multiple perspectives, thereby promoting the acquisition of technical and cognitive skills (Hidayat & Wardat, 2023).

In this context, using 3D technologies not only enriches the learning experience but also stimulates creativity and problem-solving, as students are actively interacting with the content. When applied in mobile learning environments, 3D teaching can design personalized and engaging learning scenarios wherein students construct knowledge through exploration and experimentation (Abdinejad et al., 2021).

Ultimately, integrating mobile learning with 3D technologies represents an educational frontier beyond the mere transmission of content. Instead, it fosters critical thinking and active participation, placing the learner at the center of the educational experience. This dynamic and reflective approach ensures the sustainable use of educational technologies and presents new opportunities to enhance teaching quality, making it more innovative and inclusive.

This contribution aims to describe a training initiative undertaken with university students in the Master's Degree Program in Primary Education at the University of Turin.

2. THE UNIVERSITY COURSE EXPERIENCE

The Instructional Technologies and Learning course, present in the curriculum of Primary Education Sciences at the University of Turin, aims primarily to provide second-year students with the conceptual and methodological elements related to technologies in the educational field. One of the course's sub-objectives is to train students in designing learning environments and being able to choose the principles and methods for online teaching. In 2024, the course required students to create augmented teaching lessons to pass the final exam. In total, approximately 122 augmented lessons were collected.

3. METHOD

Each student attending the course, including non-attendees, was asked to create a micro-lesson on a specific topic, including various multimedia elements such as a 3D object. The work was done individually on a topic chosen and agreed upon with the course instructor. The lesson design followed two phases:

Table 1. Project grid

Target	Characteristics of the participants
Aims	The learning goals
Discipline	For example, history, science, Italian, etc
Topic	For example, Egypt or the Roman Empire
Description of the context	Formal or non-formal context. Is the activity carried out at school or in an extracurricular setting?
Setting	How is the space organized?
Times	What are the design timelines?
Target	Characteristics of the participants
Description of the activity	Describe the multimedia elements that characterize the activity (objects, images, videos, etc.)
Work phases and reference methodologies	In which teaching moment does the activity take place? What methods are employed?
Technologies	App, Software
Expected results	What knowledge or skills are expected to be acquired?

In the second phase, students were asked to implement the design grid using a free program called Thinglink*, which allows the creation of virtual and digital environments that are not exclusively educational but suitable for such purposes. For evaluation, each product could be awarded between zero and five points, which could be added to the final exam score, with a maximum of 26/30 points. Below is the reference table with the evaluation criteria (Table 2):

Table 2. Evaluation grid

Indicator	Description	Score
1. A 3D object (downloadable from Sketchfab.com)	Students were required to identify a 3D object relevant to the lesson content on the Sketchfab platform. The 3D object can be accessed using mobile devices and, in some cases, projected using augmented reality.	1
2. At least one textual description of the content	Students were required to insert one or more textual descriptions related to the theme addressed, coherent with other elements. They were asked not to insert a referential lesson description but to add important content-related information.	0,5
3. At least one image and one explanatory video	Students were asked to balance gamification principles learned during the lesson with educational content.	0,5
4. At least one game related to the contents	Students were asked to balance gamification principles learned during the lesson with educational content.	1
5. Educational value, not just entertainment value	This included creating game environments, balancing educational elements with entertainment, and paying attention to cognitive overload. Students were expected to design a clear and coherent contents aligned with the educational design principles presented in the project grid.	2

4. DATA ANALYSIS AND FIRST RESULTS

Projects were collected through the Moodle platform, and scores were assigned. From an initial content analysis of the design grids, several characteristics emerge regarding the age group of the subjects, the frequency of chosen themes, the work phases, and the type of outcome aimed through the design process. Additionally, most students coherently integrated the 3D object into their design, aligned with their reference objectives.

The evaluations were distributed as follows: 77 students received 5 points, 30 received 4 points, 13 received 3 points, and two received 2 points. The scores were assigned based on the evaluation grid described in the previous paragraph.

The main themes included:

- The history of ancient Rome and ancient Greece
- The human body (e.g., digestive system, skeletal system)
- Geography (anthropic and natural world)
- Water recycling
- The solar system
- Science (flowers, plants, and the animal kingdom)

From this experience, some reflections can be made regarding the use of augmented lessons, as follows:

- Students were active participants in their learning process. They transformed from learners into active designers by creating educational augmented lessons with high educational value.
- They applied various elements of instructional design, incorporating the methodologies studied during the course and in other university courses.
- They developed design and technological skills, engaging in a little-known and rarely-used approach in educational settings.
- They created products that are usable outside the academic context and applicable within the educational contexts described in the design grids.

5. CONCLUSIONS

In conclusion, this experience allowed students to design integrated environments using mobile devices to work on augmented educational content. It is important to note that students had the opportunity to develop a range of digital skills and critically reflect and apply the instructional design principles learned during the course. Therefore, the added value of designing augmented lessons with university students can be expressed in two forms: a) The future teacher will know how to move from theoretical design to the practical realization of the work, thus designing complex and pedagogically valid digital learning environments; b) In line with the skills outlined in DigComp 2.2 232 (Vuorikari et al., 2022), particularly concerning the creation and reworking of digital content, students will be able to develop and implement their digital skills and, subsequently, promote a correct digital culture in their future school environments.

From these initial observations, it will be necessary to conduct further analysis of the student-generated designs using qualitative research software like Nvivo.

REFERENCES

Abdinejad, M., Talaie, B., Qorbani, H. S., & Dalili, S. (2021). Student perceptions using augmented reality and 3d visualization technologies in chemistry education. *Journal of Science Education and Technology*, *30*, 87-96.

Bruschi, B. (2021). Ambienti di apprendimento integrati e digitali per una didattica aumentata. *BRICKS*, *6*, 176–182.

Criollo-C, S., Guerrero-Arias, A., Jaramillo-Alcázar, Á., & Luján-Mora, S. (2021). Mobile learning technologies for education: Benefits and pending issues. *Applied Sciences*, *11*(9), 4111.

European Commission. *Digital Education Action Plan 2021-2027: Resetting Education and Training for the Digital Age*. 2020. Accessed [date of access]. https://ec.europa.eu/education/education-in-the-eu/digital-education-action-plan_en.

Garzón, J. (2021). An overview of twenty-five years of augmented reality in education. *Multimodal Technologies and Interaction*, *5*(7), 37.

Haleem, A., Javaid, M., Qadri, M. A., & Suman, R. (2022). Understanding the role of digital technologies in education: A review. *Sustainable operations and computers*, *3*, 275-285.

Hidayat, R., & Wardat, Y. (2024). A systematic review of augmented reality in science, technology, engineering, and mathematics education. *Education and Information Technologies*, *29*(8), 9257-9282.

Kao, M. C., Yuan, Y. H., & Wang, Y. X. (2023). The study designed a gamified mobile learning model to assess students' learning outcomes of accounting education. *Heliyon*, *9*(2).

Khaldi, A., Bouzidi, R., & Nader, F. (2023). Gamification of e-learning in higher education: a systematic literature review. *Smart Learning Environments*, *10*(1), 10.

Lisana, L., & Suciadi, M. F. (2021). The acceptance of mobile learning: a case study of 3D simulation android app for learning physics. *International Journal of Interactive Mobile Technologies (iJIM)*, *15*(17), 205-214.

Richard, N., Habinka, A. E., & Kaggwa, F. (2022). BYOD systematic literature review: A layered approach.

Sansone, N., & Ritella, G. (2020). Formazione insegnanti" aumentata": integrazione di metodologie e tecnologie al servizio di una didattica socio-costruttivista. *Qwerty*, *15*(1), 70-88.

Szymkowiak, A., Melović, B., Dabić, M., Jeganathan, K., & Kundi, G. S. (2021). Information technology and Gen Z: The role of teachers, the internet, and technology in the education of young people. *Technology in Society*, *65*, 101565.

United Nations. (2015). *Transforming our world: The 2030 Agenda for Sustainable Development*. https://sdgs.un.org/2030agenda

Vuorikari, R., Kluzer, S. and Punie, Y., (2022) DigComp 2.2: The Digital Competence Framework for Citizens, EUR 31006 EN, Publications Office of the European Union, Luxembourg.

Zeybek, N., & Saygı, E. (2024). Gamification in education: Why, where, when, and how? A systematic review. *Games and Culture*, *19*(2), 237-264.

TRANSFORMING MOBILE LEARNING EXPERIENCES IN BRAZILIAN PUBLIC SCHOOLS DURING THE PANDEMIC

Vania Carvalho de Castro
University of Illinois Urbana-Champaign, USA

ABSTRACT

This study investigates the use of mobile learning during a professional development course for English teachers in Brazil during the pandemic time. The course aimed to help educators rethink their pedagogical practices and integrate mobile learning to enhance teaching and learning. The objective of this paper is to explore how lesson plans based on mobile learning, designed and implemented by the participating teachers, promote the mobility of learners and the mobile learning experiences. This study utilized educational design-based research from the qualitative realm of investigation. The findings show that mobile learning, particularly in underserved areas, can facilitate real-world, contextualized learning experiences, empowering students to become active knowledge producers.

KEYWORDS

Mobile Learning, Public Schools, Brazil, Pandemic

1. INTRODUCTION

The use of mobile devices for various purposes in everyday life has been growing increasingly. In April 2023, 58,67% of web traffic globally was coming from mobile devices (Statista, 2024). In Brazil, for example, in 2022 there were a total of 352 million smartphones, laptops, and tablets, which represented almost 1.6 devices per person. With the number of smartphones in the country, it seems that Brazil is living in an era of digital ubiquity. Despite the widespread availability of mobile devices in Brazil, the country still faces significant educational challenges. According to the British Council Brazil/Plano DCE (2015), many English teachers do not have access to a range of technology tools nor know how to use digital technologies for educational purposes. The findings also revealed that 52% of these teachers graduated about ten years ago, and 45% do not regularly participate in teacher professional development (p. 21-22). Also, the COVID-19 pandemic intensified the challenges to the educational system.

The ubiquity of mobile phones means that these devices could potentially be leveraged to support and build the capacities of millions of educators (Unesco, 2017). Given that mobile devices are the fastest spreading technology (Pegrum, 2014, 2015; Unesco, 2013; Barbosa et al. 2020), there is a need to expand the space for learning, enabling education to happen anytime and anywhere, and to integrate mobile phones into education to provide relevant learning that engage students with real-world situations, as mobile learning encompasses not just mobile devices but also the *mobility* of learners and their learning experiences (Pegrum, 2014). Mobility involves the seamless integration of learning into diverse contexts, times, and places, supported by the ubiquitous nature of mobile devices.

This study investigates the possibilities that emerged from mobile learning during a professional development course with English teachers from public schools in Brazil during the pandemic. The goal of this course was to offer opportunities for them to rethink their pedagogical practices and integrate mobile learning towards transformative teaching. The eight participating teachers created lesson plans incorporating mobile learning during the course and implemented in their teaching during 2020. This paper seeks to answer the following research question: **In what ways do lesson plans based on mobile learning, designed and implemented by teachers during a professional development course, promote the *mobility* of learners and the mobile learning experiences?**

2. MOBILE LEARNING AND THE LEVELS OF MOBILITY

The term mobile learning refers to using all mobile devices in education through multiple contexts and social interactions in a ubiquitous way, where the learner does not stay in a fixed location (Crompton, 2013; Pegrum, 2014, UNESCO, 2013, 2017). Pegrum (2014, 2015) highlights that mobile learning is not only about mobile devices. It also refers to the 'mobility' of both learners and learning experiences. The author describes three different degrees of mobility (2014, p. 16-21):

1 When devices are mobile, but the learners and the learning experience are not. In this first stage, the mobile devices do not create a change in the learner's mobility and the learning experience. For example, when schools purchase tablets for classrooms. They may move from classroom to classroom, but students continue to learn while seated at their desks. In this scenario, tablets serve the same function as stationary computers.

2 When both the devices and the learners are mobile, but the learning experience is not. In this second level of mobility, the learners are mobile to various extents during the learning process, yet the learning experience remains unchanged. For example, in schools, students may get up with their tablets or smartphones, walk around the classroom, and interact with their classmates by asking questions, making comments, and sharing knowledge (Pegrum, 2015). However, this still represents a limited level of mobility. Therefore, although both the devices and the learners are mobile in this self-paced style, the learning experience itself remains relatively static. Connecting this theory to the present study, the participating teachers revealed that their teaching practices with mobile phones weaved back between the first and the second level of mobily.

3 When devices, learners, and the learning experience are mobile. At the third level of mobility, the real-world context is turned into the learning contexts where students' local experiences intersect with global communication channels and personal experiences intersect with their social networks (Pegrum, 2014). This is the type of mobility the scenario of this study aims to reach. Pegrum (2015) provides an example in which teachers take students out of the classroom to explore their town, they walk around the city and take pictures of historical monuments. Students then use their devices to research information about the buildings, such as who built them and when; upload photos to the classroom platform; and comment on their classmates' posts. This approach fully realizes the potential of ubiquitous learning: learning anywhere, at any time (Pegrum, 2015). In this level, the mobility applies to learners, the devices, and the learning experiences.

3. METHODS

This study utilized educational design-based research from the qualitative realm of investigation. This type of method addresses educational problems in real-world settings. One of its fundamental goals is to develop teaching/learning possible solutions for the educational scenario, primarily aimed at innovative interventions in education (Plomp & Nieveen, 2020).

Eight English teachers[1] participated in this research but only two of them were able to apply their lesson plans with their students due to the pandemic time, from April to June 2020. This paper focuses on these participating teachers. The research instruments used included 1) observations. 2) Pre and post surveys. The pre-survey aimed to outline the participants' profile and check their familiarity and access to virtual environments on mobile devices. The final one intended to capture the teachers' final perception after the course. 3) Lesson plans. The course content included Ubiquitous learning, mobile learning and the three levels of mobility, and the significance of mobile learning in the contemporary era. The course included the following Apps: Zoom (https://zoom.us/) was used for the synchronous meetings, and it was chosen due to its diversity of available functionalities during live meetings and Google Classroom (https://classroom.google.com/) was used for teachers to post their lesson plans and course activities. Besides these platforms, ten mobile applications were also used during the course: Padlet, Quizlet, Canva, Wordwall, Kahoot, Plickers, Trello, Twitter, Tik Tok, and Lyrics Training.

---

[1] All the participating teachers have given their consent in writing to participate in this research. The protocols used to collect data have been reviewed and approved by the research ethics committee (COEP) from UFMG in Plataforma Brasil. Certificate of presentation for Ethical Appreciation: CAAE: 31338620.3.0000.5149.

4. DISCUSSION AND FINDINGS

The participants' lesson plans

The lesson plans were designed for elementary and high school students. They were created on different platforms: Canva, Google Docs, and Padlet. Generally, they provided interdisciplinary activities connecting English with arts, biology, Portuguese, music, and dancing. They also incorporated some applications introduced in the course and mobile phones.

In the pre-course survey, teachers P1, P2, P4, P6, and P7 identified themselves as traditional educators, describing their teaching practices as primarily focused on content transmission with minimal use of digital tools in their classrooms. In contrast, teachers P3, P5, and P8 indicated that their teaching practices fell between content transmission and facilitating meaning-making, incorporating more collaborative learning approaches. Although P2 participated in the course, she did not answer the final questionnaire, neither she produced the lesson plan nor participated in the peer-review process.

Based on records, it was the first time the teachers studied the idea of learning anywhere at any time. The participants cited the following online educational tools for mobile learning: Edpuzzle, Playposit, Stop, Kahoot, and Duolingo. These tools were mentioned by teachers P1, P4, P6, and P7 in their lesson plans. They brought the idea of learning outside the classroom and providing technology tools to make the third level of mobility more possible. P1 produced a lesson plan about sustainability composed of 18 classes:

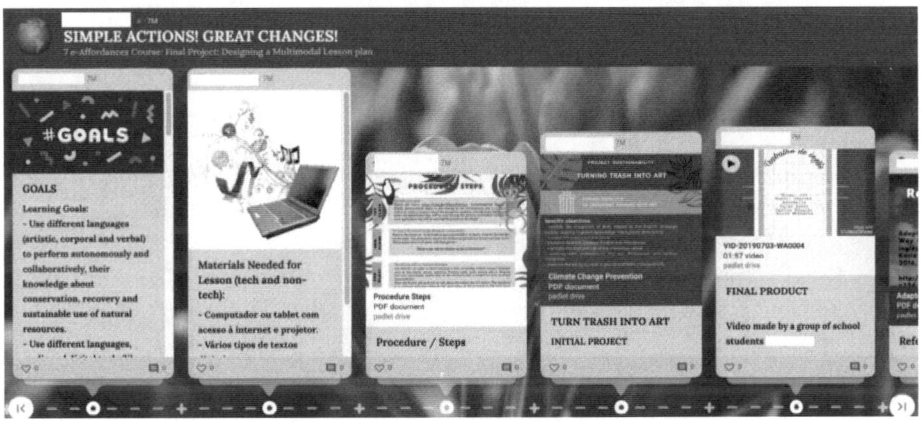

Figure 1. LESSON plan by P1 on Canva app
Source: Castro (2021, p. 218)

The teacher P1 incorporated some ubiquitous tools, such as Padlet in the third class for the students to post content: "each student should write a message about what the activity has sparked [...] This message must be posted on the Padlet so that the whole class has access in English or Portuguese language". Then, in the sixth class, they are expected to produce a multimodal artifact on Canva: "each group will produce a poster using the Canva tool (in English) the environment." Week 11th of this lesson plan is planned for the use of Kahoot with the students. P1 will create "a game to integrate and provide better knowledge about the environment, as well as interact with students."

P4, P6, and P7 did not explicitly make the lesson plan features related to learning or accessibility of learning materials anytime, anywhere. It was noted that their activities weaved between the first and the second level of mobility. P5 designed a lesson plan to encourage students to bring real world situations to the learning experience. Here is an example of a lesson plan designed by P6 for the English classes:

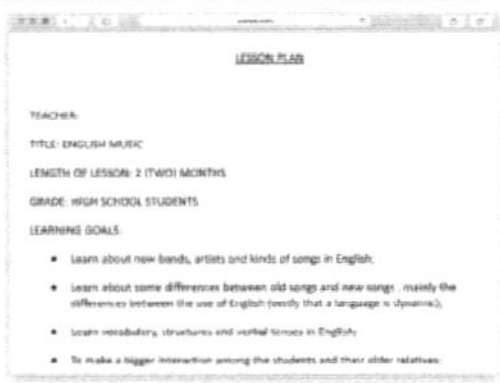

Teacher: P6 | Title: English Music

Grade: High School Student

Length Level: 2 (Two) Months

Description: Learners are expected to learn some differences between old songs and new songs, vocabulary, structures, and verbal tenses in English.

Figure 2. LESSON plan by P6
Source: Castro (2021, p. 214)

They worked on a topic closely connected to their identities using Tik Tok on their own mobile devices. The implementation of this lesson plan during the pandemic resulted in an award-winning TikTok project by a public school teacher with students using a range of multimodal effects on their phones. Brazilian students from rural areas recorded their routine using the English language. The students documented their routine habits different times a day, such as brushing the teeth, making the bed and doing classwork. They compiled the clips and narrated the video describing the actions in English:

Student 2
"brush my teeth and fix my hair"

Student 2
"brush my teeth and fix my hair"

Student 3
"I wake up, brush my teeth, drink coffee, shower, make my bed, take classes online and do my activities"

Figure 3. SCREENSHOTS from Tik Tok videos by P5's students - Part 1

They recorded videos to illustrate their routines using diverse modes (pictures, their own drawings, written and oral texts, video, songs). Student 1 drew her routine and wrote English sentences in a notebook. Then, she recorded the pages, uploaded the clips to Tik Tok, added a background song with some transition effects:

Student 1
"I wake up"

Student 1
"I have breakfast"

Student 1
"I chat with my friends on Whatsapp"

Figure 4. SCREENSHOTS from Tik Tok videos by P5's students - Part 2

They compiled the clips and narrated the video describing the actions in English. The students worked on a topic closely connected to their identities using Tik Tok on their own mobile devices. This student walked approximately 500 meters to record a video about her daily routine. In the video, she wrote her routine in large letters on a notebook and narrated it in English, flipping through the pages as she progressed.

As we can see in these examples, it was not only about teaching the English language but empowering students to be active knowledge producers through mobile devices. The real world environment became part of the learning experience. Mobile devices were used to fully capitalize on the concept of learning anywhere, at any time, reaching the third level of mobility in underserved areas in Brazil. Data collected from 32 students who participated in this activity, based on P5's lesson plan, showed a high level of mobility among the learners, the mobile devices, and the learning experience.

5. FINAL CONSIDERATIONS

The study demonstrates that the lesson plans based on mobile learning, designed and implemented by teachers during the professional development course, significantly promoted the mobility of learners and the mobile learning experiences. By incorporating mobile devices, teachers were able to create learning environments where students could engage in meaningful, real-world learning anytime and anywhere, and reaching the third level of mobility. The findings highlight the potential of mobile learning to enhance educational practices, especially in underserved areas in Brazil, by fostering learner autonomy, interactivity, and the integration of diverse contexts into the learning process. The participants expanded time and space for English teaching and learning, recognized that students need to be active in the learning process, and provided significant learning activities in their lesson plans.

REFERENCES

British Council Brazil. (2015). *Políticas públicas para o ensino de inglês: Um panorama das experiências na rede pública brasileira*. https://www.britishcouncil.org.br/sites/default/files/bncc_portuguesbx.pdf

Barbosa, A. F., Rovai, A. A., & Gonçalves, G. K. (2020). Empoderar estudantes para que se tornem agentes da transformação social por meio da aprendizagem móvel no Brasil: Estudo de caso pelo projeto UNESCO-Fazheng sobre melhores práticas em aprendizagem móvel (F. Miao & A. Domiter, Eds.). UNESCO. https://unesdoc.unesco.org/ark:/48223/pf0000373496

Castro, V. C. de. (2021). *Mobile learning and the 7 affordances of the digital in English teaching at Brazilian public schools* [Doctoral dissertation, Universidade Federal de Minas Gerais]. UFMG Institutional Repository. http://hdl.handle.net/1843/38211

Crompton, H. (2013). *Mobile technologies expanding educational opportunities* [Video]. YouTube. https://www.youtube.com/watch?v=Z2if4aQjYHA&t=1s

Cope, B., & Kalantzis, M. (Eds.). (2017). *e-Learning ecologies: Principles for new learning and assessment* (1st ed.). Routledge. https://doi.org/10.4324/9781315639215

Pegrum, M. (2015). *Assoc. Prof. Mark Pegrum: Creating the anytime, anywhere learner* [Video]. YouTube. https://www.youtube.com/watch?v=XmUdZMoJe-Q&t=34s

Pegrum, M. (2014). *Mobile learning: Languages, literacies and cultures* (Chapter 1). London: Palgrave Macmillan.

Plomp, T. (2020). Educational design research: An introduction. In T. Plomp & N. Nieveen (Eds.), *An introduction to educational design research* (3rd ed., pp. 1–23). SLO Netherlands Institute for Curriculum Development. ISBN: 978-90-329-2329-7.

Statista. (2024). *Percentage of mobile device website traffic worldwide from 1st quarter 2015 to 4th quarter 2023.* https://www.statista.com/statistics/277125/share-of-website-traffic-coming-from-mobile-devices/

UNESCO. (2017). *Supporting teachers with mobile technology: Lessons drawn from UNESCO projects in Mexico, Nigeria, Senegal, and Pakistan.* Miao, F., West, M., So, H.-J., & Toh, Y. (Eds.). ISBN: 978-92-3-100230-4. https://unesdoc.unesco.org/ark:/48223/pf0000251511

UNESCO. (2013). *Policy guidelines for mobile learning*. http://unesdoc.unesco.org/images/0021/002196/219641e.pdf

SOCIO-CULTURAL FACTORS IN MOBILE LEARNING: BRIDGING EDUCATIONAL GAPS

Mahmoud Mohanna
Université du Québec à Trois-Rivière, Québec, Canada

ABSTRACT

Mobile learning is considered an evolving learning mode, as it provides flexibility for students to learn through mobile devices. However, its effectiveness depends on socio-cultural contexts such as cultural diversity, socio-economic gaps, and technological accessibility. This paper discusses how these factors influence the adoption, implementation, and outcomes of mLearning. Drawing on case studies and examples from India, Kenya, Scandinavia, South Korea, and Brazil, it examines how mLearning can bridge educational gaps while posing challenges, such as cultural bias and digital inequality. The design of inclusive mLearning is based on the recommendations that localization, cooperation of stakeholders, and digital literacy programs should be important to ensure equitable education across diverse socio-cultural landscapes.

KEYWORDS

Mobile Learning, Socio-Cultural Factors, Digital Divide, Education Technology, Cultural Diversity, Inclusivity

1. INTRODUCTION

The integration of mobile technologies into education has redefined the learning landscape, offering unprecedented flexibility and timely access to knowledge. Mobile learning, or mLearning, facilitates learning through mobile devices such as smartphones, tablets, and laptops. Unlike traditional forms of education, mLearning emphasizes accessibility, allowing learners to be engaged with educational materials beyond temporal and location constraints (Traxler, 2007). However, the socio-cultural contexts in which mLearning operates significantly influence its implementation and effectiveness. Cultural norms, economic conditions, and technological access create the basis of how these learning platforms are going to be used by the learners. Addressing such context shall unlock the fullest potential of mLearning.

The paper investigates socio-cultural dimensions of mLearning by examining how they shape learning experiences. Opportunities and challenges brought forward by mLearning within different settings, both culturally and economically, will be explored. Based on an analysis of several case studies from five different contexts, this paper provides ways to develop both inclusive and culturally responsive mLearning initiatives. The regions were chosen for their diverse socio-cultural contexts, geographical regions, technological advancements, and unique approaches to addressing educational challenges through mLearning. In line with this is identifying the socio-cultural dynamics at play when creating and implementing appropriate mLearning solutions.

2. THEORETICAL BACKGROUND

2.1 Definition and Scope of mLearning

mLearning refers to portable electronic devices supporting learning outside, or even within, traditional classroom sittings. For Ally (2009), flexibility, accessibility, and adaptability to different contexts. Apart from e-learning, which relies on desktop devices that are stationary, mLearning emphasizes mobility, where one can learn about materials while moving around. Further, its scope extends beyond formal education to include workplace training and informal skill acquisition; it will be an adaptable tool across many domains.

Increased mobile device penetration worldwide has expanded the reach of mLearning, especially in areas where access to education is limited. The expansion underlines the democratizing potential of mLearning. However, its success depends on understanding the unique socio-cultural and economic factors influencing its adoption and implementation. It is important to recognize these influences as a means of fostering the principles of inclusiveness and impact of diverse learner needs in mLearning system design.

2.2 Socio-Cultural Theory in Education

Socio-cultural theory posits that learning is socially mediated and occurs within cultural frameworks, as developed by Vygotsky (1978). These frameworks include language, tradition, and shared values that shape the way individuals perceive and engage in education. In the context of mLearning, socio-cultural theory emphasizes the need to design platforms and content that are compatible with learners' cultural and social realities. Most of the socio-cultural theory applied to mLearning focuses on how technology interacts with culture. A mobile learning platform, for example, can be much more usable with culturally appropriate examples and materials. On the other hand, when ignored, cultural nuances lead to alienation and reduced learner engagement. Thus, socio-cultural dynamics must be understood if the aspirations of creating mLearning solutions are to resonate across diverse audiences and promote effective learning outcomes.

2.3 Relevance of Socio-Cultural Factors in mLearning

Socio-cultural factors, including cultural norms, economic conditions, and language, play a pivotal role in determining the success of mLearning initiatives. For instance, cultural attitudes toward technology can influence learners' willingness to adopt mobile platforms (Kukulska-Hulme, 2012). In regions where technology is viewed skeptically, promoting mLearning may require extensive awareness campaigns and training programs. Similarly, economic disparities affect access to mobile devices and internet connectivity, creating barriers to mLearning adoption. Another critical socio-cultural factor is language. Learners will, by far, show more interest in content delivered in their native language. Localization of efforts, or the adaptation of content within specific cultural and linguistic contexts, is essential to ensure accessibility and inclusion. Therefore, addressing such socio-cultural factors would help mLearning initiatives overcome barriers and reach the intended diverse learner population.

3. SOCIO-CULTURAL CONTEXT OF MLEARNING

3.1 Cultural Influences on Technology Adoption

Culture significantly impacts how individuals adopt and use technology, including mLearning platforms. Hofstede's cultural dimensions theory provides a framework for understanding these influences. For example, in individualistic cultures, learners often prefer self-directed approaches that emphasize personal achievement and autonomy (Hofstede, 1984). In contrast, collectivist cultures prioritize group learning and collaborative activities, reflecting their communal values. Designing mLearning content that aligns with these cultural preferences can enhance learner engagement and satisfaction. These cultural influences extend into the kinds of content that learners find relevant. Learning materials filled with culturally contextualized examples and storytelling are far more likely to resonate with learners. Conversely, disregard for cultural contexts produces content that may be abstract or irrelevant. Accounting for these cultural dimensions is crucial to crafting mLearning solutions that meet various learning needs and styles.

3.2 Language and Localization

Language is a fundamental aspect of culture, and its role in mLearning cannot be overstated. Learners are more likely to engage with content presented in their native language, as it enhances comprehension and relatability (Kukulska-Hulme, 2012). Localization, which involves adapting content to specific linguistic and cultural contexts, goes beyond mere translation. It includes incorporating culturally relevant examples, idioms, and visuals that align with learners' experiences and realities.

Poor content localization can act as a barrier towards the adoption of mLearning. For example, learners who are used to different terminology or cultural references may have difficulty comprehending some learning materials. In such cases, the need for inclusiveness in localization will make sure that mLearning platforms are accessible for people with diverse languages and cultures. With this, the mLearning initiatives could improve learner's engagement and facilitate equity in access to education.

3.3 Socio-Economic Disparities and the Digital Divide

Socioeconomic disparities are still one of the greatest deterrents to the adoption of mLearning, especially in low-income regions. According to UNESCO (2023), the digital divide is described as a wedge between those who have access to technology and those who do not; instead, it is deepening existing inequities in education. Many learners cannot afford the costs of both mobile handheld devices and subscription packages for their data. Such a digital divide calls for targeted interventions in the form of subsidized devices and expansion of internet connectivity. Public-private partnerships can thus play a critical role in these efforts by leveraging resources and expertise to bridge gaps in access. Promoting socio-economic equity, mLearning endeavors should therefore ensure that no learner is left behind in benefiting from mobile technologies.

4. CASE STUDIES: EXPLORING MLEARNING ACROSS DIFERENT SOCIO-CULTURAL CONTEXTS

4.1 India: Addressing Language Diversity through Localized mLearning

India is home to more than 1.4 billion people speaking more than 22 official languages and hundreds of regional dialects. This immense linguistic diversity entails challenges and opportunities in many aspects of mLearning. Platforms like Byju's, an educational technology company, have resolved this through successful content localization for the vast linguistic and cultural diversities of India. By providing lessons in regional languages, Byju's makes it accessible even for learners in rural and urban areas across states. This strategy not only improves comprehension, but also raises inclusivity, enabling students from marginalized communities to engage with quality education (MHRD, 2021).

This becomes apparent when looking at localization efforts in India. For example, using culturally relevant examples for teaching science and mathematics concepts increases learner identification and, therefore, an improvement in retention and application. Successful localized mLearning initiatives in India showcase the potential of culturally responsive design in bridging educational gaps in diverse societies. In addition to language localization, mLearning in India addresses infrastructural challenges like limited internet access in rural areas. Platforms such as Byju's offer offline learning features and lightweight apps, ensuring accessibility. Interactive tools like gamified assessments and voice-enabled tutorials enhance engagement and cater to diverse learning styles. MHRD data (2021) highlights increased enrollment and completion rates among students using localized content, demontrating the impact of adaptive technology in bridging educational gaps.

4.2 Kenya: Overcoming Connectivity Challenges with mLearning

Kenya has emerged as a leader in innovative mLearning solutions designed to overcome the challenges posed by limited internet connectivity. The platform "M-Shule," Swahili for "Mobile School," addresses this issue by offering offline learning tools that require minimal internet access. M-Shule uses SMS-based technology to deliver personalized lessons and assessments to primary school students, enabling them to learn in areas where internet penetration is low (Wambugu, 2020). Such tailored approaches are essential in the socio-cultural context of Kenya, where most rural households are without smartphones or stable internet. Therefore, success in M-Shule is based on how best to adapt to these constraints while at the same time ensuring quality education. It empowers parents in sending progress updates via SMS; hence, it encourages community involvement in education. This case illustrates that mLearning solutions should be designed to respond to the technological realities facing underserved communities. In addition to its adaptability, M-Shule has proved to have measurable impact on learning outcomes.

Results from a study conducted by the Kenya Institute of Curriculum Development in 2020 indicated that students who used this platform saw an improvement in literacy and numeracy skills by as high as 20% in six months. This, according to KICD, was because M-Shule could offer personalized and chunk-sized lessons that address individual learning needs. The platform also deepened community involvement by allowing teachers to monitor student performance and adjust support. Driven by simple, yet powerful technology, M-Shule can show how mLearning fosters educational development in resource-challenged communities.

4.3 Scandinavia: Emphasizing Collaboration in mLearning

Scandinavian countries, known for their egalitarian values, have integrated mLearning into their educational frameworks with a strong focus on collaboration. Applications such as "Kahoot!" and "Socrative" do focus on activity interaction and group work, hence corresponding to the cultural priorities of teamwork and inclusivity. These tools are highly exploited in both classrooms and workplaces to engage learners in problem-solving and knowledge-sharing activities (Andersen et al., 2019).

In Scandinavia, mLearning initiatives are supported by robust digital infrastructure and widespread access to mobile devices. However, their success also stems from cultural alignment. The emphasis on peer learning and collective problem-solving resonates with learners in this region, promoting deeper engagement and understanding. This case illustrates how mLearning platforms can leverage cultural values to enhance educational outcomes. Beyond engagement, these platforms have demonstrated measurable results. A study held by the Nordic Institute for Studies in Innovation, Research, and Education found that students who utilized Kahoot! and other collaborative tools produced retention rates 25% higher than traditional teaching methods (NIFU, 2019). Educators report better classroom dynamics as well, where the utilization of mLearning platforms pushed introverted or less confident students to participate in group discussions. This shows how culturally aligned mLearning solutions enhance knowledge acquisition and at the same time ensure inclusivity of the learning environment.

4.4 Brazil: Bridging Educational Gaps with mLearning

Brazil faces significant educational disparities between urban and rural areas, driven by socio-economic inequalities and uneven technological access. mLearning platforms like "ProFuturo" have sought to address these disparities by providing low-cost tablets preloaded with educational content to underserved schools. The platform also trains teachers in using digital tools effectively, ensuring that technology complements rather than replaces traditional teaching methods (ProFuturo, 2021). The implementation of ProFuturo in rural Brazil underlines that both technological and pedagogical barriers need to be addressed to ensure the successful adoption of mLearning. With a teacher-empowerment approach, with offline learning options, the program bridges the gap between education systems in both urban and rural areas. This case, therefore, points to holistic approaches: infrastructure and training, combined with cultural contexts in which the mLearning interventions occur.

ProFuturo's impact is evident in its outcomes. According to a 2021 report by the Instituto de Tecnologia e Sociedade (ITS), students participating in the program demonstrated a 30% improvement in literacy and numeracy skills within a year compared to peers in non-participating schools. Teachers reported higher confidence in integrating digital tools into their classrooms, with 85% of them indicating that ProFuturo resources improved student engagement. These results reveal how accessible technology coupled with comprehensive training can transform educational opportunities in underserved regions.

4.5 South Korea: Personalizing Education with mLearning

South Korea, a global leader in technology adoption, has integrated mLearning into its highly competitive education system. Platforms like "Classting" use artificial intelligence (AI) to provide personalized learning experiences, tailoring content to individual learners' needs and progress. This approach aligns with South Korea's educational culture, which prioritizes academic excellence and technological innovation (Kim, 2020).

High-speed internet and high-end mobile devices are so pervasive in South Korea that it has created very enabling conditions for mLearning adoption. In any case, cultural acceptance of technology as an integral component of education supports successful platforms like Classting. This case illustrates the potential for mLearning to improve learning outcomes when facilitated by advanced infrastructure and a technology-driven culture. The effectiveness of the use of Classting is evidenced by recent findings. For example, a 2020 study by KEDI showed that students who used the online platform scored 35% higher in test results compared to those who applied traditional methods. The use of AI-driven personalization increased students' performance; at the same time, it motivated them and reduced their stress by adjusting learning content to individual paces. Teachers also reported more efficiency in the class management system, as Classting streamlined administrative tasks and allowed more focused instruction. The outcome underlines the hypothesis that integrating advanced technology with cultural values can leverage the best educational outcomes.

5. CONCLUSION

This paper highlights the transformative potential of mobile learning (mLearning) in addressing educational challenges across diverse socio-cultural contexts. The case studies from India, Kenya, Scandinavia, Brazil, and South Korea demonstrate how localization, stakeholder collaboration, and digital literacy programs can bridge educational gaps by addressing linguistic diversity, connectivity issues, collaboration, and personalization needs. However, the success of mLearning depends on adapting to the unique cultural, economic, and technological realities of each region. Effective localization, inclusiveness, and overcoming socio-economic barriers are essential to creating equal opportunities for learning. These examples illustrate how mLearning not only responds to distinct challenges but also unites them under a broader framework of equitable education. The socio-cultural dimension will remain pivotal in ensuring that mLearning continues to evolve as an accessible, inclusive, and impactful educational tool for diverse learners worldwide. By integrating these principles, mLearning can reshape education for a more equitable future.

REFERENCES

Ally, M. (2009). *Mobile learning: Transforming the delivery of education and training*. Athabasca University Press.

Andersen, H.M., Hansen, S. and Pedersen, L. (2019). 'Collaborative learning in Scandinavia: Insights from mLearning initiatives'. *Nordic Journal of Digital Education*, *12*(3), pp. 45–58. Available at: https://doi.org/10.1234/njde2019.45

Hofstede, G. (1984). *Culture's consequences: International differences in work-related values*. Sage Publications.

Instituto de Tecnologia e Sociedade (2021). Assessing the impact of ProFuturo on educational outcomes in rural Brazil. ITS.

Kenya Institute of Curriculum Development (2020). Impact assessment of mobile learning platforms: M-Shule case study. KICD.

Kim, J. (2020). 'AI in South Korean education: The rise of personalized mLearning platforms'. *Journal of Educational Technology in Asia*, 12(3), pp. 45–58.

Korean Educational Development Institute (2020). Evaluating the impact of AI-driven mLearning tools on student performance. KEDI.

Kukulska-Hulme, A. (2012). *Mobile learning: A handbook for educators and trainers*. Routledge.

Ministry of Human Resource Development (MHRD) (2021). Localization strategies for digital education in India. Annual Education Report 2021. Available at: https://www.mhrd.gov.in/education2021

Nordic Institute for Studies in Innovation, Research, and Education (2019). Evaluating the impact of collaborative learning platforms on student engagement and retention. NIFU.

ProFuturo (2021). Bridging educational gaps in Brazil: The ProFuturo initiative. Available at: https://www.pro-futuro.org

Traxler, J. (2007). 'Defining, discussing, and evaluating mobile learning'. *The International Review of Research in Open and Distributed Learning*, *8*(2). Available at: https://doi.org/10.19173/irrodl.v8i2.346

UNESCO (2023). Mobile learning for all: A global perspective on inclusion. Available at: https://www.unesco.org

Vygotsky, L.S. (1978). *Mind in society: The development of higher psychological processes*. Harvard University Press.

Wambugu, J. (2020).'M-Shule: Transforming education in rural Kenya through SMS-based learning', *African Journal of EdTech*, *6*(4), pp. 24–33. Available at: https://doi.org/10.7654/ajedtech2020.24

STUDENT SATISFACTION AND ATTITUDES TOWARD CHATGPT IN HIGHER EDUCATION: COMPARATIVE INSIGHTS ACROSS ACADEMIC DISCIPLINES

Aleksander Aristovnik and Dejan Ravšelj
Faculty of Public Administration, University of Ljubljana, Slovenia

ABSTRACT

The release of ChatGPT in November 2022 marked a key shift in AI's role in higher education. Its user-friendly design made it popular among students while sparking both enthusiasm and concern among educators. While research has explored factors shaping student perceptions, the impact of academic discipline on satisfaction and attitudes remains unexplored. This paper aims to address gaps in the existing research by examining student satisfaction and attitudes toward ChatGPT through comparisons across academic disciplines. The empirical analysis uses two distinct statistical approaches, namely descriptive statistics and one-way analysis of variance (ANOVA), applied to a sample of 23,218 students. The results reveal that students found ChatGPT to be interesting and helpful, with more than two-thirds reporting interest and over half expressing satisfaction, although they still preferred human interaction due to AI's lack of social presence and human favouritism bias. Furthermore, differences across academic disciplines showed higher satisfaction among applied sciences students, who benefited from ChatGPT's technical support, while students in social sciences and humanities preferred human educators for their emphasis on critical and subjective focus. The evidence-based insights provided by this study offer significant value to policymakers and educators, supporting the responsible integration of ChatGPT into higher education while addressing the diverse needs of students.

KEYWORDS

Chatgpt, Higher Education, Satisfaction, Attitude, Global Student Survey

1. INTRODUCTION

The release of ChatGPT in November 2022 marked a major milestone in AI's role in higher education. Developed by OpenAI (San Francisco, CA), it quickly gained popularity for its natural language capabilities, enabling seamless interactions (Alessandri-Bonetti et al., 2024). Beyond mimicking human speech, ChatGPT performs various tasks (Boubker, 2024; Das, 2024) and is one of the fastest-growing AI applications, drawing both enthusiasm and scepticism from educators (Tlili et al., 2024; Twinomurinzi & Gumbo, 2023). Supporters highlight benefits like real-time feedback, personalized support, and improved access to educational resources, while critics cite concerns over data privacy, bias, student engagement, plagiarism, and misinformation. They stress the need for ethical safeguards, originality-focused assessments, and content verification to maintain educational integrity (Aristovnik et al., 2024a, 2024b; Michalon & Camacho-Zuñiga, 2023; Williams, 2024).

While extensive research has examined factors shaping students' perceptions of ChatGPT, studies on socio-demographic influences remain limited. Early findings indicate that country of residence, age, university type, and academic performance significantly affect attitudes toward ChatGPT, while gender, academic programs, and educational streams have little impact (Abdaljaleel et al., 2024; Das et al., 2024). However, the influence of academic discipline remains underexplored. Research on digitalization suggests discipline affects technology use, with engineering and architecture adopting it more than social and health sciences (Mercader & Gairín, 2020). While some studies find discipline unrelated to digital adoption barriers, others link it to confidence in technology use and equipment availability (Al-Senaidi et al., 2009; Shelton, 2014).

These findings provide a foundation for examining student satisfaction and attitudes toward ChatGPT across academic disciplines. Students generally report high satisfaction due to its instant, detailed responses and ability to clarify complex topics (Park, 2023). Greater knowledge and positive attitudes correlate with increased usage, especially among final-year students (Pallivathukal et al., 2024). Satisfaction stems from efficiency and personalized learning, while concerns over reliability highlight the need for content verification (Ait Baha et al., 2024). Computer science students stress clearer usage guidelines (Singh et al., 2023), and ChatGPT's lack of emotional awareness limits its effectiveness compared to human educators (Ajlouni et al., 2023). These mixed reactions emphasize the need for ethical guidelines and training to optimize its use across disciplines.

Therefore, this paper seeks to address gaps in existing research by exploring student satisfaction and attitudes toward ChatGPT through comparisons across academic disciplines. The evidence-based insights provided by this study offer significant value to policymakers and educators, supporting the responsible integration of ChatGPT into higher education while addressing the diverse needs of students. The remainder of the paper is structured as follows. The next section outlines the materials and methods used in the study, detailing the data collection techniques and analytical procedures. The following section presents the main results, highlighting evidence-based findings. Finally, the last section offers a conclusion, summarizing the key findings and their broader implications.

2. MATERIALS AND METHODS

The Global ChatGPT Student Survey, led by the Faculty of Public Administration at the University of Ljubljana, Slovenia, captured students' early perceptions of ChatGPT one year after its launch. To reach a global audience, the survey was available in seven languages: English, Italian, Spanish, Turkish, Japanese, Arabic, and Hebrew. It targeted higher education students aged 18 or older who could provide informed consent (Aristovnik et al., 2024a, 2024b). Data were collected from October 2023 to February 2024 using convenience sampling, promoted in classrooms and university communication platforms (Boubker, 2024; Sarstedt et al., 2018).

The online questionnaire covered multiple aspects related to ChatGPT, including socio-demographics, knowledge, experiences, capabilities, ethics, satisfaction, study outcomes, skills, labour market relevance, emotions, and general reflections. Most items used a 5-point Likert scale (1 = strongly disagree to 5 = strongly agree) (Aristovnik et al., 2024a, 2024b). The preliminary version was validated with Slovenian students (Aristovnik et al., 2024b), and refinements were made based on pilot testing. The final questionnaire and dataset are available in the Mendeley Data repository (Ravšelj et al., 2024). This paper focuses on student satisfaction and attitudes toward ChatGPT, particularly across academic disciplines.

The data analysis employed two statistical approaches. First, descriptive statistics were used to calculate the top two box scores, representing the percentage of students selecting "agree" or "strongly agree" on the 5-point Likert scale. These scores were also compared across academic disciplines. Second, a one-way ANOVA was conducted to assess mean differences in student satisfaction and attitudes toward ChatGPT across disciplines, including arts and humanities, social sciences, applied sciences, and natural and life sciences. This method identifies significant variations among three or more independent groups, allowing for population-level inferences (Ntumi, 2021).

3. RESULTS

As of the end of February 2024, a total of 23,218 students had taken part in the survey. Since completing the entire questionnaire was not mandatory, the number of responses varied across questions due to missing data. The majority of respondents were female (58.8%), studying full-time (85.3%), and enrolled in undergraduate programs (83.4%). In terms of academic disciplines (i.e., fields of study), most students were pursuing social sciences (41.4%), followed by applied sciences (34.5%), with fewer participants in arts and humanities (12.1%) and natural and life sciences (12.0%).

Students most frequently reported that using ChatGPT is interesting (70%), while just over 50% found it helpful, controllable, and satisfactory. However, only 25% agreed that interacting with ChatGPT is easier than with colleagues or that its information is clearer than their teachers' (Figure 1). The preference for human interaction stems from AI's lack of social presence (Rodway & Schepman, 2023; Yu et al., 2024), as computer-mediated communication offers weaker personal connections. The low percentage favouring ChatGPT's clarity may be due to human favouritism bias, where human-created content is rated more favourably despite comparable AI quality (Leaver & Srdarov, 2023; Zhang & Gosline, 2023). While students appreciated ChatGPT's usefulness, they valued human clarity and connection more, highlighting areas for AI improvement.

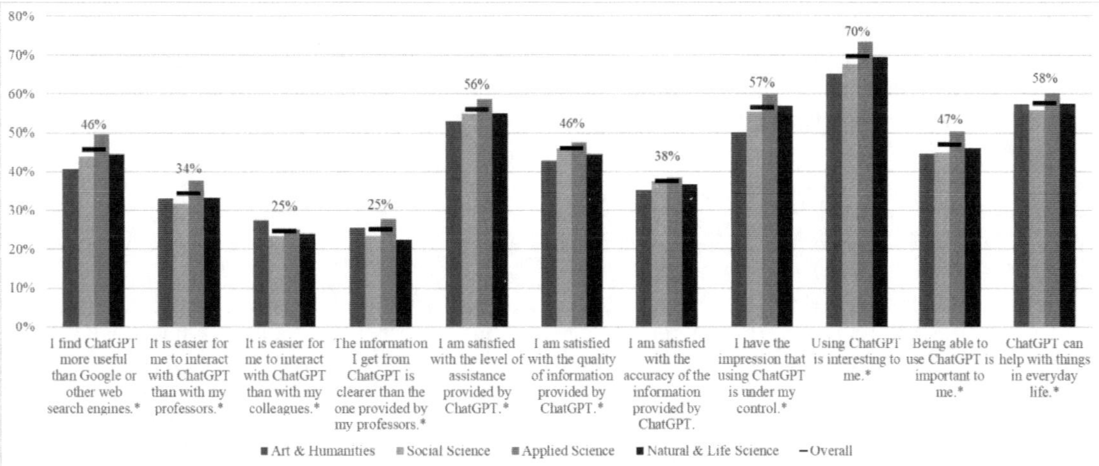

Figure 1. Student satisfaction and attitudes toward ChatGPT overall and across academic disciplines

Analysis by academic discipline reveals significant differences ($p \leq 0.05$) in student satisfaction and attitudes toward ChatGPT. Applied sciences students consistently reported higher agreement with most statements (except for ease of interaction) compared to their peers in other disciplines, aligning with overall trends. This may be attributed to their frequent use of digital tools, coding, and data analysis, where ChatGPT effectively supports practical problem-solving and technical tasks (Kumar et al., 2024). In contrast, students in social sciences, arts, and humanities who emphasize subjective analysis, critical thinking, and personal interpretation reported lower satisfaction. These disciplines rely more on human educators, whose ability to provide nuanced discussions and contextual understanding surpasses ChatGPT's capabilities. The findings suggest that students' perceptions of ChatGPT are shaped by the specific demands of their academic fields, highlighting the need for tailored AI integration strategies in higher education.

4. CONCLUSION

The study reveals that computer-mediated communication lacks the personal connection of face-to-face interactions, making students less comfortable with AI tools like ChatGPT. Human favouritism bias leads students to prefer their teachers' clarity over AI-generated content despite comparable quality (Leaver & Srdarov, 2023; Zhang & Gosline, 2023). While students found ChatGPT useful, they valued human interaction for its clarity and connection, highlighting areas for AI improvement. Satisfaction varied across disciplines, with applied sciences students reporting higher satisfaction due to ChatGPT's effectiveness in technical and factual tasks (Kumar et al., 2024). In contrast, social sciences, arts, and humanities students, who emphasize subjective analysis, showed lower satisfaction, favouring human educators.

The study's findings offer valuable insights for higher education. Institutions can harness ChatGPT's strengths in technical and factual support to enhance learning in applied sciences, where student satisfaction is highest. In arts and humanities, where critical thinking and subjective analysis are key, educators should provide guidelines for ChatGPT's use while emphasizing human-led instruction. Universities should implement training programs to help students and faculty navigate ChatGPT's limitations, such as its lack of emotional intelligence and potential for misinformation. Policymakers must establish ethical frameworks to address concerns like plagiarism and data privacy, ensuring responsible AI integration. By aligning AI applications with the needs of different disciplines and fostering human-AI collaboration, institutions can maximize ChatGPT's benefits while accommodating diverse student preferences.

This study has several limitations. First, while it focuses on ChatGPT, its status as an early, widely accessible AI tool makes it a strong representative for understanding student perceptions of conversational chatbots in higher education. The findings are likely applicable to other similar AI tools. Second, the analysis relies on descriptive statistics, limiting deeper insights. However, as part of a broader global research effort, additional context is available in a related global study (Ravšelj et al., 2025). Finally, the study depends on self-reported data, which may introduce recall and social desirability biases (Aristovnik et al., 2024a). Despite these limitations, the findings provide valuable insights into student satisfaction and attitudes toward ChatGPT, offering evidence-based recommendations for educators and policymakers in shaping the future of higher education.

ACKNOWLEDGEMENT

The authors acknowledge the exceptional assistance of numerous international partners in translating the questionnaire and/or collecting data within the CovidSocLab initiative, specifically the global ChatGPT student survey (https://www.covidsoclab.org/chatgpt-student-survey/), which served as a collaborative working platform. More information about the international partners is available in the Mendeley Data repository (https://doi.org/10.17632/ymg9nsn6kn). Moreover, the authors acknowledge the financial support from the Slovenian Research and Innovation Agency (research programme No. P5-0093, start-up research programme "Generative artificial intelligence in higher education for the future labour market", project No. Z5-4569 and project No. J5-60095). Finally, in the preparation of this manuscript, the authors utilized ChatGPT, version 4o, developed by OpenAI, for limited and supplementary purposes. Specifically, ChatGPT was employed to assist with checking the grammar, enhancing clarity, and polishing the language in certain sections of the manuscript. It must be stressed that the role of the ChatGPT was minor and purely supportive in nature. The core content of the manuscript, including all scientific interpretations, conclusions, and critical revisions, is the exclusive output of the human authors. ChatGPT did not contribute to the intellectual content or scientific insights of the manuscript.

REFERENCES

Abdaljaleel, M., Barakat, M., Alsanafi, M., Salim, N.A., Abazid, H., Malaeb, D., Mohammed, A.H., Hassan, B.A.R., Wayyes, A.M., Farhan, S.S. and Khatib, S.E., (2024). A multinational study on the factors influencing university students' attitudes and usage of ChatGPT. *Scientific Reports*, *14*(1), p.1983. https://doi.org/10.1038/s41598-024-52549-8

Ait Baha, T., El Hajji, M., Es-Saady, Y. and Fadili, H., (2024). The impact of educational chatbot on student learning experience. *Education and Information Technologies*, *29*(8), pp.10153-10176. https://doi.org/10.1007/s10639-023-12166-w

Ajlouni, A.O., Wahba, F.A.A. and Almahaireh, A.S., (2023). Students' Attitudes Towards Using ChatGPT as a Learning Tool: The Case of the University of Jordan. *International Journal of Interactive Mobile Technologies*, *17*(18). https://doi.org/10.3991/ijim.v17i18.41753

Alessandri-Bonetti, M., Liu, H.Y., Giorgino, R., Nguyen, V.T. and Egro, F.M., (2024). The first months of life of ChatGPT and its impact in healthcare: a bibliometric analysis of the current literature. *Annals of Biomedical Engineering*, *52*(5), pp.1107-1110. https://doi.org/10.1007/s10439-023-03325-8

Al-Senaidi, S., Lin, L. and Poirot, J., (2009). Barriers to adopting technology for teaching and learning in Oman. *Computers & education*, *53*(3), pp.575-590. https://doi.org/10.1016/j.compedu.2009.03.015

Aristovnik, A., Ravšelj, D. and Umek, L., (2024a). Higher education student experiences with ChatGPT: Some insights across academic disciplines worldwide. In: *EDULEARN24 Proceedings*. IATED, pp. 2232-2240. https://doi.org/10.21125/edulearn.2024.0627

Aristovnik, A., Umek, L., Brezovar, N., Keržič, D. & Ravšelj, D, (2024b). The Role of ChatGPT in Higher Education: Some Reflections from Public Administration Students. In Cheung, S.K.S., Wang, F.L., Paoprasert, N., Charnsethikul, P., Li, K.C. & Phusavat, K. (eds.) *Technology in Education. Innovative Practices for the New Normal. ICTE 2023*. Communications in Computer and Information Science, vol. 1974. Singapore: Springer. Available at: https://doi.org/10.1007/978-981-99-8255-4_22

Boubker, O., (2024). From chatting to self-educating: Can AI tools boost student learning outcomes?. *Expert Systems with Applications*, *238*, p.121820. https://doi.org/10.1016/j.eswa.2023.121820

Das, S.R. and Madhusudan, J.V., (2024). Perceptions of Higher Education Students towards ChatGPT Usage. *International Journal of Technology in Education*, *7*(1), pp.86-106. https://doi.org/10.46328/ijte.583

Kumar, J., Rani, M., Rani, G. and Rani, V., (2024). Human-machine dialogues unveiled: an in-depth exploration of individual attitudes and adoption patterns toward AI-powered ChatGPT systems. *Digital Policy, Regulation and Governance*, *26*(4), pp.435-449. https://doi.org/10.1108/DPRG-11-2023-0167

Leaver, T. and Srdarov, S., (2023). ChatGPT Isn't Magic: The Hype and Hypocrisy of Generative Artificial Intelligence (AI) Rhetoric. *M/C Journal*, *26*(5). https://doi.org/10.5204/mcj.3004

Mercader, C. and Gairín, J., (2020). University teachers' perception of barriers to the use of digital technologies: the importance of the academic discipline. *International Journal of Educational Technology in Higher Education*, *17*(1), p.4. https://doi.org/10.1186/s41239-020-0182-x

Michalon, B. and Camacho-Zuñiga, C, (2023). ChatGPT, a brand-new tool to strengthen timeless competencies. *Frontiers in Education*, *8*, p. 1251163. https://doi.org/10.3389/feduc.2023.1251163

Ntumi, S., (2021). Reporting and interpreting One-Way Analysis of Variance (ANOVA) using a data-driven example: A practical guide for social science researchers. *Journal of Research in Educational Sciences (JRES)*, *12*(14), pp. 38-47. https://doi.org/10.14505/jres.v12.14.04

Pallivathukal, R. G., Soe, H. H. K., Donald, P. M., Samson, R. S., & Ismail, A. R. H. (2024). ChatGPT for Academic Purposes: Survey Among Undergraduate Healthcare Students in Malaysia. *Cureus*, *16*(1).

Park, J., (2023). Medical students' patterns of using ChatGPT as a feedback tool and perceptions of ChatGPT in a Leadership and Communication course in Korea: a cross-sectional study. *Journal of Educational Evaluation for Health Professions*, *20*(20), p.29. https://doi.org/10.3352/jeehp.2023.20.29

Ravšelj, D., Keržič, D., Tomaževič, N., Umek, L., Brezovar, N., … & Aristovnik, A. (2025). Higher education students' perceptions of ChatGPT: A global study of early reactions. *PLoS ONE, 20*(2), e0315011. https://doi.org/10.1371/journal.pone.0315011

Ravšelj, D., Aristovnik, A., Keržič, D., Tomaževič, N., Umek, L., Brezovar, N., & et al. (2024). Higher education students' early perceptions of ChatGPT: Global survey data. *Mendeley Data*. https://doi.org/10.17632/ymg9nsn6kn.2

Rodway, P. and Schepman, A., (2023). The impact of adopting AI educational technologies on projected course satisfaction in university students. *Computers and Education: Artificial Intelligence*, *5*, p.100150. https://doi.org/10.1016/j.caeai.2023.100150

Sarstedt, M., Bengart, P., Shaltoni, A.M. and Lehmann, S., (2018). The use of sampling methods in advertising research: A gap between theory and practice. *International Journal of Advertising*, *37*(4), pp.650-663. https://doi.org/10.1080/02650487.2017.1348329

Shelton, C., (2014). "Virtually mandatory": A survey of how discipline and institutional commitment shape university lecturers' perceptions of technology. *British Journal of Educational Technology*, *45*(4), pp.748-759. https://doi.org/10.1111/bjet.12051

Singh, H., Tayarani-Najaran, M.H. and Yaqoob, M., (2023). Exploring computer science students' perception of ChatGPT in higher education: A descriptive and correlation study. *Education Sciences*, *13*(9), p.924. https://doi.org/10.3390/educsci13090924

Tlili, A., Shehata, B., Adarkwah, M.A., Bozkurt, A., Hickey, D.T., Huang, R. and Agyemang, B., (2023). What if the devil is my guardian angel: ChatGPT as a case study of using chatbots in education. *Smart learning environments*, *10*(1), p.15.https://doi.org/10.1186/s40561-023-00237-x

Twinomurinzi, H. and Gumbo, S., (2023). ChatGPT in Scholarly Discourse: Sentiments and an Inflection Point. In *Annual Conference of South African Institute of Computer Scientists and Information Technologists* (pp. 258-272). Cham: Springer Nature Switzerland. https://doi.org/10.1007/978-3-031-39652-6_17

Williams, R.T., (2024). The ethical implications of using generative chatbots in higher education. *Frontiers in Education*, *8*, p. 1331607. https://doi.org/10.3389/feduc.2023.1331607

Yu, C., Yan, J. and Cai, N., (2024). ChatGPT in higher education: factors influencing ChatGPT user satisfaction and continued use intention. In *Frontiers in Education*, *9*, p. 1354929. https://doi.org/10.3389/feduc.2024.1354929

Zhang, Y. and Gosline, R., (2023). Human favoritism, not AI aversion: People's perceptions (and bias) toward generative AI, human experts, and human–GAI collaboration in persuasive content generation. *Judgment and Decision Making*, *18*, p.e41. https://doi.org/10.1017/jdm.2023.37

PATHFINDER: INTELLIGENT CAREER DEVELOPMENT WITH SKILL GAP ANALYSIS AND PERSONALIZED UPSKILLING PATHWAYS

Kamarul Adha and Anthony F. Camilleri
Knowledge Innovation Centre, Malta

ABSTRACT

This paper presents PathFinder, an intelligent career development system that leverages large language models (LLMs) to bridge the gap between individuals' current skills and their career aspirations. The system creates sentence embeddings from user resumes and career goals, then employs vector-based matching against the European Skills, Competences, and Occupations (ESCO) database to identify skill gaps. PathFinder then generates personalised learning pathways by recommending relevant courses from educational platforms like EdX. By combining natural language processing with structured occupational data, PathFinder transforms traditional career guidance into a precise, data-driven process that aligns personal development with specific career objectives. This approach offers a scalable solution for career advancement in an increasingly dynamic job market. PathFinder was developed as part of the LCAMP Project (European Commission [EC], 2024), funded by the European Union through the ERASMUS+ Programme.

KEYWORDS

Skill Embeddings, Vector Search, Career Pathways

1. INTRODUCTION

The rapid evolution of the modern job market has made continuous professional development an imperative rather than an option. While traditional frameworks offer structured approaches to skill acquisition, they often lack the flexibility to address individual career trajectories. The emergence of artificial intelligence (AI), particularly large language models (LLMs), presents an opportunity to revolutionise career development through data-driven approaches to learning (Li, 2022). LLMs have demonstrated remarkable capabilities in understanding complex language patterns and retrieving contextual knowledge across various domains. In education and career development, these technologies excel at processing vast amounts of professional information, making them ideal tools for addressing upskilling and reskilling challenges (Proceedings of the 16th International Conference on Information Systems, 2023).

However, a significant gap exists between the theoretical potential of these technologies and their practical application in delivering actionable career guidance. This paper presents **PathFinder**, an AI-driven system that bridges this gap by leveraging LLM-derived sentence embeddings for skill gap analysis and targeted recommendations. The system's strength lies in its ability to synthesise multiple data sources - including resumes, career goals, and industry-standard frameworks - into concrete development pathways. PathFinder demonstrates how AI can transform traditional career guidance into a precise, data-driven process for navigating modern career landscapes. This development emerged from the objectives of the LCAMP Project Deliverable 5.4 which emphasises human-centric learning pathways tailored to the evolving needs of the advanced manufacturing sector. By employing a systematic approach that integrates ESCO's occupational framework and personalised upskilling pathways, PathFinder exemplifies how AI-driven tools can enhance human-centric career development processes. This initiative underscores the broader objective of LCAMP to promote innovation and adaptability in an evolving industrial landscape.

2. LITERATURE REVIEW

This literature review outlines the core technologies that form the foundation of PathFinder, focusing on how embedding models, sentence embeddings, and retrieval-augmented generation (RAG) enhance personalised career recommendations. By understanding these components, it becomes evident how AI-driven systems can transform traditional career guidance into a dynamic, data-driven process.

2.1 The Role of Embedding Models

Textual data, being unstructured, requires transformation into numerical representations for computational tasks such as similarity measurement, classification, and clustering. Traditional embedding models like Word2Vec, GloVe, and FastText addressed this need but struggled with capturing context in complex or lengthy documents. Large language models (LLMs) have revolutionised embeddings through attention mechanisms that relate words to their context across entire documents and corpora, enabling richer semantic representations (Tao et al., 2024). For this study, the BGE-M3 model, developed by Chen et al. (2024), was selected due to its ability to process multilingual data using the Multi-Lingual Document Retrieval (MLDR) dataset. This model not only understands multiple languages but also possesses extensive knowledge across diverse topics. Running locally on an RTX 4090 GPU, it generates 1,024-dimensional sentence embeddings, effectively capturing long contexts and nuanced semantics. Its open-source availability and performance make it an ideal choice for generating embeddings foundational to the analyses in this paper.

2.2 Sentence Embeddings & Vector Searching Techniques

In modern NLP applications, sentence embeddings offer a more effective way to represent textual data compared to traditional word embeddings. While word embeddings focus on individual tokens, they often fail to capture the broader semantic relationships within a document, leading to a loss of context (Rygl et al., 2017). Sentence embeddings address this issue by converting entire sentences or documents into high-dimensional vectors that preserve semantic meaning across a longer context. This transformation enables more efficient computations for similarity and relevance by mapping documents into a shared vector space, where similar texts are positioned closer together and dissimilar texts are further apart (Sawarkar, Mangal, & Solanki, 2024). For the PathFinder system, the cosine similarity metric was chosen due to its efficiency and ability to calculate the angle between vectors rather than the direct distance, making it particularly suitable for determining semantic proximity between embeddings. This approach ensures that course recommendations align with users' identified skill gaps based on nuanced contextual matching.

2.3 Retrieval-Augmented Generation (RAG) in Information Retrieval

Retrieval-Augmented Generation (RAG) has emerged as a powerful approach to mitigate the limitations of large language models (LLMs) in knowledge-intensive tasks. LLMs are prone to hallucination and have finite sequence lengths, restricting their ability to provide accurate and contextually rich responses without extensive parameter updates. RAG addresses this by integrating a retrieval mechanism that supplements LLMs with external, non-parametric memory, such as dense vector indices, which can be updated without retraining the model (Lewis et al., 2020). This approach enables RAG systems to deliver more accurate and relevant outputs by dynamically retrieving contextual information from large document collections. Furthermore, RAG enhances search and recommendation processes by refining results through semantic similarity, ensuring that retrieved documents are closely aligned with users' queries in meaning rather than merely matching keywords. As noted by Salemi and Zamani (2024), the ability of RAG systems to evaluate and rank retrieved documents based on their relevance to the task significantly improves the quality and accuracy of generated outputs, making RAG particularly valuable for applications requiring up-to-date and precise information.

3. METHODOLOGY

The PathFinder system integrates multiple data sources to provide personalised career development recommendations. These sources include EdX for course data (EdX, n.d.) and ESCO for skill and occupation data (European Commission, n.d.). Each of these sources plays a critical role in matching users with suitable learning pathways based on their career goals and skill gaps.

3.1 Prerequisites

The data required for PathFinder consists of five key components: the user's desired occupation, ESCO occupations, ESCO skills, the user's CV or credentials to display their current skill set, and course data from EdX.The user inputs, including their desired occupation and CV, are transformed into sentence embeddings to facilitate semantic matching. The ESCO occupations are similarly converted into embeddings, with the associated skills appended to provide additional context. Each ESCO skill is also embedded individually to ensure precise skill matching. Finally, course data from EdX, gathered manually using Python Selenium, is processed into sentence embeddings by combining the title, description, learning outcomes, and other relevant details. These embeddings form the foundation for PathFinder's occupation, skill, and course matching processes.

3.2 Occupation Matching

The first input used in PathFinder is the user's desired occupation, including relevant details such as responsibilities, job descriptions, required skills, and experience. This input is converted into a sentence embedding and mapped against pre-embedded ESCO occupations to identify the closest matches.The system calculates semantic similarity between the user's input and the ESCO database, selecting the top three occupations with the highest similarity scores. Each selected occupation comes with a list of associated skills, which will be used in the next step to identify skill gaps. Since many skills are shared across different occupations, a filtering process is applied to remove duplicate entries. This ensures that the system processes only unique skills, reducing both computation time and resource usage during the next phase of analysis.

3.3 Skill Matching

The next step involves matching the skills gathered from the selected occupations with the user's current skill set. The user's CV or credentials, uploaded as a PDF file, are parsed and converted into sentence embeddings to extract their existing skills. These embeddings are then compared against the required skills identified from the desired occupations.The system calculates a similarity score for each required skill by comparing it with the user's current skills. Using these scores, an average similarity value is determined to benchmark the user's skill level. Skills that meet or exceed the average score are classified as above average, while those with lower similarity scores are marked as below average. The below-average skills are flagged as gaps that require improvement and are used in the next process to recommend relevant courses for upskilling.

3.4 Course Matching

Once the below-average skills have been identified, each is compared against the course database from EdX to find relevant learning resources. The system calculates the semantic similarity between the skill embeddings and the course embeddings, selecting the top three courses that best match the context of each skill gap.The selected courses are then compiled and mapped to the corresponding skill gaps, creating a personalised learning pathway tailored to the user's specific needs. By recommending targeted courses for each deficient skill, the system provides users with actionable upskilling opportunities that align with the requirements of their desired occupation. This ensures that users can address their skill gaps effectively and progress toward their career goals with relevant educational resources.

4. BENCHMARKING

Benchmarking was conducted to evaluate the retrieval performance of PathFinder's embedding spaces for occupations, courses, and skills. Each embedding space was created using extensive attribute data to capture the context of each record. To test retrieval accuracy, a small segment from each record—such as a title or label—was extracted, converted into embeddings, and compared against the full embedding space using cosine similarity. The goal was to assess how well the system retrieves relevant results with limited input.

Table 1. Performance benchmarking results across different parameters

Embedding Space	Top-3	Top-5	Top-10	Top-25	Top-50	Sum	Total Records	Top-3 (%)
Occupation	2919	60	36	15	5	3035	3039	**96.05%**
Skill	13882	31	15	9	1	13938	13939	**99.59%**
Course	3454	25	21	48	1	3549	3549	**97.32%**

The results show that 96.05% of occupations, 97.32% of courses, and 99.59% of skills were found in the Top-3 most relevant records, demonstrating the effectiveness of the embedding spaces in retrieving contextually similar matches. These high percentages highlight the system's ability to provide accurate recommendations even with minimal input.

However, the sum of matched records is not equal to the total number of records. This indicates that some segmented records did not appear in the Top-50, likely due to insufficient contextual information. Despite these cases, the overall performance shows that the embedding model effectively captures semantic meaning, ensuring reliable retrieval and accurate recommendations in practical use cases.

5. CONCLUSION

PathFinder revolutionizes career development by leveraging LLM-based embeddings and ESCO's framework to deliver precise occupation (96.05%), skill (99.59%), and course (97.32%) matches. Its three-stage process—occupation matching, skill gap analysis, and course recommendations—bridges career goals with market demands. The system's effectiveness in addressing evolving job markets hinges on maintaining up-to-date datasets, ensuring its data-driven insights remain relevant and impactful for personalized professional growth.

ACKNOWLEDGEMENT

This research was conducted under the framework of the LCAMP Project, whose support and resources made this innovative development possible. The LCAMP Project is funded by the European Union. Views and opinions expressed are however those of the author(s) only and do not necessarily reflect those of the European Union or the European Education and Culture Executive Agency (EACEA). Neither the European Union nor EACEA can be held responsible for them.

I extend my heartfelt gratitude to the Knowledge Innovation Centre (KIC) for fostering an environment of technological innovation and supporting the development of *PathFinder*. Special thanks to Prof. Fauziah Ahmad for her invaluable guidance, and to my family for their unwavering support throughout this journey. Their collective encouragement and wisdom were instrumental in the realization of this project.

REFERENCES

Chen, J., Xiao, S., Zhang, P., Luo, K., Lian, D., & Liu, Z. (2024). BGE M3-Embedding: Multi-Lingual, Multi-Functionality, Multi-Granularity Text Embeddings Through Self-Knowledge Distillation. *arXiv preprint*, arXiv:2402.03216. https://arxiv.org/abs/2402.03216

EdX, 2024. *EdX Learning Platform*. Available at: https://www.edx.org/ [Accessed 10 November 2024]

ESCO, 2024. *European Skills, Competences, Qualifications and Occupations*. Available at: https://esco.ec.europa.eu/en [Accessed 10 November 2024]

European Commission. (2024). Learner Centric Advanced Manufacturing Platform for Centres of Vocational Excellence (LCAMP). https://lcamp.eu/

IADIS, 2023. *Proceedings of the 16th International Conference on Information Systems*. IADIS Press, Lisbon, Portugal.

Lewis, P., Perez, E., Piktus, A., Petroni, F., Karpukhin, V., Goyal, N., ... & Kiela, D. (2020). Retrieval-augmented generation for knowledge-intensive nlp tasks. Advances in Neural Information Processing Systems, 33, 9459- 9474.

Li, L. (2022). Reskilling and upskilling the future-ready workforce for industry 4.0 and beyond. Information Systems Frontiers, 1-16.

Rygl, J., Pomikálek, J., Řehůřek, R., Růžička, M., Novotný, V., & Sojka, P. (2017). Semantic vector encoding and similarity search using fulltext search engines. arXiv preprint arXiv:1706.00957.

Salemi, A., & Zamani, H. (2024, July). Evaluating retrieval quality in retrieval-augmented generation. In Proceedings of the 47th International ACM SIGIR Conference on Research and Development in Information Retrieval (pp. 2395-2400).

Sawarkar, K., Mangal, A., & Solanki, S. R. (2024). Blended RAG: Improving RAG (Retriever-Augmented Generation) Accuracy with Semantic Search and Hybrid Query-Based Retrievers. arXiv preprint arXiv:2404.07220.

Tao, C., Shen, T., Gao, S., Zhang, J., Li, Z., Tao, Z., & Ma, S. (2024). LLMs are Also Effective Embedding Models: An In-depth Overview. arXiv preprint arXiv:2412.12591.

LLM-BASED ADAPTIVE, AUTOMATIC AND DYNAMIC EVALUATION SYSTEM

Ludovic Arnould and Mohamad Al Assaad
Talan Research & Innovation Center, Paris, France

ABSTRACT

The goal of this paper is to develop an evaluation system that leverages recent advances in language processing to be automatic, adaptive, and more efficient than traditional modeling systems. From a user perspective, it would function as a dynamic chat, similar to interactions with current Large Language Models (LLMs) such as ChatGPT (Brown, 2020) or LLaMA (Dubey et al., 2024). Typically, the teacher LLM, in charge of interacting with the user, can ask general questions about the user's background, produce tailored exercises, provide help, and more. In the backend, different modules (often referred to as agents in the field of LLMs) are assigned to different tasks such as evaluating the user's responses, generating exercises, etc. Another LLM, referred to as the assistant, would supervise these agents, and provide the teacher with relevant information.

KEYWORDS

Adaptive Evaluation, Personalized Learning, Multimodal Interaction

1. INTRODUCTION

Large Language Models (LLMs) are evolving quickly, opening up new possibilities for smarter, more adaptive learning systems. This study introduces an evaluation system that uses LLMs to automatically generate, assess, and adjust exercises. With the help of multiple agents handling tasks like grading responses and creating content, the system functions as an ongoing conversation, tailoring the experience to each user's background. The goal is to enhance learning efficiency and personalization by leveraging LLMs, offering a more flexible and responsive evaluation methods.

We split our literature review into two parts: modeling of student knowledge and LLM enhanced education.

Knowledge Tracing (KT). Before the emergence of LLMs, traditional statistical methods were used to model the skill mastery of learners. We provide a simplified explanation of this setting here and refer interested readers to (Shen et al., 2024). In general, given a specific thematic area (e.g., Programming, Math, ...), a set of Knowledge Components (KC) or skills is defined in advance, along with a set of exercises linked to the corresponding skills (e.g., solving an equation could be related to the "multiplication" KC). For each student, their learning path is recorded as a list of steps, with each step containing an exercise, the related KCs, an answer, and an answer's state (correct or incorrect). Given a set of students and their learning paths, the goal is to build a system that will predict whether a student has mastered a given skill or not. This system serves as a model of the student's mastery of a predefined set of skills.

Many methods have been implemented to solve this KC prediction task. We only introduce a few typical ones here and provide a few references for a deeper exploration of the related field.

1. **Bayesian Knowledge Tracing (BKT)**

In the context of Bayesian Knowledge Tracing (Corbett and Anderson, 1995), modeling relies on several parameters. First, the prediction of the probability of transition from the unlearned state to the learned state *P(T)*, the probability of forgetting *P(F)*, the probability of guessing *P(G)*, and the probability of a mistake despite mastery *P(S)*. Then, we use the following equations to update the model:

$$(a)\quad P(L_n) = (P(L_n|Answer) + (1 - P(L_n|Answer)))P(T)$$

$$(b)\quad P(C_{n+1}) = P(L_n)(1 - P(S)) + (1 - P(L_n))P(G)$$

where $P(L_n)$ is the probability that a knowledge component (KC) is mastered at the n-th learning step and $P(C_{n+1})$ is the probability of a correct answer at the next learning step. Further computations of $P(L_n|Answer)$ involve $P(S)$ and $P(G)$. The first BKT models were introduced in the 1990s and further developed later on. For instance, Dynamic BKT (K¨ aser et al., 2017) considers the links between KCs (hierarchy, dependencies).

2. Logistic Models

Logistic regression models are widely employed for classification problems because they predict the probability of various outcomes based on certain input features. The logistic function is defined as:

$$f_\theta(x) = \frac{1}{1+ e^{-\theta.x}}$$

This function is used to extract probabilities from an input x and a parameter vector θ. For example, educational systems employed these models to test users' responses or anticipate their next learning steps (Zhou et al., 2020). These models are effective for simple tasks but may fail for more complex ones due to the comparatively straightforward decision-making process of logistic models.

3. Deep Learning Models

Deep Knowledge Tracing (DKT) relies on deep neural networks to model student knowledge states. The most used architecture is the Recurrent Neural Network (RNN) (Hochreiter, 1997), which captures the dynamics of learning and anticipates future performance based on past performance (Piech et al., 2015). Unlike traditional approaches like Bayesian KT, DKT automatically extracts latent features from learner data. The evolution of the hidden states in DKT can be expressed by the following equations:

$$(a) \quad h_t \ = tanh(W_{hs}x_t \ + W_{hh}h_{t-1} + b_h)$$

$$(b) \quad y_t \ = \sigma\,(W_{yh}h_t + b_y)$$

where W_{hs} are the input weights, $tanh$ is the activation function, b_h and b_y are the bias weights, W_{hh} are the recurrent weights, and W_{yh} are the output weights.

Other variants, such as Attention-based Knowledge Tracing (AKT), incorporate attention mechanisms to enhance DKT (Pandey and Karypis, 2019). Attention has proven its efficacy in understanding sequential data and the relationship between elements in various contexts (Vaswani et al., 2017). It has been successfully applied to KT; the interested reader can refer to (Shen et al., 2024) for further details.

We also briefly mention the use of Graph Neural Networks (GNNs) when data are represented as graphs (Nakagawa et al., 2019).

Finally, many other statistical methods are used in the field of KT, for instance Hidden Markov Models, but they are outside the scope of this work.

Integration of LLMs in education: The recent success of LLMs brought new perspectives of adaptive and automatic teaching in the educational community. Although transformer-based architectures mostly shine when processing text or audio, they might soon generate videos and illustrations answering educational needs. Several platforms have already implemented them in an educational context, whether in the industry (Khan Academy, Duolingo) or towards academic purposes (Kabir and Lin, 2023). However, they are mostly used to help the students in real time, as chatbot assistants for instance or to generate content faster. This is a rather basic implementation, and many other paths could be explored, as mentioned in several reflection papers exploring the potential uses of LLMs in education (Ng and Fung, 2024).

To the best of our knowledge, the application of LLMs in knowledge tracing remains marginally explored, with LLMs mostly being used as side modules to enrich other DKT models (Fu et al., 2024). Although the foundational technology of transformers (attention mechanisms), has been used in a traditional KT setting (cf. supra), language-driven methods have not yet been investigated in either industrial or academic settings. We believe that LLMs could revolutionize the evaluation of students and learners, offering advantages like adaptability, automation, and dynamic assessment capabilities, such as through chat interfaces, potentially enhancing both the accuracy of score predictions and the variety of exercises.

2. METHODOLOGY

In order to leverage the impressive language performances of LLMs within the evaluation process, our main idea is to build a teacher-evaluator chatbot that can interact with users to assess their level related to a given field. It is not simple to include LLMs into the assessment loop, nevertheless. Their robustness and dependability are severely limited by their hallucinations (Huang et al., 2023). For example, even when they don't provide accurate answers to the chatbot exercises, someone could use certain cues to make the LLM chatbot believe they are an expert. As a result, we suggest limiting the LLM's role to user communication and using particular agents to carry out the evaluation task (see Figure 1).

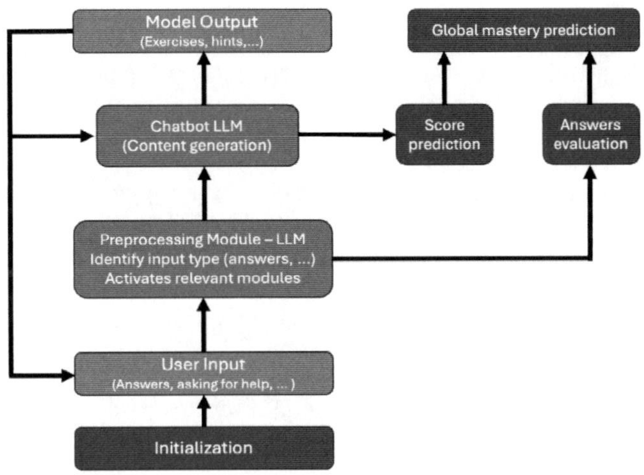

Figure 1. Adaptive Learning System Workflow: A personalized learning platform that evaluates user input, predicts performance, generates customized content, and continuously adjusts based on user progress

This system represented in Figure 1, explains the methodology of our personalized learning platform that continuously adapts to a user's progress. It begins with Initialization, where the platform prepares to interact with the user (asking for a resume of his past experiences linked to the field, etc.). The user submits their input, either by answering questions or asking for help. This input goes through the Preprocessing Module, which figures out the type of input and decides what action to take next. After that, the Answers Evaluation Module engages to assess the user's responses. If the input is an answer to an exercise, the system analyzes it and then determines the user's performance based on the answer. The Global Mastery Prediction receives evaluations and score predictions, combines several score predictions. The Chatbot LLM receives these insights and uses them to create exercises and other content that is customized to the user's current level of knowledge. Then a score prediction model is activated to predict the user's score. After that, both, answers evaluation output and score prediction output are sent to the global mastery predictions model to determine the user's overall progress and mastery level. The interaction of the user with this content creates a feedback loop in which the system analyzes the user's fresh reactions once again and the cycle is repeated.

Based on current state of the art methods, we think that this architecture faces two main challenges:

1. **Score Prediction.** The first difficulty lies in the diversity of exercises that can be provided by the chatbot (Multiple-Choice Questions (MCQ), open questions, translations in a linguistic context, mathematical reasoning, etc.). Depending on the question or answer types, different modules must be activated. For instance, an open question should be first analyzed by a dedicated LLM before being sent to a regression model. This approach was successful in a recent Kaggle Challenge in Automatic Essay Evaluation (Crossley et al., 2024). Secondly, most datasets available today come from the standard setting where questions are mostly MCQ and scores 0 (incorrect) or 1 (correct). Training a more generic model may require building new datasets and method architectures.
2. **Global Mastery Heuristic.** Assessing someone's skills on a given topic in a short time is challenging even in" real life" (Doroudi, 2020). Standard KT methods also depend on

heuristics, such as the assumption that correct answers might be guessed. This issue is magnified here as we aim to develop a general system that should operate across various topics and, ideally, generalize as broadly as possible.

Several other issues remain unresolved, primarily concerning engineering or LLM-specific challenges (e.g., LLM hallucinations, communication between modules). Nonetheless, this field is advancing rapidly, and the existing architecture could benefit directly from ongoing research without having to address every issue independently.

3. CONCLUSION

This paper proposed a roadmap to an evaluation system using modern large language models in adaptive learn- ing. Our approach allows various agents to handle distinct tasks such as personalized content generation, response evaluation and feedback. These capabilities create a more flexible and intelligent learning environment.

In the future work, additional modules can be added to the system, such as multiple input sources (audio, visual data, etc.), that could improve the evaluation ability of the system. Moreover, other insights may be useful such as reinforcement learning that can be added to the LLM-based agents of the system.

REFERENCES

Brown, T. B. (2020). *Language models are few-shot learners*. arXiv preprint.

Corbett, A. and Anderson, J. (1995). *Knowledge tracing: Modeling the acquisition of procedural knowledge.* User Modelling and User-Adapted Interaction, 4(4):253–278.

Crossley, S., Baffour, P., King, J., Burleigh, L., Reade, W., and Demkin, M. (2024). Learning agency lab - automated essay scoring 2.0. https://kaggle.com/competitions/learning-agency-lab-automated-essay-scoring-2.

Doroudi, S. (2020). *Mastery learning heuristics and their hidden models*. In Artificial Intelligence in Education:

21st International Conference, AIED 2020, Ifrane, Morocco, July 6–10, 2020, Proceedings, Part II, pages 263–278. Springer International Publishing.

Dubey, A., Smith, J., Lee, A., and Taylor, E. (2024). *The llama 3 herd of models*. arXiv preprint.

Fu, L., Smith, J., Taylor, E., et al. (2024). *Sinkt: A structure-aware inductive knowledge tracing model with large language model.* arXiv preprint.

Hochreiter, S. (1997). *Long short-term memory*. Neural Computation MIT-Press.

Huang, L., Smith, J., Taylor, E., et al. (2023). *A survey on hallucination in large language models: Principles, taxonomy, challenges, and open questions*. arXiv preprint.

Kabir, M. R. and Lin, F. (2023). *An llm-powered adaptive practicing system.* In LLM@ AIED.

K¨ aser, T., Klingler, S., Schwing, A., and Gross, M. (2017). *Dynamic bayesian networks for student modeling*. IEEE Transactions on Learning Technologies, 10(4):450–462.

Nakagawa, H., Iwasawa, Y., and Matsuo, Y. (2019). *Graph-based knowledge tracing: Modeling student proficiency using graph neural network*. In 2019 IEEE/WIC/ACM International Conference on Web Intelligence (WI), pages 156–163.

Ng, C. and Fung, Y. (2024). *Educational personalized learning path planning with large language models*. arXiv preprint.

Pandey, S. and Karypis, G. (2019). *A self-attentive model for knowledge tracing*. arXiv preprint.

Piech, C., Bassen, J., Huang, J., Ganguli, S., Sahami, M., Guibas, L., and Sohl-Dickstein, J. (2015). *Deep knowledge tracing*. In Neural Information Processing Systems, pages 505–513.

Shen, S., Brown, M., Green, S., and White, C. (2024). *A survey of knowledge tracing: Models, variants, and applications*. IEEE Transactions on Learning Technologies.

Vaswani, A., Shazeer, N., Parmar, N., Uszkoreit, J., Jones, L., Gomez, A., Kaiser, and Polosukhin, I. (2017). *Attention is all you need.* In Advances in Neural Information Processing Systems.

Zhou, Z., Miao, C., and Sun, H. (2020). *Logistic regression in educational data mining: Modeling student performance in adaptive systems*. Journal of Educational Data Science, 12(2):112–126.

EXPLORING VIRTUAL HERITAGE IN THE METAVERSE REIMAGINING TEACHING AND LEARNING IN THE IMPULSE PRE-HACKATHON WORKSHOP AT KU LEUVEN

Zoë Vandenhende[1] and Theodora Rontzova[2]
[1]*Cultural Studies Research Group KU Leuven*
Blijde-Inkomststraat 21 - box 3311, 3000 Leuven, Belgium
[2]*Library Services KU Leuven*
Mgr. Ladeuzeplein 21 - box 5593, 3000 Leuven, Belgium

ABSTRACT

The IMPULSE project (IMmersive digitization: uPcycling cULtural heritage towards new reviving StratEgies), funded by Horizon Europe, is advancing digital cultural heritage by creating immersive, collaborative, and interactive experiences that engage a wide range of audiences. A core component of IMPULSE is a series of pre-hackathon workshops leading up to a final hackathon in 2026. These workshops support collaboration across fields like education, artistic creation, and the Cultural and Creative Industries. The first pre-hackathon workshop, set for February 2025 at KU Leuven, will emphasize educational uses of the VR platform, bringing interdisciplinary participants together to co-create immersive learning experiences with digitized cultural objects. This interactive approach will encourage participants to transform traditional 2D artifacts—such as manuscripts, prints, and maps—into dynamic, 3D environments, reimagining how audiences engage with cultural heritage objects in a didactic context. The immersive VR platform will continue to evolve through input from these events, enabling richer digital storytelling and adaptive uses for cultural heritage, guided by the Community of Practice established within the project.

KEYWORDS

Immersive Learning, Digital Cultural Heritage, VR in Education, Interactive Learning, Cultural Heritage Education, Digital Storytelling

1. INTRODUCTION TO THE IMPULSE PROJECT

The IMPULSE project (*IMmersive digitization: uPcycling cULtural heritage towards new reviving StratEgies)*, funded by Horizon Europe, aims to transform the digital landscape of cultural heritage institutions across Europe. By connecting researchers, artists, cultural heritage practitioners, Cultural and Creative Sectors and Industries, local institutions and other stakeholders, the project will collaboratively explore and develop immersive narratives, engaging diverse audiences across Europe and beyond ('IMPULSE', n.d.).

Organized into several Work Packages, the project addresses important elements of this transformation, including the development of innovative digital tools, enhancement of data accessibility and interoperability, improvement of existing digitization processes, and creation of engaging and immersive user experiences. Together, these efforts strive to make digital cultural heritage more accessible, interactive, and meaningful to the public ('IMPULSE', n.d.).

A core element of IMPULSE is the creation of a versatile virtual reality (VR) platform to serve as a foundation for multi-user immersive interactions with digital heritage artifacts. This platform is being iteratively developed to accommodate a range of interdisciplinary uses, providing an adaptable space for exploring and engaging with cultural heritage in innovative ways. Throughout the project, the platform will be used to prototype various immersive experiences, reflecting the diverse objectives, user groups, and focus areas within IMPULSE (European Research Executive Agency 2023, 10-12).

2. PRE-HACKATHON WORKSHOPS AND THE IMPULSE COMMUNITY OF PRACTICE

To achieve its broader goals, IMPULSE is hosting a series of pre-hackathon workshops in various focus areas—education, artistic creation, and the Cultural and Creative Industries—leading up to a final hackathon in 2026. These workshops are intended to gather feedback, stimulate innovation, and establish a Community of Practice (IMCo) that will support the collaborative, long-term development of the project's tools and platforms. IMCo will serve as a continuous feedback mechanism throughout the project, ensuring insights and user experiences from various disciplines (European Research Executive Agency 2023, 16-17).

The first pre-hackathon workshop, hosted at KU Leuven, will emphasize educational uses of the VR platform by inviting participants to co-create immersive, didactic experiences using virtual heritage objects. Through this interactive process, participants will gain insights into the platform's possibilities, contributing to the iterative development of both the VR environment and its educational applications. Validated datasets of digitized cultural heritage artifacts from the project's Consortium will serve as ground truth data within these novel immersive platforms and virtual environments.

3. REIMAGINING TEACHING AND LEARNING IN THE IMPULSE PRE-HACKATHON WORKSHOP AT KU LEUVEN

Cultural heritage artifacts provide rich narrative windows into the past; however, traditional learning tools, such as textbooks and 2D visuals, may not fully engage students (Paolanti et al. 2023, 7). This IMPULSE pre-hackathon workshop intends to use immersive VR environments to support dynamic, learner-driven interaction that enables users to construct knowledge in real-time. Immersive VR environments are particularly effective for interactive knowledge-building and engagement, transforming static content into a constructivist, engaging experience (Baxter and Hainey 2020, 416). According to Kolb's experiential learning model, knowledge construction is most effective through iterative experiences and reflection—a process enhanced by VR, where users can repeatedly engage with learning material in interactive virtual spaces (Kolb 2022). In a VR-enabled classroom, students are no longer passive recipients; instead, they can explore digital replicas of artifacts, immersing themselves in historical contexts that might otherwise be inaccessible (Sinha 2023, 5). The metaverse, as a 3D platform, allows users to navigate virtual environments, engage in real-time experiential learning, and overcome geographic and temporal constraints (Dwivedi et al. 2022).

With recent advancements in educational technology, immersive narratives hold great potential for cultural heritage education. Through VR, cultural heritage can shift from being perceived as distant to being a vibrant, integrated experience, bringing well-documented benefits to immersive learning (He et al. 2024, 148).

The constructivist approach in VR, supported by Vygotsky's learning theories, emphasizes personal engagement and interaction, where knowledge emerges through experience and individual reflection (Ch'ng et al. 2020, 4). Unlike traditional learning models, VR fosters personal engagement, allowing users to direct their learning paths. This engagement is particularly significant in cultural heritage, where VR's immersive potential deepens users' understanding and promotes sustained interest (He et al. 2024, 148). VR environments also allow learners to personalize their focus, exploring content based on prior knowledge and curiosity (Sinha 2023, 4).

3.1 Approach and Content of the Pre-Hackathon Workshop

Within the framework of IMPULSE, the pre-hackathon workshop at KU Leuven aims to go one step further and contribute to innovative methods of teaching and learning (European Research Executive Agency 2023, 12). Beyond providing a preliminary virtual reality setting where users can log in, have ideation sessions and start learning, it facilitates an immersive and interactive environment where students, educators, and researchers are encouraged to co-create educational experiences and innovatively reuse digital heritage objects whose didactic potential would never be fulfilled.

This first pre-hackathon workshop is centered around academia, therefore the target audience and user group is educators and students in the broadest sense (European Research Executive Agency 2023, 12, 17).

The workshop envisions an emphatically interdisciplinary approach and will be welcoming participants from a range of academic fields, including cultural studies, gaming, educational studies, digital humanities, art history, and beyond, highlighting VR's potential across diverse research and educational areas. To address anticipated risks and challenges in integrating heritage into didactic VR design, such as limited content knowledge (Farrujia de la Rosa et al. 2022, 11), participants will include individuals with varying levels of expertise in both VR technology and subject matter. This collaborative approach reflects real-world teaching and learning challenges in a virtual environment for the educational prototype.

These interdisciplinary teams (participating both in person, as well as one online team) will have the opportunity to design interactive and didactic VR experiences with real cultural objects, test the innovative VR platform, and provide feedback - actively shaping its further development. Digital storytelling is a central methodology, allowing participants to craft compelling narratives using the digital heritage objects within virtual environments. This creative freedom fosters an environment where participants can explore their individual talents as well as collaborate effectively in a team (Di Blas 2022, 84). Storyboarding is a key part of this process, helping to visualize and plan original narratives. By promoting a facilitator role for instructors, we create a dynamic, inclusive, and engaging environment.

A distinct aspect of this pre-hackathon workshop lies in its focus on predominantly two-dimensional heritage objects. The aim is hereby to challenge participants to rethink how traditional 2D materials - be it manuscripts, early prints or paintings, maps and glass slides - can be meaningfully integrated into a 3D environment to support various didactic objectives. The workshop will explore novel ways to bring various collections of flat, historical artifacts to life within an immersive VR space, and therefore sustainably and adaptively reuse existing digital heritage objects that would otherwise be left behind.

3.2 Findings

At the time of writing, the pre-hackathon workshop has not yet taken place. Scheduled for February 2025, we anticipate presenting findings and insights during the upcoming conference. This workshop represents an initial stage in the IMPULSE project, and feedback from the academic and professional community will be invaluable for refining our approach.

The iterative process, supported by the IMCo, is designed to continuously incorporate participant and user feedback, ensuring meaningful and impactful outcomes. By engaging with diverse perspectives, we aim to develop a framework that enhances VR-based teaching and learning experiences, with a particular focus on the didactic potential of digital heritage.

IMPULSE is a HORIZON EUROPE project, coordinated by Uniwersytet Jagiellonski (Poland), and developed in collaboration with Katholieke Universiteit Leuven (Belgium), Alma Mater Studiorum – Università di Bologna (Italy), Universita Ta Malta (Malta), Heritage Malta, Filmuniversitat Babelsberg Konrad Wolf (Germany), Ethniko Kai Kapodistriako Panepistimio Athinon (Greece), Magna Zmien Foundation (Malta), Associazione Clust-ER Industrie Culturali e Creative (Italy), K8 Institut Fuer Strategische Aesthetik GGMBH (Germany), and Explodedview sp. z o.o. (Poland).

The IMPULSE project has received funding from the European Union's Horizon Europe research and innovation action under Grant Agreement Project ID: 101132704 – IMPULSE -HORIZON-CL2-2024-HERITAGE-01

Funded by the European Union. Views and opinions expressed are, however, those of the author(s) only and do not necessarily reflect those of the European Union or the European Commission. Neither the European Union nor the granting authority can be held responsible for them.

IMPULSE DOI: https://doi.org/10.3030/101132704

REFERENCES

Baxter, Gavin, and Thomas Hainey. (2020). 'Student Perceptions of Virtual Reality Use in Higher Education'. *Journal of Applied Research in Higher Education,* Vol. 12, No. 3, pp 413–24.

Ch'ng, Eugene, Yue Li, Shengdan Cai, and Fui-Theng Leow. (2020). 'The Effects of VR Environments on the Acceptance, Experience, and Expectations of Cultural Heritage Learning'. *Journal on Computing and Cultural Heritage*, Vol.13, No. 1, pp 1-21.

Di Blas, Nicoletta. (2022). 'Authentic Learning, Creativity and Collaborative Digital Storytelling: Lessons from a Large-Scale Case-Study'. *Educational Technology & Society* 25 (2): 80–104.

Dwivedi, Yogesh K., Laurie Hughes, Abdullah M. Baabdullah, Samuel Ribeiro-Navarrete, Mihalis Giannakis, Mutaz M. Al-Debei, Denis Dennehy, et al. (2022). 'Metaverse beyond the Hype: Multidisciplinary Perspectives on Emerging Challenges, Opportunities, and Agenda for Research, Practice and Policy'. *International Journal of Information Management*, Vol. 66, October:102542.

European Research Executive Agency. (2023). Grant Agreement No. 101132704 - IMPULSE. Horizon-CL2-2023-HERITAGE-01. Brussels, Belgium: European Research Executive Agency.

He, Xiaoyang, Dan Wu, Xin Li, and Xin Tong. (2024). 'Back to the Past: A Systematic Review of Immersive Narrative in Cultural Heritage Conservation'. *Proceedings of the Association for Information Science and Technology*, Vol. 61, No. 1, pp 48–60.

'IMPULSE'. n.d. Accessed 6 November 2024. https://euimpulse.eu/.

Kolb, David A. (2022). *Experiential Learning: Experience as the Source of Learning and Development*. Second edition. Upper Saddle River, NJ: Pearson Education.

Paolanti, Marina, Mariapaola Puggioni, Emanuele Frontoni, Lorella Giannandrea, and Roberto Pierdicca. (2023). 'Evaluating Learning Outcomes of Virtual Reality Applications in Education: A Proposal for Digital Cultural Heritage'. Journal on Computing and Cultural Heritage, Vol. 16, No. 2, pp 1-25.

Sinha, Ekta. (2023). '"Co-Creating" Experiential Learning in the Metaverse- Extending the Kolb's Learning Cycle and Identifying Potential Challenges'. *The International Journal of Management Education*, Vol. 21, No. 3.

BRIEF ON LANGUAGE ORIENTED APPROACH(LOA) OF TEACHING PROGRAMMING SKILLS

Bauminwood[1]
Artificial Intelligence College, Neijiang Normal University, Sichuan Province, 641100, China

ABSTRACT

Teaching is communication and exchange process between teachers and students. The quality of teaching depends on communication qualities, in special whether theories, ideas and methods are accurately transmitted from teachers to students. In programming course teaching, there are losses of original meaning of English textbook after translated into Chinese. In order to avoid the loss of original meaning, the author carries on using original English textbook for the software programming teaching. In the language choosing for specific documentation and programming descriptions, the author emphasizes the chosen of the technique inventor's language. With causality analysis in language and thinking, and induction method, the author proposed a new issue of Language Oriented Approach of Teaching Programming Skills, and give light to using AI to implement, such as emerged ChatGPT application. The author makes out the main points and structure of this approach, concludes the prerequisite for its use. Also the categories of Language Oriented Approach is mentioned.

KEYWORDS

Language Oriented Approach of Teaching, Inventor's Native Language, Programming Professional Training, ChatGPT Application in Teaching

1. INTRODUCTION

Since the beginning of this century, the spread of web technology has set off a new wave of learning IT technology. However, most college students majoring in computer science or software in China could not get on the trace, and had difficulty in learning. I have heard and witnessed that there are obstacles in China's computer-related or Software-related majors. More than half of them cannot work in their majors after graduation. That situation promote teachers to find ways to make effective educations.

Some teachers, including me, said that they lacked thinking mode of computer. In 2006, Jeannette M.Wing, Dean, Department of Computer Science, Carnegie Mellon University, published an article and gave the academic concept of "Computational Thinking" (Jeannette M Wing 2006), which is now given as a basic course for students majoring in computer science in university. It became a significant measure to promote the learning effect for students in computer science and related majors.

Now, in Carnegie Mellon University,the concept of Computational Thinking has been extended to the field of Algorithms and even Mathematics. In their description, "Computational Thinking is the thought processes involved in formulating problems and their solutions so that the solutions are represented in a form that can be effectively carried out by an information-processing agent." (Carnegie Mellon n.d.)

Some descriptions seem to steer into the connotation of human thinking. "Computational thinking means creating and making use of different levels of abstraction, to understand and solve problems more effectively. Computational thinking means thinking algorithmically and with the ability to apply mathematical concepts such as induction to develop more efficient, fair, and secure solutions." (Carnegie Mellon n.d.)

And in MIT, Computational thinking is set up as a basic professional course for Computer Science majors or Software majors. They use the Julia programming language to approach real-world problems in varied areas, applying data analysis and computational and mathematical modeling (MIT OCW 2020).

In practise, after nearly 20 years of unremitting efforts, although the number of computer and software-related majors has increased significantly, the quality improvement of teaching varies by country and

1[0009-0008-3501-0141]

region. In the United States and Nordic countries Software Programming education is booming, while in China and other countries slipped into another situation.

These famous American and European universities have made remarkable achievements in the education of Computer Science and Technology and become the model of computer programming education in the world. It is very different from the quality situation in China. The effect of teaching was little, so that in the past decade or more, the explosive growth of software design training institutions have sprung, directly provoked government to restrict it. Experts stood up and generally blamed poor management of universities for the problem. At the end of September 2019, China's Ministry of Education announced Opinions on Deepening the Reform of Undergraduate Education and Comprehensively Improving the Quality of Personnel Cultivating. As a result, wave after wave, quality evaluations in universities were presented in recent years.

The stark difference drove some teachers to investigate the reasons for this phenomenon. Normally, ordinary teacher would attribute this phenomenon to problems with teaching methods, such as identifying distinctly four implicit skills for novices (Benjamin Xie, et al 2019), using adaptive learning system of programming tools (Anindyaputri, et al 2020), etc.

However, I study the problem in another way. I have seen the underlying matters of the facts and thought about the reason for the decline in teaching quality in China. It is due to the inappropriate or even incorrect communication methods in teaching.

2. NEW HYPOTHESES IN PEDAGOGY

For seeking the deep reason of the effect difference, we need to rethink about the natures of learning and teaching. In my study there is a hypothesis rose. I have studied the formation process of students' learning outcomes and the process of transfer of teachers' knowledge to students, and I have a new understanding of the nature of learning and teaching. The principle of this hypotheses has three nodes.

First, Learning is process of communication with prophets, inventors, teachers and other knowledge holders. Teaching is process of knowledge transfer from the intellectuals to seekers and listeners. Second, The main tool for communication between students and teachers is language, so the language is the main tool for learning and teaching. Other teaching tools should be based on language (rarely, tool of linguistic nature). Third, there are two categories of language in learning and teaching, one is the language of communication between people and the other is the language of communication between people and computing machines. So when we here say teaching communication, both human communication and human-machine communication should be involved. Forth, thinking is a kind of self communication.

On the basis of these hypotheses, teaching methods should be reclassified into two broad categories and that is, teaching methods without computers and teaching methods with computers. Today, computers have been widely used, we want to understand the new phenomenon of the application of AI in learning and teaching, we must first figure out the teaching method without computer use. It is very helpful for development of Pedagogy.

I studied the teaching process in detail. From the perspective of teaching process, teaching is communication and exchange between teachers and students. I trust that the quality of students learning depends on the quality of communication between teachers and students. The content of communication is theories, ideas, opinions and methods. The quality of communication depends on whether these theories, ideas and methods are accurately transmitted from teachers to students. If they be, the knowledge has been caught by the students, If not, the students will enter a situation where they can't learn.

In fact, when students talk to teachers for learning, it is partly through the teachers, students communicate with thinkers, masters, inventors, engineers and so on. For example, learning the principle of the CPU are processes of communications of students with the CPU inventors, or with the holder of CPU knowledge. In these communications learning effects are realized.

I firmly believe that the teaching effect depends on the communication effect between teachers and students, and the communication content is the explanation of computer science knowledge and software products; and the learning effect depends on the degree and depth of communications between teachers and students, also the cognitive level of scientific knowledge and product standard.

In the course of communications, language is most important tool. We communicate by language. For the reason that most computer technology originated from English speaker, the knowledge need to be translated into students' native which lead to inaccurate and lack of precision. For Chinese, there are language barriers to learning IT technology. Probably, so do for people from many other non English countries.

Behind different languages there are different modes of thinking. When the same content is expressed in different languages, in fact, the content is decomposed under different thinking modes. So the results of decomposition may not be the same. There is a loss of intended meaning in the translation process. However, in modern technology teaching, we are used to translate the original to local language as teaching material. This is, in another mode to decode the original. The result may be a completely different statement than the original one. This throws the learner into a cloud of confused and obscure words. This causes the learner to miss the point of what they should get.

Almost all IT technology originated in Europe and the United States, where English is used. Linguistically, English and Chinese are completely different languages, one is an combined order language and the other is a pictographic language.

The work of programming and sending instructions to a computer is complex. Even if in combined ordered language countries, developers in non-English speaking need two language processes to work with computer: first to convert the native language to English; second to feed the English based programming language to the machine for execution. In the first process, due to the functional defects of translation itself, the semantics may be distorted or some original meaning will be lost, which reduce the accuracy and efficiency of communication between developers and computers. Those cause programmers to appear imbecile or incompetent both in knowledge acquirement and programming practice. To prevent those from happening, in educations for Computer Science and Technology majors and the relative majors, there is a great need for native English teaching materials, textbooks, and great need for English speaking.

What language are the textbooks and teaching materials expressed in? This is the primary and key issue for my teaching method design. There are different language versions of textbooks. I chose version by language which is technology inventor's native. In Computer Science and Technology, most inventor come from America, England and Nordic countries, so I chose the relevant editions of the textbook in order to stay consistent with the thinking of those inventors. This is key to gain the knowledge of computer and software both for students and teachers. Once the version of the textbook has been determined, the primary problem of teaching reform has been solved.

3. THE PRINCIPLES OF THE LANGUAGE-ORIENTED APPROACH

In reality, because software technology is an invention in English-speaking countries, other countries use translated texts as teaching materials. Due to the evolution of translation methods, there are many cases where the original meanings lost or even distorted after translating. I will give you a few examples in the field of software engineering in China. The improper translation of technical terms such as bit, database, frame, virtual machine, etc., leaves many students confused from the beginning of their studies. Without a later careful identification for these words in their original language, there is a high probability that these students will never get the handle although having accessed into the software programming industry, or never get into it at all. Assuming that AI is now used to implement education, because the basic work of translation has gone wrong, AI application will not be very helpful to students, and have an attention that the cost of AI development is very large.

Someone may contradict me by using AI technology to optimize translation functions. To answer you, optimizing technology to achieve desirable results is not something that can be done overnight. And it comes at a huge cost. Using language is a uniquely human ability, and it's quite complex. Compared with human using, it is in simple level that ChatGPT uses linguistic concepts to reason and deduce, and there are many factors that ChatGPT cannot calculate in when it comes to communication. It cannot lend itself to rigorous levels of communication and scientific reasoning.

So, we have to turn back to human language stage for solutions. We switch to use the human brain to solve the problem of efficiency in education. We make efforts to allows students to effectively learn foreign techniques which are expressed in non-native languages but in original language. We let students grasp it accurately in the context of the original language.

However, the approach is special for programming teaching. To make the problem clear, we like to give advise specific to the practical level, here is a detailed explanation of the rules of this method. The main nodes of this approach can be expressed as follow:

1.Programming teaching is a communication process between teachers and students, and students gain knowledge in the communication process.

2.The tool of communication is language, and in order to avoid communication ambiguity, the inventor's original language is advocated to use.

3.Choose the original documents of software developers and hardware inventors as teaching materials.

4.This approach is specifically designed for situations where the native language of the learner is different from the native language of the software inventor or the language of the human-computer dialogue.

5.This approach can be used as an alternative to ChatGPT application in teaching, for that ChatGPT does not take into account the language gap and does not have the desired effect.

Compared with the curriculum system design, the language-oriented approach focuses on the basic work of teaching, makes use of the important role of language in communication, and implements teaching that is conducive to students' learning efficiency. This method should be the basis of many teaching methods. Beneficiaries of Language Oriented Approach

As for the language in this issue, I promise that the language described here includes two categories of language. One is human language, the other is programming language. The latter is used to instruct computer to work sequentially. After the advent of AI area, many experts realized that ChatGPT can be applied to education as main technology. There is a rush surge in the number of recommendations to use ChatGPT for programming education. ChatGPT is implemented in programming language, so it is also the result of applying the Language Oriented approach. I regard ChatGPT educatianal application as a branch of Language Oriented approach with AI in it, what I practice as traditional Language Oriented approach does not have AI.

In fact, the application of ChatGPT to teaching practice is based on this Language-Oriented Approach. Just a specific application which is under the situation that there is no language gap. Therefore. The application of ChatGPT in teaching should be divided into two types, the first is the ChatGPT application without language gap, or in another word, the ChatGPT application in single language, and the other is the ChatGPT application with language gap. However I doesn't think ChatGPT for across language education is a well usage, such as Chinese teaching of technology from England, it actually has an efficiency loss. In fact, ChatGPT's cross-language application still has to be translated from the source language into the language of the application country. The problem of semantic loss can still occur just as same as in translation without AI.

4. APPLICATION EXPANSION AND DEEPENING OF LANGUAGE ORIENTED APPROACH

I have carried this method out as a teaching reform, practiced this method for seven years. With practice, this method has been proved to have better learning efficiency for students whose programming instruction language is not their native language (Bauming Wood 2024).

Using the Language-oriented teaching materials in instruction practice, can be benefit for several aspects, such as the students, the teachers and the employer enterprises. More significantly, the teaching effects of instruction reform as a whole has a leap progress in Pedagogy. It is greatly improve the quality of teaching practice unit for professional course.

According to author's preliminary judgment, there are three application fields of this approach: practical education, international education, and lifelong education. In practical education, especially in vocational education, the use of foreign technology requires reading the usage documents and technical instructions in foreign languages, as well as the interactive text in the human-computer interaction interface are all native languages of the inventor. The use of original languages has the effect of timeliness and accuracy for accurately mastering the technology. In the process of software coding, LOA trained personnel can easily deal with the prompt in machine monitor where human-computer dialogues open help a lot.

In international education, by going abroad to the native country of the technology invention, students can learn foreign technology more conveniently and accurately to master the technology, which itself is a LOA. Of course, without going abroad the implementation of LOA teaching locally can save the high cost of shortening the space distance is a better thing but performs learning foreign programming technology in own country.

In lifelong education, local students can first learn the language of the technical country as a foreign language, so that they can learn the frontier science and technology of the advanced technology country for a lifetime. Usage of LOA can avoid the losses of original meaning caused by translation which result in interruption of the education process.

However, all these are limited to technical education. As for social science, the main unit of society is the group, which easily takes interests as the center, and researchers will inevitably be in a certain group. it is inevitable that they will explore problems from their own interests. Countries with different languages are prone to form different concepts and theories, which have low requirements for uniqueness, logic and consistency. It is not as strictly consistent and logical as natural science and technology. So I'm not advocating Language-oriented Approach to social science teaching. However, this method should be extended to the fields of natural science and technology education, so to better promote the rapid development of science and technology around the world.

Nowadays, with rapid technological progress and great improvement of AI technology, the discussion of applying AI technology to teaching has sprung up. I suggest that the application and development of AI in teaching should be built on the basis of this approach. The basis of AI technology is character computing, which began in the 1950s and 1960s and reached its peak in the 1970s. It has proved many mathematical theorems of world-class difficulty. The underlying logic of character computing is linguistic reasoning, so AI is essentially the result of linguistic reasoning using computer technology. Today, there are many AI educational applications, although a few are not for communication functions (or nodes), but the application of AI in learning and teaching is bound to replace the brain's thinking function. People think in language. So most of the AI educational applications belong to LOA, once their functions are focused on thinking.

Next, you might want to continue optimizing AI algorithms in translation software. But no matter how optimized, at the node of understanding and communicating, machine algorithms are still less accurate and security than the human brain. We have to admit the limitations of AI, and leave some jobs to remain by human brains, which is more cost-effective. There is a trade-off between using AI and continuing to use the human brain, and there should be a balance point, exceeding which we would be better off not using AI. The trade-off between using and not using AI is a difficult thing. There is no cheap way to measure precisely, and only a rough estimate can be given here. The figure is complex for research and development but promising, and this paper does some basic mentions for it, leaving chance to the more skilled to develop later.

5. CONCLUSION

We can improve the teaching quality by designing a curriculum system, such as adding Computational Thinking courses, or we can improve the teaching quality by using Language-Oriented Approach. Evaluating my experiences and practices, latter is more effective.

ChatGPT is based on linguistic reasoning, it transfers human language reasoning into software reasoning. Meanwhile, Language-Oriented Approach focuses on linguistic communication, which is foundation of the reasoning. So, the language-oriented approach should be the basis for ChatGPT development.

There are two categories of ChatGPT education application, the first is the ChatGPT application without language gap, the second is the ChatGPT application with language gap. For the ChatGPT application without language gap, I have practised and mentioned as above. For the ChatGPT application without language gap, we have seen just as what ChatGPT has already done.

The main measures in Language-Oriented Approach include: Selecting textbook from all language version, and choosing one suitable, English is always; preparing problem sets in chosen language; executing Bilingual or chosen language teaching; giving lessons in inventor's native language; demonstrating occupational operating environment in experimental scenes. Etc.

There are prerequisites for the use of this approach, this approach is recommended if the following three conditions are met: 1. The language used is not the language reside in language-teaching. It is engineer teaching,not language teaching. 2.The language of the technology inventor is quite different from the native language of the students. 3.The language will be used in the course of employing the technology.

However, limited by time and energy, the theoretical system on the Language Oriented Approach of Teaching has not been developed. Leave it to interested colleagues. It must be promising. The issue of how to implement translation without lost of intend meaning of original language text does not developed, More themes need to be explored, such as the detail extension of use of this approach, etc. And the proposal in this paper is limited to technical education, whether the approach can be used in social science education is not discussed.

AUTOBIOGRAPHY

His original name is Bao-ming Wu, in 2024, he used the name Bauming Wood then began to use the name Bauminwood. He was born in Dashetai town, Wulat Front Banner, Inner Mongolia, China. He graduated from the School of Computer Engineering and Science of Shanghai University with a Engineering doctorate degree in computer application technology in Oct 2013. Prior to that, in January 2005, he gained the Master of Engineering (M.Eng) degree in the Department of Computer Science of Fudan University. In the first decade of this century he put forward the RCR software model. In 1997 he Invented the three-span bookkeeping method. In 2024, he proposed the Language Oriented Approach of Teaching. And he has published more than 30 articles, over 10 were in Chinese core included journals. Now, he is with the Artificial Intelligence College in Neijiang Normal University.

REFERENCES

Anindyaputri, et al, (2020). Enhancing students'ability in learning process of programming language using adaptive learning systems: A literature review. *Open Engineering*, vol. 10, no. 1, 2020, pp. 820-829. https://doi.org/10.1515/eng-2020-0092

Bauming Wood, (2024). Language oriented approach of teaching programming skills. *International Journal on Cybernetics & Informatics*, February 2024, Volume 13, Number 1, pp. 15-21.

Carnegie Mellon, (n.d.) What is computational thinking? https://www.cs.cmu.edu/~CompThink /index.html.

MIT OCW, (2020). Introduction To Computational Thinking, *https://ocw.mit.edu/courses/18-s191-introduction-to-computational-thinking-fall-2020/*

Wing, J. M. (2006). Computational thinking. *Communications of the ACM*, Vol.49 No.3, pp33-35.

Xie, B. et al, (2019). A theory of instruction for introductory programming skills. *Computer Science Education*, Vol.29: 2-3, 205-253.

CHANGES IN PARENTS' ATTITUDES TOWARD PROGRAMMING EDUCATION FOR THEIR CHILDREN

Yukiko Maruyama
Tokai University
Hiratsuka, Kanagawa, Japan

ABSTRACT

With the growing global emphasis on integrating programming education into curricula, children have increasing opportunities to acquire programming skills informally alongside their parents. This study investigated the changes in parental attitudes toward programming education and parental involvement in Japan through online surveys conducted in 2021 and 2024. The results revealed a slight decrease in the number of parents who believe programming should be taught in schools. On the other hand, parents who attend programming classes outside school and are involved in education through other actions increased. It showed that more parents were confident in supporting their child' learning programming at home. These findings highlight the need to establish supportive environments for programming education outside of school settings. However, further research is necessary to identify the factors that can encourage parental involvement in their children's programming education.

KEYWORDS

Computer Programming, Elementary School, Informal Education, Parental Involvement

1. INTRODUCTION

There is a global trend toward introducing programming education to younger generations. While implementation varies across countries, programming is being increasingly integrated into elementary and junior high school curricula, either as a dedicated subject, within computing and computer science (CS) education, or incorporated into multidisciplinary studies. This emphasis on programming skills is driven by the rapid advancement of artificial intelligence (AI) technologies, including generative AI, and the growing importance of big data analysis, making these skills indispensable in the future society.

As programming gains prominence in formal education, children also have more opportunities to acquire programming experience informally. Gerson et al. (2022) highlighted that graphical and tangible coding systems have yielded positive learning outcomes in studies with school-aged children. These systems facilitate family engagement with programming, offering valuable learning opportunities outside the classroom. Parental attitudes toward education significantly influence on those of their children's educational experiences, particularly in elementary education. Research in technology-related education, such as programming and robotics, has demonstrated the positive impact of parental involvement and collaboration in workshops on children's attitudes and learning outcomes (Liu 2012; Cuellar et al. 2013).

Japan introduced programming education in elementary schools in 2020. The Central Council for Education in the Ministry of Education, Culture, Sports, Science, and Technology (MEXT) emphasized that the primary goal of this initiative is not to teach coding itself, but to foster students' "programming thinking" (translated by the author). This concept aligns with computational thinking, highlighting the importance of problem-solving and logical reasoning skills developed through programming. Thus, coding itself is not the aim of programming education in Japan but is considered as a way to achieve the goal of programming education. According to a report published by the Ministry of Internal Affairs and Communication, there has been an increase in the number of organizations starting programming classes and lectures since 2013. Also in Japan, there have been more opportunities of informal programming education, and then parents are expected to be involved their child's education. However, according to Maruyama (2022) that investigated parental involvement at the beginning of programming education in Japan, parents' involvement in children's programming education was negligible. Notably, approximately 70% of respondents expressed a lack of confidence in supporting their children's programming learning at home.

Considering the years elapsed since the introduction of programming education and the rapid progress in AI, it is likely that parental attitudes and involvement have evolved. This study aimed to investigate the changes in parents' attitudes toward programming education and their involvement levels in Japan by comparing data collected at the time of the introduction of programming education (2021) with current data (2024).

2. METHODS

This study employed a quantitative online survey design. Data were collected in October 2021 and January 2024 using an online market research panel with approximately 13 million members. A screening survey was used to identify eligible participants: parents aged 25 to 59 with at least one child attending elementary school. The online market research company managing the panel distributed the survey invitation to eligible members until a sufficient number of responses were obtained. To ensure data quality, responses with identical answers to all questions were removed. This resulted in a final sample of 3386 (3036 sample in 2021 and 350 sample in 2024) valid responses. Demographic characteristics of the participants, including sex and age, are presented in Table 1 and Table 2, respectively. The questionnaire comprised five sections: (1) interest in and attitudes toward programming education in elementary school; (2) attitudes toward and confidence in supporting children's programming learning at home; (3) involvement in programming education and willingness to engage in programming-related activities; (4) parents' beliefs; and (5) their child's grade level. Sections (4) and (5) are not addressed in this study.

Table 1. Sex of participants

Sex	**Percentage**	
	2021	**2024**
Male	43.3	56.0
Female	56.7	44.0

Table 2. Age of participants

Age	**Percentage**	
	2021	**2024**
25–29	3.9	2.0
30–39	39.6	29.7
40–49	45.7	48.9
50–59	10.9	19.4
Average	40.9	43.3

3. RESULTS AND DISCUSSION

This section compares the results of the online surveys conducted in 2021 and 2024. All p-values reported are derived from either Mann–Whitney U tests or chi-square tests, as appropriate.

Figure 1 presents parental responses to questions regarding their interest in programming education in elementary school. While general interest in programming education remained stable across the two years, there was a significant increase in the proportion of parents who reported being knowledgeable about the educational content of programming (Q2 and Q3; $p < 0.001$, $p = 0.007$) Conversely, a slight but significant increase in opposition to programming education in elementary school was observed ($p < 0.001$). Figure 2 shows the responses to questions regarding parental attitudes toward programming education in elementary school. Although over 70% of respondents in 2024 agreed that programming should be taught to elementary school students (Q6 and Q7; $p <.001$ for both), this represents a decrease compared with 2021. This finding suggests that while parental awareness of programming education is increasing, their conviction that it should be a part of the school curriculum may be declining.

Table 3. Items assessing parental interest in and attitudes toward programming education in elementary school

Interest
(1) Are you interested in programming education in elementary school?
(2) How familiar are you with the new Course of Study (teaching guidelines issued by the Ministry of Education, Culture, Sports, Science and Technology) guidelines regarding programming education in elementary schools?
(3) How familiar are you with the computer-related topics currently taught in elementary schools?
(4) Are you in favor of or opposed to programming education in elementary schools?
Attitudes (How do you feel about programming being taught in school?)
(5) Everyone needs to know how to program.
(6) It is beneficial for elementary school students to learn programming.
(7) Programming will be essential in the future; therefore, it should be taught in elementary school.

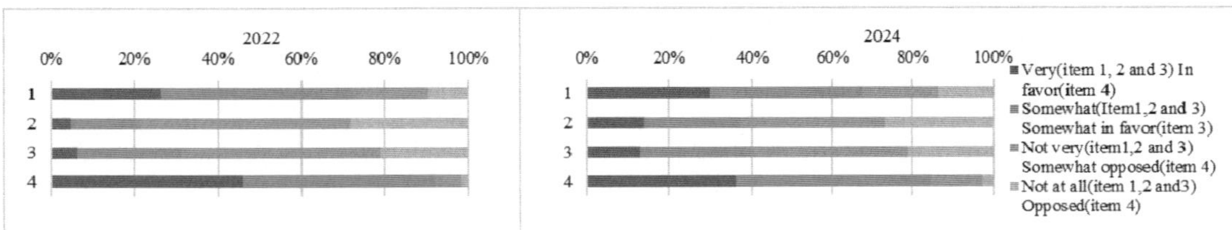

Figure 1. Answers to "interest in programming education" questionnaire

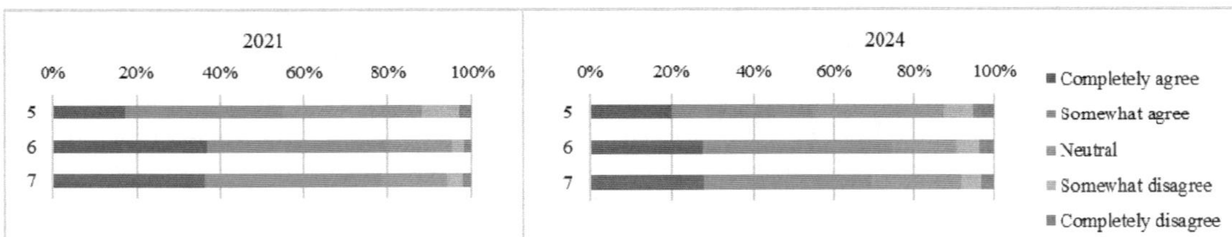

Figure 2. Answer to "attitudes toward programming education"

Figure 3 illustrates parental attitudes about and confidence in supporting their children's programming learning at home (Table 4). A significant increase was observed in the proportion of parents who felt confident in teaching programming to their children at home (Q1 and Q3; p = 0.017, p < 0.001). This suggests a growing sense of self-efficacy among parents in supporting their children's engagement with programming.

Table 4. Items regarding parents' attitudes toward and confidence in supporting children's programming education at home

(1) Do you think supplementary programming education outside of school is necessary?
(2) Do you think you will be involved in supplementary programming education at home?
(3) If you will be involved, how confident are you regarding your involvement?

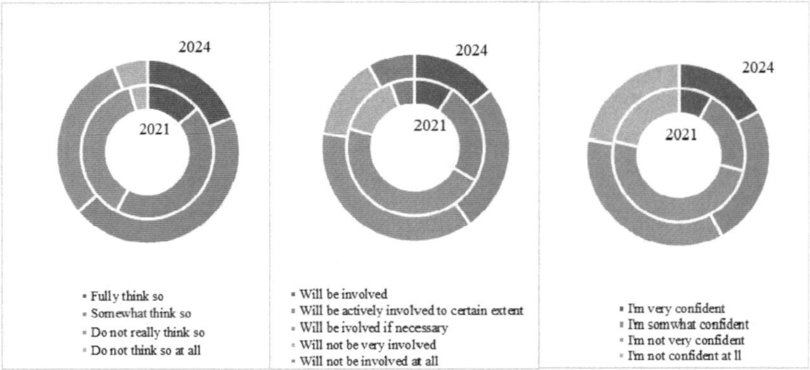

Figure 3. Answers to the "attitudes toward and confidence in supporting children at home" questionnaire

To assess parental involvement in programming education, eleven items were included in the questionnaire (Tables 5 and 6). These items were adapted from Simpkins et al. (2012), who, based on Eccles' socialization model (Eccles 1993), identified four key domains of maternal behavior influencing children's achievement-related beliefs: a) role modeling, b) encouragement and reinforcement, c) provision of activity-related experiences, and d) parent-child activities. This study examined the extent to which parents engaged in behaviors across these four domains. Items in Table 5, which focus on experiences related to programming in classes outside of school and at home, were used to measure the extent to which parents experienced behaviors related to role modeling and parent-child activity. For instance, if parents had attended a programming class with their child, this was considered indicative of both role modeling (demonstrating an interest in programming) and parent-child activity (shared engagement). Regarding items in Table 6, as for encouragement, it seems that parents' verbal encouragement influenced their children's beliefs; therefore, Q4 was considered a behavior related to encouragement. Provision of activity-related experiences was measured by whether parents bought programming related materials; therefore, Q6 and Q7 were considered as behaviors related to the provision of activity-related experiences.

Figures 4 and 5 present the results related to parental involvement. All items assessing parent-child activities (Figure 4) showed a significant increase in participation between 2021 and 2024 ($p < 0.001$ for all items). Similarly, significant increases were observed for most other involvement items (Figure 5), including encouragement, provision of programming-related materials, and discussing programming-related topics ($p < 0.001$ for Q2, Q3, Q5, Q6, Q7, and Q8; $p = 0.002$ for Q4). These findings indicate a substantial rise in parental involvement across various domains, which may contribute to their increased confidence in supporting their children's programming learning.

Figure 6 displays parental willingness to attend a programing class outside of school (Table 7). A significant increase was observed in the proportion of parents who not only wanted their child to attend such classes, but also expressed a desire to attend with their child or by themselves ($p < 0.001$ for all items). This suggests a growing interest among parents in actively participating in their children's programming education.

Table 5. Items regarding involvement in programming education

(1) Have you participated in a programming class (short-term) outside of school?
(2) Have you had programming experiences at home?
(3) Have you had programming experiences by watching TV and Internet?
(4) Have you ever enrolled in a programming class?

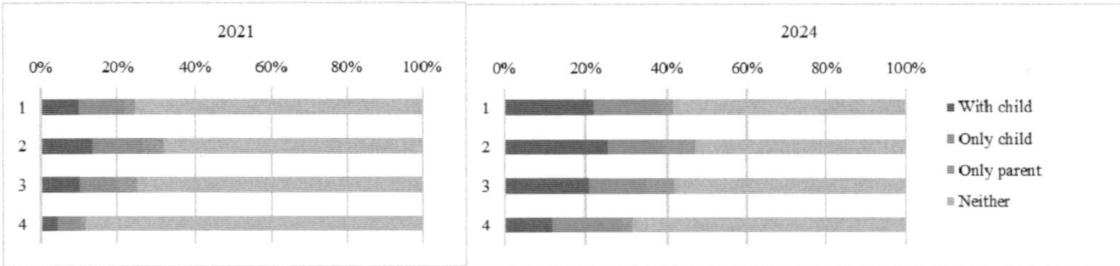

Figure 4. Answers to the "involvement in programming education" questionnaire

Table 6. Items regarding involvement in programming education

(1) Have you seen the news about programming education on the newspaper, TV, or Internet?
(2) Have you talked with other parents about programming education?
(3) Have you attended a lecture on programming education in elementary school?
(4) Have you looked into programming taught in elementary school?
(5) Have you talked with your child about programming learning and education in school at home?
(6) Have you bought a book related to programming?
(7) Have you bought a learning material related to programming?
(8) Have you looked for a programming experience event or class for your child?

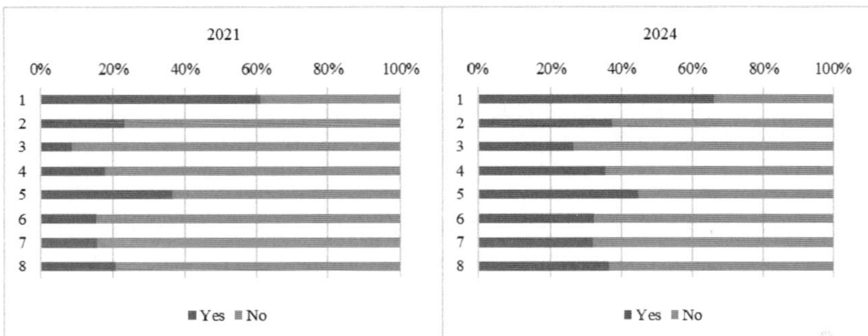

Figure 5. Answers to the "involvement in programming education" questionnaire

Table 7. Items related to willingness to attend a programing class outside of school

(1) Would you like your child to attend a programming class outside of school?
(2) Would you like to attend a programming class with your child?
(3) If a programming class specifically for parents was offered, would you like to attend it?

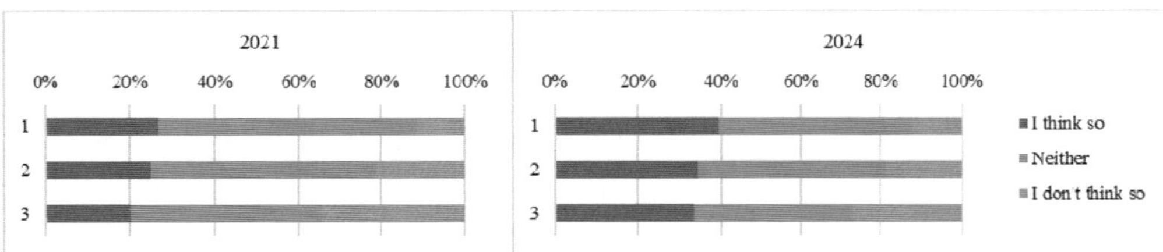

Figure 6. Answers to the "willingness for involvement" questionnaire

4. CONCLUSION

This study investigated the changes in parental attitudes toward and involvement in programming education in Japan by comparing data from online surveys conducted in 2021 and 2024. The findings revealed a nuanced picture of evolving parental perspectives.

While a slight decrease was observed in the number of parents who believe programming should be taught in schools, there was a significant increase in parental participation in extracurricular programming classes and other programming-related educational activities. This suggests a growing trend towards seeking programming education outside of formal school settings. Furthermore, parents reported increased confidence in supporting their children's programming learning at home, indicating a potential shift towards more active parental involvement in this domain.

These findings highlight the need to establish robust support systems for programming education outside of schools. Future research should explore the factors that contribute to parental involvement in programming education, including parental beliefs, perceived self-efficacy, and access to resources.

REFERENCES

Cuellar, F., Penaloza, C. and Kato, G., (2013). August, Robotics education initiative for parent-children interaction. *In* RO-MAN, 2013. IEEE, pp. 364–365.

Eccles, J. S., (1993). School and family effects on the ontogeny of children's interests, self-perceptions, and activity choices. *In Jacobs (Vol. Ed.), Nebraska symposium on Motivation: 1992. Developmental perspectives on motivation* (Vol. 40, pp. 145–208) (2nd ed.) & J. E R. Dienstbier, ed. Lincoln: University of Nebraska Press.

Gerson S. A, Morey R. D., van Schaik J. E., (2022). Coding in the cot? Factors influencing 0-17S' experiences with technology and coding in the United Kingdom, *Computers & Education*, 178, 104400.

Maruyama, Y., (2022) Parental involvement at the beginning of programming education. *Proceedings of the International Conferences on Technology and Education 2022*. Online, pp. 151–155.

Simpkins, S. D., Fredricks, J. A. and Eccles, J. S., (2012). Charting the Eccles' expectancy-value model from mothers' beliefs in childhood to youths' activities in adolescence. *Developmental Psychology*, 48(4), pp. 1019–1032.

Posters

DEVELOPMENT AND TRANSFORMATION OF ONLINE ART EDUCATION IN JAPAN

Atsumi Ide
Graduate School of Informatics, Nagoya University
Furo-cho, Chikusa-ward, Nagoya-City, 464-8601, Japan

ABSTRACT

This study examines the current state and future prospects of art-related distance education utilizing the internet in Japan. Since the early 2000s, with the advent of online bulletin boards, various formats such as on-demand and interactive education have emerged and evolved. The correspondence program at Kyoto University of the Arts has been particularly proactive in adopting online methods, offering a rich selection of short video materials for convenient mobile learning and transitioning all departments except the ceramics course to a fully online format by 2025. However, the expansion of digital learning raises several concerns, such as the risk of alterations to submitted works when relying on digital images. Ultimately, though, aesthetic judgment remains a human process. Regular exposure to high-quality artworks and the cultivation of aesthetic sensitivity are considered essential, even in the era of digital education.

KEYWORDS

Online Education, Distance Learning, Art Education

1. INTRODUCTION

While distance education providers range widely from corporations to individuals, studies examining online art education in Japan remain sparse. In its September 2020 issue, *Educational Art* explored "The Possibilities and Challenges of Online Art Education." However, as the publication is intended for educators at preschools, elementary, and middle schools, no studies have yet included higher education or lifelong learning (The Society for Art Education, 2020). This study organizes and analyzes internet-based art distance education in Japan.

2. METHODOLOGY

This study identified and categorized various online art education services using search engines. The services were grouped into five categories: (1) online bulletin boards, (2) platforms selling educational videos by companies or individual educators, (3) free on-demand education exemplified by YouTube, (4) real-time interactive instruction, and (5) correspondence courses offered by art universities. Interviews, online articles, and statements from prominent services and individuals were also collected for analysis.

3. RESULTS

3.1 Online Bulletin Boards

Toyonaka Art Institute, established by Yoshiharu Himata in 1975, alongside in-person teaching, the institute began offering free critiques through an online bulletin board in 2002. Over its first ten years, more than 5,000 artworks were reviewed, with critiques continuing until around March 2020. Categories on the board included "Drawing," "Oil and Watercolor," and "Middle School Students," with the "Drawing" category being the most active (Toyonaka Art Institute, 2020a). Users were predominantly middle and high school students aiming for art school entrance exams (Toyonaka Art Institute, 2020b). Conversely, Oekaki Art.net's "Illustration Advice Board" has provided a space for artists to exchange feedback and develop their skills collaboratively (Oekaki.net, 2024).

3.2 On-Demand Education by Companies and Teachers

Prominent on-demand art education platforms include Udemy, Coloso, and Palmie. Udemy, originating from the U.S., offers over 250,000 courses, including 3,570 related to art and crafts (Udemy, 2024). Coloso, a South Korean platform, specializes in over 1,000 courses on topics like illustration and video production (PR TIMES, 2024). Palmie, launched in Japan in 2014, focuses exclusively on illustration education. By 2024, Palmie has enrolled over 30,000 students and provides access to 236 courses through flexible subscription options (Palmie, 2024). Reflecting Japan's deep-rooted culture of manga and illustration, Palmie exemplifies an approach tailored to local artistic traditions.

3.3 Free On-Demand Education on YouTube

On YouTube, art schools like Ochabi Institute (OCHABI) and Ena Art School publish videos that explain the drawing techniques of successful art university entrants and critique viewers' works. A standout example is Harumichi Shibasaki's channel "Watercolor by Shibasaki," which has amassed over 1.81 million subscribers and is beloved for his approachable "grandpa teacher" style (Harumichi, 2024). The channel's tutorials on watercolor techniques and critiques are celebrated for their clarity and warmth. With English subtitles available, 10% of the audience consists of international viewers (Kinezuka, 2022). Feedback applicants send digital images of their artwork, which Shibasaki evaluates. He starts by highlighting the positives of the work and then, while providing suggestions, creates a new piece to illustrate his advice. Selection for feedback is lottery-based, attracting many participants from abroad, including Canada, the United States, Indonesia, and France. With over 50 years of experience teaching watercolor, Shibasaki demonstrates that a large following requires not just personal appeal but also a high level of skill.

3.4 Real-Time Interactive Instruction

The adoption of Zoom for group art classes expanded during the COVID-19 pandemic. OGURA from Grace: Academy of ART highlighted advantages such as reduced travel time for students and faster material sharing for instructors. Additionally, students could clearly hear critiques directed at peers, enhancing mutual learning (Grace: Academy of ART, 2024). ART SCHOOL SHINAGAWA / MEGURO has implemented a system where students submit photos of their artworks for instructor feedback and corrections. Through this approach, students can revise their works while studying specific corrections made by instructors (ART SCHOOL SHINAGAWA / MEGURO, 2024). Interactive art classes have brought unique advantages not found in conventional classroom teaching.

3.5 Distance Learning at Art Universities

The intrinsic value of art has historically been associated with the originality of physical works. Higher education often requires students to submit original pieces for skill-based courses such as drawing and drafting. However, The correspondence program at Kyoto University of the Arts is transitioning its programs, except ceramics, to a fully online format starting in 2025 (Kyoto University of the Arts, 2024a). In Japan, mobile devices dominate internet usage (Ministry of Internal Affairs and Communications, Japan, 2024). Research indicates that smaller, mobile-optimized content enhances learning experiences (Yu & Dean, 2019), which Correspondence program at Kyoto University of the Arts has implemented effectively. Since 66% of its students are professionals (Kyoto University of the Arts, 2024b), the system is thought to be praised for its adaptability to working individuals.

4. CONCLUSION

This study reviewed the types of internet-based art distance education in Japan. Emerging from the broadband era's online bulletin boards, art distance education has advanced alongside improvements in communication technology, enabling real-time interactive engagement. Interactive learning in art education presents advantages unique to online formats, with Kyoto University of the Arts' digital initiatives gaining traction. At the same time, the reliance on digital image submissions raises issues such as risks of modification through image editing software. Addressing how to sustain and further develop traditional analog-based skills like observation and expression is critical. Regular exposure to exemplary artworks and the cultivation of aesthetic discernment remain indispensable. Further studies should address these challenges from interdisciplinary perspectives, integrating aesthetics and information technology.

ACKNOWLEDGEMENT

This work was financially supported by JST SPRING, Grant Number JPMJSP2125.The author (A.I.) would like to take this opportunity to thank the "THERS Make New Standards Program for the Next Generation Researchers."

REFERENCES

ART SCHOOL SHINAGAWA / MEGURO, (2024). *How Online Drawing Lessons Work Instantly*, Available at: https://www.youtube.com/watch?v=ulu1TEPN7CE&t=1s&ab_channel=ARTSCHOOLSHINAGAWA%2FMEGURO (Accessed: 10 October 2024).

Grace:academy of ART, (2024). *Online Art School Grace:academy of ART*, Available at: https://www.youtube.com/watch?v=HQ5fdHUOEBw&ab (Accessed: 10 October 2024).

Harumichi Shibasaki, (2024). *Watercolor by Shibasaki*, Available at: https://www.youtube.com/@WatercolorbyShibasaki (Accessed: 10 October 2024).

Kinezuka, (2022). *A Watercolor YouTuber with Over 1.4 Million Subscribers Talks About His Life Philosophy*, Available at: https://www.kinezuka.jp/shibasaki-art/ (Accessed: 10 October 2024).

Kyoto University of the Arts, (2024a). *Kyoto University of Art, School of Correspondence Education has a new department!*, Available at: https://www.kyoto-art.ac.jp/news/press/1314 (Accessed: 7 December 2024).

Kyoto University of the Arts, (2024b). *About Distance Learning Department*, Available at: https://www.kyoto-art.ac.jp/t/about/ (Accessed: 7 December 2024).

Ministry of Internal Affairs and Communications, Japan, (2024). *Survey report on information communication media use time and information behavior in 2023*, Ministry of Internal Affairs and Communications, Japan, Tokyo, Japan.

Oekaki.net, (2024). *Drawing Advice BBS*, Available at: https://oekakiart.net/oeb09/ (Accessed: 7 December 2024).

Palmie, (2024). *Top Page*, Available at: https://www.palmie.jp/ (Accessed: 10 October 2024).

PR TIMES, (2024). *New Coloso Japan and Toyo Art School Course Opens on September 24*, Available at: https://prtimes.jp/main/html/rd/p/000000012.000144901.html (Accessed: 10 October 2024).

The Society for Art Education, (2020). *Art in Education*, Vol. 81, No. 9, The Society for Art Education, Tokyo, Japan.

Toyonaka Art Institute, (2020a). *Toyonaka Art Institute*, Available at: http://www.toyobi.com/index.html (Accessed: 5 October 2024).

Toyonaka Art Institute, (2020b). *Internet Correspondence Course Survey*, Available at: http://www.toyobi.com/cgi-bin/an/an_cc/qnaire1.cgi (Accessed: 5 October 2024).

Yu (Aimee) Zhang and Dean Cristol, (2019). *Handbook of Mobile Teaching and Learning*, Springer Singapore, Beach Road, Singapore.

Udemy, (2024). *Art & Craft Courses*, Available at: https://www.udemy.com/courses/lifestyle/arts-and-crafts/ (Accessed: 10 October 2024).

STUDENTS VIEWS TOWARDS THE ADOPTION OF MOBILE COMPUTER SUPPORTED COLLABORATIVE LEARNING IN RESOURCE-CONSTRAINED NATIONS

Ugochi Ukamaka Ugwu, Natasha Anne Rappa and Kok Wai Wong
Murdoch University, School of Education, Perth, Australia

ABSTRACT

Resource-constrained nations face educational challenges, like poor technological infrastructure and disruptions in learning, which became evident during the Covid-19 pandemic. With the deep penetration of mobile technology in these regions, this research proposes mobile learning, particularly mobile computer supported collaborative learning (mCSCL), as a viable solution for continued education in the face of disruptions. Through a scoping review and a multimethods approach, this research examined the adoption of mCSCL in resource-constrained nations, investigating the case study of a higher education institution in Nigeria. Key findings reveal that mobility and some characteristics of collaboration positively influenced students' acceptance of mCSCL. Additionally, themes derived from open-ended responses and WhatsApp interactions highlighted flexibility in learning and multimodal communication mode as some of their reasons for continuing with mCSCL.

KEYWORDS

M-Learning, Mcscl, Resource-Constrained Nations, Collaborative Learning Characteristics

1. OVERVIEW

Resource-constrained nations, especially those within Africa, are bedeviled by regular learning interruptions from strikes, pandemics, insecurities, and civil unrest, resulting in school closures, causing students to spend six to seven years for courses meant to be completed in four years (Offem et al., 2018). According to Ayoko (2022), these challenges are some of the causes of student attrition, estimated by Sani et al. (2022) to be over 30% in Nigeria. Resource-constrained nations, such as Nigeria, are defined as countries that fall within the World Bank's 2022 classifications of low, lower-middle, and upper-middle income countries (World-Bank-Group, 2023). Membership within these categories is determined by the Gross National Income per capita of the previous calendar year (Hamadeh et al., 2021). Countries identified as upper-middle, such as Malaysia, Indonesia and South Africa, were included because of their economic inequality with the bottom 50% of the population having shares of between -3.4 and 6.5% of the total national wealth (World-Inequality-Lab, 2022).

Mobile learning (m-learning) could be a practical solution to mitigating the challenges of remote learning in resource-constrained nations, given the deep penetration of mobile devices in the region (Lamptey, 2020; Mohammadi et al., 2020). The World-Bank-Group (2022) estimated the number of mobile technology users in resource-constrained nations to be over 10 billion. m-Learning defined as using mobile devices for supporting and enhancing learning anytime and anywhere (Nikolopoulou, 2020), could be personal or collaborative (Goksu, 2021). The latter is referred to as mobile computer supported collaborative learning (mCSCL), defined as the act of using mobile devices to promote collaborative learning between two or more people (Resta and Laferrière (2007). People who engage in mCSCL develop the skill of collaboration (Al-Emran et al., 2016), a sought-after skill in the workforce (Raza and Khan (2022), improve their usage of skills that promote positive relationships (Lukyanov et al., 2021) and have access to social support from peers (Ansari & Khan, 2020). However, m-learning in developing countries is also challenged by contextual factors like the high cost of mobile devices, limited Internet data, small screen size, power outage, poor bandwidth, and the cost of training workshops for both teachers and students, and cultural factors like traditional attitudes toward education which may favour in-person learning over online learning (Kacetl & Klímová, 2019; Klimova, 2019) .

Against this backdrop in resource-constrained nations and the prospect that mCSCL using WhatsApp could help address these identified challenges, be an alternative method of learning in the region, and benefit its users, this research conducted a case study to examine the views of students in a Nigerian higher education institution on the adoption of mCSCL. To holistically examine students' views about mCSCL adoption, the study adopted the following research questions; RQ1. What considerations are required to implement mCSCL in resource-constrained nations? RQ2. To what extent do the characteristics of mobile technology influence students' decision to make use of mCSCL in resource-constrained nations? RQ3: To what extent do the characteristics of collaborative learning influence students' decision to make use of mCSCL in resource-constrained nations? RQ4: What are the prospects and challenges of mCSCL in resource-constrained nations?

2. METHODOLOGY

This study employed a multimethods approach (quantitative and qualitative methods) (Clark & Ivankova, 2015). Initially, a scoping review based on PRISMA guidelines identified key considerations for m-Learning implementation and answered research question one. This was followed by a three-month intervention study with 250 higher education students using WhatsApp. The students participated in a collaborative learning intervention of General Mathematics III, after which they completed an online survey combining both closed- and open-ended questions to capture a broad range of perspectives. Using a research model comprising constructs from mobile learning characteristics (mobility and collaboration – unpacked by positive interdependence, individual accountability, promotive interaction, and appropriate use of social skills), and the technology acceptance model (perceived usefulness and ease of use, and behavioural intention) (Davis et al., 1989), the quantitative data from the closed-ended survey questions were analysed using Structural Equation Modelling (SEM) (Hair Jr et al., 2021) to explore the factors affecting students' acceptance of mCSCL, and thus, addressing research questions two and three. In the qualitative component, the thematic analysis of open-ended survey responses and screenshots of WhatsApp discussions only provided reasons for continuing mCSCL, not discontinuing it. Participants' responses revealed two broad categories—personal/social and technological considerations, along with five themes supporting their desire to continue using mCSCL. Analysis of screenshots identified two categories (communication methods and learning/collaboration) and four themes. These findings, including the participant observation, provided deeper insights into the prospects and challenges of mCSCL adoption as well as facilitated data triangulation (Miles et al., 2019), and thus, answered research question four.

3. SUMMARY OF FINDINGS AND CONCLUSIONS

The literature search, addressing RQ1, revealed growing interest in m-Learning in resource-constrained countries, with an increasing number of publications from 2012 to 2023. The study further highlighted the popularity, benefits, and challenges of mobile devices, their impact on learning achievement, and the importance of theoretical frameworks in forming research design (Ugwu et al., 2024). RQ 2 and 3 explored students' acceptance of mCSCL using a Technology Acceptance Model (TAM) integrating mobility and collaboration (unpacked with its characteristics as established in Johnson and Johnson (2009)) as external variables. The findings revealed students' willingness to adopt mCSCL as mobility, individual accountability, promotive interaction, and social skills had a significant influence on either or both perceived usefulness and perceived ease of use, which in turn influenced behavioural intention; perceived ease of use was equally a strong predictor of perceived usefulness (Ugwu et al., accepted). For RQ 4, the analyses of open-ended survey responses, WhatsApp screenshots, and participant observation, triangulated findings, which identified nine key themes that illustrate students' verbatim responses as to why they wished to continue using mCSCL (Ugwu et al., in review). Influenced by mobile technology characteristics and collaborative learning characteristics, this study suggests that mCSCL holds significant potential to improve learning in resource-constrained nations. Also, the positive student experiences as denoted in their responses, indicate that mCSCL could be a viable solution to learning disruptions if the challenges in implementation are addressed.

Being a very popular application in resource-constrained nations, Educators and students could leverage the scalability nature of WhatsApp to set up class groups for discussions, share resources, organize collaborative problem-solving activities, post questions, share answers, and engage in peer learning. Also, policymakers could show their support for mCSCL by supporting blended learning, ensuring access to affordable mobile data and smartphones through collaboration with telecom companies to guarantee broader access to mobile learning opportunities for all students, and promoting open educational resources for easy mobile access.

In terms of limitations, this study in focusing on a Nigerian higher education institution has produced findings that may not be fully generalizable to other resource-constrained nations due to differences in cultural, economic, and technological contexts. Other limitations include an imbalanced gender ratio, no representation of lecturers' perspectives, and reliance on WhatsApp as the sole mCSCL platform. Additionally, the study's focus on TAM may overlook other relevant theories. Rapid changes in mobile technology and educational policies may also affect the relevance of the findings over time.

REFERENCES

Al-Emran, M., Elsherif, H. M., & Shaalan, K. (2016). Investigating attitudes towards the use of mobile learning in higher education. *Computers in Human Behavior*, *56*, 93-102.

Ansari, J. A. N., & Khan, N. A. (2020). Exploring the role of social media in collaborative learning the new domain of learning. *Smart Learning Environments*, *7*(1), 1-16.

Ayoko, V. O. (2022). Understanding the falling-out that contribute to school dropout and the way forward: analysis of governement failure, cultural believes, disasters, pandemic and forced migration. *Proceeding Book*, 46.

Clark, V. L. P., & Ivankova, N. V. (2015). *Mixed methods research: A guide to the field* (Vol. 3). Sage publications.

Davis, F. D., Bagozzi, R. P., & Warshaw, P. R. (1989). User acceptance of computer technology: A comparison of two theoretical models. *Management Science*, *35*(8), 982-1003.

Goksu, I. (2021). Bibliometric mapping of mobile learning. *Telematics and Informatics*, *56*, 101491.

Hair Jr, J. F., Hult, G. M., Ringle, C. M., Sarstedt, M., Danks, N. P., & Ray, S. (2021). *Partial least squares structural equation modeling (PLS-SEM) using R: A workbook*. Springer Nature.

Hamadeh, N., Van Rompaey, C., & Metreau, E. (2021). *New World Bank country classifications by income level: 2021–2022*. Retrieved 05/10/2024 from https://blogs.worldbank.org/en/opendata/new-world-bank-country-classifications-income-level-2021-2022

Johnson, D. W., & Johnson, R. T. (2009). An educational psychology success story: Social interdependence theory and cooperative learning. *Educational Researcher*, *38*(5), 365-379.

Lukyanov, S., Popov, N., Sikarev, I., Rumyantseva, E., & Petrieva, O. (2021). Digital learning technologies within geo-information management. E3S Web of Conferences.

Miles, M. B., Huberman, A. M., & Saldana, J. (2019). *Qualitative data analysis - International student edition: A methods sourcebook* (4th edition. ed.). SAGE Publications, Inc.

Nikolopoulou, K. (2020). Secondary education teachers' perceptions of mobile phone and tablet use in classrooms: benefits, constraints and concerns. *Journal of Computers in Education*, *7*(2), 257-275.

Offem, O. O., Anashie, A. I., & Aniah, S. A. (2018). Effect of strikes on management and planning of educational activities in Nigerian universities. *Global Journal of Educational Research*, *17*(1), 1-8.

Raza, S. A., & Khan, K. A. (2022). Knowledge and innovative factors: how cloud computing improves students' academic performance. *Interactive Technology and Smart Education*, *19*(2), 161-183.

Resta, P., & Laferrière, T. (2007). Technology in support of collaborative learning. *Educational psychology review*, *19*, 65-83.

Sani, G., Oladipo, F., Ogbuju, E., & Agbo, F. J. (2022). Development of a Predictive Model of Student Attrition Rate. *Journal of Applied Artificial Intelligence*, *3*(2), 1-12.

Ugwu, U. U., Rappa, N. A., & Wong, K. (2024). Key considerations for implementing mobile learning in resource-constrained nations: a scoping review. *Interactive Learning Environments*, 1-18. https://doi.org/10.1080/10494820.2024.2412069

World-Bank-Group. (2022). *Mobile cellular subscriptions*. Retrieved 28 September from https://data.worldbank.org/indicator/IT.CEL.SETS)

World-Bank-Group. (2023). *World Bank Country and Lending Groups*. Retrieved 28 September from https://datahelpdesk.worldbank.org/knowledgebase/articles/906519-world-bank-country-and-lending-groups

World-Inequality-Lab. (2022). *Global economic inequality: insights*. Retrieved 28 September from https://wir2022.wid.world/chapter-1/

MICROCREDENTIALS FOR MICROCOMPETENCES IN EDUCATION

Vlado Stankovski
University of Ljubljana, Faculty of Computer and Information Science
Večna pot 113, 1000 Ljubljana, Slovenia

ABSTRACT

The evolving landscape of education and workforce demands has led to the rise of microcredentials, offering a flexible and competency-based approach to lifelong learning. This paper explores the role of microcredentials for microcompetences, focusing on their significance in education and professional development. Unlike traditional degree programs, microcredentials provide modular, verifiable, and skill-specific certifications, ensuring learners acquire targeted competencies aligned with industry needs. The paper examines the implementation of blockchain-based verifiable credentials, ensuring security, authenticity, and interoperability within European education frameworks. Through case studies from EBSI-VECTOR, ESSA, NOO Ultra, and TRUSTCHAIN, this study highlights the practical adoption of microcredentials in higher education, vocational training, and corporate upskilling. The paper further discusses their impact on educational personalization, workforce mobility, and digital trust. Challenges such as standardization, credential stacking, and cross-border recognition are addressed, with recommendations for policy alignment and technological advancements. This research contributes to the ongoing discourse on the future of credentialing, advocating for scalable, secure, and transparent digital certification ecosystems in education.

KEYWORDS

Microcredentials, Microcompetences, Blockchain, Lifelong Learning, European Education Frameworks

1. INTRODUCTION

The rapid digital transformation and evolving job market dynamics have created a pressing need for flexible, competency-based learning solutions. Traditional education models, characterized by long-degree programs and rigid curricula, often fail to address the immediate and changing skill demands of industries (European Commission, 2022). As a result, microcredentials for microcompetences have gained traction as an alternative credentialing system, allowing learners to acquire specific, verifiable skills in a short time, fostering lifelong learning and employability (Brown et al., 2021). The emergence of blockchain-based credentialing systems has further strengthened the security, transparency, and trustworthiness of digital certificates, supporting interoperability across educational institutions and job markets (Xu, 2024).

In today's knowledge-driven economy, employees must continuously upskill and reskill to remain competitive. However, traditional education pathways do not provide the flexibility required for learners to quickly adapt to emerging job roles (Smith et al., 2020). Employers also struggle to assess actual competencies, as formal degrees do not always reflect practical, job-specific skills (Gauthier, 2020). Furthermore, existing credentialing systems are often centralized, fragmented, and difficult to verify, leading to inefficiencies in credential recognition and cross-border mobility (European Parliament, 2022). These challenges necessitate alternative, verifiable, and modular approaches to education that can be tailored to industry demands while ensuring secure and portable skill validation.

Numerous European initiatives and research projects have focused on developing scalable solutions for microcredentialing. Projects such as EBSI-VECTOR, ESSA, NOO Ultra, and TRUSTCHAIN have explored the integration of digital credentials in education and employment sectors (European Commission, 2022). Several studies emphasize the importance of verifiable digital certificates in enhancing trust, security, and interoperability in learning systems (Andrade et al., 2021). Blockchain-based credentialing, in particular, has been recognized as a promising solution for decentralized and tamper-proof verification (Xu, 2024).

However, significant challenges remain in terms of standardization, accreditation, and policy alignment across different education and industry ecosystems (Mikulecky et al., 2022).

This poster examines the role of microcredentials in modern education systems, emphasizing their impact on workforce development, mobility, and trust. Specifically, it investigates how blockchain-based verifiable credentials can enhance the transparency, security, and interoperability of digital certification.

We provide:

- A comprehensive analysis of microcredentials for microcompetences, focusing on emerging European policies and industry adoption trends.
- A review of decentralized digital credentialing systems and their implications for lifelong learning and employment
- Dashboard example at https://www.friacademy.com/api/student_panel/Dashboard
- An application for microcredentials for microcompetences in education.
- Case studies from leading European projects, highlighting successful implementations, challenges, and future directions.

This study contributes to the ongoing discourse on digital identity and trust-based credentialing by offering a structured framework for microcredential implementation. Key contributions include a strategic model for integrating verifiable credentials in educational institutions and enterprises (Brown et al., 2021); policy recommendations for ensuring cross-border recognition and standardization of microcredentials (European Parliament, 2022); an analysis of blockchain and decentralized identity solutions that enhance the security, privacy, and authentication of credentials (Xu, 2024); and an evaluation of real-world pilots, demonstrating the scalability and adaptability of microcredential frameworks in higher education, vocational training, and corporate upskilling (Gauthier, 2020). By addressing these aspects, this research bridges the gap between education and industry needs, advocating for a scalable, trust-enhancing, and interoperable microcredential ecosystem.

2. MICROCREDENTIALS

Our solution for Microcredentials is built on a blockchain-based infrastructure that ensures the security, integrity, and interoperability of digital credentials. At its core, it employs W3C Verifiable Credentials (VC) and Decentralized Identifiers (DID) standards, providing a tamper-proof, self-sovereign, and user-controlled approach to credential issuance and verification. By leveraging blockchain, once a credential is issued, it remains immutable and cannot be altered, making it resistant to fraud. The use of decentralized identity management eliminates reliance on central authorities, giving individuals full ownership over their digital credentials and allowing them to selectively disclose information based on privacy-preserving principles.

To facilitate seamless verification and automation, the solution integrates smart contracts that govern the issuance, validation, and revocation of credentials. These smart contracts are deployed on the blockchain and operate autonomously, ensuring that credentials are issued only by authorized institutions, verified in real-time, and revoked when necessary. The architecture supports auditability and compliance with regulatory frameworks such as GDPR, eIDAS 2.0, and the European Blockchain Services Infrastructure (EBSI). Compliance with EBSI ensures that the system is interoperable across EU member states, supporting cross-border credential recognition in education, employment, and regulatory sectors.

The modular and scalable design of the platform is based on a microservices architecture, enabling seamless integration with existing educational institutions, HR systems, and industry certification bodies. It is built to support both cloud-based and edge computing environments, ensuring efficiency, security, and real-time access to credentials. The multi-stakeholder framework allows universities, employers, and regulatory agencies to participate in a decentralized ecosystem where credentials can be issued, managed, and verified without centralized bottlenecks.

A key feature of the system is the digital wallet that allows users to securely store, manage, and share verifiable credentials. This wallet is designed with privacy-enhancing technologies, enabling individuals to control which credentials they share and with whom, using zero-knowledge proofs and selective disclosure mechanisms. Credentials stored in the digital wallet can be accessed through multiple platforms, including mobile applications, web interfaces, and enterprise systems, ensuring broad usability and accessibility.

The platform also incorporates AI-driven analytics and credential intelligence. Machine learning models analyze credential issuance and usage patterns, identifying skill gaps, job market trends, and fraudulent credential activities. This intelligence provides recommendations for upskilling opportunities, guiding learners toward personalized education pathways based on their career goals and industry demand. Fraud detection mechanisms further enhance the trustworthiness of credentials, ensuring that only legitimate and verified digital certificates are used in professional and academic contexts.

By aligning with the European Learning Model, the system supports microcredentials that enable modular learning and credential stacking. Learners can accumulate credentials from multiple courses, certifications, or work experiences, gradually building towards larger qualifications. The platform ensures that work-based learning components are formally recognized, making it easier for professionals to transition between industries, upskill, and demonstrate competencies in a verifiable manner. Partnerships with accreditation bodies such as ASIIN and the European Qualifications Framework (EQF) further strengthen the credibility of the issued microcredentials.

The application of verifiable credentials extends beyond education into multiple sectors, including the labor market, supply chains, and social security. In employment, the system streamlines hiring processes by allowing instant verification of skills, degrees, and work experience. In supply chains, credentials play a role in verifying product authenticity, compliance certifications, and ethical sourcing. Additionally, the system supports digital identity verification for healthcare professionals, legal entities, and public administration, enhancing security and transparency across various domains.

This comprehensive technical framework ensures that the verifiable credentials solution is secure, privacy-preserving, interoperable, and adaptable to multiple industries. By integrating blockchain, decentralized identity, smart contracts, and AI-driven analytics, the system provides a future-proof digital credentialing ecosystem that aligns with global standards and regulatory requirements. It represents a fundamental shift in how credentials are issued, shared, and verified, paving the way for a more trustworthy, efficient, and decentralized approach to credentialing in education and beyond.

3. CONCLUSION

The piloting with the European Software Skills Alliance (ESSA) has provided valuable insights into the implementation and practical adoption of microcredentials for software professionals. The testing process involved developing and deploying a structured digital badge system, designed to recognize competencies in various software roles such as Developer, DevOps Expert, Solution Designer, Test Specialist, and Technical (Software) Specialist. The process emphasized aligning microcredentials with industry standards and workforce needs, ensuring that issued credentials effectively demonstrate relevant skills and expertise.

The piloting focused on validating how learners and professionals engage with microcredential frameworks in real-world settings. Participants included students, software professionals, and employers who interacted with digital badges and verifiable credential mechanisms to assess their usability, credibility, and impact on professional development. Employers were involved in evaluating whether microcredentials accurately represented job-ready competencies, while learners tested how these credentials could be stacked, shared, and integrated into career progression.

The results highlight the critical role of standardization and interoperability in digital credentialing systems. Ensuring that microcredentials are recognized across educational institutions and industry sectors proved essential for their adoption. The testing revealed that seamless verification and integration with existing hiring and upskilling processes increased the perceived value of the credentials. Learners reported that microcredentials enhanced their ability to showcase specialized skills, particularly in fast-evolving domains such as software engineering and cloud computing. Employers recognized their potential in streamlining recruitment by providing a trustworthy and transparent representation of competencies.

One of the key findings from the piloting was the necessity of flexible learning pathways. Participants benefited from the ability to earn, stack, and share credentials dynamically, rather than committing to long, rigid degree programs. This modular approach allowed individuals to customize their learning experiences, focusing on targeted skill acquisition while maintaining professional responsibilities. The testing also revealed the importance of decentralized and privacy-preserving verification, where individuals could selectively disclose credentials to potential employers and institutions without compromising personal data.

The piloting also examined technical scalability, ensuring that the infrastructure could support a large-scale credentialing ecosystem without compromising security, authenticity, or user control. The digital wallet and verification mechanisms underwent stress testing to assess their performance under high transaction loads. The system successfully maintained real-time verification speeds, ensuring that credentials could be issued, revoked, and validated instantly, a critical factor for widespread adoption.

Overall, the ESSA piloting demonstrated the practical viability of microcredentials in professional software education, confirming their value in skill validation, workforce mobility, and employer trust. It underscored the importance of collaboration between education providers, industry stakeholders, and regulatory bodies to ensure that digital credentials are widely accepted, interoperable, and future-proof. By integrating standardized frameworks, user-friendly verification processes, and industry-aligned skill assessments, the pilot has laid the groundwork for scaling microcredential adoption across broader education and employment landscapes.

ACKNOWLEDGEMENT

The research and development reported in this paper have received funding from the Research Agency of the Republic of Slovenia (ARIS) under the Research Programme P2-0426, Digital Transformation for Smart Public Governance (1/1/2022 - 31/12/2027), the project 621751- EPP-1-2020-1-BE-EPPKA2-SSA-B (ESSA project: European Software Skills Alliance), and the NOO ULTRA 8.05 project Microcredentials for Microcompetences.

REFERENCES

Andrade, A., Eichsteller, M. and Praeger, R., (2021). Microcredentials and Digital Learning: A Framework for Policy and Practice. Springer, London.

Brown, M., Nic Giolla Mhichíl, M., Beirne, E. and Mac Lochlainn, C., (2021). The Global Microcredential Landscape: Charting a New Credential Ecology for Lifelong Learning. Journal of Learning for Life, 5(2), pp.45-63.

European Commission, (2022). Council Recommendation on a European Approach to Microcredentials for Lifelong Learning and Employability. Publications Office of the European Union, Luxembourg.

European Parliament, (2022). Microcredentials and the Future of Learning: Policy Developments and Challenges. Brussels, Belgium.

Gauthier, T., (2020). The Value of Microcredentials: The Employer's Perspective. The Journal of Competency-Based Education, 5(2), pp.1-8.

Mikulecky, P., Vrabec, M. and Kolman, P., (2022). "Blockchain-Based Digital Credentials in Higher Education: Opportunities and Challenges." Proceedings of the European Conference on Digital Education Policies, Prague, Czech Republic, pp.87-102.

Smith, J., Williams, L. and Taylor, R., (2020). "Reimagining Credentialing in the Digital Age: The Role of Verifiable Microcredentials." International Journal of Educational Technology and Innovation, 12(3), pp.125-140.

Xu, Y., (2024). Development of Blockchain-Based Academic Credential Verification System. Open Access Library Journal, 11(09), pp.1-20.

THE BIRTH OF THE DIGITAL IMAGE: HOW IS TRUTH BEING CREATED ON THE INTERNET?

Petra Kočková, Kristýna Kiliánová and Kateřina Kostolányová
University of Ostrava, Czechia

ABSTRACT

With the advent of digital technologies, the Internet has become a vast repository of visual content, including images and videos. These digital artefacts play a key role in our perception and understanding of reality. Distinguishing between truth and manipulation is currently a significant challenge, especially for younger individuals who have been socialised in a digital environment. This pilot study aims to explore the processes involved in the creation, manipulation and dissemination of digital images. The study focuses on how primary and secondary school students perceive digital visual content and how they respond to its potential manipulation.

KEYWORDS

Digital Literacy, Critical Thinking, Deepfake, AI, Media Education, Visual Manipulation

1. INTRODUCTION

With advancing digital technologies, the Internet has become both a repository and a tool for creating and manipulating visual content. AI-powered tools, such as deepfake technology and GANs, can generate highly realistic yet artificial images, blurring the line between reality and fabrication (Farid, 2019; Goodfellow et al., 2014). While these technologies have creative applications, they are also used to spread misinformation and manipulate public perception (Wardle & Derakhshan, 2017).

For a generation immersed in social media and digital tools, media literacy is essential. This study addresses the challenges of AI-driven image manipulation by equipping students with critical skills to recognize and evaluate digital content.

AI and manipulation: truth or fiction? In recent years, artificial intelligence has become a key tool not only for the creation of digital content, but also for its manipulation. Applications such as DALL-E or Midjourney allow the generation of visual scenes based on textual descriptions, which has wide applications in education, art and commerce. On the other hand, these technologies open space for abuse. Deepfake videos have already been used to spread false political statements or misinformation in crisis situations (Chesney & Citron, 2019). For young people, who are often exposed to this content, it can be difficult to distinguish between what is real and what is fake.

Why is this important for students? As primary and secondary school students are one of the most active groups on social media, it is essential that they understand not only how digital images are created, but also how they can be manipulated. Digital literacy must include knowledge of how to recognize and verify synthetically generated images. As Buckingham (2003) says, "Media literacy is a key prerequisite for critical citizenship in the information society".

This study therefore provides a systematic approach to teaching students how to navigate the digital world and empowering them to distinguish between truth and fiction. The aim is not only to improve their critical thinking, but also to equip them with concrete tools and skills that they can apply in their daily lives.

2. METHODOLOGY

This study explored how primary and secondary school students perceive digital visual content and recognize manipulated images. Conducted in the Moravian-Silesian region of the Czech Republic, it involved 184 students (90 primary, 94 secondary) from both urban and rural schools, ensuring diversity in geography, social background, and digital literacy levels.

Data were collected via online questionnaires distributed through Google Forms. The questionnaire assessed:

- **Demographics** – Age, gender, and self-assessment of digital skills.
- **Knowledge & Attitudes** – Students' understanding of image manipulation and their perceptions of digital content.
- **Visual Analysis** – Students evaluated 10 images (authentic, digitally altered, and AI-generated) and justified their classifications.

Teachers supervised data collection during class time to ensure standardized conditions. Ethical approval was obtained, with informed consent from schools, students, and legal representatives. Participation was voluntary, and responses were anonymized.

Data analysis was conducted on two levels:

1. **Quantitative analysis**: The percentage of students who correctly identified manipulated and authentic images was analysed. Furthermore, results were compared between age groups (primary and secondary school) and between pupils from urban and rural areas.
2. **Qualitative analysis**: Open-ended responses in which pupils gave reasons for their decisions were analysed to identify common errors or gaps in their abilities. The most common arguments used by pupils in evaluating the images were evaluated.

This research approach provided the first valuable insights into pupils' visual literacy skills and their critical approach to digital media. However, this is only the initial phase of a pilot study that serves as a basis for further data collection. The research will continue to be conducted to broaden the sample of respondents and deepen understanding of the issues under investigation. The interim results of the study will be used to optimize educational activities and develop teaching materials that will support students' ability to recognize digital manipulations and critically evaluate visual content.

3. RESULTS

The pilot study yielded intriguing insights into the capacity of primary and secondary school students to discern manipulations in visual content. A noteworthy finding was that the success rates of primary school (primary) and secondary school (secondary) pupils were nearly equivalent. It was hypothesized that older students would demonstrate superior performance due to their greater experience with digital technologies. However, this hypothesis was not confirmed. The mean success rate for correctly identifying the veracity of images was 70% for primary school pupils and 72% for secondary school pupils. This discrepancy is inconsequential and rather indicates that visual literacy is not substantially influenced by age or educational background.

A further noteworthy finding was the gender difference. Girls, irrespective of whether they were in primary or secondary school, exhibited a higher success rate than boys. The average success rate for girls in primary school was 75%, while the average success rate for boys was 65%. In secondary school, the same pattern was observed, with girls having a 78% success rate and boys 66%. This difference may be attributed to the girls' greater attention to detail in analyzing the images or a different approach to the task.

The principal findings are as follows:

The success rates of primary and secondary school pupils were found to be comparable, with the difference between the average success rates of the two groups being negligible.

A noteworthy gender disparity was observed, with female students exhibiting a higher success rate than their male counterparts, a trend that was discernible in both age groups. The most common errors were as follows: Pupils demonstrated particular difficulty in recognizing images that had been subtly altered, for example through slight changes in color or the addition of detail. Conversely, gross manipulations (e.g. completely unnatural scenes) were readily identified. These findings indicate that students are generally capable of recognizing overt manipulations but may encounter challenges in identifying more subtle alterations. It would be beneficial for future educational activities to priorities the enhancement of this skill, with a particular focus on the development of proficiency in the utilization of digital content analysis tools.

4. CONCLUSION

The pilot study highlights primary and secondary students' ability to recognize digital manipulations and the need to enhance visual literacy. Success rates between the two groups were similar, challenging the assumption that age and experience improve analytical skills. A gender disparity was observed, with female students outperforming males, possibly due to differences in attention to detail. While students could identify obvious manipulations, they struggled with subtle alterations, emphasizing the need for improved education in digital analysis. These findings support future research and curriculum development to strengthen students' critical evaluation skills in an era of increasingly sophisticated digital content.

REFERENCES

Beck, K. and Ralph, J., 1994. Patterns Generates Architectures. *Proceedings of European Conference of Object-Oriented Programming*. Bologna, Italy, pp. 139-149. Buckingham, D. (2003). *Media education: Literacy, learning, and contemporary culture*. Polity Press.

Chesney, R., & Citron, D. K. (2019). Deepfakes and the new disinformation war: The coming age of post-truth geopolitics. *Foreign Affairs, 98*(1), 147–155.

Farid, H. (2019). *Fake photos: The rise of manipulated visual content*. Cambridge University Press.

Goodfellow, I., Pouget-Abadie, J., Mirza, M., Xu, B., Warde-Farley, D., Ozair, S., ... & Bengio, Y. (2014). Generative adversarial nets. *Advances in Neural Information Processing Systems, 27*, 2672–2680.

Mitchell, W. J. T. (1992). *The reconfigured eye: Visual truth in the post-photographic era*. MIT Press.

Wardle, C., & Derakhshan, H. (2017). *Information disorder: Toward an interdisciplinary framework for research and policymaking*. Council of Europe. Retrieved from https://rm.coe.int/information-disorder-toward-an-interdisciplinary-framework-for-researc/168076277c

AUTHOR INDEX